Doing IT Right

Technology, business, and risk of computing

Harold Lorin

MANNING

Greenwich
(74° w. long.)

The publisher offers discounts on this book when ordered in quantity. For more information please contact:

Special Sales Department
Manning Publications Co.
3 Lewis Street
Greenwich, CT 06830
or
73150,1431@compuserve.com
Fax: (203) 661-9018

Copyediting: Margaret Marynowski
Typesetting: Stephen Brill
Cover Design: Peter Poulos

Many of the designations used by manufacturers and vendors to distinguish their products are protected as trademarks. Wherever these designations appear in this book, and we have been aware of the trademark claim, they have been typeset in initial caps or all caps.

Library of Congress Cataloging in Publication Data

Lorin, Harold.
    Doing IT right : technology, business, and risk of computing / Harold Lorin.
      p. cm.
    Includes bibliographical references and index.
    ISBN 1-884777-09-0 (pbk.)
    1. Information technology—Management. 2. Management information
systems. I. Title.
    T58.64.L67 1995
    004'.02465—dc20   95-37678
                                          CIP

1 2 3 4 5 6 7 8 9 10 — BB — 00 99 98 97 96

Printed in the United States of America

thanks

To my good friends in the industry, who share their concerns and disappointments. To Ted Gerbracht of Merrill Lynch, Fran Smyth of Bear Stearns, and Paul Aspinwall of IBM for very helpful early reviews of the manuscript. To Steve White of MTS for the generous contribution of so many figures, which his staff developed for our seminars. To the management of the manticore consultancy for also permitting the use of some manticore visuals. To my good graduate students, who keep me current. But also to Eckert and Mauchley, who may or may not have invented computers, but who created my first darling, whom I shall remember and love forever.

> *"To the unsung heroes of the IBM System Research Institute, who struggled but failed to make them believe what was coming."*

HAL LORIN

about the author

Harold Lorin is a consultant to organizations in Europe and the United States in areas of information technology strategy. He is an author of books on the technologies of hardware, software, and distributed computing, and has contributed many articles to journals and trade publications, including MIS Quarterly, ACM SIGOPS, ACM SIGARCH, IEEE JSAC, Computers and Communications, and Datamation. He has presented at SHARE and GUIDE meetings, Hewlett-Packard customer seminars, ACM and IEEE seminars, and American and European unversities, including the Massachusetts Institute of Technology, Stanford University, and Cambridge University. He has developed professional seminars for CAP-Gemini Institute, National Technology University, and other organizations in Europe, Asia, and Australia. He serves as advisor to high-technology start-ups in objects and high-performance imaging. Before founding the manticore consultancy, he was a ranking faculty member of the IBM Systems Research Institute, IBM Consultant. He is Senior Adjunct Professor at Hofstra University. He is a frequent reviewer of technology articles and books for IEEE, Computer Communications, and the IBM Systems Journal.

contents

Basics book 3   Operating systems basic functions

preface

This book addresses the Wittgensteinian problem of knowing what you do not know. It provides an intellectual framework in which the topics of information processing are related to each other. It describes some useful and constructive attitudes toward managing IT, and discusses technical topics suitable for management, which needs some notion of a technology's position in the market. For technologists, it provides some idea of how other technologies affect what they do.

Technology must be understood in the context of its profitable use. Many books discuss management in a manner independent of the particular attributes of what is managed, and they discuss technologies without distinguishing between industry standards and arcane projects known only to eleven graduate students. There seems an almost inexplicable lack of treatment at the meeting ground where investment decisions must be driven by an assessment of the capability of the technology and the investment risk.

This book addresses the empty center between management and technologists. At one time, IBM mediated between technologists and management, and the empty center was not so dangerous. But now the center is empty in a time of rapid change. Organizations are floundering in architectural vacuums, without the skills necessary to make the transition to new technologies, and with no significant idea of the relative costs and profit potential of various systems' structures.

This book undertakes to define the center in which IT management and the technologist can meet. It hopes to provide a common view of the industry and its dynamics, a commonly held set of the key issues of IT and a shared view of the key technologies.

It also hopes to broaden the horizons of technologists so that they will understand how an area of specialty relates to the general system structure; how other technologies impact an area of specialty; how future developments in other areas may change the specialty by merging with it or requiring new functions; and how costs and benefits are viewed in the eyes of management.

Difficult decisions about content and balance must be made in such a book. The guiding principle is to focus on technology and those vendors operating at the enterprise level. The cost of this is a focus on IBM, Microsoft, Novell, DEC, Sun, AT&T, and others capable of being primary vendors, with a gloss over specialized vendors whose products will fill boxes in the blueprint. This is deeply unfortunate and a disservice to splendid companies like SynOptics, Cisco, 3Com, and Banyan, but there is no real choice if room is to be left to build the center with an artifact not unusably large.

The book assumes a level of computer literacy an IT manager would have merely by listening to vendor presentations. Technical people are less likely to hear these presentations. They tend to be even less informed about technologies not their own than their managers.

A sort of book within a book, "The Basics Book" provides supporting discussions for readers who can profit by a review of underlying principles and technologies. The boxes in the text provide commentary that may establish a basic principle, discuss a related topic not necessarily useful in the main flow, or explain a technical point beyond the interest of some readers. The reader can decide which boxes are useful. The book can be read without the boxes.

There is no shortage of books on operating systems, communications, distributed computing, etc., of which this author is himself culpable, but there is little integration of the technology, market, and economic factors that can define a meeting place for management and technology.

The book has many sources. Primarily, it comes from the efforts of the IBM Systems Research Institute. The Institute tried (apparently unsuccessfully) to draw the attention of IBM professionals and managers to changing technologies and new industry dynamics and the risks and opportunities for IBM. It also comes from my experience with the needs and activities of graduate students in Computer Science at Hofstra University. They remind me that, behind the white papers, strategy statements, and statements of direction, people are trying to develop systems in a world independent of the hype.

Some material comes from my work with clients concerned with strategy and risk issues, from participation in technology start-ups, and from professional seminars developed with various organizations, including IBM, Hewlett-Packard, MTS in the U.K., and other organizations in Australia, Italy, and Germany.

HAL LORIN

chapter 1

Out of control

EXECUTIVE SUMMARY Various industries are moving together, like con-tinental plates, to form an "information industry" whose structure, stability, product set, and major players are not yet known. One of these, the "computer" industry, is itself a complex web of shifting niches and subniches, whose boundaries over-lap in confusing ways for both producers and consumers of computer resources.

In a time of rapid change, our notions about management become as unstable as what we are trying to manage. It is not clear how IT and using organizations should relate to each other in an industry as complex as computing. It is clear that IT cannot be the sole arbiter of the use of information technology in producing revenue and profit. It is equally clear that there must be a focal point for large investments in complex and unstable technologies. Between these poles are many views.

The chaotic state of the industry manifests itself in the confusion of products, product packaging, and vendor niches that parallels the petroleum industry for complexity. But there is one major trend: the focus of competition is moving from the wellhead to the pump.

Investment in information technology requires due diligence and defensible processes. In order to achieve this, managers must understand enough about the technology to put the right questions to technologists. Technologists must under-stand enough about each other's technologies to see how they work together, and enough about business to understand notions of investment and return.

Out of control

Before the "desktop revolution," there was little conviction that 25 years of in-formation technology had had significant payback. There was a low rumble of feeling that it had delivered less than its promise, had not clearly paid for itself, and often seemed irrelevant or even obstructive to business. During that time, IT acted as the keeper of the flame, the agency responsible for the promulgation (or retardation) of information technology into enterprise culture.

All the dazzle of "empowerments," "productivity revolutions," and "human augmentation" that has come with the micro has swept away those doubts. As doubts of the utility of computing have faded, so has the control of IT, and with it any effective control over IT strategy and investment by the enterprise.

Clearly, an enterprise has information needs beyond those of its individuals, groups, and departments. It is a legitimate user of information with a requirement that the information it gets be good. It is ultimately the last bill payer as well, with a responsibility to stockholders to know how hundreds of millions of dollars (pounds, yen, or deutschmarks) are being spent.

There must be a center of control and a competence associated with high technology resources whose acquisition and use require expertise, judgment, and dedication. But the center cannot be the whole. There must clearly be rational divisions of responsibility and function, as there must be a rational balance between orderly response to challenge and quick, innovative aggressiveness.

But what is the nature of this enterprise control? After a decade of computing that is "distributed," "client/server," "open," "network-oriented," etc., has the IT bureaucracy learned something it did not know before? This not-knowing caused the control of technology to fall from its hands. Does it understand that computing is entering an era of even more dramatic and intense change; that the role of the building blocks are redefined and transformed in periods of months; that an inherent cost of a new system must be the cost of migrating from it? Does it understand something about cost and benefit, profitability, flexibility, efficiency, and aggressiveness in the enterprise? Or is it still fixated on DASD utilization and n-year-long architectural studies, as it was when the 3330 and MVS were the glories of their time? Are the institutional processes associated with IT appropriate for managing in a fluid, chaotic industry with more of the attributes of high fashion than of capital markets?

The unhappy retort is that where practices are unsavory, they are as unsavory as they have always been. The more things change, the more they stay the same. By and large, in many dark spots in the world, the heart of the IT beast is as it was. It remains insensitive to benefits as opposed to costs, has few formal procedures for quantifying benefits per user, or wholesome processes for assessing costs or risks. There is no "due diligence" in the technology acquisition process. Budgets, although stressed by arbitrary ad hoc cuts, are effectively out of control, with levels of waste that derive from basic misunderstandings about what is worthwhile to manage, what is manageable, and what costs more to manage than to leave alone.

Enormous sums are spent on "enterprise architectures" that have little or no effect on development projects or technology acquisition. Such "architectures" do not define components in a way that might guide or constrain investment.

By and large, the leaders of IT are not sufficiently technical to recognize or assess the levels of sophistication of their staffs, the degree to which the technical staff understands best industry practice, and what is needed to discipline and guide the budget.

Many have been busy being "proactive" in the business, leaving no one to watch the multimillion dollar technology investments that still appear to businessmen as barriers, not facilitators, to strategic opportunity.

The technical staff has been little changed by a decade of presentations about "integration," "openness," and "interoperability." "Do it now" prevails as strongly as ever over "do it right." There is little sense of systems as coherent wholes. For example, decisions are made about security, recovery, objects, storage management, etc. without any regard to the overarching systems management frameworks in which these functions must exist and coexist.

Unhappily, the members of IT either know too much or too little about information technology; some are unable to see the trees, while others are unable to see the forest, and the distribution of these afflictions has cost us all.

On the other side of this, there is the scenario of solid professional groups who have been reduced to ineffectiveness by the ill-considered decentralizations of computing: IT groups who do not know what the IT assets of the enterprise are, or who are unable to force systems management into the mainstream or mandate enterprise-wide security despite the obvious need for such infrastructure technologies as part of the lighting and plumbing.

Of course there are leadership organizations whose IT structures and processes have matured over the decade and produced dramatic incidents of "getting it right," of moving on to new technologies at a proper time and on a proper cost curve. But billions of dollars are either under the control of staffs for whom time has not changed or are out of control completely, with the amount of spending unknown, making the mismanagement of this resource a disservice to the company and its stockholders.

Dynamics of industry

Changes in technology create new markets with new dynamics. Fluctuations in rates of change transform the structure of industries.

When segments of a market are disappearing and combining, and boundaries are increasingly fuzzy and in flux, buyers and suppliers must modify their practices. They must not be caught in dying niches or using obsolete equipment.

Vending companies must redefine their core business and competence. They must seek allies or acquisitions in technology segments that begin to impact their traditional niches. Telephone companies must integrate cable and wireless and television and computing. Computer companies must integrate common carrier networking and entertainment products. Data base companies must integrate software development offerings and skills. Using companies must adjust to the changing forms of offered products, to new sets of vendors, new deals, and new combinations of offerings and capabilities.

As the computer, communications, consumer electronics, and "edutainment" industries merge and mingle, there are mega changes in the dynamics and definition of electronic product. Within the segment that was the computer industry there is genetic change. Once dominated by IBM in a small oligopoly of vertically integrated giants, it has fragmented into an industry as complex as the petroleum industry. There is competition all over the industry, but especially at the pump. It is at the pump that industry dominance is achieved.

There are major companies that did not exist when some IT managers entered their professions. Apple, Microsoft, Novell, Lotus, Sybase, Cisco, Borland, Oracle, Informix, SynOptics, and Sun have invented, defined, and redefined market segments. Start-ups have challenged industry giants for key revenue. That many now consider it "safer" to follow the Microsoft Windows path for desktop software than to take a "risk" with IBM OS/2 suggests the magnitude of industry change, and the influence of competition at the pump.

Processes of industry fragmentation and recombination are partially (but only partially) due to the lateness of early leaders to recognize change. Leaders often see new technologies as "toys," constrained to niches not competitive with mainstream products. They do not anticipate how traditional market segments fade and recombine to create new forms of competition. Focusing on the needs of the current market, established companies forget that the customer often does not know what it wants until it sees it.

Competition may lead to divergence or similarity. In the early industry, each member of the oligopoly marketed strongly linked unique hardware and software products "bundled" into single packages. Each achieved a market share protected by the cost of change. IBM products often served as de facto industry standards, but much of the systems technology was vendor specific. Univac, Burroughs, IBM, and Honeywell equipment had particular personas and cultures. IBM cloning came in the first maturity, led mostly by the Japanese.

Competition now breeds similarity. Systems and components from different vendors must work together over shared networks. There is great interest in standards and similar software interfaces, behaviors, and packaging. There is a whiff of "commoditization." It is not likely that computer technology will be like pork bellies and copper, but it is becoming much like VCRs and automobiles. Enterprises and consumers want assurances that products from different vendors will work together and that new features will not require massive reinvestment.

The complexity of the industry and its unstable nature are part of what IT must manage. Managing it well requires a knowledge of the nature of what is to be managed. While there are surely management skills common to all industries and situations, it is a different thing to manage an oil field than a broadcast network. One must know something about what is being managed as well as the goals of its management.

System and industry structure

Figure 1.1 is a conventional rendering of system structure. Each layer consists of elements dependent on the services of the layer below. The hardware layer consists of a basic technology layer that defines what a machine is made of, and an architecture layer that defines how it looks to software.

Upperware	
Application development tools *Applications: mail, word processing, spreadsheets*	
Middleware	
File systems *Database managers* *Interface managers*	*Security managers* *Transaction managers*
Baseware	
Base operating system *Network software*	
Hardware	
Hardware/software interface/architecture *Design* *Technology*	

Reprinted by kind permission of MTS, Ashford, Middlesex, England.

Figure 1.1   System structure.

Elements of the hardware layer determine the underlying capability of a computer system. The speed of the processor, the size of its memory, the organization of the pathways between the elements, and the operations that can be performed are the concerns of the semiconductor and computer segments of the information industry. These concerns determine what is on our desktops or laps and in our printers and toasters, how long it will be there, and what we are paying for it.

Above the hardware layer, the software layers are often described as baseware, middleware, and upperware. In actual product, the boundaries between the layers (and the structures within) are fuzzy and are obscured by packaging and pricing. Internal componentry and layer-to-layer relations are in constant flux but, in a general way:

1 *Baseware* is closest to the hardware—it is software that manages the hardware resource. Baseware hides the hardware attributes from middleware. It offers services like reading and writing disks, refreshing the screen, etc. Exemplars of baseware are the DOS operating system, and the base Unix System. From the point of view of middleware, baseware is an extension of the hardware.

2 *Middleware* defines the key underlying concepts of computing. Our ideas of a document, or a file of information, or a data base, are defined here. Middleware uses baseware and provides services of data access and storage, and program control for the use of upperware.

3 *Upperware* is what is immediately interesting to an end user. Word processing programs, spreadsheets, mail programs, programs to develop programs, etc. exist in countless numbers at the upperware layer. Historically, these are the "applications" of computers, although the line between what is an "application" and what is a "system service" is constantly shifting.

Terms like "operating systems," "communication managers," "file systems," "data base managers," "presentation managers," etc. are used informally to represent functions in different layers. It is not always clear what these terms mean. "Operating system" is sometimes used to represent baseware, or baseware plus selected middleware elements, or an entire collection of system software.

Figure 1.2 provides a more complete picture of the software structure. It is not for "study" at this time; it is shown now to suggest the scale of software complexity and the reasons why software coherence is so difficult to achieve. It indicates the major layers and the particular technologies associated with those layers. The benefits, functions, and costs of these elements are in large part the topic of this book.

Value of software

Ideally, each layer adds greater benefit by adding greater functionality and usability. When computing hardware is expensive, baseware increases value by maximizing the efficiency of hardware. It maximizes sharing and utilization. When hardware is inexpensive, upperware increases value by providing for user productivity. Software perceived as too complex to own and use (a burden, rather than a tool) will have trouble as costs of ownership become high relative to the cost of hardware.

The core functions of a software environment are to:

1 Define a machine persona. Provide attractive and appropriate access to services for users, application developers, systems managers, and administrators.

2 Define and manage the resources of computing. Guarantee the availability, correctness, integrity, and security of data and programs. Enable the sharing of resources for multiple users on a single computer or across a network. Provide for interaction between users in a single system or across a network.

Figure 1.3 shows how greater value has shifted toward upperware. When machines were absolutely expensive, it was critical to manage the hardware well. Baseware resource management contributed value at the cost of end-user

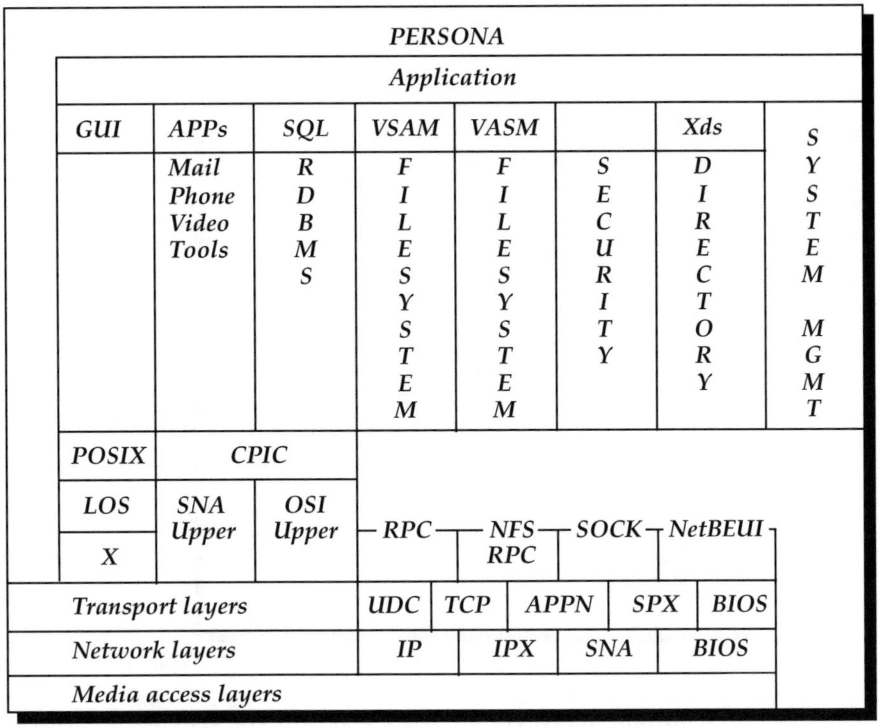

Figure content:

PERSONA							
Application							
GUI	APPs	SQL	VSAM	VASM		Xds	S
	Mail	R	F	F	S	D	Y
	Phone	D	I	I	E	I	S
	Video	B	L	L	C	R	T
	Tools	M	E	E	U	E	E
		S	S	S	R	C	M
			Y	Y	I	T	
			S	S	T	O	M
			T	T	Y	R	G
			E	E		Y	M
			M	M			T
POSIX	CPIC						
LOS	SNA Upper	OSI Upper	— RPC —	NFS RPC —	SOCK —	NetBEUI ⌐	
X							
Transport layers			UDC	TCP	APPN	SPX	BIOS
Network layers			IP	IPX	SNA	BIOS	
Media access layers							

Reprinted by kind permission of MTS, Ashford, Middlesex, England.

APPS	Applications		RDBMS	Relational Data Base Management System
CDE	Common Desktop Environment		RPC	Remote Procedure Call
CPIC	Common Programming Interface for Communications		SNA	Systems Network Architecture
GUI	Graphical User Interface		SQL	Structure Query Language
IP	Internet Protocol		TCP	Transmission Control Protocol
NFS	Network File System		UDC	Unix Datagram
OSI	Open System Interconnection		VSAM	Virtual Storage Access Method
POSIX	Portable Operating System Interface for Unix		XDR	External Data Representation
			Xds	Interface for Directory Services

Figure 1.2 Software structure.

inconvenience and professional support. As end users' productivity has become key, upperware contributes relatively more value. In effect, competition shifts from the wellhead to the pump.

The cost of all functions must be less than their value. There is great disagreement on when and whether this is so. Cost of ownership arguments have been developed against every form of computing. Mainframes, minicomputers, client/server, and workgroup computing—buzzwords of our time—

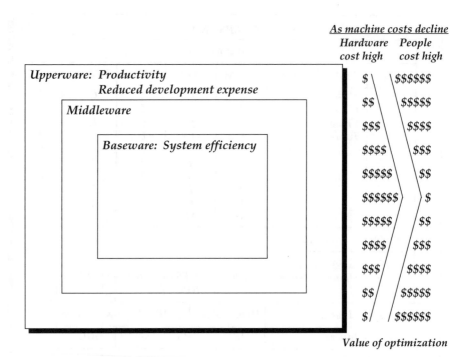

Figure 1.3 Software value. As people become more expensive than machines, the dollar value of optimizing people becomes higher than the dollar value of optimizing machines.

suggest an approximate notion of how enterprise power should be organized. Each has enemies that claim the cost of ownership and operation are insupportable. A great part of the cost derives from the acquisition, tending, operation, and evolution of software.

IT decisions and system structure

Upperware requires middleware. Middleware requires baseware. Software requires hardware, which in turn requires semiconductor technology, which in turn requires semiconductor design and manufacturing technology.

Each layer has many competing personalities (Pentium vs. PowerPC, OS/2 vs. MS-DOS/Windows, etc.) and is in itself quite complex, with many elements of differing interdependencies. Developing enterprise IT systems requires systems decisions in key areas:

1 To what degree should baseware, hardware, or upperware be standard within the enterprise, within departments, within any operational unit? What is the benefit of an enterprise operating system standard? What is the downside? To what degree and on what basis can heterogeneity be allowed at various software levels?

2 To what degree is availability of middleware a gating function for baseware, or of upperware a gating function for middleware? Should it be necessary that selected middleware elements run on all baseware platforms? What inconveniences arise if some middleware runs only on some baseware? Some baseware only on some hardware, etc.?

3 What is a proper strategy for packaging vs. customization? Is it better to buy component by component or layer by layer, or to buy highly integrated environments in which baseware, middleware, and upperware are priced and packaged as a unit?

These questions, and their resolution, determine the personalities of enterprise computing systems and the range of vendors with which IT must deal. Someone must decide what is to be bought and who it is to be bought from. There is a clear argument for IT to decide the hardware, baseware, and middleware elements of all systems, and to decide from the viewpoint of manageability and efficiency.

The structure of the industry determines how many vendors must be involved in technology processes. Some IT organizations have continuing liaison with upwards of 75 vendors. User departments in these companies have some equally long, partially intersecting lists.

System and industry structure

Software structure is a metaphor for industry structure. Figure 1.4 shows industry segments. As in the petroleum industry, there are complex integrations and separations, and a variety of relations between companies drilling, pumping, transporting, and refining hardware and software products.

The semiconductor (technology) industry has diverged from the "computer industry." Intel, National Semiconductor, Advanced Microdevices, and Cypress are technology sources not themselves participants in the computer or software market. They compete in a capital-intensive segment for the business of the computer companies: IBM, Compaq, Dell, Hewlett-Packard, and DEC.

	Microsoft	IBM	Lotus	Oracle	Novell	Intel
Spreadsheets, mail, word processors	•		•			
Interface managers	•	•				
File systems/data base managers	•	•		•	•	
Operating systems/network operating systems, e.g., Microsoft, Novell, Univel, HP, DEC, IBM, Sun, SCO	•	•			•	
Computer packagers, e.g., IBM Apple, Compaq, HP, DEC, Sequent, NCR, Sun — Communication, e.g., Wellfleet, Cisco — Drives, e.g., Conner						
Architectures/technology companies		•				•
Semiconductor/technology companies		•				•

Reprinted by kind permission of MTS, Ashford, Middlesex, England.

Figure 1.4   Structure of computer industry.

The computer companies choose a technology on which to base their computers. They determine how to package this technology and the degree to which they will add specializations and proprietizations of their own.

The degree to which a computer maker specializes its machine or conforms to industry standards reflects its position in the industry. Leadership companies generally attempt to differentiate and provide unique features. Other companies are content to produce low-cost "clones" or "compatibles."

Computer software, especially baseware, was long associated with particular hardware. Much early software ran only on a single machine type or within a single machine family. Vertical companies had various "bundling" strategies. Over time, for example, a major vendor would offer services and software free with hardware, or would "unbundle" and charge individually for hardware, software, and services support.

Whether the layers were bundled or unbundled, however, there was a strong link between particular hardware, baseware, middleware, and upperware personalities. In contrast, bundling (MS-DOS, Windows, Softnet Fax, e.g., with an IBM Thinkpad) now involves the products of many companies and complex licensing agreements.

Software segments

There have always been software companies with no hardware revenue flow and vendors producing applications and middleware for other people's machines. In a market with a single company holding nearly 80% of mainstream market share, a proper strategy is to create software for the industry-dominant machine. When the machines tend to be large and the market small, this software can be "pricy" and profit margins large.

The independent software companies of the mainframe era tended to be niche companies that were more symbionts than competitors, in that their success depended on the success of IBM. Insurance industry applications on a mainframe required the IBM baseware and middleware. Systems management software required a particular system to manage.

The emergence of a mass personal computer market dominated by a semiconductor company (Intel, not IBM) changes the rules. A software company maximizes profit by running on as many machines as possible, from different vendors, making itself available for different hardware and loosening the bond between hardware and software. Prices are set in accordance with consumer and mass market dynamics, aiming for market share and volume. More and more software at all levels is available regardless of whether a machine is from IBM, Compaq, Dell, ASR, or even Apple or Sun, which do not use the Intel chips.

The loosening relation between particular hardware and baseware is paralleled by loosening relations among baseware, middleware, and upperware. A middleware vendor must decide what baseware environments it will run with (Unix, Macintosh, Windows, OS/2, or MVS). An upperware vendor must decide what middleware (Oracle, Sybase, DB2, or CICS) it will run with.

A software company must decide in what layers to operate and how broadly to cover the layers. It must decide whether to specialize in a small niche or position itself as an "enterprise" player with a broad product line. Microsoft makes software at many levels, from operating system (baseware) to application packages (upperware). Its level of vertical integration has been a concern for the government because of the potential for it to force acquisition of its operating system in order to run its applications. This practice, once considered normal in the industry, is now viewed as a possible constraint of trade.

Decisions of upper-layer suppliers are critical to the success of lower-layer products. OS/2 and Apple Macintosh, for example, experience problems attracting upperware developers, who see greater return on early development for the Microsoft Windows family. Available upperware is critical to the success of middleware and baseware.

Figure 1.4 shows that many companies straddle layers. IBM provides OS/2 for its PC hardware and AIX for its RS/6000s. It also provides a DB2 data base for its AIX baseware. Similarly, Hewlett-Packard, DEC, and other systems vendors straddle layers. As a consequence, there are upperware, middleware, baseware, and hardware layers that still are strongly linked to each other.

There are vertically defined companies that operate in "towers" defined across layers. For example, they may provide some of the baseware, middleware, and upperware needed for communications or for storage management. Figure 1.5 shows a tower for communications, data base management, file management, and document management. It also shows baseware shifting up as a tower serving specialized towers. A company may offer a full range of software and services within a tower, with product at each layer. Such offerings lead to specialized systems, such as data servers or communication servers.

Counterforces

The fragmentation of the industry into semi-independent layers is balanced by a counterforce of integration. This integration is both product- and company-oriented. Oracle and Sybase integrate their middleware data base managers with Novell baseware to present a consistent image and become "automatic" participants in the Novell networking market. Lotus and Microsoft integrate various upperware products (data base, spreadsheet, word processor) into packages that have a common look and feel and a single price. Microsoft moves to acquire Intuit (but backs away when the government frowns), Novell acquires WordPerfect, and SynOptics and Wellfleet merge. There is a rebirth of bundling—but the bundles straddle vendors, and the bundles may be horizontal.

In addition to the integrating acquisitions, there is a constant flow of alliances, consortia, and partnerships that address particular (often ephemeral) market concerns. IBM and Apple, Novell, Unix Systems Laboratories, Wellfleet and SynOptics were among the bruited or actual affiliations of the past year.

Segments, niches, and boundaries are constantly shifting. Companies face the danger of becoming too generalized, or of not offering a sufficient range of

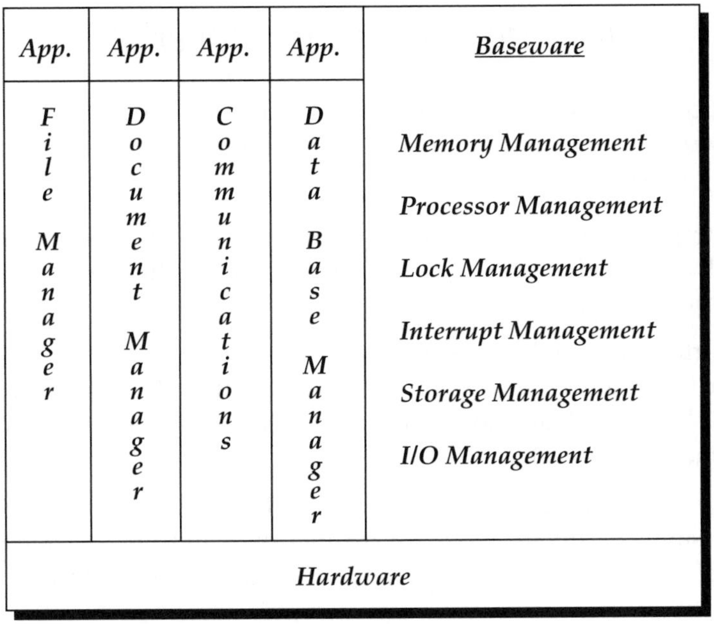

App.	App.	App.	App.	Baseware
File Manager	Document Manager	Communications	Data Base Manager	Memory Management Processor Management Lock Management Interrupt Management Storage Management I/O Management
Hardware				

Figure 1.5 Tower concept of software.

product to sustain the revenue flow. Novell is an important example of a company in the midst of repositioning. The leader in the local area network communications niche, it became concerned that first-generation client/server technology was not sufficient to sustain growth. It is currently attempting to use partnerships (with AT&T and Wellfleet) to penetrate wide area networking. It is forming alliances and acquiring technology to compete in the upperware segment with AppWare. It is expanding its own technology to address enterprise-wide networking issues. Some see this as a necessary expansion of product line. Others see it as a loss of focus. In an industry with shifting segments, the problem of product range is common to all companies, from IBM to my smallest start-up clients.

Apple is another company growing out of its niche. The forces of integration of desktop and larger systems into networks, the sheer number of Microsoft Windows systems, and the power of Intel and Intel packagers press in on Apple's once tidy and secure niche. It is forced to allow cloning of its product, to support Windows software, and to move onto a machine (PowerPC) hoping to become an industry standard.

Paradigms of computing—putting it together

There has been much said about "shifting paradigms" of computing. There is a certain amount of confusion and some self-interest involved in this, but there is a prevailing sense that:

1 Total enterprise computing must consist of a population of machines of different scales and personalities that must cooperate to define an enterprise information asset.

2 An important relation between two machines is the client/server relation. Software helping the interaction between a person and a machine runs on a desk or lap (client), and software giving access to data runs on a shared larger machine (server).

3 A minimal cost of change must be achieved. This involves "scalability" (use of a single hardware and software environment from "palmtop" to "teraflop") and "portability" (enabling programs to run on different platforms).

4 Access to information must not be restricted by artificial technology boundaries. It must be possible to access any information from anywhere, across different vendors and environments.

5 Conferencing and group work situations must be simulated by information technology at a level that includes visualization, document sharing, and modifications in multimedia.

6 Electronically stored data must include "unstructured" data beyond current files and data bases. Graphics, image, video, voice, and touch must enable advanced visualization of data and ease human/machine interaction.

7 The access device at the interface between human and system must be meaningful to the senses of the human. The PC must be a multimedia device, offering a range of entry and reaction methods, integrating the personas of the telephone, television, computer, stereo, copier, etc. in a way that involves the human.

Deciding when, for whom, and how the above will come to an enterprise, and at what cost, must be the responsibility of IT. There are disputes about both benefits and costs, and many mythological creatures intrude rudely on the discussion. The mythologies are serious because they distort proper views of the decision space and set up obstacles to clear thinking and clean doing.

The mythic beast of centralized computing

The Loch Ness monster of information processing is a nasty creature called "centralized computing." This beast embodies the (incorrect) idea that a single enormous machine in a single enormous data center can provide all of the information technology for an enterprise. It is accessed by "dumb" terminals throughout the company, but nothing called a "computer" exists in the enterprise other than the single enormous machine. Naturally, it is controlled by an enfranchised priesthood that dispenses rights of access to a community of dependent clients. The high point of this odd view was the Multics system in the late 1960s, which envisioned huge data centers and four machines serving America.

Whether or not this is an attractive idea is not at issue. The truth is that there are no exemplars of this beast. All companies of serious size have both multiple machines and multiple data centers. There are different degrees of operational centralization, and there are tendencies to have more or fewer data centers with more or fewer machines in them. But no machine represents more than about one-thirtieth of total enterprise computer power in a corporation of significant size.

The "centralized vs. distributed" decision is a choice about the relative percentage of computer power represented by any particular machine or data center. It is theoretically possible to decide whether a particular environment can be best served by one, one hundred, or one thousand machines. It is possible to distribute workloads and data resources in a number of different ways. Apples compete with oranges all the time.

Changes in technology cause price anomalies and discontinuities between older machines and newer machines. Technologies (bipolar, ECL) developed for a small market of large machines aim for high performance. These technologies, specially designed, manufactured in limited quantities, form the basis of "traditional" mainframes. Technologies (CMOS) developed for mass markets concentrate on cost effectiveness. They are slower but more price/performance effective. The new chip technologies will soon be the basis of all machines, including new generations of mainframes (enterprise servers).

Changes in technology have caused a redefinition of machine classes. Mainframes, minicomputers, and microcomputers have given way to superservers, enterprise servers, department servers, group servers, and personal servers. These share a common technology and have much common architecture. They are "scalable" machines. An ideal of baseware, middleware, and upperware is to be able to run on machines of any scale and in populations of arbitrarily small or large size. This notion of scale combines with an idea of "open" standards to minimize the cost of migration and coexistence.

The mythic beast of open

Bigfoot. Ideally, in the new world, an enterprise may move from 5 large machines to 50 smaller machines and versions of the same software environment can be configured to support the new topology. The software does not present a constraint to migration polices.

In this "open" world, scalability and portability, interoperability, and migratability are perfect. Virtual mainframes that form thousands of computers into the image of a single computing resource can be formed with components from diverse vendors using various baseware, middleware, and upperware elements.

This is another mythic beast, seen only in the fog by distraught stragglers. There are severe limitations on scale, interoperability, portability, and compatibility in the industry. Unexpected limitations and costs characteristically hinder progress toward the enterprise resource.

Unhappily, at the present, baseware, middleware, and upperware elements do not run on any machine of any size. There are definite barriers to data sharing and access to function that derive from machine type and machine scale. Overcoming these barriers is called "open distributed computing," and it is something of our Holy Grail in that, like the Grail, many are no more sure of what it is than they are of where it is.

New capabilities, old glories

Software requirements and capabilities spring from new hardware. Video, voice, and high-performance transmission are hardware potentials that must be enabled by software. Hardware advance imposes new requirements and, at the same time, makes them easier to achieve. As computer storage and memories grow in size and computer logic becomes faster, programs that took hours can take seconds. Graphics, artificial intelligence, and on-line data bases waited years for fast hardware at low cost so they could enter the mainstream of computing.

New hardware technologies—such as high-resolution image and graphics hardware, high-performance digital video, extremely low-cost, high-volume digital storage, high-performance optical storage, and low-cost broadband communications—will require new software elements. Each of the new software elements must be put into a structure where it interacts with other software elements. How well this is done will affect users' impressions of the usefulness of the software environment. It is often not clear how a new function should be positioned in a software structure. Should optical images be held in special optical data managers or integrated with traditional file managers, for example? This problem is becoming part of our considerations for the future of data bases and objects.

In the presence of remarkable and destabilizing rates of change, there is a vast population of older systems generally referred to as the "legacy." The nature of this legacy is uncertain, as the word means different things to different folks. To some it means any IBM mainframe running its proprietary software. To others it means particular applications that run only in a particular environment. To others it means components of systems developed before the current generation of hardware and software technologies.

Something must be decided about this legacy. Is it a rich heirloom we were lucky to inherit or a terrible white elephant forced upon us by the innocence of our predecessors? Is it to be replaced immediately, at some reasonable rate, or integrated into new computing environments? If it is to be integrated, by what process will the integration occur? How will things move from old to new? How will the old itself become the new?

While we are making decisions about what is in the data center, we are creating a second legacy that may or may not be even more difficult to dispose of—a legacy of obsoleting personal machines and small client/server systems that have great difficulty participating in enterprise computing. While we were watching and giving presentations about integration and collapsing barriers, we created a set of dismembered systems without regard for their reintegration.

Due diligence

We see our possibilities through technology. It is a dangerous error to despise technology with patent phrases like "technology cannot solve management problems, but management can solve technology problems." It is equally dangerous to believe that unmanaged technology can achieve goals and reap rewards.

Technological change at the rate we are experiencing is destabilizing for the institutions that use it, as well as for the institutions that create it. There has been severe disappointment in the payback of technology investments, even in relatively stable and manageable times. There have been cost overruns, project delays and failures, and low software quality in the most stable times. In dangerous times like these, the level of management and technology skills needed for the effective integration of new capabilities is higher than at any time since the beginning of information technology.

The "devil is in the details" has two dimensions of truth. One is that a lack of knowledge of details involves extraordinary risk. The other is that the inability to get beyond the details involves equal risk. We are all familiar with projects that flounder because of some minuscule showstopper buried in old code. We are equally familiar with projects that flounder because they have not considered issues of integration and longer-term evolution.

Changes in technology clearly require a response from the culture responsible for its acquisition, evolution, and use. Different organizations of different skill sets are required. Different metaphors and abstractions are needed to articulate system concepts and directions. Different working groups and group relations must be formed around technology as its own internal structure changes.

Changes in technology and industry structure present a number of challenges to the IT culture. In particular, IT must define processes of due diligence in technology investment:

1 The rate at which new technologies will be acquired. What are the risks of early commitment? What is the cost of skills needed to use the technology? What is the best method of introducing the technology?

2 The rate at which old technologies will be retired. What must be migrated and what may be replaced? What is the cost of migration and replacement? What residual role can the old technologies play?

3 The various new technologies that are key to the future. Are there technologies that will enable new business strategies? Are there technologies that solve long-standing problems? Are there emerging technologies that are a precondition for profit?

4 The most profitable of different system structures competing for the same applications. How should work and data be dispersed around the enterprise resources? What are the relative costs of different systems structures? What balance of investment in networking capacity vs. larger systems is appropriate?

5 How new technologies affect system architecture. Will new components fall into current frameworks? Will new frameworks be required to integrate new functions? How will image data be brought on line? How will objects be brought to systems?

6 How the new industry structure must affect acquisition. Must IT be more aggressive in acting as its own system integrator? How will multiple vendors be effectively managed? How will requirements be coordinated across multiple vendors? How will vendors be chosen?

7 The modifications needed for IT organization and function. Are new skills necessary? Are new groupings of skills required? Are some new management processes required? Is a new relation with user entities required?

The next IT "era" will have more vendors competing for attention. It will have even higher user expectations. It will have even greater rates of change. It will have new sets of decisions to be made and risks to be evaluated. In order to navigate these rough seas, it is essential that:

1 IT management understand the nature of the technologies in which they must invest: what they are; what they do; how they compare; and which are industry dominant. What are the up- and downsides of the current state of the art? What is the probable next stage and the cost of getting to it?

2 IT technologists must develop and understand the broader framework in which new technologies will be introduced. They must understand which elements depend on each other. They must be able to identify potential problems with technology and estimate the rate of technology maturity. They must understand the benefit/cost framework for justifying the investment.

IT management must be able to listen, and IT technologists must be able to articulate the nature of technology. IT technologists must be able to listen, and IT management must be able to articulate the business and IT strategies that technology will serve.

The enterprise must trust IT as it trusts its corporate counsel to be the holder of its brief. It is as grotesque to place attorneys in every operational department as it is to place senior systems programmers, planners, and systems integrators in those departments. No more so, and no less so.

The key technologies

Conventional wisdom is that the dominant paradigm of computing is one of flexibility, heterogeneity, and customizability. Different divisions of work across different populations of computers on differing network structures will represent mosaics of resources in "heterogeneous distributed computing systems." We could, in fact, make this so.

Building large, robust networks of interacting computers is difficult when computer hardware and software on different systems come from the same culture. There are things that are hard to do on two machines that are easy to do on one. When differing system personas, hardware, baseware, middleware, and upperware are trying to interoperate, the difficulties increase. Multi-vendor and multiplatform systems have serious barriers to cooperation and sharing across elements on the network. Limitations exist in how different products can "talk" to each other. An articulated aim of the industry is to overcome these limitations and increase the capacity of systems to cooperate. But sometimes the industry has less will and weight than a vendor who does not see profit in going that way.

The technologies required for heterogeneous distributed computing and the processes needed for their management define the scope of this book. It is hoped that a meeting ground between management and various technology disciplines is defined by these topics.

Look and feel

Technology that defines the interactions between human and machine: what users do to make something happen, what mental models are used, and how the computer indicates what choices exist. Software elements involved are Windows and OS/2 Presentation Manager (and their multimedia extensions), X Windows, Motif, OPEN LOOK, NeXT, Apple, Common User Access, and Common Desktop Environment. Each of these is either a set of standards for how a computer and a person should interact or a programming framework in which to enforce those standards or both.

Access

Technology that enables a user to gain access to a system entry point. After gaining access, the user must be granted rights to individual and particular resources across the network. Access involves authentication (proving the user is the user), authorization (checking what the user is allowed to do), and encryption (masking data except for privileged users). Access controls exist in operating systems, communication managers, and specialized security packages in various forms around the network. Particular technologies include Resource Access Control Facility (RACF), Access Control Function (ACF II), Unix Access List, AS/400 user profiles, data base management views and schema.

Locate resources

The ability to find data or function anywhere in a network. This requires common naming conventions and the ability to search through directories of resources at various machines. Some form of global directory is required. An emerging technology is International Standards Organization (ISO) X.500. Support for X.500-like global directories is available from Novell NetWare 4.0, Sun ONC+, and Microsoft Windows NT, and is part of the commitment of OSF DCE.

Communicate

Establish contact across the network. Various conventions (protocols) exist for network traversal. These define the formats and events of data exchange between programs running on different systems. They are implemented in communications software that processes network messages. Among the industry-pervasive protocol suites are IBM's Systems Network Architecture (SNA), DEC's Digital Network Architecture (DNA), the Transmission Control Protocol/Internet Protocol (TCP/IP) available from a broad spectrum of vendors, and Sequenced Packet Exchange/Internet Packet Exchange (SPX/IPX) from the Novell Corporation and various licensees.

Interaction between programs across the network

Application programs wishing to communicate across the network need technology to invoke the services of the communications software. There are various models of program interaction, including Common Programming Interface for Communications (CPI-C), Remote Procedure Calls (RPC) and message transfer mechanisms such as Message Queuing Interface (MQI). Each of these represents the behavior and interface (semantics and syntax) for a model of program relations.

Access to remote data

Technology that enables a program or a data system to access data in a remote data system. It includes distributed data base management technology from many vendors: Gupta, Informix, Sybase, Oracle, Ingres, and others. It also includes data warehouse technology that enables data from diverse sources to be gathered together into a unified format.

SOME BASIC SOFTWARE

Unix is the trademark name for an operating system developed in the early 1970s. Unix more truly characterizes a family of systems using similar technologies and interfaces. The pure Unix (SVR5) system is owned by Novell. There are Unix variants offered by numerous vendors, including Sun Microsystems (Solaris), Hewlett-Packard (HP-UX), DEC (OSF/1) and IBM (AIX). The right to call a system Unix is controlled by the X/Open Consortium.

Windows is a family of operating systems developed and marketed by the Microsoft Corporation. These systems are the de facto standard for laptop and desktop operating systems. The initial version depends upon MS-DOS (Microsoft-Disk Operating System) as baseware. Newer versions (Windows NT, Windows 95) are integrated offerings. There is also an NTAS (NT Advanced Server). Windows runs primarily on computers that use Intel technology, but NT can be taken to other machines.

OS/2 is a product of the IBM Corporation for Intel-based machines. It is a complete operating environment. The current version, Warp, is highly integrated with communications (once again) part of the package.

Apple Macintosh System 7, still thought by some to be the quintessential friendly system, runs on Apple hardware. The chief difficulty of the system is that it does not scale and has many unique interfaces.

NetWare is a system providing local area connection from Apple, Windows, DOS, OS/2, and Unix to larger NetWare client systems providing data and administrative support. It is used to link single-user machines to shared machines (servers) over a technology of local area networking (the distance of a building or a corporate park). While NetWare is a product of the Novell Corporation, NetWare communications functions are available from a large number of vendors for different operating systems. NetWare runs primarily on Intel-based computers, but elements of NetWare directly concerned with communications run on all architectures and machine models.

Systems management

Managing the software, applications, data, use, and network of a heterogeneous system involves many dimensions and individual technologies. All systems vendors provide technology for network and systems management that enables resource control, problem determination, and problem resolution. Aspects include storage management, recovery, security, software distribution, and remote workload management. The dominant industry protocol is the Simple Network Management Protocol (SNMP), the basis for most products in this area. Serious extensions to SNMP are embodied in SNMP 2 and in the Communication Management International Protocol proposed by the ISO. There are key products from IBM, DEC, Microsoft, Novell, Hewlett-Packard, Sun, Tivoli, and others. Bringing industrial strength to the network means establishing storage management, archiving, security, and recovery on a network-wide basis that is as good as what mainframes do for dumb terminals.

Other important technologies

These are the enabling operational technologies of heterogeneous distributed computing. Other technologies are involved with the development of the software necessary for such systems. Of particular interest are the tools and toolkits used as part of Computer Aided Software Engineering (CASE). Increased productivity and program quality is a long-time key IT concern. This decade may have the technology to solve chronic software development problems.

After a discussion of some aspects of IT, the book addresses those aspects of the hardware and software technologies that should form the common knowledge of manager and technician. The technician will achieve a broader view of technology frameworks, costs, and risks. The manager will achieve a deeper understanding of the nature of the technologies upon whose success his or her career depends.

chapter 2

The playing field

EXECUTIVE SUMMARY *In the face of destabilizing rates of change, decisions must be made about what rates an enterprise wishes to establish for itself. Different transitions of leadership, pacing, or laggardness, with their attendant risks, occur when technology generations last two years rather than five. Decisions must be constantly revisited at the various layers of a system. Architectural styles as well as individual components change significantly. We move from mainframe host/slave to client/server, and will surely move onto another scenario in a few years, and we must begin to manage the transitions as much as the stopping points.*

An enterprise must have a cohesive strategy for evolution based upon a perception of its own needs, current costs, and points at which no change becomes more expensive than change. Hardware and software elements combine and recombine to form fundamentally new offerings and systems structures.

The key technologies must be identified, and evolutionary strategies must support each technology. The enterprise should be aware of what constitutes aggressive behavior and what constitutes dangerous slowness in installing new technology.

Plus ça change

It is proverbial in the computer industry that most companies operate at the state of the practice, a generation behind the state of the art and two or more generations behind the leading edge of advanced technology. Four generations of computing are represented at any time, since there are companies operating a generation behind the state of the practice.

In simpler times, a generation of computing lasted about five years. Change was gradual and evolutionary; nondisruptiveness was integrated into management and technology mindsets. Updates, mid-life kickers, and new versions were introduced at a leisurely rate by vendors happy to squeeze the last drops of profit out of an older system and not challenged by much direct competition.

The movement from idea through proof of concept, through pilot, to industrial strength is considerably faster now. Hardware and software obsolete quickly and, as a result, so do our skills. A generation may last less than two years. The risks or benefits of the state of the practice, the state of the art, and the edge of the art have changed as "behindedness" comes more quickly. In some layers, five years behind may mean three generations behind, and in some industries that means "out of the game."

The rate of change is so rapid that the processes used to assess and manage technology investment are not flexible and quick enough. The complexity of the market has given rise to a new set of decisions involving comparisons of unlike technologies (apples and oranges) for which we have no set methodology. The technology has provided a potential whose value we have no true way of measuring: why, how, and how much is a product engineer producing better, more profitable product on a three-dimensional multimedia screen.

In times of rapid change, there is broad difference of opinion about what is a "safe" policy for technology acquisition and investment. Some feel it is necessary to "reinvent" the enterprise in accordance with new technological opportunities. Others feel this is dangerous and will disrupt business function and distort technology investment.

Some feel it necessary to preserve and integrate older technologies (mainframes); others feel it necessary to replace older technologies as quickly as possible. Some feel it necessary to introduce new software cultures as quickly as possible; others feel it unwise to break old cultures.

Information technology has architectural periods like cultures. One progresses (or at least changes) from Hellenistic to Norman to Gothic to Modern. These shifts are driven by technological and cultural changes. To exist, a modern building requires glass and steel, of course, but it also requires attitudes, values, and esthetics.

At the moment, "client/server" is a dominant architectural style and a metaphor for change (see Box 2.1). In early 1995, few companies participating in various surveys still thought it merely a buzzword and few thought there was a decision to be made other than how and when it would be done. The architectural concept matured because the glass and steel it needed matured and the attitudes it needed developed alongside.

There are many significant examples of the successful development of money-saving and reliable systems involving a smallish server and a set of personal computers. There is a small counter-reformation, with instances of an expanded use of mainframes, or of the introduction of larger servers to replace groups of smaller servers. This is only to be expected.

Counter-reformation claims that there are unacceptable hidden expenses in client/server reflecting great uncertainties about the cost of change; tendencies to decentralization; unexpected costs involved in new development and migration; and what change is an unavoidable change or merely an impulse to the future.

WHAT IS CLIENT/SERVER?

The best answer seems to be "I don't know, but I know it when I see it." There are different views of whether client/server represents an organizational style or a specific set of hardware and software technologies. For some, client/server means decentralization, loss of IT control, and local and departmental application development. For others, it merely means a partitioning of function across the network so that systems services can be accessed from a personal computer running an application in direct contact with a human. The IT organization surrounding such networking and service technology is orthogonal to the structure of the system.

The phrase client/server is sometimes used to mean a specific configuration of computers— a client requesting services (data, for example) and a server providing a service. But it is also used to suggest any form of computing in which distribution occurs and it is necessary for more than one machine to operate in order to perform a user request.

Client/server, whatever it may be, is progressing despite rumbles of a counter-reformation. Recent surveys confirm some disappointments in first-generation systems, but the great bulk of organizations were pleased to have undertaken it.

Change, when rational, occurs when it is too expensive not to change. But the assessment of this is complex and partially judgmental. The measurement of cost involves more than comparisons between the prices of different systems. There are legal and tax issues relative to depreciation and investment credits. There are secondary costs of power, maintenance, and credit. There are costs associated with risk assessment and the possibilities that new technologies will be delayed or unstable on arrival. There are issues of whether denied benefits or lost opportunities should be counted as costs.

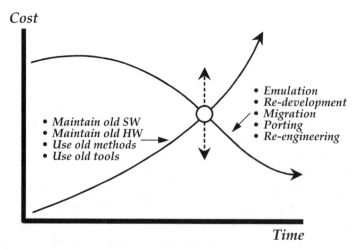

Cost

- *Maintain old SW*
- *Maintain old HW*
- *Use old methods*
- *Use old tools*

- *Emulation*
- *Re-development*
- *Migration*
- *Porting*
- *Re-engineering*

Time

Figure 2.1   Cost/change curve.

WHAT IS VALUE?

The assessment of value is one of the arcane arts of information technology. There are wildly different views. Narrow views often measure value by cost avoidance or cost reduction. The value of the system is a reduction in unit cost to accomplish a certain activity. A somewhat more aggressive view associates value with revenue that the system can generate; for example, additional business volumes or a new line of business using interactive television ordering.

An intriguing view is that the value of a system is the worth of the information it produces. A system contributing information that is part of a $10,000,000 decision is more valuable than a system producing information that is part of a $1,000 decision. In this sense, information used by the enterprise may be more valuable than information used by a department.

Time may also be factored into appreciations of value. Units of information have different rates of decay. Yesterday's commodity contract prices have little value to a trader today. The value of a computer system may be the difference in value of information it can produce at a much earlier time.

Value may be calculated as the difference between the benefit and the cost of maintaining and operating a system. Some propose the calculation of value as the cost of replacement. That is, if one spent $10,000,000 fifteen years ago to develop an application that can now be replaced for $500,000, the value of that application is $500,000.

Figure 2.1 shows a crossover point where the cost of no change exceeds the cost of change. At the crossover point, the cost of new system elements and the cost of introducing them are seen to be less than the cost of continuing the older system. An aggressive company will include lost opportunity costs in the assessment, a more conservative company will not. Among the cost elements are

- maintaining older hardware vs. the acquisition of new
- extending older hardware vs. the acquisition of new
- older hardware environments vs. new environments
- older software maintenance vs. redevelopment
- redevelopment of older vs. new system
- acquiring new skills for new system
- acquiring new skills for older system
- migration skills
- denied systems features:
  - portability between vendors
  - lack of interoperability
  - lack of new technologies for end user and network
  - inability to run new software
- denied strategic benefits:
  - rapid response to business need
  - differences in rates of productivity.

WHAT IS THE LEGACY?

Exactly what has been inherited and whether it is a boon or a burden is often a matter of some dispute. Extreme partisans of change use "legacy" as a pejorative and a label for technology that is expensive to maintain and operate and that is no longer contributing information of value to the enterprise. Any older IBM 390 running IBM proprietary software is by definition part of the burdensome legacy. (Older proprietary systems using older technologies from any vendor are viewed the same way.) Such equipment and its software must be removed as quickly as possible since they drain off IT resources beyond their value in the form of hardware and software maintenance.

More moderate folk suspect that the old technology mainframes are in fact part of a burden, but that software running on them may well be contributing considerable value to the enterprise. They sometimes use the word "legacy" to indicate a set of older, stable infrastructure applications around which the business is built. They do not see the older mainframes as something to dump, but as something that must be "integrated" into a new generation of computing.

Much argumentation goes on about whether integrating older systems or replacing them is more economic and, in fact, exactly what the difference is between the two activities.

The crossover may occur because migration tools make the process of change inexpensive or because the dramatic low cost of the new technology overcomes any resistance.

There are great problems in discovering the critical point. The metrics for value (see Box 2.2) are informal and intuitive. The metrics for cost are less solid than they appear to be when risks, depreciation periods, inflation rates, costs of credit, etc. are factored into sophisticated assessments.

There is little safety in numbers, or in anything else. For aggressive companies, there is the risk that new technologies do not have industrial strength, that they lack supporting services, utilities, and tools. It is possible that skills will be difficult or expensive to acquire, and that there will be unexpected new forms of complexity and costs. For conservative companies, there is the danger of late realization of applications, of productivity disadvantages with competitors, of missed strategic opportunities, and of dependence on a single vendor strategy.

Change strategy

Figure 2.2 shows three rates of change associated with different views of the value of computing. It maps the percentage of investment in "legacy" technology (see Box 2.3) over time. An aggressive company, a moderate company, and a conservative company introduce new technologies at different rates, driven by their appreciations of value, cost, and risk.

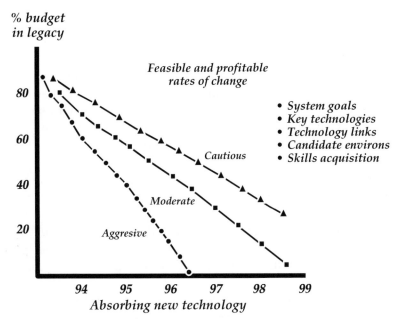

% budget
in legacy

Feasible and profitable
rates of change

• *System goals*
• *Key technologies*
• *Technology links*
• *Candidate environs*
• *Skills acquisition*

Cautious

Moderate

Aggresive

80

60

40

20

94   95   96   97   98   99

Absorbing new technology

Reprinted by kind permission of MTS, Ashford, Middlesex, England.

Figure 2.2   Rates of change.

These rates of change represent strategies. Often one hears of a "DCE (Distributed Computing Environment) strategy" or "a Windows strategy," where a product or technology choice is used to describe an enterprise direction. This is a wrong view and demonstrates the extent to which there is confusion about what a strategy is. Product acquisition decisions must derive from a strategic statement of the goals of an enterprise over time.

Strategy: "Use state-of-the-art technology introduced at a rate appropriate for avoiding competitive disadvantage and providing return on investment within two years of introduction. Use technology derived from de jure and de facto standards from dependable vendors able to provide adequate support."

Strategy: "Use advanced technology introduced at a rate appropriate for assuming industry leadership. Accept high percentages of project failure in order to win high-leverage success. Use the shortest possible depreciation periods and assure that no back-level technology is used by principals of the company. Introduce early product for evaluation, and assess vendors primarily on technology quality rather than financial stability."

Strategy: "Minimize the cost of information technology. Outsource all functions that can be outsourced on favorable contract terms. Change technology only in response to industry changes when older technology is fully depreci-ated. Use only industry-dominant financially stable companies as service or technology sources."

These three quite different statements represent strategies. They create frameworks within which one acquires and uses technology. They derive from views of the competitive and regulatory environment of an industry. An enter-prise must determine if it believes there is profit to risk in technology leader-ship, or that the greatest profit is pacing the industry, or that there is no risk in lagging behind.

An aggressive company is positioned between the state of the art and the practice. It is using technology for production within two years of beta test and is commonly a beta-test site. It is pressing vendors to stretch their technology reach, searching for more aggressive vendors, depreciating product at very fast rates, and reorganizing itself at frequent intervals. It tends to be "project ori-ented," and since it is willing to accept risk, it will take fast solutions that may not endure.

A moderate company is at the state of the practice. It is using product within four years of beta test and is essentially tracking vendor curves for rates of change. It uses write-offs of longer duration, and its organizational structure is relatively stable. It is risk averse to the extent that there must be evidence of industry experience and success with a product before it will introduce it.

A conservative company is behind the state of the practice. It introduces technology six to ten years after beta test. It is primarily cost driven, and often must be pushed by its vendors to replace product coming off support cycles. It uses long depreciation periods, and has a rigid organizational structure, tend-ing to be very centralized.

There is a great deal of frantic reporting in the trade press and even in some highly partisan professional literature. Sometimes it is difficult to assess what the mainstream of the "moderate" company truly looks like in key areas. The following sections represent what is likely the predominant strategy at differ-ent layers.

Hardware

The number of larger mainframes being retired is quite low. There is a strong tendency to prolong the life of the large mainframe. This tendency is stronger in companies that own them than companies that lease them. The depreciation rate for these systems has fallen from an average of about seven years to about four years. A fully depreciated mainframe is not a bad asset.

POSITIONING MATRIX

A = Aggressive M = Moderate C = Conservative X = Very aggressive	Done	Testing	Doing	Prototype	Exploring	Planning	Thinking	Reject	Aware	Unaware
Replace some older mainframes	A	A	M	M	M	C	C	C	C	C
Object applications	A	A	M	M	C	C	C	C	C	C
Upper CASE and I-CASE	A	A	M	M	C	C	C	C	C	C
End user applications	A	M	M	M	C	C	C	C	C	C
Multimedia mail	A	A	A	M	M	M	C	C	C	C
Multiple production C/S	A	A	A	M	M	M	C	C	C	C
Mission-critical C/S	A	A	A	A	M	M	M	C	C	C
Relational data bases	M	C	C	X	X	X	X	X	X	X
Object data bases	X	X	A	A	A	A	M	M	C	C
Open disciplines–DCE, X/Open	A	A	A	A	M	M	M	C	C	C
Unix	A	A	M	M	C	C	C	C	C	C
No new applications on legacy	A	A	A	M	M	M	M	C	C	C
Downsizing projects	A	A	M	M	M	M	M	C	C	C
Workgroup computing	X	A	A	A	M	M	M	C	C	C
Re-engineering	X	X	A	A	A	A	M	C	C	C
LAN management system	A	M	M	M	M	C	C	C	C	C
Integrated LAN/WAN	A	A	M	M	M	M	C	C	C	C
Multiprotocol networking	A	A	M	M	M	M	C	C	C	C
Heterogeneous distributed data	A	A	M	M	M	M	C	C	C	C

Reprinted by kind permission of the manticore consultancy, New York.

The mainframe is being positioned as a full participant in network-oriented computing by bringing new software technology to it. Open, client/server software technologies (representing de facto standards from X/Open and other organizations), which are discussed later in this book, are being aggressively produced for older mainframe software by all major vendors.

There is a more significant replacement of older midsize machines with departmental servers. While the larger water-cooled mainframe is hanging on fairly well, smaller, older machines, like the IBM systems that traditionally run

WHAT IS A SERVER?

A clever man at a development lab once said to me that "midsize machines were in big trouble but servers were doing fine." The words "mini-computer" or "midsize machine" reek of antiquity. But "group server," "department server," and "enterprise server" are wonderful new things. What is the difference between them? Why are the Sequent WinServer, the HP 9000, and the IBM RS/6000 perceived differently from the IBM AS/400?

It is not at all clear. All of the contemporary servers are microchip based, running with Intel chips or with high-performance RISC chips (see Chapter 3). They are "open" in the sense that they run industry de facto standard communications software and offer pervasive data managers from independent vendors. They interact with a variety of clients running different operating systems. Although not necessarily Unix based, they offer technology from the Unix culture through the X/Open Consortium or the Open Software Foundation. They have a set of software development tools designed to split work between a desktop or laptop machine and a tending server. Those that do not offer that much Unix technology (Windows, OS/2) at least offer Unix-style or Novell-style communications.

The midsize machine, on the other hand, is not chip based, runs proprietary software, often offers only a vendor proprietary communications technology, interacts with fewer clients, and has a definite unique character. AS/400, DEC/VMS, and HP/MPE are exemplars of software environments for midsize systems. There are fewer client/server development tools and they offer fewer services to the clients in way of backup, recovery, etc.

But it is a subtle thing, becoming more subtle as the midsize machine vendors bring "client/server" technology to position the older machines as fully legitimate servers. But whether the AS/400 will ever be perceived as a server in the sense that other machines are remains to be seen.

the VSE operating system, are under heavy attack. IBM seems to be more willing to propose its own AIX products as VSE replacements, and is trying to position its AS/400 as an "open server," something very difficult to do with the particular packaging of that machine.

Systems software

There has been a rapid penetration of Unix into the IT culture, even in companies that are not aggressive. Unix has become the operating system of choice for larger servers and is now safely part of the IT mainstream. Whether Microsoft's attempts to dislodge it with Windows NT will be successful is not clear as of this writing. There will likely be significant Windows NT penetration.

A large number of companies are introducing software technologies that position the older systems as servers. Extensions to the mainframe IBM operating

36

system MVS, called MVS Open Edition, include a Unix-like look and feel, and interfaces that conform to emerging Unix standards. This positions MVS as a participant in network-oriented systems involving multiple vendors.

A reasonable strategy for a cautious company is to move onto microchip versions of the 390 while developing applications that use the Open Edition interfaces. In this way, they may reduce the cost of new capacity and introduce new software cultures at a modest rate. At some time in the future, the software environment may be moved to a PowerPC-based new generation mainframe.

There is a rapid introduction of communications culture from the Unix world. TCP/IP is now the mainstream communications standard for all vendors in almost all environments involving long-distance networking. Similarly, Novell NetWare is being introduced into multiple environments as a de facto standard for local area networking.

The moderate company is already multicultured, with important Windows, Unix, and older systems instances. There are fewer and fewer instances of "pure shops," where a single vendor dominates across all the software layers.

Applications

The mainstream strategy seems to involve these elements:

1 Continued reliance on informal narrative design and specifications documents. COBOL remains the primary programming language, but there is significant penetration of C. Continued use of the traditional development models.

2 Significant, but not dominant, use of relational data technology.

3 Infrequent use of user-developed programs, with well over 70% of development done by IT programming staffs.

4 Development for mainframe is often limited to "commodity applications," where GUIs have no clear value, and to the maintenance of older applications.

5 Some client/server successes with small networks out of the control of IT. Few on-line transaction or mission-critical systems.

There is a shift in make vs. buy decisions for software, with an increasing tendency to buy wherever feasible. This helps establish portable software with common interfaces within an organization.

What is an architecture?

The search for an architecture in IT is like the search for the Holy Grail. It is generally believed that between a strategy and a system design there is something called an "architecture," the function of which is to define a structure that will enable certain activities to occur within it.

Attractive as it may seem, the architectural metaphor has some dangers for IT. Buildings are not constructed to be amorphous and flexible entities changing with fashion and reconfiguring easily. Each period has an architectural style that comes from its culture. In this regard IT is consistent, as its architectures take on metaphors like "distributed" or "client/server" in a way similar to Hellenic or to Gothic styles. But Hellenic buildings are rarely transformed to Gothic buildings, while it may be necessary to transform mainframe to distributed architectures.

Despite its elusiveness and despite the dangers of the building metaphor, some framework for technology must exist. There must be appropriate constraints, guidelines, and standards with which to operate the processes of establishing information technology.

Most architects and construction contractors agree that renovating an old structure is generally more costly and complex than creating a new one. This explains why buildings on a site are so often torn down and replaced rather than renovated.

The metaphor of a building architecture is not really satisfactory for systems because of the rates of change. Recently, a new metaphor has been substituted—a metaphor of city planning. How much this will contribute to understanding remains to be seen, but it might well be more satisfactory because it abandons the fiction of eternity.

In IT there is a tendency to start from the top and to go down to details. However, starting from the top has the danger of confusing the architecture with the business plan. An architecture may be closely linked with the business plan, just as a building is closely linked with its uses and purposes, but architecture is only a statement of the structure in which the business plan can operate. It is well understood that the system deriving from the architecture should:

1 Not constrain the enterprise from realizing strategic goals.

2 Enable the enterprise to restructure and reform itself as business practices suggest.

3 Enable the enterprise to adopt new technology at a rate consistent with its industry goals.

2.6   MVS AS A GOTHIC CATHEDRAL

The operating system for the large 390s has evolved over the years as the 20th century's version of a Gothic cathedral. The first generation had an inspiration and began to build the first version without much documentation and no "architecture" as such, just as if it were the first generation of a cathedral built under the hand of a master, without documents.

A second generation understood that it would be a good thing to document what was being built. It improperly and incompletely attempted to do so, leaving future generations with unreliable ideas of how the thing held together.

A later generation decided that the original concept was wrong and undertook major conceptual changes, restructuring modules, and elaborating functions, just as the stone pillars of some 12th century cathedrals were covered with marble in the 16th century.

A still later generation regretted the modifications of their predecessors and decided to return the structure as much as possible to its original form, ripping out modules, recombining elements, as the buildings were restored to their pristine form.

Thus, an old piece of software has a long history, only partially documented, reflecting the unreliable opinions of generations of builders, and a population of modules as varied and complex as a cathedral with a 4th century crypt and an 18th century clock tower.

Too close a linkage between the IT architecture and the business plan or enterprise architecture will surely be a problem at some future time. IT architectures must not constrain business change.

If the word "architecture" is properly used in an IT context, there must be artifacts and processes equivalent to those existing in the construction industry. These processes and artifacts must provide goals, constraints, and measures of success. Therefore, an IT architecture must contain:

1. A definition of the interfaces that can exist within the enterprise system and a statement of their sources. This is the equivalent of an architectural standard-parts catalog. The included interfaces define a "profile" for the enterprise system. The profile will define the portability of elements of the enterprise system.

2. A definition of the behaviors (protocols) that can exist within the enterprise. A protocol concerns what software does, as opposed to how it is invoked. The communications world is concerned primarily with protocols—defining behaviors, independently of interfaces. The protocols will define the extent of component interaction within an enterprise.

3. A statement of the distributability of elements consisting of interfaces and protocols. This provides for an ability to reconfigure function and data across a network as underlying layers change.

Most IT architectures must address a renovation process from existing systems with a current population of hardware, networking, and software. IT cannot "shut down" the old structure while the new structure is emerging. Some definite process for retiring elements of the old system and for preserving others must be defined.

A renovation architecture must include an adequate description of older elements that must be associated with the new architecture. It must also include the methodologies that will transform old elements into new elements—in particular, the way that interfaces and protocols of the new architecture will be introduced. There must also be a statement of process and sequencing that indicates the order in which elements will be replaced (or modified and preserved) and denotes dependencies. Finally, there must be a statement of the time it will take to achieve the "renovations."

All of this seems quite simple enough, but it is rarely done; and as a result, enterprises are in constant confusion and are supporting insupportable costs of change.

Responsibilities and principles

It is the responsibility of the technical staff to create implementable, flexible architectures that constrain the costs and risks of information technology. It is the responsibility of management to sufficiently understand the architectures so as to constrain product acquisition strategies.

In the current atmosphere of uncontrolled spending, architectural efforts are funded and flounder because of uncertainty about what an architecture is and what it is to achieve. Enormous sums are spent on documents that do not impact the behavior of development in any way.

IT management is unable to control expense because it does not understand what an architecture is and what an architecture is supposed to do.

An architecture:

1 Is a statement of vision but also a statement of constraints. It must provide limits for design efforts (as design must limit development).

2 Must be costable within a broad range. Expenditure levels must be inferable from architectural statements.

3 Must identify industry standard parts to be used in development and construction.

4 Must provide support for a broad window of business strategies.

5 Must provide for the evolution and replacement of components over time. Migration costs must be built into the architecture.

Technologists and management must guarantee to an enterprise that the thing called "architecture" has these features.

Uncertainty and dispute

A real danger is that the position of an enterprise is inappropriate for the times and for the industry it is in. In times of rapid technology change, coupled with sometimes dramatic changes in regulatory environments, entire industries are destabilized. The strategy must be appropriate within an economic context.

There are dangers for all strategies. The aggressive company faces the possibility that new technology is not industrial strength. There may be a lack of the usual infrastructure utilities and services, a difficulty finding skills, unexpected costs of migration, and new forms of complexity not initially well understood.

On the other hand, overly conservative companies face rising costs and lost opportunities. There will continue to be long lags in application development, maximum software maintenance costs, increasing skills costs as older skills become arcane, and dependence for change on the self-enhancing strategy of a single vendor or small set of vendors.

There is great difficulty in organizing the decision space. Many costs attributed to client/server are investments in Open technology that will be common to all platforms—MVS Open Edition ("looks like Unix, feels like Unix, works like MVS") as much as for Windows NT or OS/2 or Unix itself. The costs of achieving the skills needed for MVS/Open will be the costs of achieving the skills for client/server.

There is concern that distribution will lead to a decentralization that is very expensive and loses control. This argument started in 1956, and we still do not have it right. Distributed-computing resources and distributed control of computing budgets, while not orthogonal, are only loosely connected. While there are strong arguments for decentralizing application acquisition and development, there are impelling arguments for sustaining an operational infrastructure to track technology, support enterprise applications, and control operational costs. This has nothing to do with the relative costs of client/server or mainframes.

WHAT IS INDUSTRIAL STRENGTH?

At the heart of the conservative argument is the idea that only older mainframe systems like MVS have a robustness appropriate for corporate information processing. The argument is that they alone have the technology, the tools, and the attitudes appropriate for mission-critical transactions. Industrial strength is defined across elements of availability, recovery, backup, synchronization, and security at large-system scale.

Advocates of the "new paradigm" claim that "industrial strength" at a single machine is no longer a key criterion, that industrial strength must be provided across the network. Modern industrial strength means backup, recovery, and storage management across the network, something the older mainframe software does not do.

Achieving industrial strength on the network finds systems like MVS and Novell NetWare racing for the center. The IBM Storage Division Distributed Storage Manager running on MVS moves MVS to industrial strength, as new versions of Windows NT and NetWare achieve industrial strength on servers. When all this matures, "industrial strength" will be available in a system regardless of the size of its elements and the age of its software. Network-oriented companies have surely overcome any notions that group, departmental, or enterprise servers are toys.

Self-serving and inconsistent statements and counterstatements abound to support intuitive views. For example, mainframe advocates will notice that mainframes run 86% of the total time, while PC LANS run only 36% of the time. This is offered as part of a defense for mainframes as transaction engines. But client/server buffs will point out that almost all mainframe transactions are triggered during normal office hours. Therefore, mainframe late shifts are running batch programs whose value may not be clear.

There is considerable disagreement about system stability. MVS mainframe availability is 99.6% and PC LAN capability is 92%, on average. But MVS must be accessed from a network, a network-centric theologist will say, and networks do not have the stability of individual nodes. Distributed computing can avoid single points of failure at a low cost.

There are continuing arguments about the cost of ownership. Traditionalists say that personal and administrative costs make distributed computing intolerably expensive. The counterstatement is that costs of distribution and

	Cost per User	Revenue per User	Profit per User
Mainframe	$2,797	$1,347	$−1,450
Distributed	2,162	2,445	278
Decentralized	9,347	13,400	4,053

Table 2.1   Per-user cost analysis.

decentralization are being muddled. Distribution can be centrally and effectively managed.

Table 2.1 confirms that decentralized computing is expensive, but centrally managed distributed computing and mainframe computing have quite similar per-user costs. The data in the table are a result of a project to determine costs and benefits using accounting methods in which costs of mainframe operations are calculated to include software revision and application maintenance costs, and costs of acquiring skills for "open" are allocated to all systems. Notice also the Profit per User column, which reminds us that more costly systems can be more profitable if they have bigger payoffs. Unhappily, the payoffs go to the user, and the costs accrue to IT.

chapter 3

Kinds of computers

The reader is advised to read the first chapter in The Basics Book, *"The Queen in the Hive," for a review of underlying principles and technology.*

*E*XECUTIVE SUMMARY *Many of the basic bright ideas about software have been around since the "big bang" waiting for hardware fast enough to make them feasible. It is the dramatic shift in the basics of hardware design and technology that has fueled the current period of instability. New classes of machines—application servers, data base servers, network servers, enterprise servers, group servers, etc.—populate the space that used to be occupied by mainframes, mini-computers, and desktop machines.*

In the new technology environment, the properties of classes of machine tend to blur, and the very specific attributes of "small," "large," and "medium" machines seem more like points on a scalable continuum. Systems seem buildable across different partitions of work and distributions on different populations of machine.

A great deal of uncertainty about the meaning of words like "mainframe" has developed. What is a new 32-microprocessor multimillion dollar system? Is it a new generation of mainframe, or a new kind of system for which a place must be found in the IT culture?

The industry seeks ways to enable comparing the apples and oranges that must be compared to each other.

The existence of a small number of highly scalable hardware systems has an enormous impact on software, which must respond to new configuration and co-existence requirements.

Hardware

Hardware (the part of a system one can kick) is still the basis of it all. A computer is one or more processing units, some memory, disk storage, and I/O adapters that allow it to use printers, CD-ROMs, floppy disks, high-performance monitors, speakers, faxes, etc.

Over the years, the logical structure, design, and technology used to build computers has changed dramatically. This has been reflected in important changes in cost and capability and in the redefinition of the segments of the

Architecture		Packaging Range ($)	Characterization
IBM S/390	CISC	75,000–6,000,000	midsize to mainframe
IBM AS/400	CISC[1]	10,000–1,000,000	small to midsize
IBM PowerPC	RISC[2]	5,000–10,000,000	laptop to superserver
DEC VAX	CISC[2]	3,000–4,000,000	desktop to midsize
DEC Alpha	RISC	4,000–1,000,000	workstation to enterprise server
Intel 386	CISC	800–2,000,000	laptop to parallel
Intel 486	CISC	1,500–2,000,000	laptop to parallel
Intel Pentium	RISC/CISC	2,500–2,000,000	laptop to enterprise
SPARC	RISC	4,000–1,000,000	workstation to enterprise
PA-7100	RISC	4,000–1,000,000	workstation to enterprise
MIPS RS4200	RISC	5,000–750,000	workstation to enterprise

[1]Very complex.

[2]Complex for its type.

Table 3.1   Architecture examples.

computer marketplace. It was once clear that a large machine differed in many ways from a small machine. It used different basic semiconductor technology and a radically more complex unique design, and it looked different to a program. Now the industry is moving to a set of scalable systems built around essentially the same technology, with many common points of design.

The old terminologies of computers—"mainframes," "minicomputers," "midsized machines," "microcomputers,"—have given way to a new terminology that reflects the new packaging of computer systems. "Enterprise server," "departmental server," "group server," and "personal server" suggest the scale of a computer from those which provide services across an organization down to a personal system. "Application server," "data server," "network server," and "security server" reflect specializations of computer systems now affordable with current technology.

The various kinds of computers are built around a family of underlying architectures (see Table 3.1). A hardware architecture is a set of rules a program must obey to function correctly. Examples are the IBM 390 family, the DEC Alpha, and the Intel Pentium. Each of these machines represents a set of programming rules that a compiler must obey when it creates a program. The product packaging of an architecture defines its market range or scalability.

FUNDAMENTAL STRUCTURES

The uniprocessor is a single processor with memory, input/output, and special-function adapters. It spans a large range of performance levels. A minimum uniprocessor in 1994 was in a package under $1,000 and likely contained an Intel 486 clocked at 33 MHz with 4 MB of memory. A large uniprocessor consisted of a RISC chip clocked at 150 MHz with 64 MB of memory at a price of over $5,000. The performance range spans personal computers, through engineering workstations, to departmental systems servicing multiple users accessing the system through their own devices.

The asymmetrical multiprocessor has two or more processors of different architecture or design, each of which is dedicated to a specialized function. One version is the coprocessor. A math coprocessor may provide fast execution of floating-point operations, enabling a personal computer to take on engineering tasks. The processors share memory.

The multicomputer has processors that do not share memory. It can be used for compatibility between different chips or for special functions like imaging and video. For example, one computer may have Intel architecture, and the other computer may be a high-performance signal processor managing images.

The symmetrical multiprocessor has two or more identical processors that share memory and other systems capabilities. Any program can move from one processor to another at the convenience of the system. The processors are perfect peers.

This class of machine has a tremendous range, from two-processor group servers in the $15,000 range to enterprise server mainframe challengers like the Sequent Symmetry, with up to 32 processors in configurations costing from $200,000 to $2,000,000. The symmetric multiprocessor imposes special requirements on an operating system.

A CISC architecture has many powerful instructions that attempt to do things with the fewest instructions. A RISC architecture has very simple instructions and achieves speed by doing many of them in parallel.

Computer organization

The microprocessors, memories, buses, special function chips, storage devices, etc. are assembled into computer systems of various size, cost, performance, and other features. Some fundamental machine organizations are shown in Figure 3.1.

These computer structures represent variations in product packaging that occur at different price levels. The packaging has different goals. The multiprocessor, for example, is used to improve the performance of a system without using more expensive technology. The coprocessor is often used to enhance performance for particular operations, such as floating-point operations. The multicomputer is often used to achieve compatibility. Thus, a Macintosh running on a non-Intel architecture would permit the introduction of an Intel processor and memory to run Intel-based programs.

Interesting trends: the massively parallel system

"Massively parallel" is a generic term for systems that have from 500 to 1,000,000 processors. Originally they were thought to be useful mainly for applications with enormous volumes of calculation. However, the parallel organization is found useful for critical operations in data management, and the parallel data base engine has become mainstream, most recently integrated into AT&T/NCR systems architectures (the Teradata engine, consisting of thousands of Intel processors).

The massively parallel system is a fine-grained multiprocessor. This means that each processor is small and adds relatively little to the total computational power. Applications are decomposed to maximize the parallel potential. For example, to sort a million numbers, the lists are partitioned so that multiple processors can sort sublists in parallel and then cooperate to conjoin the sorted sublists.

There are two types of massive parallelism: SIMD (single-instruction multiple-data) and MIMD (multiple-instruction multiple-data) machines. In the SIMD machine, a set of processors execute a single instruction in lock step. It is an extension of the uniprocessor model. The MIMD machine is an extension of the multiprocessor model, where sets of processors may collaborate within an application, but each processor has local controls.

There are a number of SIMD massively parallel machines at or near the market. These include the GF-11 from IBM and the DECmpp 1200. The DECmpp is based on the Intel i860 architecture (an inexpensive RISC chip from Intel

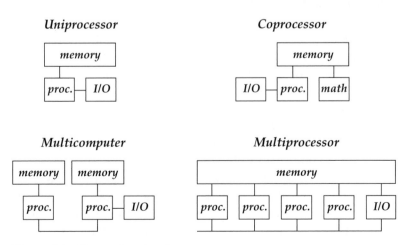

Figure 3.1   Computer structures.

MASSIVELY PARALLEL

Mature computer scientists cannot remember a time when parallel computing was not about to burst upon us. This poor author wrote in 1972 (*Parallelism in Hardware and Software*) describing structures much like those being discussed now, and was preceded by research in the 1960s. In 1972, it seemed that the constraints were: it was hard to define and create programs that could be partitioned and harder to use the same number of processors over their activation to about the same degree, a requirement of parallel efficiency.

Our mathematics is essentially convergent and our thought processes sequential. Some say massive parallelism will not be mainline until there are easier notations for describing parallel operations. Others say massive parallelism will not be mainline until software can find the parallel potential for itself without worrying the programmer. Both, for the moment, seem to be right.

We used to think that weather prediction was an application. If one could reduce the elapsed time necessary to process all of the data, one could improve weather prediction. We now understand that is wrong. We will never be able to predict the weather. There are too many butterflies flapping too many wings.

primarily intended for controllers) with a range of 1,000 to 16,000 processors and a price range of $175,000 to $1,800,000 dollars. There are emerging entry-level massively parallel SIMD systems at around the $75,000 level.

Massively parallel MIMD machines include the Thinking Machine, with up to 65,000 processors, and the Teradata Data Engine. These, like SIMD machines, are rarely used as stand-alone general purpose computers. They are commonly associated with some large-scale general purpose system or are nodes on networks supporting general purpose systems.

Interesting trends: the specialized engine

Now that hardware seems cheap, the economics of specialization begin to have more appeal. Early specializations were attempts to cut hardware costs by reducing the generality of operations. Specialized sorting engines, specialized data base machines, and specialized scientific calculators (vector processors) had little success because the functions they performed required most of the hardware of a general purpose processor.

The new specializations involve configurations of standard hardware. Specialization does not come from architecture, but from combinations of standard elements. The Intel-based Teradata is an extreme example. This machine is marketed by AT&T Global as a data base engine that can be accessed from a network or from a mainframe. It has a large (4K) population of microprocessors, which together represent an enormous parallel capability suitable for query processing.

Economics of hardware

Figure 3.2 shows a U-shaped diminishing-returns curve that reflects ideas of economy of scale. This curve drove the industry for the first twenty years. It states that within a technology period, for a range of architectures, there is an optimum price/performance ("bang for the buck") knee. To the left of that knee, cheaper machines give disproportionately bad performance. To the right of that knee, more expensive machines do not give proportionate performance improvements. This image of computing led to the idea of consolidated workload machines shared by as many users as reasonable.

The x-axis of the curve is price, the y-axis a function of price/performance. Computers are frequently measured by their price/performance ratio, a ratio of price divided by some statement of speed. Unhappily, it is difficult to determine the price of a computer (discounts, private deals, gray markets, "street prices") and almost impossible to determine its performance, since the behavior of a program or a set of programs is affected by so many factors of hardware, software, and use. The concept is firm but the metrics are a little shaky.

The minicomputer of the 1970s seemed to shift the knee so that the mainframes thought to be at the knee began to look less efficient, until an argument could be made for a 4-to-1 price/performance disadvantage by the middle 1970s.

But the microchip broke the curve by breaking the assumption of a common technology envelope for products in the marketplace at the same time. Figure 3.3 shows two curves, one based on the older technologies used by 1980 mainframes and midsize machines, and one based on the technologies of microchips.

Many interpreted the technology discontinuity as a fundamental break in the economy-of-scale curve, an indication that larger systems could never again be as cost efficient as aggregations of smaller systems. This is currently

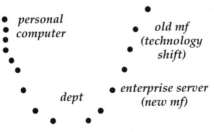

Machines have minimum circuit count and slow technology. Cheap but slow. Big increases in performance for increases in cost. Costly. Small.

personal computer

old mf (technology shift)

dept

enterprise server (new mf)

Machines have maximum circuit count and/or fast technology. Fast but costly. Small increases in performance for large increases in cost.

Machine price/performance ratio is optimum

Figure 3.2   Price/performance curve.

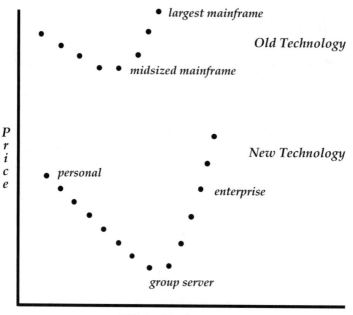

Figure 3.3 Technology discontinuity.

not so clear as it was. One sees in Figure 3.3 that there are versions of personal computers and workstations less efficient than larger versions. That is to say, within a technology envelope, there still seems to be some economy of scale.

At the present, the discontinuity between microprocessor-based machines and "legacy" machines is real. Computational power runs at about $500 per million instructions per second (MIPS) performed for microprocessor-based machines, and $40,000 for mainframes using older technology. As one would expect, market dynamics have cut the price of mainframe power approximately in half (vendors are discounting 40% to 60%), but a great gap still exists between machine classes. This gap will in time be closed by newer-technology mainframes; this is already happening in the form of "enterprise" servers. What is not known is where the enterprise servers, using microchip technology, will join the re-established unified curve when they mature. Presently, a large enterprise server runs at about $15,000 per MIPS.

Until 1994, mainframe prices were decreasing at an annualized rate of about 15%, while micro-based system prices were decreasing at a rate of over 30% per year. While mainframe cost per MIPS had declined from nearly 50 cents in 1982 to under 10 cents in 1994, the ratio of mainframe to mini- and micro-based systems cost had increased from under 7 to nearly 20. For the desktop machine, the ratio is over 100 to 1. In 1994, the cost of 1 MIPS on a micro-based departmental server is around one cent, and the cost on a desktop machine less than half a cent.

Performance is influenced by memory and storage sizes as well as by processor speed. Storage technology prices are about $2,000 per gigabyte of storage for desktop to enterprise server systems, and about $4,000 per gigabyte for classical mainframes. These numbers are expected to settle at about $2,000 per gigabyte for all systems within 4 years (by 1999).

The price of a computer system may be viewed in a broader context as a component of "total cost of ownership." Technologists will often consider associated costs as part of the "price" of a system. For example, Computer A may cost $200,000 and Computer B $125,000 for equivalent functionality. However, the IT community may feel Computer B is more expensive because programs for it are more expensive, it is more expensive to operate and manage, it is more expensive to put it on the network, etc.

Metrics for performance

There are many factors affecting price and performance, and many metrics. Comparing systems or understanding true cost is an arcane art indeed. As the industry matures, it becomes more anxious to compare machines of different architectures. Various artificial benchmarks have been created to reflect the performance of various hardware platforms. Transactions per second are frequently used for commercially oriented systems, and SPEC measurements for engineering systems.

Benchmarking is not as pristine a venture as one might think, and there is considerable accusation and counteraccusation about whether certain test cases, or even architectures, are "rigged" to perform well in accordance with details of a benchmark definition.

The following measures of performance and price/performance appear in the trade literature and in advertisements:

- MIPS (millions of instructions per second)
- Transaction Processing Council's transactions per second (TPS) in order of complexity:
  - TPC-A
  - TPC-B
  - TPC-C
  - TPC-D
  - TPC-E

- SPECint92 (integer processor performance)
- SPECfp92 (floating-point processor performance)
- SPECmP92 (multiprocessor performance)
- Whetstones
- Dhrystones
- Composites-Intel (defined operations per second)
- Cost per transaction (TPS/system cost)
- Cost per MIPS (MIPS/system cost)
- Vendor private benchmarks (from many vendors)

They are all based upon the performance of a particular machine on a standardized set of software programs defined by some neutral group. The transaction per second figures are commonly used as a measure of system throughput for commercially oriented systems. The SPEC figures are commonly used as measures of computational efficiency in scientific/engineering environments.

The metrics above provide performance that can be divided by system cost to develop a metric for price performance. Cost per transaction or cost per MIPS are price/performance metrics.

To assess the cost of various options for enterprise computing power, it is necessary for technicians to understand how various combinations of machines of different sizes will perform together, and what these combinations will cost.

A system's architecture

The language of computing contains the words "mainframe," "minicomputer," "midsize machine," "server," "personal computer," "laptop," "notebook," "workstation," and "client." We have only approximate ideas of what the things suggested by these words truly are. Closely connected are words supposed to describe market dynamics in the industry: "rehosting," "downsizing," "rightsizing," "client/server," "upsizing," and "workgroup distributed." We have only an approximate notion of what these words mean as well. Fuzzy words make it very difficult to perceive what are hard major trends and how ideas legitimately cluster together.

Any particular system will represent about one-fiftieth of the computing resources of a large organization, so the myth of centralization must be abandoned. The decision before us is how to effectively partition total enterprise computing power, given the available classes and kinds of computers and

Class	Use	Attributes	Price Range ($)
Supercomputer	Sci/eng	High FLOPS	2,500,000–25,000,000
Highly parallel	Sci/eng/data base	1K–64K proc	100,000–7,000,000
Mainframe	Gen purpose/comm	Old technology	700,000–25,000,000
Mini-supers	Sci/eng	Symmetric MP	100,000–1,500,000
Enterprise server	Gen purpose/comm	Symmetric MP	200,000–2,000,000
Department server	Gen purpose/comm	Symmetric MP	50,000–500,000
Group server	Gen purpose/comm	Microprocessor	7,000–25,000
Super minis	Gen purpose/comm	Symmetric MP	200,000–3,000,000
Workstations	Sci/eng	Single-user/Unix	5,000–50,000
Personals	Gen purpose	Single-user	1,000–5,000

Table 3.2   System classes.

networks (see Table 3.2). This must be done with various political, historical, and software constraints and in a confusion of machine classes.

"Downsizing," "rightsizing," etc. are about the competition between fuzzily defined classes of machine. Applications and systems may be configured across a number of different computing structures. Small machines, workstations, and midsize servers compete with each other, replace each other, or complement each other according to details of workload and need.

Enterprise computing is some combination of interconnected computers of different classes consistent with strategic goals and cost constraints. This section will look at the general nature of the building blocks.

Building block: the personal computer

The personal computer is most likely an Intel-based desktop or laptop computer with 8 to 64 MB of memory, 240 to 540 MB of disk storage, and a $1,000 to $5,000 price tag. The price depends primarily on how elaborate the interface is. Active matrix color is very expensive in a laptop, increasing the price from around $1,200 to near $5,000 for machines quite similar in other regards.

An alternative personal computer is an Apple with a Motorola 680x0 or a PowerPC engine running Macintosh software.

Multimedia equipment, especially CD-ROM, is rapidly becoming part of the basic package; and video, sound, and pen-based capability are coming on rapidly at prices between $1,500 and $2,500. Built-in fax modems, networking capability, and wireless are common options. Software is often bundled into the price.

An important enterprise decision is the hardware base that will be on executive, professional, and support staff laptops and desktops. Small price differences can have a large budget impact across large populations.

The decision about desktop capacity must be made in the context of networking and server capability. There is a direct trade-off between investing in personal systems and investing in server capacity. This trade-off will not only affect hardware investment, but software investment as well. Whether to have a fully functional data base manager on each desktop or to share a server data base manager from smaller clients is a decision of significant economic impact.

The percentage of stand-alone personal computers is rapidly declining. In the office, less that 20% of desktop computers are not network connected as of the end of 1994. Consequently, the processes of acquiring personal computer power are increasingly constrained by systems concerns and issues.

The depreciation period for a personal computer is another concern. IT should set carefully defined standards for what kinds of computer power are required to keep enterprise employees at least as productive as the competition. Upgrading to graphics- and image-capable systems—for example, that will allow professionals or support staff to create presentations—will not only eliminate outside costs but eliminate response-time delays. The economics of the desktop requires sophisticated measures of productivity.

The cultural split between the Apple machines and the Intel machines is being bridged by Apple. Penetrating business environments requires an ability to run Microsoft client software. IBM and other Intel-based companies can solve this problem at a software level. But Apple, with its non-Intel technology, must also provide a hardware solution. The solution is by no means novel—an Intel chip (DOS Compatibility Card) is provided to run Microsoft software. Apple software arranges for the two cultures to run "seamlessly." The intent is that whatever two Apple programs can do together, they can do with a Windows program.

Building block: the workstation

The workstation has traditionally differed from the personal computer in a number of ways. It is overwhelmingly a RISC-based machine, it usually runs Unix, it has a larger monitor (19" or 21"), and it costs from about $3,000 to $25,000, depending on its image and graphics capabilities. Often it is specialized for various trades and disciplines. Workstations compete fiercely on a raw-performance basis.

The SPARCstations, Alphastations, AIXstations, etc. are commonly measured by SPECint or SPECfp measures of integer arithmetic or floating-point arithmetic performance. The results are constantly changing—the vendors leapfrog each other—and the reader should be aware of the need to have the latest issue trade press publications before claiming to know which is the fastest machine. The following is a late-1994 snapshot of workstations:

- RISC-based: PA-RISC, PowerPC, Alpha, SPARC
- Engineering/scientific
- Many commercial applications
- Strong Unix culture
- Many packages
  - IBM RS/6000
  - HP 9000
  - DEC 300s
  - SPARCstations
  - Silicon Graphics
- Underlying chips
  - DEC Alpha 21064A   (SPECint = 170)
  - DEC Alpha 211641   (SPECint = 300)
  - SGI MIPS R4000   (SPECint = 175)
  - HP PA-RISC 7100   (SPECint =   80)
  - HP PA-RISC 7200   (SPECint = 175)
  - PowerPC   (SPECint =   60–300)
  - SPARC 94   (SPECint = 250)
  - SPARC 95   (SPECint = 375 projected)
  - Pentium 66   (SPECint =   67)

The boundaries between the personal computer and workstation segments may be blurring. The increasing power of Intel processors and buses and the entry of the PowerPC into the PC market suggest a merger of the segments. In the merged segment, units will be priced in a single continuum of power, and the distinction between personal computer and workstation will disappear.

Part of any such segment merge must be the availability of the same software over a multitude of packaging. Microsoft Windows family operating systems must run on non-Intel systems, and Unix must run on a wide band of Intel configurations. Similarly, the data base vendors, e-mail vendors, application development vendors, office suite vendors, etc. must offer product on all platforms at similar prices for similar power.

	Small	Medium	Large
Processor	DX2/66 1/Pentium60	2/DX2 Pentium66	4/DX2 Pentium66
I/O	Fast SCSI-2	Fast SCSI-2	Fast SCSI-2
Storage	550 MB to 112 GB	1050 MB to 140 GB	1050 MB to 140 GB
Use	Comm service	App services	Downsizing
Software	NetWare	NT and Unix	NT and Unix
Performance	50–150 TPS(A)	200–300 TPS(A)	300–400 TPS(A)
Price	$6,000	$9,000	$14,000

Features:
  Monitors condition and performance.
  Fault prefailure timing: 3 year prefailure warranty.
  RAID levels 1, 4, 5; hot pluggable drives; on-line spare drive; off-line backup processor.
  ECC RAM.
  Recovery.
  CD-based hardware configuration/software installation.
  CD-ROM standard.

Table 3.3   Typical smaller servers.

The convergence of workstation and personal computer occurs while there is some uncertainty about what the function of a desktop vs. a laptop vs. a notebook is. Current management trends suggest a larger population of workers in a "virtual office," connected by workgroup, computing across a network. There is some possibility that desktop computers will not be replaced as they age. In their place, there will be "docking" stations allowing portable computers to connect to large monitors and LAN-connected systems in the office.

All of us will work in cyberspace, checking in from time to time.

Building blocks: servers

A server offers service(s) to a workstation or personal computer client. There seems to be no more precise definition that does not lead to technical/theological argument. A server is a primarily software-defined abstraction crossing a wide range of machine sizes.

Group servers

Priced in a range from $6,000 to $15,000, these are versions of personal computers running appropriate server and communications software. They are represented by systems like the Compaq Proliant Servers. There are Apple group servers, but as a group they are predominantly Intel machines and commonly run NetWare server software from Novell.

Table 3.3 shows some examples of typical small servers. The numbers are vendor claims, but vendor names are removed.

Such systems are gaining industrial strength, and though they are rarely used for "mission-critical" applications as of yet, they have fault-tolerant and recovery features that are surely beyond any notions of their being "toys." Note that the larger versions run NT or Unix.

Here is a low-end Unix server family, based on proprietary RISC chips, from a leading Unix vendor with a broad product line reaching into enterprise servers:

Model	TPS	Price
1	80	$5,969
2	125	$8,319
3	155	$11,319

Various vendors are constantly comparing their systems in terms of transactions and SPECints. The following is given only to establish a general range of server performance:

Server	SPECfp92	SPECint92	Price
A	160	185	$16,000
B	121	126	$18,000
C	90	100	$15,000
D	90	120	$16,000

Departmental servers

These are represented by a broad range of systems priced from about $25,000 to $150,000, with an enormous range of performance. Many of these are Intel based, but there is a significant RISC-based and Unix presence. It is at this level of system that the presence of RISC and Unix is most strongly felt. The following departmental servers run proprietary software with X/Open interfaces:

Model	Users	Min. (2 I/O)	Max. (4 I/O)
Very small	8	$12,000	$16,000
Small	64	$40,000	$45,000
Larger	100	$60,000	$65,000
Largest	100	$80,000	$85,000

An uncertain boundary lies between "servers" and "midsize." Midsize systems are traditionally "multiuser" systems, aimed at supporting terminals rather than personal computers. Servers are intended to provide services to communities of workstations or personal computers. A number of companies make systems in the midrange pricing area, but there are differences in the extent to which midrange machines are seen as servers. Among those systems most accepted as servers are those from Unisys, Data General, Sequent, and Sun and the HP 9000 and IBM RS/6000. Those least perceived to be servers are the IBM AS/400 and the IBM ES/9000 midsize machines. The HP 3000 and DEC VMS systems are somewhere in between.

Real differences between midsize machines and servers are due to perceptions that are software defined. There are software technologies that must appear in the software of a server. If they are absent, a machine is viewed as an obsoleting midsize. These software technologies come from the de jure and de facto standards discussed in Chapter 7.

Enterprise servers

Enterprise servers, the new generation of mainframe, can cost in the area of $2,000,000 and deliver in the range of one-half to one-third the mainframe performance at one-tenth to one-third the price. Examples of RISC-based enterprise servers are shown in the table:

System	Proc	OS	TPS	Max. Users	Price
EP1	1/12	Unix	1,500	4,500	$175,000–$650,000
EP2	1/8	Prop	1,500	2,700	$225,000–$680,000

Enterprise servers are both RISC and CISC based and run both Unix and non-Unix software. The Sequent WinServer is an Intel-based symmetric multiprocessor running Windows NT Advanced Server. Other Intel-based enterprise servers come from AT&T and DEC. RISC-based servers running Unix come from Hewlett-Packard and IBM, among countless others.

These systems are the mainframe in a pizza box. They offer a direct challenge to the future of the top-of-the-line system and will certainly become the next generation of machine.

Ah . . . the mainframe

What is it? Traditionally it:

• supports thousands of users
• has an IBM MVS, VM, or VSE operating system or a near copy

3.3   THE GLORY OF THEIR TIME, PART I (SEE BOX B1.11, page 328)

Mainframes were the glory of their time. They have gigabyte primary storage, eight gigabytes of expanded storage, can sustain data rates from I/0 of 10 million bytes per second, and can be combined into multiple system complexes with performance rates in billions of instructions per second. They can service 400 to 500 disk spindles holding terabytes of data. They can support 5,000 interactive on-line users and can process 3,000 transactions per second using specialized transaction software. At this writing, the fastest of these machines was thought to be the Amdahl 5995, which could provide 311 MIPS in full configuration. It cost around $30 million list price (the street price of this class of machine is 40% to 50% of list).

They have been improving over the years. Since 1985, they are 50% more powerful and have over 4 times more memory. Yet there is about them an atmosphere of another time. While their basic problem is that they are off the price/performance curve, they have other problems equally important—the ability of their operating systems to operate comfortably in network-oriented computing structures, interacting with systems of other vendors, and running portable applications.

But they are beautiful, awesome, and a joy to us, like the memory of our first love. Here is an example:

- 4 system complex
- IBM ES/9000 900 (6-way)
- Vector processor per engine
- 1 gigabyte primary store
- 8 gigabyte expanded store
- 256 I/O ESCON 10 MB data rate
- 4 systems approach 1 BIPS
- 400–500 DASD spindles
- Terabyte range
- Workload
  - TSO 500 users on-line
  - IMSff 200 tps
  - IMSFP 1,000 tps
  - CICS 1,000 tps

- has 390-type architecture
- has bipolar technology
- has 4 to 8 way MP
- has IBM-compatible disk storage
- has SNA communication protocols
- has an enormous data farm

This definition limits the population to the set made by IBM, Fujitsu, Hitachi, Amdahl, NEC, and a handful of others. The market for this kind of system was around $32 billion in 1993, with marginal growth since 1987.

It is not likely that the mainframe is dead in the sense that its model of computing is dead. The enterprise server model is a mainframe model. But it is based on a new technology and priced on a different curve.

IBM's 1994 announcement of microchip-based 390s suggests a path to the future. Without breaking the software culture, a mainframe user can move function onto 390 parallel-processor microchip "offload engines," priced at about $15,000, rather than $40,000, per MIPS. These query engines run data base functions at enterprise server prices.

By 1998, all mainframes will be microchip based and a single curve of price/performance will be re-established in the industry.

How fast the current generation will be replaced is not clear. The current average age is a surprisingly low three years. Yet the depreciation periods are shortening dramatically. There seems to be an annual 30% decline in the value of a mainframe. A machine leased at a rate of $45,000 per MIPS in 1993 will have a market value of $10,000 in 1997. This so alarms some leasing companies that they are backing away from the mainframe business.

Yet the beast hangs in. There has only been a small drop in total revenue in the period 1990–1993 and well under a 10% drop in the number of in-place large systems. There even seems to be some potential for growth of current systems.

In places, the mainframe culture is surprisingly intact. The bulk of computer investment is still in mainframes, with over 50% of their budget associated with mainframe culture for some companies. However, a growing number (around 20%) now have less than a 10% allocation for mainframe technology.

About 60% of installed mainframes are purchased, about 15% are leased from a vendor, and about 15% are leased from third parties. The depreciation periods have recently been shortened from a prevailing 7 to a prevailing 5 years.

Hardware markets and systems software

The shift in hardware market segmentation has transformed the nature of software. In earlier times:

1 Hardware was expensive relative to people. Economics dictated the largest possible machines intensely shared. Operating systems were to maximize the efficiency of hardware. There was an assumption that computing environments would be staffed by highly trained professionals who would earn their meager keep by keeping the hardware warm.

2 Particular software did not cross machine cultures. Vendors offered operating systems, etc. for their own machines.

3 Small, medium, and large machines were substantially "different." Programs did not scale. Each class of machine required particular software appropriate for its class.

4 Applications programming was important in most companies. There were relatively few independent software vendors.

These factors led to software that was architecturally specialized, difficult to use, aimed at particular machine classes, and preoccupied with being both industrial strength and efficient in largely centralized environments.

In the current market:

1 Hardware is cheap relative to people. Productivity and quality of work require user friendliness in interfaces that consume enormous amounts of computing power.

2 There is limited economy of scale and an apparent anomaly (perhaps temporary) at the top of the line. Old mainframes are off the price/performance curve and the strategy must avoid new investment in these resources. Some form of "offloading" is required, but exactly what form is uncertain.

3 Software as an industry has become largely autonomous of its hardware base. Software suppliers in operating systems, data bases, communications, software development software, et al. aim software at multiple platforms. Hardware must attract the favor and interest of independent software vendors. Availability of de facto industry software is a key hardware acquisition criteria.

4 Scalable architectures go from "palmtop to teraflop." Intel architectures span packages from hundreds to millions of dollars. A similar destiny seems intended for the DEC Alpha and the IBM PowerPC. The differences between large and small systems lie in systems configuration and topology. Software must scale the architectural range.

5 New applications mostly run on smaller machines and are mostly acquired from software vendors. There is a reduced level of "homegrown" applications, and spreadsheet, data base, and e-mail have become more and more critical.

These conditions lead to a software industry stressing:

1 End user efficiency and attractiveness. Systems compete on the way people "feel" about them. New multimedia applications use sound, CD-ROM, speech, etc. for information access, interaction, and application development.

2 Network-wide industrial strength. Recovery, security, backup, and applications management are extended to the network.

3 Interoperability at all systems levels. Data to any requester from any source, regardless of data formats, data file or data base management system, operating system, communications protocols, or underlying hardware.

4 Large sets of common applications. Systems must have the ability to run industry-dominant applications and attractive new applications.

The change in the software industry derives from the transformation of hardware economics and the development of a consumer market for digital technology. This is linked to a rapid maturing of communications technology, which we will discuss next.

Networking

> *The reader is advised to read the second chapter in* The Basics Book, *"Communications," for a review of the underlying principles and technology.*

EXECUTIVE SUMMARY A necessary (but not sufficient) condition for enterprise computing is the network connection of computers. The interconnection of computers of various cultures complicates the already difficult issues of networking.

Networking is understood through a model of the International Standards Organization called Open System Interconnect (OSI). While the concepts are accepted, the products using them frequently support only obsolete versions of the standard.

As an alternative to OSI, there are pervasive de facto standards, including the IBM Systems Network Architecture, the DEC Digital Network Architecture, the local area protocols of the Novell Corporation, NetWare SPX/IPX, and the standard of the Unix community, TCP/IP.

The various protocols support diverse concepts of how programs across the network interact. Conversations, messaging, and remote procedure calls represent the semantics of program interaction. They are supported by various programming interfaces. The programming interfaces themselves represent an attempt to achieve uniformity, portability, and interoperability between systems.

The pressure to connect machines from different cultures has resulted in a reform of networking product that enables the integration of various protocols within the same product set. It is now possible to choose various interfaces and protocols on almost all operating system baseware. This capability will eventually reduce network complexity by eliminating (or reducing) the need for conversion gateways.

There has been intense focus on interoperability over the past decade. Now new issues are emerging that impact the networking culture. Multimedia access requires considerably enhanced network capability, and connection to Internet-based network services raises a number of security issues.

Networking

The ability of computers to exchange information across distances beyond a few thousand feet depends on technology associated with networking. Wide area networking (telecommunications) permits cooperation between systems without geographical limit; local area networking permits communication within the range of a building or a corporate campus.

An underlying force is the digitalization of communications and television, providing an information technology base identical to computers. Digitalization provides the possibility of common receivers and common pathways for the television and telephone model of communications and for the consequent merger of computers, telephones, televisions, faxes, etc. into a range of consumer machines. Digitalization combined with new transmission media provides the ability to transmit at rates consistent with the needs of high-quality television and image broadcasting.

Change in technology leads to the current interest in a data superhighway that would enable impressive new capabilities. A technology is emerging that will make it common to transmit text, video, voice, and image as part of a single "message." Various industry predictions call for 80% of the capacity of telecommunications lines to be data and image by the mid to late 1990s. At the end of the 1980s, only 20% of the capacity was used for this purpose.

Improvements in transmission media are paralleled by the development of computers dedicated to various network functions. An entire industry of suppliers (Wellfleet, Cisco, CCOM, etc.) of intelligent routers, gateways, hubs, and bridges has developed over the last few years. These are integrated hardware and software units whose performance is defined by resident software.

Until recently, local area network (LAN) culture and technology has been quite distinct from that of wide area networks (WANs). A key difference between LANs and WANs has been speed. Over the years, the ratio of speed between LANs and WANs has gone from around 10:1 to over 150:1. The last ratio is based upon standard 10 Mb/s Ethernet LANs and 64 kb/s WANs. As LANs drive to 100 Mb/s, the ratio becomes even more dramatic. As a result of the differences, response times between LAN- and WAN-based systems can seriously diverge, and different product cultures have developed around LANs and WANs.

However, on the WAN side there are portents of change. Physical technologies are expected to allow speeds about 2,400 times faster than current speeds within a few years. Standards for WANs that provide for speeds in the 64 kb/s to 2,488 Mb/s range have developed. The technology promises the possibility of sending diverse media on the same physical network. Exactly how difficult this is can be seen from the table below that gives the bandwidth requirements for various types of communications media.

Function	Bandwidth (Min.–Max.)
Telephone	8–64 kb/s
Interactive text	4.8–64 kb/s
Text mail, fax, bulk	4.8–64 kb/s
Freeze-frame TV	56–64 kb/s
Compressed video conf.	1.544 Mb/s
Standard TV	34 Mb/s
High-quality TV	540 Mb/s

Since voice and data (and diverse media within data) have different transmission attributes, integration in old technologies was somewhat limited. Phone calls generally are short and require very short, uniform delays on the network, but tolerate long connect times. Data interaction, on the other hand, can be quite bursty, with short messages and long idle times, and is tolerant of some delays during transmission (this is no longer true for multimedia). To integrate diverse media requires technologies that just overpower the problems.

Software-defined networks

Much of the behavior of networked systems is defined by industry standard protocols at hardware and software levels. A generic conceptual framework for protocols in the WAN technologies comes from the International Standards Organization (ISO) architecture for Open Systems Interconnect (OSI) (see Chapter 2 in *The Basics Book*).

The industry has a number of proprietary network architectures that are more or less compliant with the layers and standards of OSI. Among these are IBM's Systems Network Architecture (SNA), DEC's Digital Network Architecture (DNA), the Unix community's Transmission Control Program/Internet Protocol (TCP/IP), the SPX/IPX protocol of the Novell Corporation, and the AppleTalk protocols of Apple. Each of these communications architectures

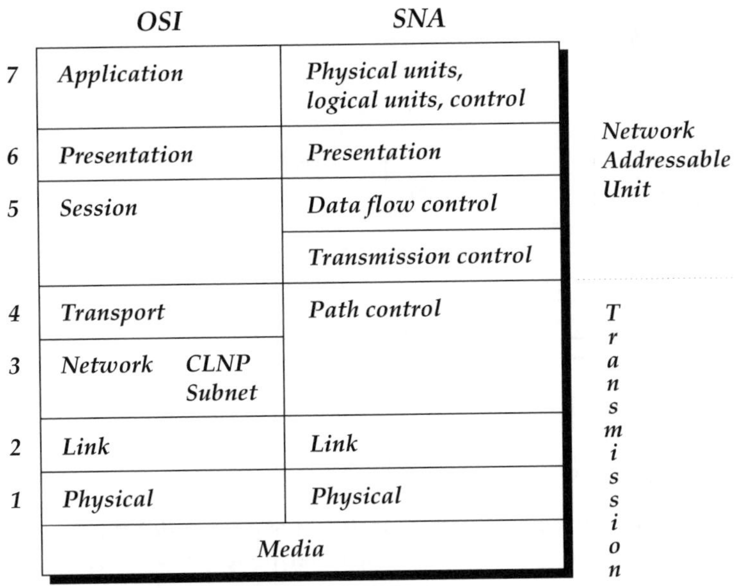

	OSI	SNA	
7	Application	Physical units, logical units, control	Network Addressable Unit
6	Presentation	Presentation	
5	Session	Data flow control	
		Transmission control	
4	Transport	Path control	Transmission
3	Network CLNP Subnet		
2	Link	Link	
1	Physical	Physical	
	Media		

Figure 4.1   SNA on OSI.

includes some of the standards of OSI and IEEE (Institute of Electical and Electronic Engineers) at various layers.

Systems Network Architecture

IBM was early to recognize the need for protocols to interconnect computers and terminals. In 1974, it offered Systems Network Architecture (SNA) as a complete communications environment. Figure 4.1 shows SNA on the OSI model. SNA correspondence is imperfect in the distribution of functions across layers, and there are some OSI concepts of network quality not in SNA.

The primary protocol of SNA, LU 6.2 (Logical Unit version 6.2), intends to provide "industrial strength" to a connection between systems. It provides sessions that hold conversations (sustained defined equivalents of a telephone call) capable of multiple interactions, multiple connections, and guaranteed recovery. SNA APPC (Advanced Program-to-Program Communication) is an interface to the LU 6.2 protocols for the mainframe environments. It is a de facto standard for IBM mainframes. It is clearly intended as a wide area technology.

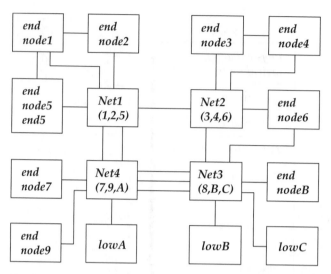

Figure 4.2 APPN provides a meshlike association of peer nodes. Some of them, the end nodes and low order nodes, have limited function.

Other IBM systems and a large number of vendors offer access to LU 6.2 systems through SNA gateways, which convert another protocol into LU 6.2 for mainframe access. DEC was an early provider of DECnet to SNA gateways. Since it now seems that not all mainframes are going to immediately disappear, companies with ambitions in the enterprise arena are providing gateways to SNA. Microsoft and Novell are recent examples of companies now providing their own product to connect to SNA systems. On its own, the definition of SNA has been expanded to include protocols other than LU 6.2. Protocols for local area networking, as well as OSI and the Unix community TCP/IP, are now part of the capability of SNA.

Associated with SNA is a family of layer 7 programs for document exchange (DIA), file distribution (SNA/DS—SNA Distributed Services), and systems management (SNA/MS—SNA Management Services). These programs were primarily developed for the mainframe, and while they may distribute data between various systems, there are no exact equivalents on all IBM platforms.

Advanced Peer-to-Peer Networking

Advanced Peer-to-Peer Networking (APPN) is an extension of SNA that enables communication between smaller computers. It is positioned as an

KEY SNA CONCEPTS

SNA is hierarchic in that it was built to provide access to a mainframe "host" by terminals or limited-function control units. A "host" has network control and responsibilities enabled by its possession of a "System Services Control Point" (SSCP). The SSCP is used to initiate sessions, support directory and routing functions, and monitor the system. The basic SNA network is a family of terminals interacting with a host that has an SSCP.

The mainframe implementation of SNA involved two software components: (1) a mainframe program called Virtual Telecommunications Access Method (VTAM), running (approximately) layers 5 and 6, and (2) a Network Control Program (NCP) running layers 1–4 on a front-end communications controller. However, a network could not be live unless its associated mainframe was up, subjecting network robustness to machines running complex applications workloads.

Now SNA provides host-to-host communication and multiple "domains." A domain is an administrative grouping of resources under common control. Peer-to-peer communication between mainframes is now common in SNA.

SNA has a set of defined network logical units with varying capabilities. Network logical units consist of physical units and logical units. A physical unit (PU) can be a nonprogrammable terminal, a controller, a small processor, or a mainframe. PU definitions define functions associated with the control of physical hardware on the network. A logical unit (LU) is a definition of the logical end points of an SNA connection. All SNA relations are between logical units of various types. The key logical units of SNA are LU 6.2 (full function) and LU 2.1, which provides a protocol for smaller system peer-to-peer interaction. LU 6.2 is sometimes called APPC (Advanced Program-to-Program Communication). An extension of LU 2.1 is called APPN (Advanced Peer-to-Peer Networking).

alternative to TPC/IP (see section "Other Protocols" later in this chapter). IBM has licensed it to other vendors, but there has been something of a rocky history with the terms. APPN has received favorable comment in independent tests of its performance. However, it does not, at the time of this writing, seem to be seriously challenging the growth of TCP/IP.

Figure 4.2 shows an APPN network with network, low entry, and end-point nodes. The figure represents the mesh quality of APPN, and the ability to have multiple connections between nodes. End-point and low-entry nodes have limited functions (see Box 4.2). Figure 4.3 is a layer rendering of APPN.

DECnet

The design intent of the first versions of DEC's Digital Network Architecture (DNA or DECnet) was to provide peer-to-peer communication between minicomputers running DEC operating systems. DEC systems tend (still) to be interconnected families of midsize machines and require peer-to-peer messaging

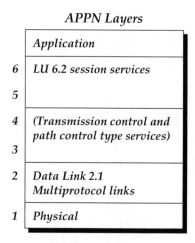

APPN Layers

	Application
6	*LU 6.2 session services*
5	
4	*(Transmission control and*
	path control type services)
3	
2	*Data Link 2.1*
	Multiprotocol links
1	*Physical*

Figure 4.3   APPN structure.

to support sustained interaction between equals. Since DEC has always been faced with the necessity of coexisting with IBM and other vendors, it has been a provider of "gateways" (DNA/SNA) from early days.

Figure 4.4 shows the DECnet structure. Its layer structure corresponds to OSI. The original layers did not. DEC restructured DNA to conform to the OSI model in the mid-1980s. Note the OSI standards offered at every level, and their correspondence with DEC DNA protocols.

Pathworks is a broader DEC framework built to work with all major protocols on Open VMS, Unix, and OS/2 platforms.

Other protocols

There are other proprietary architectures offered by Unisys, ICL, Siemens, etc. None of these have the penetration or posture of SNA and DNA. It is likely that

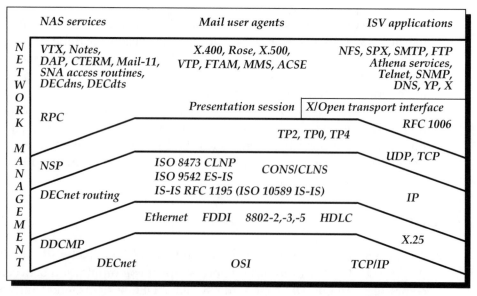

Figure 4.4   DECnet/OSI.

APPN is built on the T2.1 node concept. T2.1 provided a host-independent connection for "independent" logical units, not dependent on VTAM and NCP. Used for System/38 interconnect, a T2.1 node has some of the function of LU 6.2, including multiple and parallel sessions and multiple links. Control-point functions were placed in all T2.1 nodes so that configuration, session, and address management functions could be performed by any T2.1 node on the network. This is a significant departure from the previously strong, hierarchic host-to-dumb-terminal bias of earlier SNA.

APPN extends the concepts of T2.1 to provide peer-to-peer meshed networking with intermediate routing through intervening nodes. It provides dynamic configuration of the network, multiple links between T2.1 nodes, and considerably reduced overhead in establishing sessions.

The architecture defines three node types:

1 Network Node: A node that provides session level functions, and routing and directory services for its own logical units and the logical units of attached nodes. A network node and its adjacent end-point and low-end nodes constitute a domain.

2 End Node: The end node cannot perform routing functions and, consequently, cannot provide passthrough and intermediary routing services. It can perform session services for its logical units and can establish a session with another node. It can be attached to more than one network node, but is defined to participate in only one domain. An end node participates in the network as the destination or origin of a session.

3 Low-Entry Networking End Node: The LEN, sometimes called the "non-APPN" node, participates in the network as the destination or origin of a session. However, it cannot pass control information between itself and a network node and, consequently, cannot register its resources as part of the domain. It can perform its own session services.

The continued existence of T2.1 is due to the David-like struggle of the IBM Rochester laboratory against the orthodox Goliaths in Corporate Headquarters and Raleigh. Many now baking in the sun of low-level networking were most aggressive in trying to kill T2.1 for years. Readers may remember that LU 6.2 was the *only* communications technology announced as System Application Architecture (SAA).

DNA and SNA will have a presence for some time but that other proprietary protocols will give way to TCP/IP, OSI, and emerging converged protocols over time.

TCP/IP—the Internet protocol

This is the greatest example of a university project supported by a government developing a commercially important product. The Internet was born from a government desire to interconnect the networks of military centers, universities, and other facilities. The DARPA-funded activity to build networks of networks laid the basis for what is now the most alluring and perhaps most fragile first form of the information highway.

Networks have boundaries and limits. They have different addressing conventions, use different physical media, and have different message formats. A technology is required for crossing network boundaries. The protocol family for this technology is generically called Transmission Control Protocol/Internet Protocol (TCP/IP).

When software is discussed, the same words can represent a particular program, a set of programs, a culture, or an industry. Figure 4.5 shows TCP/IP in its broadest meaning. This includes a set of applications at layer 7. These are:

1 Simple Mail Transfer Protocol (SMTP). The basic electronic mail facility of the Unix community.

2 File Transfer Protocol (FTP). For transferring files over the network.

3 Virtual Terminal (Telnet). Provides remote log-in.

4 Remote Execution (REXX). Permits a user to remotely initiate a remote program.

5 Network File System (NFS). The de facto Unix remote file system.

In addition to the utilities at layer 7, there is a set of pervasive interfaces to TCP/IP shown as Sockets and RPC. These are discussed shortly. Not shown are administrative services providing for network configuration, gateway/router definitions, and directory or time services.

There is a protocol provided for systems management called Simple Network Management Protocol (SNMP), which currently represents the dominant protocol for systems management in both the Unix and non-Unix environments. It is discussed in Chapter 13.

Often someone saying "TCP/IP" does not mean to include the Network File System, SNMP, remote execution, or the interfaces, but merely the mail program, the file transfer, and the log-on. This is the base TCP/IP culture.

The core TCP/IP

The heart of TCP/IP is at layer 4 and below. There are two transports, Transmission Control Protocol (TCP) and User Datagram Protocol (UDP), and a network layer, Internet Protocol (IP). Beneath the IP layer is a physical layer that supports various physical networks and physical network standards. TCP provides connection-based transport. UDP provides a connectionless datagram service.

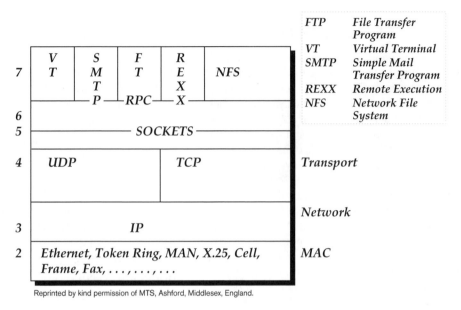

Reprinted by kind permission of MTS, Ashford, Middlesex, England.

Figure 4.5 TCP/IP.

Initially, TCP/IP was unique to the Unix culture. It provided connectability for different versions of Unix running on different machine architectures. It crossed address domains and provided a link between wide area and Ethernet networks.

Now it is the apparent primary building block of the "Information Highway." The installation rate of TCP/IP ran at a nearly 4-to-1 ratio compared to installations of OSI product in the early 1990s, when OSI was thought to be the inevitable coming thing.

Radio programs, interactive magazines, uncountable information sources, and service businesses are built around the network; and there is a organization, Internet Engineering Task Force (IETF), responsible for its growth and direction. There are an estimated 25,000,000 Internet users and over 4,000,000 users in the U.S. corporate community.

There are numerous service providers that offer access to the Internet, or to part of the Internet, for a fee. The American network services companies Prodigy, America Online, and CompuServe offer access to the Internet for their subscribers. Successful access is supported by a technology, the network browser, that enables end users to navigate through offerings in a reasonably convenient way. All the commercial services provide access to a concept of the network called the Worldwide Web. This is a browsing and navigational facility that allows a user to discover where information is held, using an interface somewhat like a yellow pages. Access to the Web may be arranged without the use of the commercial services.

The rapid growth of Internet availability, the recent inclusion of video, graphics, and television capacity, the growing availability of various kinds of data sources, and the ability to transmit mail and documents of greater size make it a possibility that Internet services and not current e-mail programs and office suites will be the predominant technology for wide area communications in this decade. IBM's purchase of Lotus, in the heat of the Microsoft network offering, may have been just a little too late.

Internet services are astonishingly diverse and useful. No one really should be without it; but on the other hand, to connect a company to the Internet can involve considerable risk. An employee signing onto the Internet through a commercial network service can expose the company to viruses and violations that can have disastrous results.

Local area networking

Many products, product families, and protocols are available for local area networking. LAN protocol stacks are "leaner" than wide area stacks. Addressing is considerably simpler and routing can be almost trivial on small LANs in a single office or building. There are more optimistic assumptions about media quality.

Large peer-to-peer networks may use a protocol product called VINES, from the Banyan Corporation. IBM and Microsoft offer LAN product in various forms to support a protocol called NetBEUI. By far the dominant de facto LAN technology is SPX/IPX (Sequenced Packet Exchange/Internet Package Exchange) from the Novell Corporation NetWare culture.

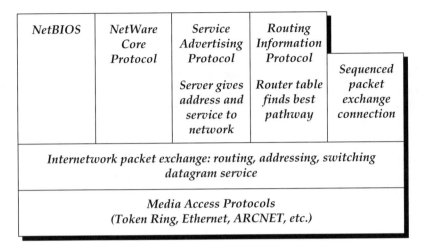

NetBIOS	NetWare Core Protocol	Service Advertising Protocol	Routing Information Protocol	
		Server gives address and service to network	Router table finds best pathway	Sequenced packet exchange connection
Internetwork packet exchange: routing, addressing, switching datagram service				
Media Access Protocols (Token Ring, Ethernet, ARCNET, etc.)				

Figure 4.6   NetWare protocols.

NetWare

NetWare technology contains the pervasive protocols for local area networking, SPX/IPX, as well as support for other protocols. It also contains elements of a complete network operating system. Figure 4.6 shows the protocol structure.

The NetWare Open Data Link supports 32 different protocol stacks with appropriate routing for each stack. SNA LUs are not part of link set, but a gateway is provided to SNA. The primary protocol stack for NetWare is SPX/IPX, similar in concept but "lighter" in weight than TCP/IP. NetWare will also provide protocol support for NetBIOS/NetBEUI, AppleTalk, TCP/IP, and X.25. IPX is a datagram service, while SPX is a connection-based service operating at OSI layers 4 and 5. The SPX/IPX protocols are now available outside of the NetWare context from Microsoft in Windows, as an SNA protocol, and from other Unix and operating system vendors. There are some limitations on what services can be reached from what platforms.

NetBIOS

Another LAN protocol family is NetBIOS/NetBEUI. NetBIOS is the protocol and NetBEUI is an interface to the protocol. The protocol is a connection-based transport layer with some session-level services. These protocols are available with Microsoft and IBM LAN Server and LAN Manager products for Windows and OS/2.

VINES

Banyan VINES (Virtual Network Solution) is an important offering in the LAN segment that also offers integrated WAN support. It is respected for its scalability and ease of use. It is integrated with Unix and shipped with Unix. VINES provides the NetBIOS SMB (messaging format) and private transport and network protocols, SPP (Sequenced Packet Protocol), RTP (Routing Update Protocol), and VIP (VINES Internet Protocol). VINES provides a remote procedure call (see "Remote Procedure Calls" in the next section) for applications development. A major feature of VINES is its directory services at an enterprise level, StreetTalk.

Interfaces

Figure 4.7 shows a set of application programming interfaces (APIs) introduced into the structure of the protocols. Application programs use APIs to activate the communications software. Until recently, the interfaces defined for communications software were operating system specific. No standards existed that corresponded to standards for the protocols. In the last few years, the interface to communications has received more formal attention. A number of industry standards have evolved.

Models of program interaction

At the heart of an interface is a mental model of program interaction. This defines what services can be requested and the possible results of such requests (successful completion, failure, need for further interaction, etc.). The industry currently distinguishes between three models of program interaction: dialogues or conversations, messaging, and procedure calls; each has a unique API or set of APIs.

Dialogues or conversations

A "conversation" is a connection-based relation between two programs using layer 4 (transport) and layer 5 (session) behavior. Conversations occur within sessions. A conversation is a sustained interaction between two end points.

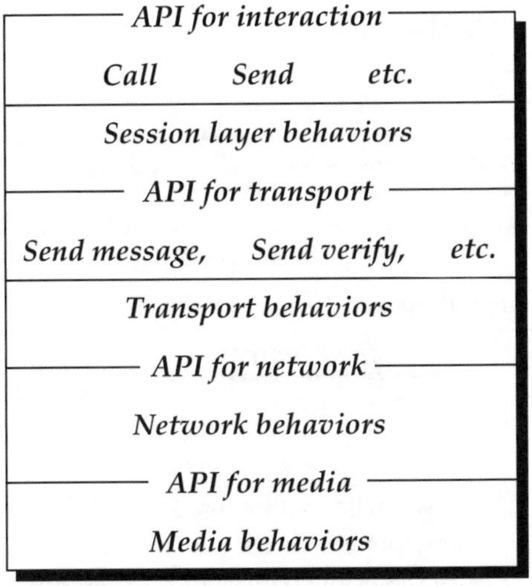

Reprinted by kind permission of MTS, Ashford, Middlesex, England.

Figure 4.7 Protocol and interface layers.

LU 6.2 is a protocol that supports the model of a conversation. It has had, in the past, various APIs. The OSI equivalent is an ASCE dialogue.

There are a number of specific interfaces to LU 6.2. An emerging industry standard for a conversation interface is the Common Programming Interface for Communications (CPI-C). CPI-C defines a set of commands for the control of conversations. A subset of these commands, the starter set, is intended for use by applications programmers who are not expert in communications technology. The core functions of CPI-C establish a conversation and its attributes, and send and receive messages over the conversation. The model of program interaction presented to an application is a model of direct connection to another program.

CPI-C is the only fully defined interface for services at layers above 4. As such, it is being extended and promulgated as a standard for higher-level services for other protocol stacks. Figure 4.8 shows the extension of CPI-C to serve

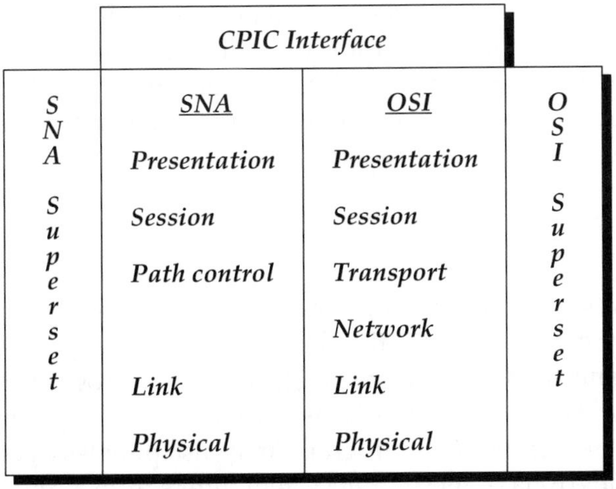

Figure 4.8 CPI-C over SNA/OSI.

CONVERSATIONS

The mental model of a conversation is a direct link between two programs. In the intervening technology there are message-format functions, and staging, routing, and buffering functions on both sides of the wire. The figure shows some of the intervening mechanisms. The intervening mechanisms are not

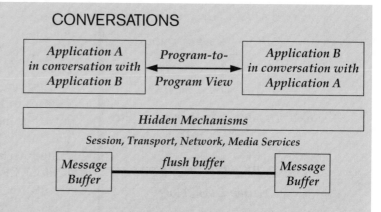

revealed to the programmer in the starter set. They are concealed in two ways: (1) commands that operate on buffers are not provided, and (2) parameters that define intervening structure are not shown. Parameters for buffer size, for example, are not available at the CPI-C starter interface.

Information required by the system to set up conversation attributes is provided by systems programmers or communications programmers using advanced CPI-C. This provides more discrete control over the relation. For example, whether a program asking for a message but finding no message should wait or continue to run is an attribute established by the advanced CPI-C Set command.

as an interface for both the SNA protocol stack and the OSI protocol stack. There is a defined subset of CPI-C that a program can use to preserve portability over SNA or OSI layers. CPI-C has been accepted as an interface in the API set promulgated by X/Open.

The ability to use CPI-C as an interface to either the behavior of the OSI or the SNA protocol stack provides an example of a "protocol-independent interface" that can be used by a program regardless of what communications protocol it is using. Making interfaces protocol independent is a relatively new idea, which is becoming important in the industry.

Messaging

"Messaging" is a relation between a program and a queue. A relation between programs is derived from the relations they have with message queues. Figure 4.9 shows this. Program A puts a message on Queue Alpha. Program B takes a message from Queue Alpha. Program A's and Program B's basic view of the world is through Queue Alpha. Other programs may also put messages or take messages from Queue Alpha. A messaging system differs from a conversation in the visibility of the queue (buffer) to sending and receiving programs.

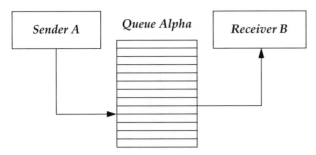

Figure 4.9 Messaging involves a relation between senders or receivers and an intervening queue of messages. A sender task is complete when a message gets safely to the queue.

Messaging systems may be connectionless or connection based. Datagram services are connectionless messaging systems. In a connection-based messaging system, the system is responsible for end-to-end guarantees and packet ordering. Messaging systems lend themselves to rather elaborate program relation structures and quite flexible definitions.

Messaging behavior is fully supported at the transport layer (layer 4). A number of interfaces for messaging are essentially layer 4 interfaces. Unix Named Pipes is fundamental to the Unix culture. IBM's MQI (Message Queuing Interface) is evolving into a de facto standard outside of the Unix community. Industry de facto interfaces to layer 4 are Streams, Sockets (see Box 4.5), and NetBEUI. Txi is a developing vendor-neutral interface standards. Work is being done to make a number of these interfaces transport-layer independent, but at the present time NetBEUI is associated with NetBIOS and Unix pipes with TCP/IP.

Remote procedure calls

There is an odd hybrid beast called the remote procedure call (RPC), supposedly an extension of the procedure call of programming languages. The procedure call invokes a "subprogram," which operates and then returns a result to the caller. The RPC enables this across a network. The RPC shares with the procedure call the concept of one call, one return.

There are a number of widely used RPCs. Two of them are:

1 The RPC of the Sun Microsystem Open Network Computing (ONC) architecture. It includes the NFS, REXX, an RPC, and a directory.

2 The RPC of the Distributed Computing Environment (DCE) from the Open Software Foundation (OSF). It is based on technology from Hewlett-Packard

MESSAGING

This paradigm, now associated with the communications culture, is equally a computer science paradigm that addresses the interaction of two programs that do not share a memory space. Send/receive mechanisms are appropriate for non–memory sharing programs whether or not they are separated by a wire. The figure shows some possible queuing structures. A messaging system may have the model that a queue starts on one side of the wire and finishes on the other, or it may have the model of queue-to-queue transfer across the wire.

Sockets is an extension of the file input/output concepts of Unix. It is primarily an interface to TCP, but it is now being used as an interface to other transport layers. It provides a facility to establish a connection by creating an identified socket over a selected protocol family. Usual programming techniques bind a program to a developed socket definition containing a socket address, a protocol family, and addressing information.

Commands are provided for connection-based and connectionless messaging. For connection-based messaging there are commands to send (SEND), to write (WRITE), and to write with verification checking (WRITEV). There are also read, read

S/R a: Sends to Q1, Q2, Q3; broadcast to S/R b, c, e.
Receives from Q4 from S/R c, d.

S/R b: Sends to no one.
Receives from Q2 from S/R a.

S/R c: Sends to Q4 to S/R a.
Receives from Q1 from S/R a.

S/R d: Sends to Q4 to S/R a.
Receives from Q5 from S/R e.

S/R e: Sends to Q5 to S/R d.
Receives from Q3 from S/R a.

verify, and receive verify. For connectionless messaging, the commands are Sendto (containing the address), Sendmsg, Receivefrom (Recvfrom), and ReceiveMessage (recmsgv).

and DEC. The base technology comes from the Hewlett-Packard Apollo Network Computing System (NCS) architecture. OSF is a consortium initially developed to promulgate common interfaces and structures for Unix products. Its function is changing somewhat in the 1990s and is currently unclear.

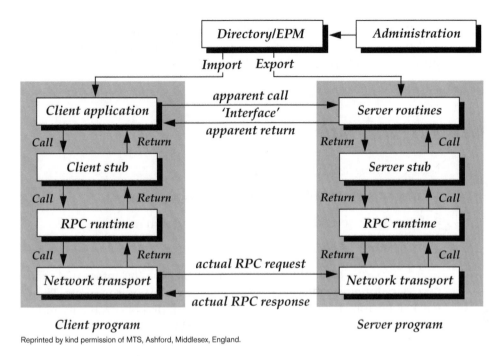

Client program   Server program

Reprinted by kind permission of MTS, Ashford, Middlesex, England.

Figure 4.10   RPC operation.

Figure 4.10 shows the flow of an RPC. When a program calls for execution of a remote program, it invokes a surrogate program provided by the system. This surrogate, called a stub, intercepts the call and prepares it for the network. The stub is generated by the system from parameters provided in an auxiliary language specific to the RPC. This language defines what functions the stub is to perform. The basic function is to prepare a communications packet for the underlying transport layer, commonly TCP/IP or UDP/IP.

Other functions may occur in the stub. The stub may be responsible for finding the called program in the network and establishing a connection, for performing security checks, or for appropriate data conversion when the called program is on a system with different encodings from the calling program. The stub passes a prepared packet to the transport layer, starting the process of communication.

On the receiving side, the transport layer requests the remote program to be executed by the operating system. The operating system starts the stub of the called program. The stub prepares the received packet so that it looks like a local call. It passes it to the invoked program, which runs to a result and issues the equivalent of a return.

On the return, its stub is invoked, performs its functions and passes the result packet to the transport layer. On the calling side, the message is decomposed into a returned result, and the caller invoked.

Network integration

Network integration has three aspects:

1 Integrating protocols to minimize access boundaries.

2 Integrating voice, data, and other transmission media.

3 Integrating LANs and WANs.

Advances in technology establish a basis for the integrated transmission necessary for new conferencing and visualization environments. There is major work to be done to bring together networks of diverse protocols and to smooth seams between local and wide area networking.

Protocol integration

Computer systems that are built around different network protocols have difficulty communicating with each other. The Internet protocol (TCP/IP) does not solve this problem for systems that are SNA, DNA, or OSI based.

Integration has two aspects: interoperability and portability. Interoperability permits programs in different environments on different protocol stacks to communicate. Portability permits a program to run on different protocol stacks.

Protocol independence

Enabling a program to run without change on any protocol reduces the difficulty of cross-system communication. Programs can be placed in environments where a needed protocol stack exists.

Such capability is achieved by "protocol-independent interfaces." An example of this is CPI-C over SNA and OSI. Other protocol-independent interfaces are developing at the transport level for APPN, TCP/IP, SPX/IPX, and NetBIOS.

THE REMOTE PROCEDURE CALL

Procedure invocation is language specific. The remote procedure call (RPC) provides a language-independent semantic for invocation across a wire. However, there are important semantic and syntactic differences. Strange beasts stalk the earth, like the local RPC, which gives the syntax and semantics of RPCs to locally called procedures.

An essential problem is that RPCs are not procedure calls at all, they are truly process invocations. The true procedure call invokes programming on the same dispatchable unit as the calling program:

1 The caller is deactivated while the called program runs.

2 The calling and called program share resources beyond the parameter list handed to the called program.

3 The calling program has a large set of parameter-passing options. Parameters may be passed by values or by pointer to them.

With the RPC, the invoked program runs across the wire in a different resource domain. There are restrictions on the parameters to be passed and on how they are passed. The transparency of a call cannot be sustained. Acquiring the skills to use the RPC is a substantial undertaking.

The RPC of ONC is stateless, running on UDP datagram services. "Stateless" means the system retains no record of the status of the relation between caller and callee, and recovery is independently achieved on either side of the wire. This design must assure that nothing can occur in which the failure of one side would disable the other. The DCE RPC runs on either TCP/IP or UDP/IP. The DCE enhancements to the Hewlett-Packard (Apollo) RPC provides statefullness. This permits a more complex relation but makes recovery more complex.

Using a protocol-independent interface allows a program to run on any of the protocol stacks that it supports.

Some of the protocol-independent interfaces are "vendor neutral." They originate in consortia or standards organizations. Among these are Txi from the X/Open Consortia. Others are generalizations of older de facto interfaces. Sockets, originally a TCP/IP interface but now intended to be usable with other stacks, is among these.

Interoperability

It is convenient when programs running on one protocol stack communicate with programs on another without the requirement of porting and modification. Programs on different stacks cannot talk because different formats and system states are defined for different architectures. An OSI network layer cannot interpret messages or provide the behavior of an SNA encoding from path control.

Interoperability across networks is achieved by:

1 Gateway functions converting the formats of a sending protocol to those of a receiving protocol. Gateways translate at all levels of the protocol hierarchy to bridge between networks. A gateway is shown in Figure 4.11.

2 Stack crossover. This allows "navigation" through protocol stacks. It is a step to protocol convergence. As shown in Figure 4.12, it is possible to start communications with CPI-C and then to "cross over" to SPX at the appropriate level. The crossover is accomplished by use of "compensators" or

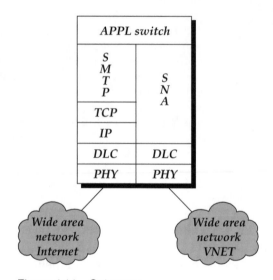

Figure 4.11   Gateways.

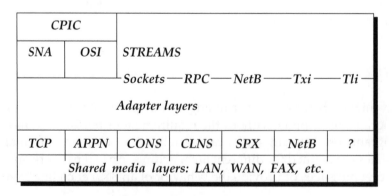

Figure 4.12   Cross-stack interoperability.

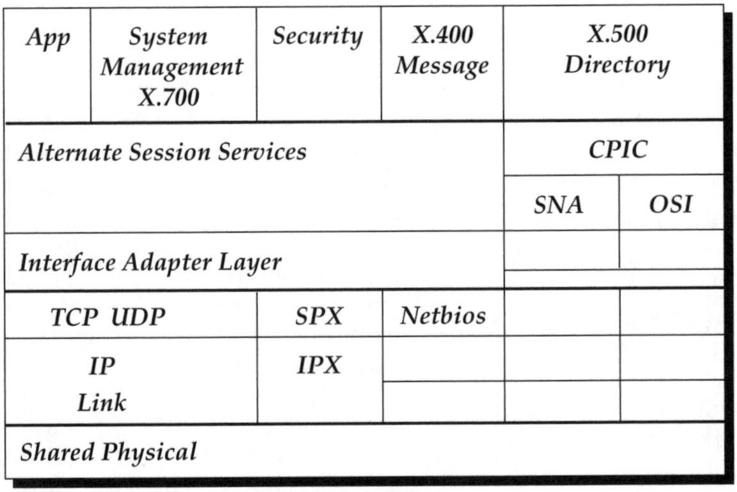

App	System Management X.700	Security	X.400 Message	X.500 Directory	
Alternate Session Services				CPIC	
				SNA	OSI
Interface Adapter Layer					
TCP UDP		SPX	Netbios		
IP		IPX			
Link					
Shared Physical					

Reprinted by kind permission of MTS, Ashford, Middlesex, England.

Figure 4.13   Restructured services: common higher-layer services for all session, transport, and network protocols.

"adapters." At each appropriate level, a compensator receives a package from the layer above and converts it into formats appropriate for the layer beneath. A program using CPI-C or any private LU 6.2 interface can "come out to the wire" through IP and look to a receiving program like an IP user. On the way from an IP user, conversion is made so that the sender looks like an SNA user to a receiver.

A constraint of interoperability is that naming, security, systems management, and recovery have been unique to the protocol stacks underlying them. These are layer 6 and 7 services, and their uniqueness to particular protocol stacks makes it difficult to manage interconnected systems.

Figure 4.13 shows a significant restructuring as a step in integrating network environments. This, in concert with the reform of the lower layers, could significantly reduce internetworking boundaries. Directory, systems management, and X.400 messaging are described later.

LAN/WAN convergence

Network convergence requires crossing boundaries between LANs and WANs. When this is achieved, an end user or an application can use LAN software and pass transparently onto a WAN. This involves a gateway (which may

Portability and migration costs depend on how much program modification is involved in moving to a different environment.

Three program properties affect portability:

1 The interfaces used by the program for services like I/O, communications, recovery, etc. at run time.

2 The interfaces to parameterize its environment at start-up or tear-down time. (These statements are not made in the programming language but in a command or operator language of the software complex.)

3 The structure of the program as influenced by the various process and memory models of its underlying environment.

The minimum cost is to run the "binary" on the target machine as it runs on the source machine. This is sometimes possible. Often it is necessary to recompile the run-time interfaces, use the same control statements, and leave program structure alone. Sometimes it is necessary, moving from one operating system to another, to create new control statements.

The great question is how often it is necessary to rewrite and restructure a program, even if its interfaces are "pure," in order to get performance in the presence of changed memory and process models. A CICS program running with MVS runs in a very different operational environment than a CICS program running on AIX, despite the identity of CICS interfaces. Many who have done easy ports have found it necessary to invest in significant restructuring post facto in order to get performance.

Some in the past have said that a machine-independent program is a program that will not run on any machine.

---

be an office PBX) and software to extend the addressing and routing conventions of LANs.

LAN software has differed from WAN software in a number of important aspects. It has made more optimistic assumptions about line quality at layers 1–3. It has had much simpler routing algorithms, since LANs (even those considered large) do not scale to the size of WANs and do not face the intervening intermediate nodes between sender and receiver. The culture is primarily defined by the lower four layers. LANs tend to be installed at departmental levels and to proliferate as implementations of small client/server systems.

Different products and vendors have existed in WAN and LAN worlds. A program or programmer knows when it is interacting through local area or wide area facilities because of different APIs. Systems administrators install wide area and local area software independently.

Gateways to interface local and wide capability (generally to translate between TCP/IP and SPX/IPX) are common. In addition to the Novell/AT&T undertaking, Wellfleet has developed wide area routing capability for NetWare nodes in a gateway.

Recent products provide "seamlessness" by supporting LAN protocol stacks as part of a network architecture and by providing protocol-independent

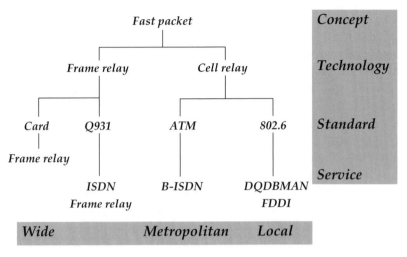

Figure 4.14   Fast packet technology.

interfaces for LAN- and WAN-oriented stacks. In addition, the bottom layers (media) are now shared by both WAN and LAN transport and network layers.

A program may now use the same interfaces at layer 4 to interact with a system a few meters or 1,000 kilometers distant.

New technologies and protocols

Hardware advances lead to new software concepts. An overarching term for the changes due to high-speed technology is "fast packet technology." Fast packet assumes low error rates, low delays in passing through intermediate network points, and highly unpredictable traffic patterns.

There are two fundamental organizations of fast packet. Frame relay is a two-layer concept currently being implemented; cell relay is a one-layer concept just lingering above the horizon. Whether to implement frame relay networks or wait for cell relay is a difficult choice that organizations must make. Figure 4.14 is a rendering of the relationship between certain concepts and terminologies.

Fast packet discards some classic notions of communications. In order to accommodate integrated voice and data, the idea of variable-sized packets (for minimizing data transmission overhead) is discarded. This increases the overhead for data, particularly in cell relay, but is excellent for voice. Because of the increased confidence in the technology and the need for greater speed, error checking is taken out of the lower-layer functions. End users are expected to transmit lost frames if necessary.

The cell relay protocol is the basis for a multiplexing and switching technology called ATM (asynchronous transfer mode). ATM is a methodology permitting intensive use of bandwidth by enabling sharing between identified cells on the network. ATM is the basis for B-ISDN (Broadband Integrated Services Digital Network) offerings.

Public network offerings of integrated voice and data have been available for some time. The ISDN, supporting voice, data, facsimile and limited video, has been available for both circuit switching and packet switching services across narrowband and wideband facilities. The ATM base takes the capability of ISDN into the multimedia time frame by providing data rates and robustness at the levels of B-ISDN.

Asynchronous transfer mode

ATM is expected to be the instrument that brings high-performance computer networking into our homes and offices, and onto our desks and laps. It assumes the availability of high-quality fiber optics transmission and a set of international standards for transmission rates. These digital signaling standards (unhappily, divergent in the U.S. and Europe) define initial transmission rates in a three-level range from megabits per second (DS1), through 6.3 Mb/s (DS2), to 44.7 Mb/s (DS3). Standards for higher speeds are also pretty much in place.

The standardization of speeds provides a basis for definition of a B-ISDN. The B-ISDN definitions provide for synchronization, framing formats, and

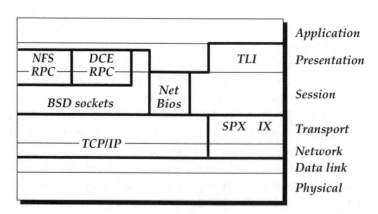

Figure 4.15   UNIX network interfaces.

optical rates that allow complex documents with voice, image, and text to be transmitted as coherent units. The standards lead to a definition for a Synchronous Optical Network, or SONET (named Synchronous Digital Hierarchy in Europe—unhappily, with different speeds).

ATM is a switching and multiplexing technology for B-ISDN. Its goal is to integrate multimedia transmission elements. It is capable of multicast, and can interoperate with existing LANs and WANs.

ATM has both LAN and WAN applicability and can be used as a layer underneath various transport layers with various needs.

Operating systems and networking

A key trend in operating systems is the integration of network and local function. The tight bonds between a particular protocol and a particular operating system are breaking rapidly. Many protocols are available with particular operating systems. TCP/IP is pervasive through non-Unix operating systems. LU 6.2 is offered for platforms other than MVS. The following operating systems provide protocols or gateways to LU 6.2, TCP/IP, and SPX/IPX:

- IBM: MVS, VSE, VM, OS/400, OS/2, AIX
- DEC: VMS Open, ULTRIX, Windows NT
- AT&T: Unix SVR4, Windows NT
- Hewlett-Packard: MVE Open, HP-UX, Windows NT

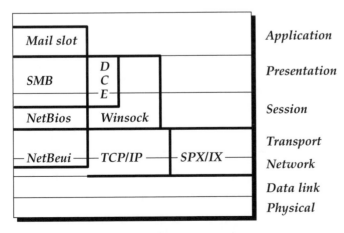

Figure 4.16   Windows NT network interfaces.

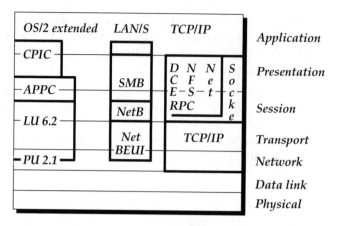

Figure 4.17   OS/2 network interfaces.

- Sun: Solaris, SunOS
- Apple: Macintosh OS, A/UX
- Microsoft
  - DOS 6.0 (486)
  - Windows 3.1 (486)
  - Windows for Workgroups (486)
  - Windows 95
  - Windows NT Client (486, Alpha, PA-RISC)
  - Windows NT Server (486, Alpha, PA-RISC)
- Novell
  - NetWare 4.0 (486, PA-RISC, SPARC, PowerPC)
  - UnixWare (Univel): SVR4.2 with NetWare

Figures 4.15 through 4.17 represent available interfaces and protocols in various operating systems.

chapter 5

Software infrastructures

The reader is advised to read the third chapter in The Basics Book, *"Operating System Basic Functions," for a review of the underlying principles and technology.*

EXECUTIVE SUMMARY   The behaviors, good and bad, that dominate our thinking about computing come from the characteristics of software. In machines—network hubs, application servers, clients, workstations, etc.—there is a defining functionality contributed by software elements. These disparate elements define a "software environment."

The software industry is highly fractured and unstable. There is a mosaic of vertical and horizontal offerings. Underneath the chaos, however, there are a number of relatively stable industry-pervasive software platforms. These are Unix-based systems, Windows-based systems, Novell-based systems, and those derived from the older proprietary software of the "legacy."

These systems compete with each other in different ways. They try to break market limits by running on more hardware architectures, or on a wider range of models of architectures. They try to emulate each other's behavior in order to minimize the barriers of moving from one to the other. They undertake marginal value-adds in key areas to ride trendy waves.

Pricing software is like pricing airline tickets. It is an unstable maze of deals, special offers, and one-time opportunities that clearly position these products in a deeply competitive mode.

Software environments

A point of Chapter 1 was that the boundaries between software layers are often fuzzy. "Operating system" sometimes means baseware, sometimes baseware plus selected middleware, and sometimes the entire collection of software that exists in a system. For this reason, this chapter substitutes the phrase "software environment" for the aggregation of programs living on a machine that are not applications. This includes operating systems, network operating systems, file systems, presentation managers, communications managers, data base managers, mail managers, etc. As we go, the reader will realize that the system/application boundary also becomes fuzzy as word processors and spreadsheets become integrated into basic packages.

CHAPTER 5:   SOFTWARE INFRASTRUCTURES

BUNDLING AND INTEGRATION

Unix, OS/2, Windows, NetWare, and MVS are names variously used to represent a base system, an environment, or a culture. In its largest sense, the name MVS represents a subindustry of over 1,600 companies that provide competitive or symbiotic product for the IBM base system. In its smallest sense, it means around 8 million lines of programming primarily concerned with managing the hardware of 390-style machines.

There are various "bundling" options for Unix, OS/2, and Windows that include or exclude various middleware or communications features. The conveniences of "bundling" are, commonly, a lower price per function, easier installation, and control. The inconvenience of bundling is buying a function one does not wish. For example, if a communications capability is part of the OS/2 priced package but one wishes to use Novell software for communications, it is not economic to pay for the OS/2 communications software as part of a bundle. If IBM observes that it may be losing market share for this reason, it will "unbundle" the communications manager.

Vendor decisions about "bundling," how software will be packaged and priced, vary from product to product and from time to time. In the Unix world, separate pricing for various layers is common; one buys a base Unix system and communications, data base managers, etc. separately. In the non-Unix world, there seems to be a growing tendency to integrate function priced and packaged as a single unit.

Integration of function may be more than a pricing strategy. Sometimes elements are more truly integrated in that common services and features such as security, recovery, directory, and end user interfaces are shared among elements at the same or different layers. This is a great convenience, as it increases the usability of systems while cutting the cost to set them up and operate.

Many technologies are common to all programs; searching lists, sorting lists, calculating values, putting messages on queues, indexing, calling for services from another program, and asking for input or providing output are common activities.

There are concepts particular to particular layers. The idea of a table of "relations," a two-dimensional table with columns and rows, is unique to a relational data base manager like Informix, Sybase, or Oracle. Only a data base manager has the power to browse through the attributes of data, finding elements that conform to selection criteria. Similarly, the protocols of sending or receiving a message are unique to communications programs concerned with implementing de jure or de facto standards. The transforms needed for rotating three-dimensional visualizations are unique to presentation managers.

As the industry has fragmented, elements at certain layers come as complete packages. They are fully integrated with their own security, recovery, naming conventions, directory, and end-user and administrative interfaces. In a system environment containing a number of elements, the multiplicity of specialized versions of an essentially common function becomes expensive and inconvenient. Some functions are common to all layers and common to all programs within a layer. A system that has a single directory for all its resources is more convenient to use and install than a system with fragmented directories in each layer.

Systems populations

There is a large population of software environments. Some of these have common base systems and differ mostly in the upper layers. Others reflect the historical linkage between the layers. In general, there is still a strong tendency to think of software environments in terms of the base system, to speak of OS/2, Windows, NetWare, and Unix environments, despite a commonality of applications, communications protocols, data bases, mail programs, etc.

There are various (and admittedly fuzzy) key attributes for the baseware that traditionally defines an environment:

1 Scalability: the range of machine on which it runs. Unix and Windows NT run from laptop to enterprise server, including symmetric multiprocessors. OS/2 and NetWare have just extended their range to large departmental servers.

2 Generality: various environments run in niches. A general-purpose system straddles many niches, but none to date has straddled all. VMS as a server system, Unix as a desktop system, OS/2 as a transaction processing system, and any of them as a real-time system are unusual applications. However, systems evolve. The current extensions of VMS (VMS/Open) position it legitimately as a server. The addition of CICS to OS/2 positions it as a transaction machine.

3 "Openness": this, we shall see, has many aspects. One is the degree to which the system supports de jure or de facto standards; another is the number of machines the system will run on; and another is the availability of applications.

Attributes are often more perceived than real, but they have true market impact. Unix, thought of as a "scientific" system, had difficulty entering commercial markets. Thought of as a desktop system, OS/2 may have trouble penetrating the enterprise server market. Perceived as a small system environment, NetWare may have trouble penetrating to departmental or enterprise servers.

PC Mobile or Desktop ($900–5,000)	Workstation ($3,500–20K)	Group Server ($3,000–10K)	Department ($10K–100K)	Enterprise ($100K–2M)
OS/2	SunOS[1]	SunOS[1]	SunOS[1]	VMS
MS-DOS	Solaris[1]	OS/2	OS/2	MPE
DOS	AIX[1]	Windows AS	Windows AS	HP-UX[1]
Apple System 7	HP-UX[1]	NetWare	NetWare	AIX[1]
Apple A/UX[1]	SCO ODT[1]	AIX[1]	AIX[1]	MVS
Windows	Windows NT	HP-UX[1]	HP-UX[1]	VM
Solaris[1]	UnixWare[1]	UnixWare[1]	UnixWare[1]	Windows AS
Destiny[1]		Linux[1]	VSE	Unix[1]
UnixWare[1]			VM	SunOS[1]
NetWare			MVS	Unisys
			VMS	Amdahl
			MPE	AIX/ESA
			Linux[1]	Linux[1]

[1]Unix or Unix derivative.

Table 5.1   Platform systems by machine size.

Table 5.1 shows scalability for major software environments. Tables 5.2 and 5.3 show the scalability and portability of a set of competing software environments. Table 5.2 shows the availability of platforms by package pricing for architectural ranges. Table 5.3 shows availability by architecture only.

What limits a market?

All software environments have niches they were developed to serve. Breaking out of these niches, going on to other platforms, taking on new functions, and coexisting with various networks represents an investment on the part of a vendor. This investment must be justified by a perceived market for the product in another context.

As a result, there are remaining links between hardware and software environments. Not all operating systems run on all machines, not all data base managers run on all operating systems, not all operating systems talk to all

Environment	Price Range (dollars)	Architecture
OS/2	1,500–25,000	Intel, PowerPC[1]
DOS	1,000–5,000	Intel
Windows	1,500–5,000	Intel, PowerPC[1]
Windows NT	2,500–5,000	Intel, PowerPC[1], Alpha, PA-RISC
Windows NT AS	5,000–2,000,000	Intel, Alpha, PA-RISC
Apple System 7	1,500–10,000	680x0, PowerPC
NetWare	5,000–25,000	Intel, PowerPC[1]
Solaris[2]	4,000–50,000	Intel, SPARC, PowerPC
SCO ODT[2]	2,500–50,000	Intel
AIX[2]	4,000–1,000,000	PowerPC
HP-UX[2]	3,000–750,000	PA-RISC 7x00
OSF/1[2]	5,000–22,000,000	VAX, Alpha, 390
OS/400	10,000–1,000,000	Power PC
VMS/Open	5,000–3,000,000	VAX, Alpha
MPE/ix	10,000–1,000,000	PA-RISC 7x00
VSE[3]	75,000–250,000	390/390ESA
MVS[3]	250,000–22,000,000	390/390ESA
VM	75,000–22,000,000	390/390ESA

[1]The status of software for the PowerPC is not certain as of this writing. There seems to be an IBM intent to run OS/2 in some version and an intent by Motorola to bring Microsoft Windows NT to it. Novell has stated its intention to run NetWare.

[2]Unix or Unix derivative.

[3]These systems coexist in over 80% of their occurrences, offering complementary services.

Table 5.2   Environment, price range, and architecture.

networks, etc. These limitations are a constant and constraining problem for enterprises trying to achieve maximum flexibility and accessibility.

Limitation: Architecture it runs on

The number of sales or licenses of an environment will always be less than the architecture on which it runs. IBM MVS runs only on larger versions of the 3x0 architecture and, as a consequence, is dependent on the market penetration of

IBM 3x0	Intel	SPARC	PA-RISC	PowerPC	Alpha	MIPS
AIX/ESA	OS/2	SunOS	MPE	AIX	VMS	Windows NT
VM	Windows	Solaris	HP-UX	Windows NT	OSF/1	Unix
MVS	Windows NT		Windows NT	OS/2[1]	Windows NT	
VSE	Windows AS		Windows AS	Apple OS	Windows AS	
	NetWare					
	MS-DOS					
	DOS					
	Unix SVR4					

[1]The status of software for the PowerPC is not certain as of this writing. There seems to be an IBM intent to run OS/2 in some version and an intent by Motorola to bring Microsoft Windows NT to it. Novell has stated its intention to run NetWare.

Table 5.3   Platform systems by architecture.

that system for its survival and future. IBM might want to enlarge the domain of MVS to midsize or even small systems running 390 microchips. The success of this effort depends not only on the success of MVS as a midsize or small server platform, it depends on the success of 390-style midsize and small systems.

DEC is now contending with the need to port older VMS software from the older VAX architecture to the new Alpha. This is an unprecedented undertaking. No such attempt to port a software environment across a broad scale for commercial users has previously been made. When IBM made the shift from IBM 709X to S/360, it introduced new software, with only marginal attention to cohabitation and coexistence with earlier systems.

The availability of Windows operating systems on RISCs depends on the degree of penetration not only of Windows NT, but of RISC systems into the commercial market.

Software vendors at all levels (baseware, middleware, and upperware) recognize the need to draw revenue on top of as many platforms as possible.

Limitation: Scale

It was once conventional wisdom to need different software for "small," "medium," and "large" machines. This was partly due to architectural differences between the three classes and to workload characteristics that derive from scale.

Penetration and market share were at the basis of the great Microsoft/IBM disaffection. IBM was interested in the private packaging of Intel architecture with a proprietary microchannel bus. The best interest of Microsoft was to run on as many packages of Intel as could possibly be achieved. They wished to maximize their revenue by broadening the base to all Intel-based systems, making MS-DOS a "generic" platform that would run on hundreds of hardware packages. Such strategic divergences—one company viewing software as a hardware "drag-on," another as a robust revenue flow without regard to hardware—cannot be reconciled.

Despite its vision, Microsoft didn't develop an entirely portable version of DOS or Windows. This may be because it was constrained by Intel, or that the market for non-Intel architectures in the mid-1980s did not offer enough inducement. The only major packager of Motorola architecture was Apple, whose Macintosh was entirely integrated with its software, leaving no market for a non-Macintosh platform. The RISC machines were Unix dominated, and versions of MS-DOS at that time could not offer the functionality of Unix to Unix users at larger workstations. Windows NT may loosen the bond between Intel and Microsoft. Part of the market strategy of Microsoft will likely be to have portability approaching that of Unix. If PowerPC and other RISC architectures make serious penetrations, there will be NT versions for them. If NT makes serious penetration, the non-Intel vendors will see the necessity of offering NT.

Different models of the "same" machine often have significant differences in secondary attributes. Memory sizes are naturally larger on larger machines. Input/output capability is much higher, and the organization of I/O more complex. Raw machine-speed differences might require different programming styles for different systems.

An interesting detail is the minimum machine on which an environment will run. Once, DOS had considerably less function than Unix and could run on much smaller and, consequently, cheaper systems. As DOS, Windows, and OS/2 grow, their hardware requirements begin to approach that of Unix. As minimum machines grow larger, Unix and non-Unix systems will have more direct competition on the desktop or laptop. It is likely that minimum machines will run Unix, OS/2, Windows, and Windows NT equally comfortably.

At the top of the scale, symmetric multiprocessing (SMP) has a deep impact on baseware, middleware, and upperware layers. SMP is a hardware direction that uses microchips in a tandem memory-shared set to achieve performance. A system must have some particular design characteristics to take efficient advantage of the SMP architecture. It is difficult for baseware not initially designed to run SMP to achieve hoped-for performance.

Hardware differences lead to workload differences. A software complex expecting 5,000 users faces problems different from a software complex expecting

PORTABILITY

To be portable, software must be free of dependencies on unique machine characteristics. Much of this can be done by writing software in a machine-independent language with compilers for a number of architectures. C is such a language, as is C++, Modula, and some proprietary languages at major vendors. These languages differ from COBOL and FORTRAN in that they permit definition and manipulation of elements at a level closer to architectural features.

Some percentage of software (there is disagreement about how much) depends on the details of a particular architecture. This is because the notation of the higher-level language does not permit the direct manipulation of certain features. In this case, it is necessary to program in notations closer to "machine" code, which reveal particularities of the architecture and are always architecture specific. Some critical functions are written in machine code because they must be optimized for performance, and many programmers feel that hand optimization of critical sections is necessary for speed. There remains disagreement about the relative efficiency of higher-level languages and a master systems programmer.

Naturally, the economics of porting require as much common code as possible. The feasibility of a successful, affordable, marketable port from Intel 486 to Intel Pentium is quite high because of the common core architecture of Intel-packaged machines. However, even here, differences in bus logic, I/O adapters, screen features, etc. require modification. A port to or from Intel and a RISC might well require more effort because of the particular need to optimize a RISC pipeline. To do this, it might be necessary to not only provide machine-level code, but to rearrange C code.

When the source system is not in a universally available language, the port becomes very difficult. Most of VMS for VAX is written in a language at about the level of C; a port to Alpha was reasonable if a compiler for the DEC systems programming language was available on Alpha or if the VMS was rewritten in C. DEC chose the latter path, as have some major independent software vendors (SAS, for example). However, DEC made major optimization of VMS for the Alpha pipe, and has so far shown no interest in a portable VMS for Intel or for other RISCs. Considerably more than the VMS baseware has been ported to Alpha. A quite large range of DEC middleware and upperware is coming over so that DEC can support VMS cultures on Alpha.

32 users, or a software complex expecting 1 user. There are differences in the sophistication of the security model, the recovery model, the process model, the memory model, etc.

Basic functions like ordering a list, searching a list, or managing a queue are done differently, depending upon the expected size of the list or queue. In addition to differences in algorithms for basic software functions, there are needs for complex scheduling functions to allocate the attention of the processor among large populations of users doing unrelated work.

Currently, there is considerable interest in scalability. Versions of Unix have the widest range, followed by Windows NT. IBM and Novell are working on more scalable versions of OS/2 and NetWare.

MULTIPROCESSOR ISSUES

Multiprocessing introduces requirements for program synchronization, locking, and sequencing that have profound effects on the structure and performance of software. Consider this multiprocessing problem: program A running on processor 1 and program B running on processor 2 get the same value from memory (*ab*), modify it, and replace an (erroneous) result. The initial value of location *ab* is 31. The proper final value is 38 (= 31 + 3 + 4).

Time	A: Processor 1	B: Processor 2
1	Get value in *ab*	Other business
2	Add "3" to value	Get value in *ab*
3	Store new value in *ab* (= 34)	Add "4" to value
4	Other business *ab* = 34	Store new value *ab* = 35

In a symmetric multiprocessor, synchronization must occur instruction by instruction. During the period times 1 to 4, the system must impose "mutual exclusion" so that processor 2 cannot get the value from *ab* until processor 1 has stored its finished value.

Multiprocessor hardware has mutual exclusion logic. However, software must include locking, release, and coordination functions that exclude error without diminishing performance. The upper figure shows a bad SMP software environment. The dotted lines show processors in application operation, the & lines show processors in platform operation, and the $ lines show processors waiting. A processor puts a "lock" on entry to baseware. Only one processor can execute code in baseware at a time. Other processors attempting to pass the gateway are

```
P1:    $$$$$$$$$$$$$$$$$$&&&&&&&&&&..................&&.........$$$$$$$$$

P2:    .............$$$$$$$$$$$$$&&&&&&&&.......&&&&&...........&&&&&&&&

P3:    &&&&&&&&......$$$$$$$$$$$$$$$$$$$$$&&&&&&&&&.............$&&&&&.......

P4:    ........&&&&&&&&&&.................$$$$$$$$$$$$$$&&&&&.............
```

Time intervals = 64
Total processor intervals = 256
Wait times: P1 = 25/64, P2 = 11/64, P3 = 18/64, P4 = 12/64
Total wait time = 66/256 = 0.26
Total application time = 127/256 = 0.50

```
P1:    &&&&&&&&.....................&&.......................

P2:    ..........&&&&&&&&........&&&&&......................

P3:    &&&&&&&&        &&&&&..........&&&&&................

P4:    ........&&&&&&&&&&..............&&&&&...............
```

Time intervals = 64
Total processor intervals = 256
Total application time = 193/256 = 0.75

prohibited until the lock is released. Since a processor may spend as much as 40% of the time in baseware, exclusion of other processors has an enormous impact on efficiency.

In the lower figure, the baseware has been restructured so it is possible for multiple processors to work in baseware at the same time. Much smaller "critical sections" are defined and protected by locks. A critical section is the minimum program area where parallel execu-tion cannot be permitted without a paradoxical result. While the overall performance of the system in the lower figure is much improved over that in the upper figure, there is a consid-erably "heavier" locking structure, and more time to weave through locks at different granu-larities to find safe parallelism. The perform-ance of the SMP may well suffer because of the weight of the locking system with well-de-fined critical sections.

Limitation: Other platforms and older applications

An environment must face other environments in the market. Competition is not only for customer installations, but for the attention of independent soft-ware vendors that make middleware and upperware software not made by the environment vendor. The market for an environment is limited by what is available above it (what it supports) as well as by what it runs on.

Environments have evolved cultures that secure their position. To replace them, one must show considerable advantage and a minimal cost of "migra-tion." An environment might replace another if it can convince key people that:

1 It is going to be pervasive and will force no limitations on machine choices.

2 It is well priced and performs well. There are "good deals" for multiuser use and a long-term commitment.

3 It provides an appropriate environment for a wide range of workers, and widely used upperware will be available.

4 It is "more advanced": it has more powerful multimedia (perhaps), more impressive visuals, and less-burdensome system cares.

5 The migration is simple and well supported by technology. Old software can be run, and a prior system can be continued in the context of the new system. Data can be brought over from the old system with minimal inconvenience.

A dominant player like Microsoft has no concerns about showing market penetration. However, IBM OS/2, DEC VMS, and Unix vendors must provide a reason for an upperware developer to develop for the platform.

The Unix community has attempted to develop a model of Unix that will lure upperware and other developers. The COSE (Common Open Software

5.5 SORTING SCALE

An example of scale and differences in programming comes from sorting a list. A short list is best sorted by treating it as single linear list; longer lists are best sorted by treating them as hierarchic tree structures. A list requires about $n^2/2$ comparisons to sort using the simplest linear methods. If the list is short, this can be accomplished in less time than it takes to set up the complex algorithms to build and handle a programmed tree structure. On a good day, a programmed tree structure can sort a list in $(n/2)\log_2(n)$ comparisons, a number much less than $n^2/2$ for large lists.

Environment) agreements define a common look and feel to all aspects of Unix. A developer can minimize the cost of developing for IBM AIX, HP-UX, or Sun Solaris by developing for the common interfaces of COSE. The market for the development is the combined market of all COSE-compliant systems. For a customer, this also means that software will be portable from one version of Unix to another.

The movement toward common interfaces (APIs) diminishes the distinctiveness of a platform personality for application programs. Figure 5.1 shows that, over time, the percentage of newly developed applications using APIs unique to a particular platform will dramatically decline. The number of portable applications, developed to operate on different platforms, will increase, and there will be a general convergence of platforms.

While using common APIs is a way of providing a platform-independent future, there is yet the problem of what to do with the past and present. How does a new platform deal with displacing an older one?

Emulation is an old game in the computer industry. A system offers the appearance of another system by imitating its interfaces and behaviors or by making the old system part of itself. Thus, it is possible to run DOS and Windows programs with Unix, OS/2 programs with Windows, and Windows programs with OS/2. A user can theoretically maintain the programs of the old operating system and use the features of the new one for newer programs.

A key issue is what the system should look like to an end user. A critical set of interfaces are those that determine touch and feel to a human. Solaris Wabi runs Windows applications but without the Windows touch and feel. OS/2 and Windows try to look like each other. There is clearly a

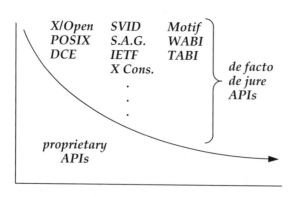

Figure 5.1   Common vs. proprietary APIs.

EMULATIONS

One can capture a prior system by:

1 Running it as an application. Examples are VM running MVS or Unix or VSE as a guest system. VM is "baseware baseware" in that a part of it is a minimum function "hypervisor" or "microkernel" that mediates between a "guest" platform and the hardware.

2 Providing "adapters" for the APIs of another system. An application program runs using its usual APIs, but these are translated into functions and services provided by the new system. A translation function surrounds the application, which thinks it is running in the old environment. Sometimes this translation emulates an older machine as well as an older platform. A balance of emulation and translation is a characteristic of many systems. The binary code of an application is emulated (in software or microcode) until a call is made for a system service; then, native functions are executed that emulate the original environment.

3 Providing direct support of the APIs of the old system, in effect implementing all of the behaviors with new code in a new environment—recompiling Windows, for example, to run with Unix in place of DOS.

There is also the option of "coexistence." The old platform runs as an alternative system in the same machine, and the new and old interact with each other somewhat as in heterogeneous networking.

There are instances of all approaches. IBM OS/2 emulates Windows 3.1 (but OS/2 Warp will not emulate Windows 95 as of this writing). Windows NT provides Windows 3.1, OS/2, and a new Win32 interface. Sunsoft provides a Microsoft Windows API through an emulator called Wabi (Windows Application Binary Interface). This emulates Intel instructions until it encounters a call to DOS or Windows. It translates the call and invokes X Windows or Unix for the service. Windows applications have a Motif or OPEN LOOK touch and feel. There are restrictions on Windows functions but it permits Sun Solaris to emulate many Windows applications. A third-party vendor, Insignia Solutions, has licensed code from Microsoft and recompiled DOS and Windows for Unix, providing a Windows desktop in a Unix environment. Macintosh interfaces are to be available for Apple Unix, and there are available Mac System 7 interfaces for Solaris and Silicon Graphics. Apple provides a 486 chipset with up to 32 MB of private memory that permits DOS applications (including Windows 3.1) to run concurrently with Mac. A user can switch between environments. Many Unix environments run DOS Merge, which enables users to exchange data between Unix and DOS.

decision to be made about how important sustaining touch and feel is for which applications and which users.

It is not clear how acceptable the market model is that old applications run with the old interfaces, but new applications will be developed in the "superior" interfaces of the new system.

There is an alternative form of competition in which the look and feel of the platform is used as a direct selling point. All older platforms are integrated into a common framework that has a common "persona" under which all software operates.

	AIX	HP/UX	Windows NT	OS/2	SCO	Solaris	UnixWare
Borland Interbase	•	•	•	•	•		•
Informix	•	•	•		•	•	
Ingres	•	•	•	•	•	•	•
Objectivity	•	•	•			•	
Oracle7	•	•	•	•	•	•	•
Sybase 10	•	•	•	•	•	•	

Table 5.4   Data bases available (shipping or announced).

An indication of the degree to which independent software vendors create product to run in multiple environments is shown in Table 5.4 with regard to data bases.

A product may be more or less integrated with a system on which it runs. For example, a data base may have a different look and feel from its underlying platform, different cataloging and directory, different data representations, and create, in effect, its own sub-universe. On the other hand, more integration would present a common data format, a common directory, and a common look and feel behind the standard GUI of the platforms.

The market dynamic

The environment market has a fuzzy internal structure as well as soft boundaries with other layers of a system. There is always change, and software planners always get it wrong. There is a constant attempt to define niches in which a product looks dominant and pervasive, and to convince everyone that new players or new product cannot successfully intrude. But as it turns out, there is no Unix vs. non-Unix market as such, no MVS vs. VM market as such—there are only applications and users searching for appropriate platforms.

There is now reason to believe that the market where software is sold is entering a new phase. The wild and violent buccaneer period in which companies entered the industry without capital, struggled, and then "elbowed" into major enterprises seems to be over. There is considerable consolidation running in parallel with niche redefinition and reformation. There are some truly dramatic reversals of fortune among major players, and some truly massive competitions developing between megacompanies. IBM's acquisition of Lotus is a manifestation of industry consolidation.

A competitive framework will involve Unix vs. non-Unix environments for different classes of systems. As Microsoft tries to push Windows NT into the closet or glass house, Unix vendors will try to defend their position and perhaps try to push Unix to the desktop. Competition more or less creates the Snow White image of the earlier industry, except that IBM is one of the dwarfs. This competition between Unix and Windows family products is likely to be more central to the industry than any struggle between OS/2 and Windows-oriented products.

Another competition will be for positions at the enterprise tier. Novell, in particular, has understood that it is not possible to settle in a niche. The comfortable, stable, highly profitable niche called "small local area networking" is decomposing quickly in the face of technology and conceptual changes. Desktop machines may be frequently replaced by wireless remote portables. Networking capability is being integrated into other platforms. And the focus of acquisition in client/server is moving up the layers to products like e-mail, development toolkits, spreadsheets, word processors, etc.

As a consequence, it is necessary to become a broad-based supplier of products at all levels and, in particular, to be a supplier of enterprise technology. Hewlett-Packard, Sun, Microsoft, and others have shown recognition of the need to play enterprise and to spring from a suffocating niche. The technologies for enterprise are:

- Systems management for heterogeneous distributed systems
- Integrated application development tools, focusing on objects
- End user interface software and kits to develop interfaces
- Global standards-conformant directory technology
- Cross-protocol network-integration capabilities.

But everything is ebb and flow. There is now an apparent tendency for companies to search their ethnic roots and find the "core" business. If that core business is still healthy, that is possibly a reasonable strategy. It is not necessary that Hewlett-Packard, for example, provide all of the storage management bells and whistles for HP-UX on its own. On the other hand, if that old "core" business is rotten, the search for it can be unhappy indeed.

Another competition will be for the role of "integrator" of information technology in the form of consultancy and services. This phenomenon links the software market to the education and consultancy market in ways not yet easy to predict.

The degree to which companies will "outsource" platform software acquisition and operation is a matter of some debate. There is a sense that it is cost efficient to outsource to a services company, but also there is a concern about giving up control. There is something inconsistent about claiming to the Executive Board that IT is a strategic weapon, and then contracting with another company to make key decisions in that area.

Much technology has crossed product and vendor boundaries. For example, the NetWare protocols are available from IBM, Microsoft, and others, as well as from Novell. Similarly, the NetBEUI protocols of LAN Manager and LAN Server are available in NetWare. TCP/IP is available from almost everybody.

One has a choice—for example, between Novell and Microsoft—of choosing the Novell protocols in a Novell systems structure and personality, or in a Microsoft systems structure or personality. Similarly, one can choose NetBIOS protocols in a Novell or Microsoft personality.

What drives a decision is not the primary technology, which is common to many, but secondary characteristics, like systems personality, cleanliness of integration, performance, vendor relations, and anything else we might think of, such as price.

Unix in the market

The evolution of Unix in the market is especially instructive. The establishment of Unix at the center of IT culture comes after decades of marginality on academic campuses and in the wiring closets of telephone companies. Now versions of Unix are pervasive, from laptop computers to large enterprise servers. It is the operating system of choice for workstations and midrange servers running OLTP (On-Line Transaction Processing). It has a dominating presence in technical applications.

The Unix market has segments of its own. Many Unix systems are descendants of a system called System V Release 3 (SVR3) from Unix Systems Laboratories (USL). Rather than following USL leadership and moving to System V Release 4 (SVR4), major vendors have used SVR3 technology and leavened it with selections from another branch of Unix, BSD (the Berkeley Software Distribution), and some proprietary features to produce the "proprietary" Unixes. Among these are IBM/AIX, SunOS, and Hewlett-Packard HP-UX. DEC Unix for Alpha is a version of OSF/1, the base operating system of OSF. There are other vendors offering "proprietary" Unix, including the Santa Cruz Operation

KEY UNIX

Unix systems are available from software vendors and from systems vendors who have created versions for their own hardware. The Unix systems from vendors who are likely to play an enterprise role are:

- Apple A/UX: POSIX, SVID, BSD 4.3, and Apple technology. Runs on Macintosh and Quadra.

- DEC: ULTRIX, OSF/1. ULTRIX runs on VAX- and MIPS-based systems, SVID, and POSIX. OSF/1 is based on the Mach Microkernel. It is available from other vendors for other architectures.

- Hewlett-Packard HP-UX 10.0: SVR3, Hewlett-Packard technology, and OSF standards. Runs only on PA-RISC.

- IBM AIX/RS/6000: SVR3, DSD 4.3, IBM technology, and OSF standards. Runs only on RS/6000 platform. But there are AIX versions for mainframe and Intel architecture. Little in common between various AIX platforms.

- SCO Open Desktop: Leading workstation Unix vendor with a pervasive version.

- Sun Microsystems (SunSoft) Solaris v2: SVR4, SunOS 5, OPEN LOOK. Runs on SPARC and Intel architectures.

- Novell SVR4, SVR4.2, and UnixWare: The USL canonical systems. Runs on Intel, MIPS, and other architectures.

(SCO) Open Desktop. There are a large number of SVR4 offerings, including those from AT&T Global, Sequent, Unisys, and Fujitsu.

Unix will likely never run mainframe workloads, but there may be few such workloads to run in the future, and Unix has a credible batch capability. Differences of opinion still exist about the future of Unix. Some believe it will be the standard operating system for all but desktop machines, others that it will be only a competitor of Windows NT.

A perhaps more interesting question is "What is the future of Unix technologies?" One sees the older operating systems moving from proprietary postures to Unix technology. POSIX, TCP/IP, X Windows, DCE, Sockets, and Spec 1170 have become part of MPE/ix, MVS, VM, VMS, and other proprietary systems. There is some loosening in the concept that Unix and Open are synonymous terms.

A great issue for Unix is establishing itself on PC-class machines. It already has a presence on the desktop at the workstation level, and the development of inexpensive PowerPC and Alpha chips for personal computers could provide a platform for Unix.

As personal computers become larger and as all operating systems grow, the machine cost barrier for Unix will diminish. Windows 95 is expected to require a 16 MB machine, about the size that many Unix users have been comfortable with. There was a hope among Unix vendors that a Unix desktop at the PC

5.8 ELEMENTS OF A DESKTOP UNIX

Communications	TCP/IP
Software organizer	IXI.X desktop manager
End user manager	X Windows 11 R4
End user standard	Motif 1.1
DOS coexistence	MS-DOS 5.0 as an application
Windows look and feel on DOS	Windows 3.0
Distributed data	NFS
NetBIOS Support	LAN Manager Client
Base System	Unix SCO 3.2
Hardware requirement	12 MB memory, 120 MB disk

level might be established. This would permit a client/server presence that could arguably reduce operational costs.

Unix as the universal system does not seem to be happening at this time. The presence of Windows is too pervasive to overcome—even corporate shops may not be able to resist the consumer product. When Windows seems to stumble, it seems to be OS/2 and not Unix that picks up the desktop slack. Hewlett-Packard is aggressively growing its Windows-supported Vectra line of PCs. However, tides turn, and approaches like Sun Microsystems' emulation of Windows may yet carry Unix to Intel desktops. For the moment, the Unix vendors seem focused on fighting off Windows NT as a server.

Novell is offering a desktop version, SVR4.2, called "Destiny." Novell is also interested in integrated NetWare with Unix, both on server and client platforms. Sun Microsystems has ported its Solaris package (Unix, X Windows, OPEN LOOK) to Intel architecture, and IBM has announced an intention to offer it with the PowerPC. This system is a packaging of a base Unix, communications capability, and OPEN LOOK. It also offers the Windows API (Wabi).

Motif, OPEN LOOK, VUE, and the newly defined CDE provide touch and feel similar to that of OS/2 and Windows. Many people not in the Unix culture do not feel that even behind these interfaces Unix is sufficiently invisible to non-Unix users.

Availability of applications is profoundly important. Unix has a large portfolio of applications, especially in certain industries like publishing. Various data bases (Informix, Oracle, Sybase, AIX/DB2) run on Unix, but the set is not the same at the consumer data base level, where there is a large population of non-SQL data bases. Also there is delayed support in Unix for the office suites of the type marketed by Microsoft and Lotus containing spreadsheets, word processors, and e-mail.

The announcement of Windows NT, and its positioning as server competition, drew the attention of Unix vendors. They felt vulnerable to the presence of a single scalable operating system. An irony was that the Unix compatibility and portability of myth and story was now clearly its greatest lack. An informal set of meetings (COSE) was established to undertake the convergence of Unix APIs. IBM, Hewlett-Packard, Sun, SCO, and Novell undertook to establish a common interface at all levels (DEC joined in later). The work was naturally most difficult where it was most important, in the end user interface and network management areas.

Market conditions change so rapidly that what looks like a reasonable strategy in a first quarter looks humorously obsolete by the third, and in the interim not much has happened. Agreements were extended to include object conformance and achieve object interoperability, and some plan for formalizing COSE was developed. As of this writing, nothing is clear. X/Open seems to be readying for promulgation of Spec 1170.

Windows in the market

Windows is a generic name for a family of Microsoft operating systems. The Microsoft Windows family platform product line contains a number of systems.

1   MS-DOS 6.x: A base operating system.

2   Windows 3.1: An end user interface environment that runs on various versions of MS-DOS (and competitive DOS) and that Microsoft has licensed to run on other operating systems.

3   Windows for Workgroups: A version of Windows with integrated communications permitting peer-to-peer resource sharing.

4   Windows 95: The successor to Windows 3.1 that will integrate the base operating system, extend the user interface, and bundle in access to on-line services (unless the U.S. government says no and can prove that Microsoft's bundling of net access with a base operating system is improper competition).

5   Windows NT Client: A version of Windows that brings it close to Unix in functionality, clearly aimed at corporate environments.

6   Windows NT Advanced Server: A scalable version of NT intended to run on departmental and enterprise servers using both Intel and RISC architectures. It has integrated communications, advanced multitasking, and other features of a large server system.

7 A forthcoming pure object-oriented, distributed system: Cairo.

8 LAN Server products that provide support for LAN systems independent of Windows; in particular, LAN Server runs with DOS and IBM OS/2.

Windows 3.1 is represented as an entry environment for palmtops and laptops, Windows for Workgroups for larger laptops and desktops with extension to "Intel workstations," and Windows NT running on the largest desktops, Intel and RISC workstations, and Intel, RISC, and SMP servers. Microsoft has said it will always position NT to be a complete superset of any technology in smaller systems like Windows for Workgroups, Windows 3.1, or Windows 95.

Windows products compete with OS/2 on single user systems and small servers; with Unix on single user systems and larger servers; and with NetWare products for local area networking, peer-to-peer workgroups, and smaller client/server systems.

Windows for Workgroups

Windows for Workgroups (WfWG) is a packaging and extension of Windows 3.1. WfWG provides peer-to-peer networking for intensely interactive resource sharing. The system allows a node to designate which resources may be seen by other nodes. Systems directories may be seen from remote nodes, printers may be shared (with or without designation of a printer server), mail servers can be designated to facilitate mail exchange within a workgroup, and meetings and appointments can be scheduled with Schedule+. Access to non-WfWG systems requires extension to the system. Spreadsheets and graphics can be shared across the network with the ClipBook, a shared persistent data base extension of the Windows 3.1 Clipboard. Object Linking and Embedding (OLE), the Microsoft object technology, is extended across the network, enabling remote application initiation.

Various workgroups with different security rights to various resources can be defined. WfWG has built-in connectivity to LAN Manager, Novell NetWare, and Banyan VINES. It can be accessed from non-WfWG platforms.

Windows NT

For the IT manager, it is the future of Windows NT that may be of most concern. NT is an attempt to create a single environment for client and server. It is a challenge to OS/2 on the desktop and Unix on the server, as well as to products like AS/400, Hewlett-Packard MPE/ix, and VMS/Open.

Sensitive to the complexity of introducing a corporate-level platform, Microsoft announced NT with great caution, pointing out it was not "grandmother's operating system" and suggesting that it expected to see a long curve of introduction. That has in fact happened, whether in accord with Microsoft's expectations is not clear.

NT is, depending on one's view, two operating systems or two configurations of the same system. The Advanced Server has componentry appropriate for servers and lacks some client technology.

NT is open in the sense that it is easily portable from one Intel packaging to another and less easily, but reasonably, portable to other chips. There are versions running on DEC Alpha, versions intended for PowerPC (at least by Motorola), and rumors of versions running (albeit poorly) on PA-RISC, although Hewlett-Packard has made no suggestion it will market NT.

NT has attracted intensive support. Its use will not constrict choices for data bases or office packages. Ingres, Sybase, and Oracle are among very early developers for the platform. NT has positioned itself against OS/2 by providing environments in which it can run 16-bit OS/2 and DOS applications, with little constraint on their relations with 16- or 32-bit Windows applications. NT offers multiple communications protocols, including NetWare SPX/IPX, TCP/IP, NetBEUI, and SNA. Microsoft, despite a minimum Unix flavoring of its own, is happy, on inquiry, to name the vendors that will supply X Windows, ONC+, and other elements of the Unix culture on NT.

On the negative side, there is concern about the currently limited number of applications, and about NT interoperability with Unix, MVS, or AS/400. There is also some lingering concern for its robustness.

But the greatest concern seems to be about Microsoft's intentions and directions, the shifting statements of relations between Windows 95 and NT, and the shadow of Cairo in the background.

Nonetheless, it is only Unix and Windows that currently scale from laptop to teraflop, and the temptation of a single operating system across the range is strong. NT developers clearly knew something about midsize operating systems, since they were led by Dave Cutler, lead designer of the VAX VMS operating system. The structure of NT is discussed in the third chapter of *The Basics Book*.

Windows 95

Windows 95 extends the end user interface and makes Windows independent of MS-DOS. This system is a Windows 3.1 consumer follow-up intended to improve the Windows family image relative to OS/2 Workplace Shell and Apple.

After a number of delays, most lately in the beta test cycle, the system was released in August of 1995. It is targeted at Windows 3.1–class machines.

The product is positioned as a full-function client. It offers some of the technology that is now in NT, and Microsoft is positioning it as a subset of NT. This suggests that NT will acquire the new, more Mac-like interface shortly after the arrival of Windows 95.

Windows 95 provides preemptive multitasking, integration with NetWare, OLE, and support for NT and NT applications. It also is bundled with access software for on-line interactive services (unless...). Initial sales have been strong, and the expectation is for rapid intrusion and 30 million copies by the end of 1995.

Windows At Work

Less visible at the moment but equally intriguing is Microsoft's vision of the integrated office, Windows At Work. This integrates copiers, printers, fax, voice, hand-held devices, and mail as managed network nodes, emulating and extending the flexible access to services that mainframe users have been offered. Windows At Work intends to achieve unified document formats, directory, and security in a small version of Windows with a common end user interface, print format, etc. The package allows one to use a fax as a document scanner, edit faxes in applications, and do voice annotation of documents. Clearly, it is an ambitious undertaking that will step on many toes, as there are developing standards for multimedia and phone integration outside of the Microsoft context.

Microsoft has achieved some level of participation from 60 companies. Manufacturers of printers, copiers, etc. will license elements of Windows At Work that they require. Peripheral units will be managed as network nodes.

The entire system will provide a unified document format, consistent directory, security, and document distribution across an integrated office using Windows elements and configurations. The Microsoft SMS network manager will be used as the management technology. This technology is also to be used with NT.

Environment pricing

The prices, deals, and special offerings of platforms bring airline fares immediately to mind. There are rapid changes, strange combinations, and unguessable

OS Software	Price ($)
Introductory DOS 6	49.95
Solaris (SunOS, ONC+, MP Deskset, Open Windows)	
Client	795.00
Workgroup server	4,995.00
Enterprise server	59,954.00
Development kit	495.00
UnixWare	
Personal edition	495.00
Development kit	599.00
TCP/IP-NFS	295.00
Encryption	95.00
Personal utilities	49.00
C2 Secure	109.00
Server	2,490.00
DOS Merge	399.00
NetWare on SPARC	5,000.00
NetWare 4.0	
10 users	2,400.00
100 users	8,795.00
500 users	26,395.00
1,000 users	47,995.00
Windows NT AS	2,995.00

Table 5.5   Operating system software pricing (mid-1994).

terms. Bundling baseware with data bases and telecommunications facilities is common, and sudden unbundling also occurs in a maelstrom of market shift.

Often, in the consumer market, the platform seems to have no price at all, as it is given as part of total product pricing, often with an office suite or at least a word processor. Windows, OS/2, and DOS are all given away by computer companies (e.g., Dell, IBM, Compaq), as are spreadsheets and word processors.

As of the end of 1994, software products at all levels in the Unix culture remain expensive relative to DOS, Windows, and OS/2. Versions of products that sell for $100 to $250 for Windows may cost $500 to $1,200 in the Unix culture. The rate at which these prices normalize will be determined by the rate at which Unix becomes part of the consumer mainstream, a rate partially determined by the success of the PowerPC, COSE, and X/Open.

Dramatic discounts are available for multi-unit license packages. One hundred copies of the same product, for example, can win a 30% discount from Microsoft. There are other deals in which a commitment to run the software on all of the machines at a site can win a 50% discount, or up-front commitment to a two-year usage level can win a 40% discount.

Pricing for a server is both higher and more complex than pricing for a personal system. A version of a server platform may cost $3,000 to $5,000, with various terms and conditions. Server software is licensed per user or per site at rates that reflect a vendor's desire to obtain market share.

Table 5.5 shows some examples of pricing (as of mid-1994). They are furnished only as examples, have not been confirmed by the vendors in any way, and surely will differ by the time the reader has opened this book.

A careful understanding of how software is used can save a good deal of money on software. Software costs are often given as the part of the cost of client/server computing that makes it expensive compared to mainframes on a per-user basis. However, investment in a software server with an understanding of usage patterns can reduce the need for software copies. For example, if there are 500 users of a product, it is not necessarily true that one needs 500 concurrent licenses that allow 500 simultaneous users. If it were known, for example, that the most popular packages were concurrently used by 60% of the users, and the least popular by 25%, then the number of concurrent licenses could be reduced and significant monies saved without diminishing accessibility and availability.

Large-scale software prices are dropping at a fast rate; there are many "street" deals, and it is difficult to generally say what large-scale software costs. Nevertheless, we present in Table 5.6 the result of an investigation done for a seminar on downsizing with a client.

Various combinations of systems are necessary in an enterprise. A representative configuration might be 4 departmental servers and 200 personal systems. At the prices given above, the software bill would be $4 \times \$20,000$ for the servers and $200 \times \$750$ for the clients. The maximum software cost for a platform with communications and a data base manager would be $230,000, as opposed to $360,000 for the mainframe.

Comparative software costs are hard to come by in a reliable way because of the turbulence of the market. Discount deals, special deals, and private deals abound for both mainframe and nonmainframe software. The exercise used published list prices for various user and site licenses and purchase prices to come up with a total software cost for different classes of system.

No words of caution on this can be too extreme. As this is read, the world will have changed yet again, new deals will be made, new prices announced. Still, this is an interesting exercise because it reveals alternatives and demonstrates concerns.

Key trends summary

There appear to be a number of major environment trends:

1 Increasing scalability, with more of a laptop to teraflop presence for Unix, OS/2, and Windows.

2 Increasing integration of networks and local operating systems. Platform systems now offer multiprotocol support, separately charged or bundled into the price. Since Windows, OS/2, and Unix have powerful networking

System Type[1]	OS	DBMS	System/Mgr	Interface	Total
BIGMF	100,000	200,000	50,000	10,000	360,000
SMF	10,000	25,000	–	2,000	37,000
CMOSG/S 1	5,000	5,000	–	–	10,000
CMOSG/S 2	5,000	5,000	–	–	10,000
RISC D/S	10,000	10,000	–	–	20,000
RISC E/S	20,000	50,000	–	–	70,000
RISC W/S	2,000	2,000	–	1,000	5,000
PC Desk 1	250	500	–	–	750
PC Desk 2	50	300	–	–	350

[1]Key to abbreviations: BIGMF = big mainframe, SMF = small mainframe, CMOSG/S 1 = small group server, CMOSG/S 2 = midsize group server, RISC D/S = department server, RISC E/S = enterprise server, RISC W/S = RISC workstation, and PC Desk 1 and 2 are personal computers.

Table 5.6   Software costs (in dollars).

capability, the place for a distinct "hard-boundary" network operating system is less clear. More application functions are being integrated, including data bases, mail, and access to network services like America Online, Prodigy, CompuServe, and (maybe) the Microsoft network.

3   Increasing convergence of Unix offerings, perhaps not behind COSE as it sits today, but certainly enough to present a unified front against the anti-Unix (Windows NT).

4   Increasingly common middleware and upperware, including shared development technology as well as shared file systems and data base managers, with largely common code.

5   Increasingly powerful multimedia interfaces, with CD-ROM an assumed machine feature and with support for imaging, video, and graphics built into the interface managers.

6   Expansion of the relational model behind "smarter" SQL to enable the manipulation of image and graphics objects.

7   Increased use of objects as a basic structuring unit, and the creation of object-oriented baseware.

8   Increased compatibility and emulation, and the eventual disappearance of the baseware and much middleware from the view of users and application developers.

chapter 6

Distributed and client/server computing

119

EXECUTIVE SUMMARY For nearly two decades the phrase "distributed computing" has been used to designate a class of systems whose characteristics never seem to be stable or clearly defined. Probably the phrase is better thought of as a characterization of enterprise systems emerging as a result of shifts in the relative costs of machines, networks, and people.

There are countless paradigms, topologies, and definitions used to describe distributed computing. There are serious disagreements about the relations between distributed computing, client/server, workgroup computing, etc. This book takes the view that client/server and workgroup computing are concrete instances of an abstraction called distributed computing.

The morphology of distributed computing is important because it suggests how systems might migrate in the future. An important aspect of IT investment is to prevent legacy after legacy, and to organize systems with some notion of how it will be when they must be evolved.

This chapter discusses various dimensions of distributed computing in terms of the resources that may be distributed, the relations between resources that are distributed, and where the technology may be taking us.

Distributed computing

Shifts in the underlying economics and capabilities of computer hardware that lead to workstations, highly parallel systems, superservers, etc. also lead us to distributed computing.

Distributed computing is less a kind of system than a set of attitudes responding to new hardware and communications capabilities. It has been with us for some time in various forms. It started with clusters of minicomputers, then transformed to PCs attached to minicomputers or mainframes. In this generation, it is associated with client/server and "rightsizing," in which there is tremendous interest, political and technological.

Distributed computing involves the partitioning of workloads, data, and applications across connected computing systems. It provides an ability to access

End user device function	End user interface standards function	Application function	Application function	Data access function	Data
(a)	(b)	(c)	(c)	(d)	(e)

| *n* | *n* | *n* | *n* | *n* |

Network

a/n/bcde	Host oriented non-programmable terminal
ab/n/cde	Host oriented programmable terminal
abc/n/de	Client/server (simple model)
abc/n/cde	Co-operative processing
abcd/de	Distributed database management
ab/c/c/d/de	Fully distributed

Figure 6.1 Network-oriented computing: the split of work is an investment decision.

resources on computers significant distances away. Ideally, it makes available to any person from any site all resources of computing with complete transparency as to source.

Distributed computing is a protean phrase used for systems of different functions and structures. There is a chaos of near phrases conveying some identical or similar idea: "distributed data," "distributed processing," distributed transactions," "cooperative computing," "client/server," "workgroup computing," "peer-to-peer computing." Vendors and consultants coin words that have no inherent meaning and use them carelessly.

The structure of a distributed system is an investment decision. Figure 6.1 shows the various points at which a system can be "distributed." Networking function is represented by a point (*n*) at the base of the vertical line. Various splits come into fashion at various times. The current favorite client/server split is represented by the double line.

Evolution and morphology

Distributed computing is enabled by the availability of smaller computers and peripherals priced so that significant amounts of computing power can be organized at prices equal to or less than a single mainframe of equal power.

TRANSPARENCY

Idealizations of mature distributed computing have been put forth by many people, including this author. "Transparency" is a Grail of systems theorists. It means that no end user or running application program needs to know where in the network something is. This information is restricted to administrators and systems people who must deal with the infrastructure directly. Programmers and end users are entirely unaware whether a program or data is on their machine, in the next town, or on the next continent.

This goal is not likely ever to be achieved in its purest form. Some awareness of the context in which a resource is located seems to keep creeping into systems. A programmer using a remote procedure call may not know where the called program is, but knows it is not local, for example. Some data base systems have naming conventions that include the system name of the computer on which it was developed (the "birthsite"). Some now even doubt that transparency is achievable for application developers or that it is even desirable. It is necessary to partition applications with an awareness of the topology across which they are being partitioned.

In the 1960s, end user nonprogrammable terminals began to be located at remote distances from mainframes. The arrival of minicomputers in the mid-1970s gave rise to systems that consisted of interconnected smaller machines located at distant geographic sites. These early systems had nonprogrammable terminals that communicated with local minicomputers. The computers interacted with each other at a less intensive rate than a nonprogrammable terminal interacting with a remote mainframe. The intent was to reduce absolute reliance on a network and on a single remote central unit. The local smaller machines could work autonomously for long periods. The model is a peer-to-peer system of cooperating autonomous systems.

In the early 1980s, personal computers led to a "downloading" of certain functions from central machine to desktop. The desktop computer improved the human/machine interface, could run some applications, and could work for periods of time without interacting with a central machine. The model is an asymmetric split of function, with varying degrees of dependency on a "host" or a "server." Investment is made in the desktop to diminish investment and reliance upon networking resources.

Recent advances in the quality and efficiency of network technology have again shifted views. Interdependency between distributed machines can be increased, and "virtual mainframes" or "enterprise systems" can be built of tightly linked systems with intense interaction across long distances.

Distributed systems develop in two ways: from the offload of large centralized systems and from the interconnection of systems not previously interconnected. Frequently the offload of larger systems is called "downsizing," while the interconnection of machines is called "networking." An associated

HOST-CENTRIC

Who does what is something of an issue. There are various splits of work between clients and servers, and different kinds of dependencies.

As late as 1990, IBM executives gave presentations assuming orders of magnitude more computing power in mainframes. The favorite IBM model at the time was to keep the program close to the data. When a personal machine needed "serious data," it would go to the host where the data base was. When a personal computer needed "serious computation" it went to the host where a part of its "cooperative computing" application would compute. The personal computer was highly dependent on the host for its resources. Local resources were frequently downloaded from the host. The notion of host-centric computing involved continued development of applications for the host with the personal computer limited to functions supporting the end user interface.

Some claim the tide turned on (part of) IBM when a product built around these concepts was killed as it tried to get out the door. The "host-centric" nature of cooperative computing became too much, in early 1991, even for IBM management.

Ironically, at the current time, the server is being positioned as a reconstructed host, with more and more infrastructure duties, although the notion of the mainframe as an application-execution site does seem to have had its day.

phenomenon, "upsizing," refers to reconsolidation of elements to enterprise servers. Winds shift quickly in computing; as of this writing, the stronger tendency is for dispersion from larger to smaller systems, although there is a small countertrend as well.

Forms of distributed systems—choices

Three attributes of distributed systems are shape, granularity, and resource.

Shape is the relation between elements for control, data access, and application performance. It determines whether systems are peers, or whether there are master/slave dependencies or client/server dependencies, and what these dependencies are.

Granularity is the size of distributable units. Are entire data bases to be dispersed, or should a single data base be split up? Granularity determines features like network size, instances of particular elements of software, and number and size of machines.

Resource is the particular aspect of computing being dispersed. Some systems disperse parts of applications, others data, others control over systems operations, others some notion of a transaction.

Figure 6.2 shows various shapes of distributed systems. Figure 6.2*a* shows a peer-to-peer system, Figure 6.2*b* a client/server, and Figure 6.2*c* a system with

Peer

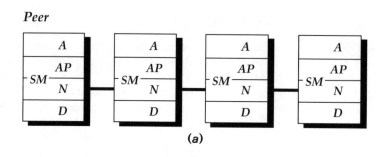

(a)

Client/server

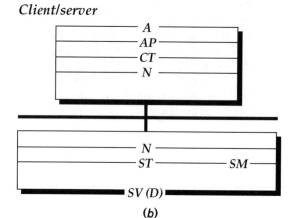

(b)

D   Data
AP   Application
SM   System management
N   Network function
A   Access
CT   Client technology
ST   Server technology
SV   Service

Smart network

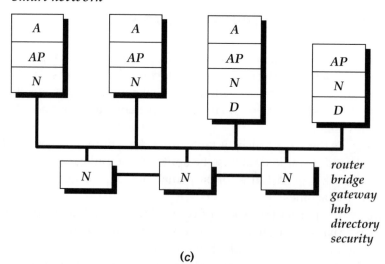

router
bridge
gateway
hub
directory
security

(c)

Figure 6.2   Shapes of distributed systems.

additional function pushed into the network. In Figure 6.2, the functions of a computer system are given as

- Data (D)
- Application (AP)
- System management (SM)
- Network function (N)
- Access and interface (A)
- Client technology (CT)
- Server technology (ST)
- Service (SV)

A system may be symmetric (built of cooperating peers) in its data flow, but asymmetric (specialized systems management servers) in control.

Peer to peer

Figure 6.2*a* shows all functions on all machines. Peer to peer is the model for relational data base and workgroup computing. In distributed relational data bases, each data base manager is an autonomous self-contained unit. Relations between managers are fundamentally "symmetric." In workgroup computing, each member of the group has an independent computer cooperating in a group session.

In peer to peer, any system can offer any service. Machines may be organized regionally rather than functionally, so instead of file servers, etc. one regional system may offer all services within the domain of the region. Machines may be small or large.

Symmetric systems may have asymmetric features. For example, end user interfaces may be isolated on desktop systems and the peer-to-peer relation established between servers. There are often some specialized servers with special functions.

Client/server

Client/server systems, discussed for more technical readers in "Client/Server—Development Views and Technologies," are asymmetric. Figure 6.2*b* shows access to the system (A), application program (AP), network (N), and some specialized technology on the client. The specialized client technology (CT) is what protects the application program from the communications awareness necessary to reach a service over the wire.

On the server side, there is network (N), the technology that defines the relation between client and server (ST), and the service (SV); in this case, the service is data. Systems management (SM) exists to the side to show that the server has some responsibility for the welfare of its client. There are many variations in the relations between clients and servers. Some servers have an arm's length relation with clients. Other servers have a more or less tending relationship: server and clients are more clearly part of a single system.

Group, departmental, and enterprise servers may combine and bundle services differently. A server may be generalized and offer a multiplicity of services. A group server will tend to offer a specialized service to a small group of end users. A departmental server may offer multiple instances of the same service or multiple services. An enterprise server may offer an environment quite similar to a traditional mainframe on a rather large machine.

"Smart network"

Figure 6.2c shows a system in which many functions are moved out of machines that have applications or data used by applications. Nodes 1 and 2 are clients with access, application, and client technology. Node 3 has a local data base that uses the network to talk to other data bases in a peer-to-peer relation. Node 4 is a data base server that talks both to the data base on Node 3 and to the clients at Nodes 1 and 2.

Functions like security, recovery, and directory (finding where things are) have been moved out of the client, server, and application nodes and into the network nodes. Network systems do more than their usual routing, gateway, and switching functions and become a systems infrastructure backbone.

Granularity

There is a "rightsizing industry" that will, by consultation or publication, help decide whether a particular workload, data base, or application should reside on a single mainframe, on 10 enterprise servers, 100 departmental servers, 1,000 group servers, 10,000 personal computers, or various combinations of these.

This naturally depends on the ability of the workload to be partitioned, the manageability of different populations, the cost and capability of interconnecting network structures, the relative prices of hardware of different sizes of machine, and the availability of software for different sizes of machine.

Breaking up a consolidated workload into independent units can be done with reasonable ease. Cutting into existing applications or data bases to find smaller partitions of function and data is difficult and expensive. Workloads that exist only because of the assumed economics of large systems and consolidation will easily break apart. Workloads that involve complex sharing patterns and some degrees of integration will tend to cohere.

Granularity involves relations between data, applications, and users to determine who is using what and how, and who is sharing. The effect of separating some data from its applications, or data bases that have been together, is not trivial and must be understood before being undertaken.

The size of distributed elements determines how big the network will be. Scale is a key aspect of systems management. Larger systems with hundreds or more nodes on a network require more sophisticated management technology. In larger systems, techniques like replication and duplication can (or must) be used to achieve higher reliability and improved performance.

Distributed elements

The elements of a system that can be distributed are data, programs, and control (systems management) functions.

Distributed data

A distributed data system is one in which data is dispersed around the system and accessed from remote sites.

There are three methodologies for distributing data:

1 Partitioning, in which parts of a data base are dispersed on a defined basis. The dispersion may be "functional" or "regional." A functional dispersion puts data related to accounting at one site and data related to inventory at another, for example. A regional dispersion places all data (accounting, inventory, etc.) on a system devoted to the activity of a particular part of the enterprise.

2 Extraction involves the selective duplication of subsets of data for a particular purpose. For example, critical data may be extracted and placed on a machine that will offer fail-soft services if the main data source goes down.

CONSISTENCY AND CONFORMITY

Systems that have "loose consistency" permit periods of time during which copies diverge. When change to a copy is made, changes to other copies are made at the convenience of the system. This approach is suitable with data for users who do not require the latest changes, but are content to work with day-old data.

With "tight consistency," data changes must be made at all copies before a transaction is completed. No later transaction may see data until everything is conformed. This requirement makes it necessary to:

1 Request permission to change data. Units with copies are notified. They lock local data (neither read nor write access). The lock may be on a file or a record in the file or a data base or a table in a data base or a row or column of a table.

2 Make tentative changes at a controlling site. Promulgate the changes to all copy holders and begin synchronization. The changes are written in a scratch pad (log) at all sites.

3 Synchronize modifications at all sites. A common paradigm is a "two-phase commit,"

in which a "master" (commonly the site where the change was requested) waits for other sites to confirm they are set up to make the change. When all sites have reported, the master sends out a commit. This directs sites to make the permanent change and report. All sites respond with an intention to commit. Changes are made and reported. When all changes are reported, the transaction is considered to be complete. Locks are released and response is made to the user(s).

There may be failures in the commit process. In case of some failure, the master directs operational sites to "back out" of the change, restore data, and report. When this is done, the master aborts the transaction and reports failure to those using the program.

These functions may be performed by a file manager, a data base manager, or a transaction manager. The need to conform data is not restricted to replicated copies. Related data bases—indicating, for example, the suppliers of items, the inventories, and the sales volumes—may have a need for synchronization.

3 Replication places exact copies of data bases around the system and guarantees that each copy is always identical to each other copy.

It is often difficult to "decompose" data into unique dispersible sets because of the internal structure of the information and because of reference patterns. While improved interconnect technology is diminishing many distribution constraints, intensity of reference is still a constraint. If a number of departments require access with about equal frequency from equidistant locations, it is not useful to disperse data to any particular group.

Replicating rather than partitioning is effective for data that is infrequently changed but often "browsed." As rates of change become more frequent, and as patterns of change become more complex, replication becomes more difficult. Frequent changes from a single source are easier to manage than frequent

When it is not possible to accomplish static partitions of the data by systems analysis, dynamic copies may be made of entire data collections or parts of data collections. For example, parts of a file may be "cached" forward to an end user device as it is needed for performance convenience. The dispersed data is not considered to be a replicated copy of the data from the dispersing site and has no formal system status. The movement of data forward in this way is a simulation of memory management hierarchy in computer hardware, where data is copied forward to a cache memory on a processor chip from a memory chip while it is being used.

When reference is made to part of a file, a section of it is moved forward to the referring system, on disk or in memory. The referring system browses the data or modifies the data, and the changes are posted back to the resident file according to some semantic that approximates hardware caching rules within a machine. In Unix semantics, all changes are immediately posted back to the file site to enable immediate change availability to all file sharers. This simulates "push-back" or "write-through" hardware caches. In file semantics, changes are not pushed back until the file is closed by the local user. This is a somewhat imperfect emulation of a "write-in" cache.

changes from multiple sources. As interconnect technology improves, replication is becoming a more mainstream technology, but it is still constrained because of the complexity of guaranteeing identical copies.

In many relational data base systems, data is extracted by "snapshots." Data is brought to a local data base on request. Changes to the home data are reported to the snapshot at an agreed rate.

A copy of a file or data base may be requested by a system and transferred to its own local file or data base system. It is the equivalent of copying a file from a hard disk to a floppy disk. The transfer creates a new file in a local file system. The new file is distinct from the old file, has a different system-wide name, and there is no conformity relation between them.

A form of extraction that is becoming key is the "multidimensional warehouse." Data from operational data systems is extracted onto a dedicated server where it is summarized and otherwise aggregated to support decision making. The data is organized by subject rather than by organization or application and various views are allowed on the data. On-line analysis of the data is provided through development tools, and the data can be imported to desktop software like spreadsheets and word processors. The data warehouse can be static, that is, designed without capability of extension, or dynamic, permitting redefinition of what aggregrations and elements should be associated with the subject. Source operational files may be relational data bases or file systems. This is discussed in greater detail later.

Distributed file systems—choices

The manner in which data in remote file systems is accessed will impact the cost of a network, the size of desktop systems, and software that will be used. There are a number of approaches to granting access to remote data in file systems:

1 Enable a personal computer to emulate a nonprogrammable terminal. The computer accesses files at a "host" system as if it were a terminal. This technique is well known to users of IBM VM, for example. Many organizations have purchased desktop computers only to enable employees to emulate terminals most of the time.

2 Enable a personal computer to define a "phony" disk drive that holds files actually on a distant mainframe. Local drives A: and C: are augmented by X:, Y:, or Z:, which are defined across space on a host disk system.

3 Define a distributed file system that has a front-end part and a back-end part. The front-end part enables application programs to call on file services as if the file were local. The back-end part contains the file system and associated services. This is the file data form of the client/server model.

All distributed file systems permit a user at a client system to access data on a remote file system as if it were local. They differ in the recovery services, security services, and directory services associated with file access. They also differ in their memory and network management aspects in the degree of sharing that is reasonable and in the unit of distribution. However, the underlying paradigm is common: access and change file data as if it were local.

The technology of distributed file systems is client/server. File system–to–file system interaction, where one file system is a requester to another, is a limited phenomenon.

There are a growing number of distributed file systems. An industry-wide de facto standard, absolutely dominant in Unix environments but also pervasive outside of the Unix world, is the Network File System (NFS). This file system is part of an architecture supported by Sun Microsystem's Open Network Computing (ONC+). It is possible to access the NFS from Unix or non-Unix clients. The file system itself runs with many operating systems (MVS, VMS, MPE/ix, Windows NT) that are not Unix. It runs on the UDP (datagram) transport protocol. The technology associated with the NFS is the dominant de facto Unix distributed computing software culture. The NFS, Lock Manager, RPC, Yellow Pages, and REXX are fundamental to Unix and systems that coexist with Unix. Sun promulgated this technology by freely licensing at a very low cost to many sources. There are many sources of the NFS for various operating

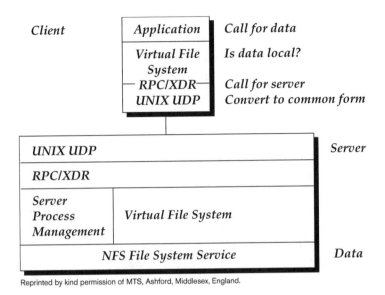

Figure 6.3   Network File System structure.

systems, each of which conforms to the architecture. ONC is open in the sense that it runs on many platforms and is available from many sources; however, its architecture is tightly controlled by Sun. Recent extensions to ONC, ONC+, have improved some aspects of NFS performance and have provided an enterprise quality directory technology. Access to NFS from non-Unix clients is available through NFS-PC. Figure 6.3 shows the NFS.

Another distributed file system associated with Unix is the Distributed File System (DFS) of Distributed Computing Environment (DCE). It is derived from the Andrew File System at Carnegie-Mellon University. DFS differs from NFS in that the server assumes dependency on the part of its clients. The file system on the server is cached forward to clients, but the server watches the use of data. It will not permit multiple write tokens, and if a writer comes onto the system, it removes read privileges from clients using possibly changed data.

The NFS and the DFS present two quite different views of the relation between a client and a server. In the context of NFS, there is no assumption of the relative size of client and server. The models on which it was based were administratively independent large systems at independent military or university facilities. Issues of recovery, data synchronization, and security were left largely to the independent administrations of each system. A large mainframe might be the server for one academic discipline and a client for another academic discipline.

There are remote access file systems outside of the Unix culture. Novell provides a file server that permits various clients to access file data as if they were dealing with a file system of their own culture. The Novell file system can look like an OS/2 file to an OS/2 application, a DOS file to a DOS application, etc.

Distributed relational data base

Relational data bases represent data as two-dimensional tables. This model has the great advantage of eliminating the need for programs to navigate through data by presenting data that conforms to selection criteria as a well-formed table.

Distributed data bases involve data base managers requesting data from each other. Each may be autonomous, fully capable, separately managed, and geographically distant from another. The computing model is peer to peer.

The technology for distribution with identical data bases includes recognition that data is remote and synchronization between data bases whose view of the world is identical. Recovery, security, and synchronization are done within identical language, naming, and data organization.

Achieving a distributed data base involves data partitioning or integration at high levels of abstraction. The technology of distributed data base is ahead of the technology of distributed data base planning. The tools needed to determine where data should be placed across an enterprise network are lacking.

In undertaking distributed data solutions, it is essential that flexibility and modifiability be built into the system in case the initial "cut" of data is wrong, or the business changes its own structure.

Relational data base operations are set theoretical functions: union, intersection, set difference, product, etc. It is impossible to determine the complexity of an SQL statement by inspection; therefore, it is difficult to understand whether any particular SQL function can be satisfied across a distributed network. There are various limitations on the complexity of distributed relational operations that can be taken to the network even with identical managers.

Distributed software

Software can be distributed independently of data. The distribution can be in one of two ways:

1 Complete applications or systems software functions can be dispersed around the network and replicated as necessary. Individual machines become cookie cutter examples of particular software environments.

2 A particular application or software package can be partitioned so that parts of it exist at different points in the system. Some programming theorists like to partition applications into "end user" parts, "computational" parts, and "data intensive" parts. End user parts, interacting intensively with human users, should be on machines physically close to humans, the computational part should be on a system most efficient for computation, and the data access part on a data server of some kind.

Program decomposition, the art of creating distributed programs, is in a somewhat early stage, except for simple client/server divisions. The slow maturity of parallel applications development may serve as a model for the rate at which truly distributed applications will emerge.

The integration of separately created applications into "mega applications" seems to be moving more quickly. Various applications, perhaps represented to a user as icons on a screen, are placed into a larger framework, much in the way that a multimedia document is created. The placement of these applications within the unifying structure links them together so that they can share data, controls, and interfaces. Embedding spreadsheets into word processing programs and film clips into text documents are examples. Embedding applications from the network into a visually coherent single application is an extension of integrated "office suites."

Entire applications may be duplicated at different machines. Each user population communicates directly with a local application, which then accesses local or remote data as needed. If remote data is to be accessed, the application may be structured so that a local program communicates with a remote "cousin" to ask for the data.

There are various operational and administrative problems with program replication. It is necessary that programs be identical at all systems. Upgrades, new versions, patches, etc. must be uniformly applied so that the behavior of all program copies is identical. In addition, many applications are now available with contracts that specify rules for total users, total simultaneous users, total copies, etc. These rules must be rigidly enforced, since more lenient contracts usually involve higher costs. Frequently, a program distribution mechanism that "caches" copies of programs forward to end user stations from a kind of server is preferable to permanent distribution and maintenance of multiple copies.

Distributing control

There is no issue more central to distributed computing than the ability to manage systems remotely and the ability to disperse aspects of control across a

DEGREES OF DISTRIBUTION

There are various degrees of distribution possible within multiple data base managers. These are commonly defined as:

1 Remote request: A single "select" statement in the Structured Query Language (SQL) is passed by one data base manager to another. The requested manager returns a requested table. The entire span of the unit of work is a single statement. This applies to inserts and updates as well.

2 Remote unit of work: A group of SQL statements referring to various tables in the system is sent to the site where those tables exist. The unit of work is a list of SQL statements calling for selection of data, modification of data, or insertion of data at one remote site in the system. The first data base sends the entire list to a single remote data base for response.

3 Distributed unit of work: A group of SQL statements referring to various tables in the system is distributed to the sites where the tables exist. The unit of work is a list of SQL statements calling for selection of data, modification of data, insertion of data, etc. and ending with a statement calling for synchronization of the unit of work. The first data base manager to see this list determines where in the system the referenced tables exist and disperses each SQL statement to its proper site. Remote systems respond with tables, which are transmitted to the application. Each data base manager is responsible for its own SQL statement.

4 Distributed request: A group of SQL statements or a single SQL statement refers to tables not wholly contained at a single system. Tables are fragmented so that some rows exist at one site and other rows exist at another site. A single SQL statement is distributed to the sites containing various rows. These rows may represent a regional split of a huge data base treated as a logical unit by the enterprise.

population of machines. It is necessary to enable recovery from remote sites, to judge the load of a remote machine, and to determine software usage patterns on remote machines from multiple points in a large system. A lack of ability to properly manage is often given as a serious cost inhibitor to distribution.

Control is defined by systems management technology (see Chapter 13). It includes data, software, network, error, desktop, storage, load, and change control. These elements may be grouped together in a centralized manner or they may be dispersed around the system. Network management may be distributed across various domains capable of local control. There may be a centralized network manager that is distinct from a centralized storage manager, which is yet further distinct from a centralized application manager.

Various forms of distributed control are needed to support diverse administrative and operational environments where interlinked computer systems may not map onto organizational structures. Control topologies may be orthogonal to data, program flow, and institutional structures.

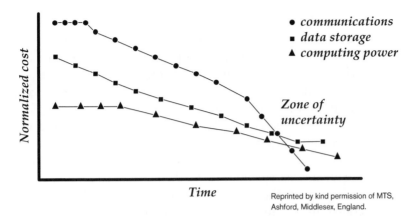

Figure 6.4 Efficiency curves showing a shift of limiting resources over time and that exchange impacts systems design. The design minimizes dependence on the limiting resource.

The feasibility of certain kinds of distributed systems is determined by the ability to control the dispersion. The costs of uncontrolled systems, even at the level of small client/server projects, are prohibitive.

Systems control for distributed systems of moderate size is in a relatively mature condition. However, as networks become large, and since they contain diverse and heterogeneous elements, system control becomes an increasingly critical constraint.

Economics and system structure

Figure 6.1, on page 121, showed a general notion of how software can be split, and Figure 6.2 showed some possible shapes. There are very fine grains of distribution that Figure 6.1 does not show, and there are multitudinous variations of topology not shown by Figure 6.2. Each variation represents an investment decision—a balancing of investment in networking, end points, and server populations.

Figure 6.4 shows a set of curves representing conjectural improvements in efficiency for various resources over time. Each resource of computing is represented by a curve showing its "abstract efficiency." The figure intends to show various relationships between the resources. The abstract efficiency of a resource is its price/performance relative to other resources of computing. The idea is abstract because of the difficulty in quantifying and normalizing price/performance for all resources.

The figure shows there is always a constraining resource whose relative efficiency is such that designers try to minimize its use in the system.

The constraining resource is relatively most expensive, least reliable, least available, slowest, or has other negative attributes. There may be more than one constraining resource. The constraining resource for performance may not be the constraining resource for reliability. However, in general, a single efficiency number suggests which resources are best minimized and which are best maximized within a design period.

The constraining resource may change over time. When communications is the constraining resource, investment is made in desktop storage, memory, and logic in order to minimize the dependency on networking. When large system software is a constraint, the tendency may be to disperse from the large system. Various matrix manipulations are required to discover a set of feasible (one never discovers optimum) topologies within various constraints.

When communications are expensive relative to memory, storage, and logic, functions tend to move to the desktop. When communications are efficient relative to storage, logic, and memory, some functions tend to move back to the center. For example, data bases may be moved back from desktop machines to a group server, and application programs may be moved back to an application server providing better software licensing arrangements and usage control.

An important aspect of computing is the uncertainty over time of the relative efficiencies of resources. Rates of change for some technologies are not well understood, and pricing dynamics for many are changing unpredictably and erratically. There is a resulting need for configuration flexibility, a design care that data bases, software, and elements of control can be reconfigured at a minimal cost as resource efficiencies change, and at different periods it becomes more efficient to centralize data bases or disperse them. Network topology will be in constant flux.

Client/server—development views and technologies

Various vendors, authors, and consultants present different views of what client/server is. One view is that client/server is a way of thinking about the business. The viewpoint associates client/server with notions of re-engineering and business strategies. It involves processes of analyzing information flow across an enterprise or business unit and dedicating smallish networks to particular applications. Little specific technology is associated with client/server computing in this view.

This writer prefers a more technology-oriented view that distinguishes client/server as a form of distributed computing and that separates a bit more how one thinks about the technology architecture and the business architecture. Client/server is a particular instance of distributed processing in which there is an asymmetric flow of data, requests, and control.

There is great danger in not understanding client/server in a context of change. Over time there will be changes in views of where services should reside in the network, and client/server imposes particular constraints on changing configurations.

At one time, it may be convenient to export data bases to group servers, or even to desktop systems where they partake in peer-to-peer sharing. During other periods, it may be better to import back to enterprise servers. Shifts in the network will change instances of when data access is managed by data base technology or by client/server technology. This change is sometimes driven by the business and sometimes by changes in resource efficiency.

Client/server technology and variations

Client/server is a technology used in the absence of a service at a particular site. The technology provides a mediator between an application asking for a service, the network that will reach the remote server, and the server itself. It is primarily a software-defined relation between two computers in which one is typically dedicated to a single user and one is shared between users. There is no necessity that the client be a smaller system than the server. Historically, the notion of client/server grew out of relations between machines of the same size allowing access to specialized data bases.

Client/server faces issues of interoperability and connectability. Linking technologies are necessary to permit, for example, Macintosh to talk to Windows NT Advanced Server, MVS, or HP-UX; or to permit Windows desktop systems to talk to Unix servers; or to permit Unix desktop systems to talk to VMS. The sources and nature of this technology will be addressed in Chapter 7 as part of "open."

The basic technology of client/server is:

1 Server software appropriate for a group or a departmental system supporting 25 to 256 users, or for an enterprise service supporting populations in the thousands.

2 Server ability to support clients running various operating systems, in particular, Windows, DOS, OS/2, and Mac System 7.

3 Server facilities consisting of market-pervasive data base managers or file systems (for example, Oracle, Sybase, Informix, NFS).

4 Support of de facto communications protocols, particularly TCP/IP, SPX/IPX, and NetBIOS, with gateway capability to SNA and DNA.

5 Technology to generate linkages between clients requesting services and servers across the wire. The linking technology acts as a local surrogate for the service. When a client application is started, the system provides "stubs." These stubs are activated when the application program calls for a service. They operate to prepare the request to be sent across the network to the equivalent stubs on the server side.

6 Development toolkits to create applications using simple data references that can be satisfied across the network.

Figure 6.5 contains another picture of a simple client server system. It contains new elements:

1 The "side language" which is used to generate the client stub and the server stub. This side language is the instrument by which the application developer describes the service it wants from the server.

2 A library of programs which are used to perform functions associated with the passing of messages between client and server.

Various client/server environments have different capabilities. Some permit parts of the application on the server. In the pure paradigm, all application code is on the client; but exceptions are many. This is partly because of the vague boundaries between systems services and applications and the usefulness of some application programming near the data system. Some systems provide infrastructure services on the server, such as data access synchronization or storage management.

Toward a next generation

Current client/server technology tends to isolate small servers in particular applications environments. The second generation of server technology must address a reintegration of computer functions.

A goal in the early 1990s, from which we seem to have been diverted, was to increase the coherence of computing systems by reducing the barriers between them. Somehow, in pursuit of that goal, we have fragmented and isolated data and applications at a level we could never have achieved on the mainframe.

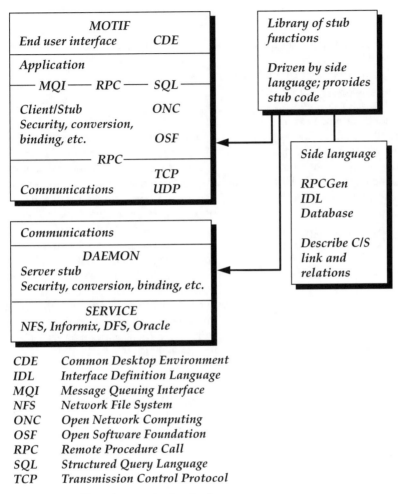

CDE	Common Desktop Environment
IDL	Interface Definition Language
MQI	Message Queuing Interface
NFS	Network File System
ONC	Open Network Computing
OSF	Open Software Foundation
RPC	Remote Procedure Call
SQL	Structured Query Language
TCP	Transmission Control Protocol

Figure 6.5   Client/server technologies.

As a second generation of client/server develops, there is a focus on reintegration of systems. This sometimes takes the form of moving applications back to larger servers: to departmental servers, for example, from group servers, or to enterprise servers from departmental servers.

Sometimes the reintegration focuses on server/server issues and the definition of relations between servers. The links between two servers can be supported by local or wide area interconnects, or even by fast input/output technology. Sets of servers working together are sometimes called "clusters." Clusters represent the current generation of a system class that first started in the 1960s and was brought to a form of maturity by VAX clusters in the 1970s.

STUBS

The stubs are programming provided by the system that links an application program to the service by performing certain functions and preparing a package for the communications software. The stub is entered by a call (directly or indirectly) for a service. The stub is generated from the macros in the service library in accord with the side language. The application issues a request for a service. This request is intercepted by the stub. The stub performs certain functions on behalf of the application:

1 It performs any directory lookups that might be required to find the service.

2 It contacts the service to establish a service relation.

3 It develops a package to give to the transport layer.

4 It performs any data conversion necessary between the client and the server. This may be done from the client or server side.

5 It performs any security functions appropriate for the service. This may be done from the client or server side.

The client/server passes a message down to the communications protocols. On the server side, the communications manager receives the package and invokes the server stub. The server stub deconstructs the communications package and passes the request to the service as if it had been a local request.

The service performs the requested function and passes data or notice of completion to its stub with the equivalent of a "return." The stub prepares a package and passes it to the communications manager. On the client side, the data or notice is passed up by the client stub to the client application as if the service had been local.

Servers can be clustered by networking with each other, or by being attached to a shared "data farm" so that they in effect look like a single source of load to that data farm, or by both techniques. It is by no means a new idea.

Common services

Figure 6.6 shows a group server running a file system service. Bundled into the file system are private naming, directory, security, and recovery functions. Each file system has private notions of how these functions should be performed. As a result, it is tremendously difficult to perform functions across multiple file systems for complex transactions. Such technology is typical of first generation systems that have been developed largely as stand-alone systems for small groups.

Tying servers together in any way is enormously difficult because of the private versions of what should be system-wide functions.

Figure 6.7 shows a reformed picture of file services, directory services, security services, and recovery services. These infrastructure services are mapped across all file systems, and can be isolated on specialized servers or combined

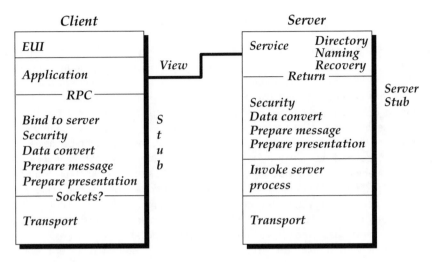

Figure 6.6 Functions across multiple file systems.

with each other and with file services in various ways. The common availability of infrastructure services diminishes barriers between systems.

The system in Figure 6.7 contains infrastructure services common to all file systems, data base managers, and other servers. Such technology permits the interconnection of servers to form cooperating multiserver systems.

App	System Management X.700	Security	X.400 Message	X.500 Directory	
Alternate Session Services				CPIC	
				SNA	OSI
Interface Adapter Layer					
TCP UDP		SPX	Netbios		
IP		IPX			
Link					
Shared Physical					

Figure 6.7 Restructured services: common higher layer services for all session, transport, and network protocols.

CASUAL VS. CARING

Two models of client/server are the "casual" and the "caring."

In the casual model (of the de facto standard Open Network Computing), the client is understood to be outside the cell of the server. The client and server live in separate worlds with an agreement that lets the client access the data and resources of the server in some way. Clients and servers may be machines of equal complexity and capability. A client for biology data from a particular university may be a server for chemistry data to that same institution. Client/server in the casual model is a service between peers who require no tending from each other.

The technology for such a relation is an arm's-length technology with minimum recovery and synchronization services associated with the User Datagram Protocol (UDP). A "stateless" model, in which the server remembers little or nothing about the status of the client, supports the limited relation that exists between client and server.

The "caring" model is stateful and derives from a paradigm of computing in which the server has a closer relation to the clients. The client and the server are assumed to be in the same cluster and cell, and the client is assumed to be a less capable computer than the server. The client may even be diskless, with no permanent storage capabilities at all. There is a strong notion that the client family and the servers are members of a single system, and that the server must tend the clients much in the way that a mainframe host would tend users of a dumb terminal.

In such a system, the server is considerably more aggressive in recovery and coordination between clients. For example, in a caring system, if a client asks to change data and if there are readers of the data subject to change, the server will notify the clients of the obsolescence of the data, perhaps even forcing the client to suspend processing and re-request the new data after the changes are completed. The DCE Distributed File System is like this.

Grouping of services

Servers come in three basic sizes: group, department, and enterprise. Grouping services on servers involves decisions that span many aspects of modern computing. The issues involved are (at least):

1 The price/performance characteristics of different classes of system—the relative efficiency of mapping 100 data bases on 100, 10, or 1 server(s).

2 The efficiency relationships between investment in communications technology and computer technology for both hardware and software.

3 The ability to run different upperware software on different middleware and baseware.

4 The available software development tools for developing applications of different scale and degrees of portability.

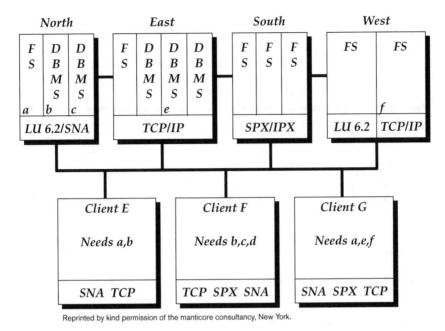

Figure 6.8 Multiserver. The lower-case letters refer to functions or data needed by a client that are resident in the indicated environment.

5 The levels of integration and the methods of integration available on a single computer as opposed to on the network.

6 Industrial strength on an enterprise server as opposed to network-centric systems. Older systems must recognize the need to offer systems management support to workstations and PCs. Network systems must offer the backup, archiving, and high availability associated with mission-critical computing.

Advocates of the "new paradigm" claim that industrial strength at a single machine is no longer a key criterion, that industrial strength must be provided across the network, and that systems growing up from the bottom and those coming down from the top are in a race to arrive at scaled network industrial strength.

Figure 6.8 shows a multiserver where each server provides multiple services on a regional basis.

We are moving back to a centric, almost mainframe, mind-set with this system. The art is to be able to group services elegantly without reintroducing some of the problems of mainframe complexity, cost of ownership, and bureaucracy.

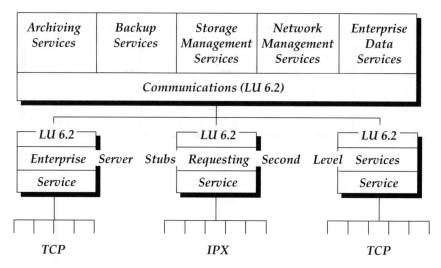

Figure 6.9   Multi-tier servers.

The system is more complex than a first generation system in that it is a composite of peer to peer and client/server. It is an attempt to relink business functions and enable sharing of data and function. Each server is larger and more complex, and the relations between them are more tightly drawn.

Figure 6.9 shows a variant system in which there are two tiers of servers: a first tier of operational servers and a second tier of enterprise-wide infrastructure services like archiving, storage management, etc.

The relations between servers

A key aspect of the relations between servers is what barriers exist between them and the expenses associated with overcoming those barriers—if, in fact, they can be overcome.

The relations between servers actually shifts attention from client/server issues to peer-to-peer distributed computing models. A server will interact with another server when it recognizes that:

1   A requested resource is at another server.

2   A needed function is unique to another server.

3   There is a need for an infrastructure server to find out where an object is, to establish a link with another server, and to determine security aspects of a data access request.

Key elements in the relations between servers are the problems of systems administration and management. Families of servers are sometimes called "cells" and sometimes called "clusters." A cell is an administratively defined unit where system responsibility spans all units. A cell is expected to have a common organizational responsibility, although it is not expected to be technologically homogeneous. A cluster, on the other hand, is technologically homogeneous and represents a family of interlinked systems with a maximum technological basis for resource sharing.

Heterogeneous servers in cells face the problem of systems management limitations across technology boundaries just in that area where common management is most key.

Another aspect of client/server relations is the extent to which there is a nominated "home" server through which a client accesses the system. It is responsible for linking the client to all other servers from which it must gain service. It does not necessarily lie on the pathway between the client and other services, but is a point of control for client access to the system. Various aspects of downloading applications, licensing control, synchronization, and data backup are taken on by a primary host server.

chapter 7

Open interoperable systems

147

EXECUTIVE SUMMARY   Problems of interconnecting similar systems are complex enough. When one desires to connect systems with different software environments at baseware, middleware, and upperware layers, problems compound dramatically. Even after connection is made, there are difficulties in sharing data, recovery, security, and management across product boundaries.

There have been a number of quite different approaches to increasing the ability to work together. They all go under the rubric of "open." An open system carries with it the notion that it has a maximum ability to interoperate, or even to run the programs of other systems. One way of achieving this is to "homogenize" systems. This involves making a choice and imposing a single set of interfaces and protocols on all systems. These may come from de jure standards organizations, dominant vendors, or industry alliances. Another way to achieve "open" is to install various kinds of "adapters" that accommodate the behaviors of other systems. These adapters come in many forms. They may be protocol programs that simulate the behavior of another protocol, or they may be interface modules that allow one API to be transformed into a call the protocol is expecting.

The processes and organizations through which open standards are developed are quite diverse. It is sometimes difficult to judge the depth to which vendors are committed to support the interfaces and protocols of the alliances they join. Despite market forces for similarity in offerings, vendors still naturally pursue profits in an increasingly competitive industry.

Yet, standards from IEEE, X/Open, OMG, and other organizations discussed in this chapter would be dangerous to ignore when planning development strategies.

The dimension of heterogeneity

Limits on sharing among systems put limits on the business. New opportunities often require new "slices" and "dices" of resource existing across diverse

CHAPTER 7:   OPEN INTEROPERABLE SYSTEMS

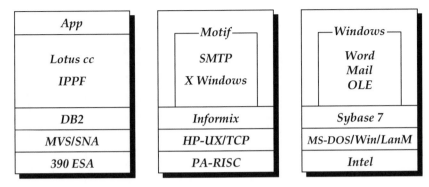

Figure 7.1 Various towers.

computer systems. The inability to integrate resources restricts the ability of an enterprise to respond to opportunity.

Computers differ in many details. Some differences do not affect their ability to intercommunicate and interoperate. But other differences represent barriers to the sharing and access of resources.

Figure 7.1 shows a layered view of three computer structures in three cultures. Each tower represents a system with particular data formats, program interfaces, and naming conventions. The sharing or movement of data or programs from one tower to another is severely restricted by the particular features of each. Even after interconnect, it is sometimes impossible for a user of one tower to find, access, transfer, or manipulate a resource on another tower.

Sharing and common use is restricted by:

- Different data organizations
- Different interfaces to access data
- Different rules for security and access
- No methodology for finding resources on a network-wide basis
- No application development systems that span towers
- No technology for joint management of diverse towers
- Different "look and feel," making access from anywhere difficult.

These are constraints associated with heterogeneous systems. The difficulties of using resources from different environments are not particular to distributed processing. Figure 7.2 shows that complex mainframe environments also have boundaries that restrict data from being shared among subsystems. Different towers have private directories, differing interfaces, diverse naming conventions, etc. that make it difficult to cross boundaries even though a single machine is shared.

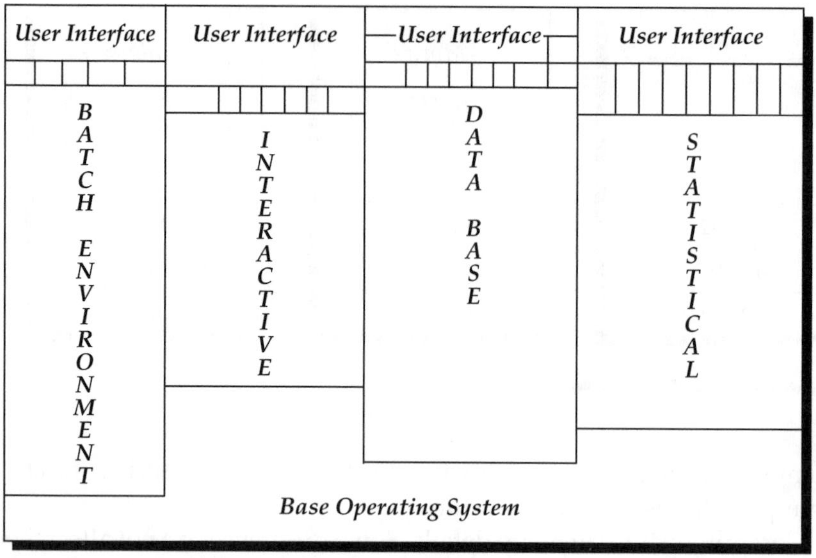

| User Interface | User Interface | ─User Interface─ | User Interface |

| B A T C H E N V I R O N M E N T | I N T E R A C T I V E | D A T A B A S E | S T A T I S T I C A L |

Base Operating System

Reprinted by kind permission of the manticore consultancy, New York.

Figure 7.2 **Mainframe complexity: differing levels of operating system support, duplication of operating system functions, private directories, unique data formats, unique program interfaces, and different user interfaces.**

It was a common experience, in the early days of personal computing, not to be able to move data from a word processor to a data base program, or from a networked information system into a word processor. Boundaries are defined by software developed without regard to other software, and they exist regardless of software distribution across a wire.

"Open systems"

"Open systems," "cooperative computing," and "heterogeneous distributed computing" are phrases used to describe systems that lower the barriers between interconnected computers. Motives for increasing the cooperation between systems are diverse—some technological, some business-oriented.

Opening a culture to technologies coming from multiple vendors is thought to enable a user to be more aggressive in the business. Multiple-vendor systems provide:

- An ability to determine one's own rate of technology change
- Benefits of price and product competition between vendors
- Lower cost of application development by the use of standards
- Easier migration from system to system over time.

One way of achieving an open system is for everyone to produce and use product that is exactly the same—a commoditization of computer product at all levels. Another way is for every tower to be modified so that it works with every other tower. Aspects of both approaches are being pursued.

Vendors have different ways of stating how they are open. There are many colorations of open (see Box 7.1). There are many problems with the standards that might be used to achieve open.

Standards do not span the range of systems requirements. They have conflicting versions and options that make them incompatible. The de jure standards process lags behind the rate of technology change, and new technologies must be deployed before standards are mature. De facto standards show their "ethnic" origins (Sun, Novell) and are less environment independent than one would like. There are competing and alternative de facto standards. The rate of delivery of product supporting standards is uncertain.

There have always been standards of some sort in the industry. During the years of IBM dominance, IBM effectively set standards. "Open" meant that IBM would publish enough to enable symbiont competition. That role is partly filled now by Microsoft and Intel.

Vendor-defined proprietary standards remain the basis for the large bulk of existing systems. These do not provide a solid basis for reducing development costs and increasing interplatform interoperability, portability, and migratability.

"I am open because . . .

   . . . I support de jure standards on my platforms" (e.g., IBM)
   . . . I support de facto standards on my platforms" (e.g., Hewlett-Packard)
   . . . others use my standards, I make de facto standards" (e.g., Microsoft)
   . . . I offer my standards on other vendor platforms" (e.g., DEC)
   . . . I communicate with my competitors" (e.g., Sybase)
   . . . you can use my proprietary standards everywhere" (e.g., Novell)
   . . . my product defines this niche" (e.g., Sunsoft).

Make a choice

One way to achieve open is to make a choice, which means choosing a single set of consistent standards. Ideally, there would be a standard interface and behavior (syntax and semantics) for each component of each layer of a computer system. This standard would be supported by all vendors desiring to sell product to the enterprise.

Making a choice means defining an enterprise "profile" of interfaces and protocols that work together, are consistent with each other, and that represent a complete definition of a system. The source of such a profile might be an international organization, an industry group, a vendor alliance, or a single vendor. Many major vendors have defined a set of interfaces and protocols that constitute a profile.

DEC and IBM communications architectures were expanded into system-wide system profiles in the 1980s to include more elements at the middleware and upperware levels. IBM's Systems Application Architecture (SAA) and DEC's Network Application Support (NAS) were collections of interfaces and protocols that the companies delivered on their own systems that spanned a system domain.

In the current market, there seems to be an interest in systems profiles that are more "vendor neutral," not under the control of a single business unit. Standards tend to be set by international agencies, consortia, alliances, etc. Although many of these come and go quickly, there is a growing body of convergent technology among vendors. And, of course, it is difficult to refute the clout of Microsoft with nearly 100 million or so systems: "Whatever I do is open."

Make no choice

"Make no choice" is the world of gateways, adapters, boundaries, multiprotocol stacks, virtual file systems, etc. It is a world in which boundaries are lowered by creating links between all existing product.

IBM SYSTEMS APPLICATION ARCHITECTURE

Systems Application Architecture (SAA) is worth a book on its own and has received a number of them, none sufficiently critical.

In 1987, IBM announced a major strategy to provide common interfaces for all of their "strategic" operating systems. They invented the notion that MVS, VM, AS/400, and OS/2 were strategic, but that DOS, CICS, VSE, and IMS were not strategic. There was, as the reader can imagine, a certain amount of clarification about the status of CICS, VSE, IMS and DOS. AIX, the IBM Unix, was outside the fold at first, reflecting a deeper cultural split than usual, even for IBM. Some attention was given to SAA/AIX interoperability until it became more important to focus on AIX as a good Unix player.

SAA was a portability announcement, defining a Common User Interface, a family of Common Programming Interfaces (CPIs), and a communications base (LU 6.2). As part of the SAA announcement, IBM took great pains to show how the organizational processes of software creation would be reformed to make SAA happen. A great SAA process was invented with SAA project offices, SAA design councils, SAA strategy councils, etc.—all the paraphernalia of corporate paralysis.

All of this has now blown by us, and we again can hear the quiet chirping of birds in Purchase (sold by IBM) and Somers. What went wrong? Nobody, including IBM, ever believed it would happen; no one, including IBM, ever really wanted it to happen; and the perception fathered the reality. IBM did not relax short-term profit goals for the various platforms to encourage them to support the interfaces. IBM did not reform its software development processes to get some common code for all of this duplication across platforms. IBM did not enforce its processes. And then IBM was blindsided by "open." SAA was too little, too late, and always unloved.

The techniques of interoperability are:

1 Make different things look the same. For example, provide a single data access language that spans data models, data base managers, and file systems to deliver the appearance of one system.

2 Make different things look the same to each other. Provide gateways that convert requests, data flows, and responses into forms a program is "comfortable" with and recognizes. For example, map data formats used by a COBOL MVS compiler into formats used by an AS/400 Report Writer.

3 Define a set of common behaviors and interfaces so that some subset of functions can be done together.

De jure standards

Two international sources of de jure standards are the International Standards Organization (ISO), the originator of the Open Systems Interface (OSI), and the

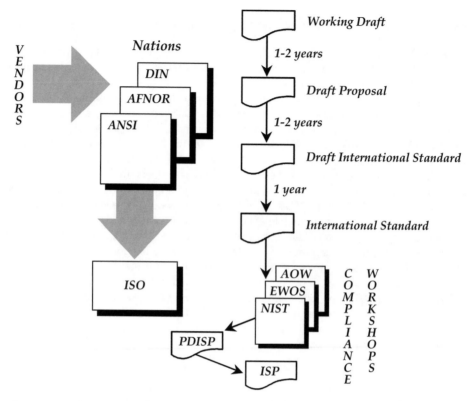

Figure 7.3 Standards process.

Institute of Electrical and Electronic Engineers (IEEE). The ISO has traditionally been communications-protocol oriented, while IEEE has developed both behaviors and interfaces at hardware and software levels.

A de jure standard is an international standard mandated by governments and published by an international organization and agencies of participating governments. The standard has different meanings in different places. In some European countries, compliance is a requirement for conducting business. In the U.S., compliance is often a requirement for doing business with the government or certain contractors on certain projects.

The development of a standard goes through various stages in a consensus process involving (in the case of the ISO) national standards organizations, vendor companies, and user companies that participate in the "working groups" of the standards organizations. These working groups are committees of experts focused on a particular area of technology.

A developing standard goes through various stages. Figure 7.3 shows a five-year process in which an evolving standard moves through the stages to a Draft International Standard and, finally, a Standard. The standard itself is a large narrative document that is distributed to vendors for vendor development of compliant product.

A standard need not entirely define a product. A product can support a standard while offering unique functionality in addition. Only some features are necessarily determined by compliance with a standard. There are numerous examples of products that support the same standards but that are effectively different in critical features to the point that they cannot interact with each other.

Standards may contain options that permit vendors to support the standard in ways that preclude product interaction. Various vendors can be standards-compliant without being able to interoperate because of different pathways through the options.

Vendors must determine whether a product is in compliance. After publication of a standard, there is a "poststandards" process, in which the standards organization provides mechanisms in the form of "workshops" and "test suites" to determine compliance. A product must show the behavior specified by the standard. But because of optionality, support of the standard does not guarantee interoperability. Interoperability must be independently tested as part of the poststandards process.

In a time of rapidly moving technology, the processes of governmental and semigovernmental agencies superimposed upon vendor politics have not been effective in providing timely products in key technology areas. Products often support back level standards and require years to support standards that have already taken as long as five years to emerge from the de jure process.

The general use of international de jure standards has not spread as rapidly as was hoped when the "open" issue became so heated in the early 1990s. After a good deal of focus on de jure standards, there seems to be a general recognition that the de jure standards process is not going to produce timely products.

International Standards Organization

The world of de jure international standards organizations is quite complex, including treaty organizations, United Nations agencies, and other artifacts of bureaucracy. The relation between these organizations involves networks of co-committees, standing consultative groups, and the usual paraphernalia of international institutional interaction. Kafka would be proud of us.

The ISO is an organization with broad interests, from boilers to remote procedure calls, and a source of international telecommunications standards (many ISO telecommunications standards come from CCITT, Consultative Committee for International Telephony and Telegraphy, and ITU, International Telecommunications Union).

The goals of the ISO are to:

- Develop international standards
- Facilitate the exchange of goods and services
- Encourage cooperation: "Intellectual, economic, technological, scientific."

The ISO has developed nearly 8,000 international standards since 1946. Its membership includes more than 90 countries, and its activities are organized around technical committees. Some claim that the process can be compressed to a series of phased stages that will bring a new work item to an international standard within two years. This is a very optimistic assessment.

Often a de jure standard is a reaction to de facto standards. The attempt to define an ISO standard relation to TCP/IP is a fine example. Much de jure standards work exists in areas where there are already de facto standards. A justification is the "ethnicity" of de facto standards that show the language, operating system, or data model tradition out of which they have emerged.

7.3   TAXONOMY OF ISO

The current activities and key technical committees of an international organization are interesting for the view they provide of the taxonomy of problems in technology. As problem definitions shift, committee structures (over time) are modified to reflect current views of problems and their relations.

ISO Technical Committee 97 is the locus of most activity of our interest. It consists of subcommittees and working groups as follows:

Subcommittee 21: Information Retrieval, Transfer and Management

Working Group-1: Reference Model, Security, Naming, Addressing

Working Group-3: Relational Data Architecture, SQL

Working Group-4: OSI Management, Directory

Working Group-5: FTAM, JTM, Term Management

Working Group-6: Presentation Layer, Session Layer, Authorization

Working Group-7: Open Distributed Processing

Subcommittee 6: Telecommunications and Information Exchange (L 1-4)

This structure may well have been modified as of the publication of this book, but the subcommittee and working group structure will surely remain in place; and changes between this list and the current list will show how the computing industry has evolved in the period.

Ongoing or recently maturing ISO standards that concern this book and may affect the direction of computing are:

DIS10026   Transaction Processing
DIS9805   Commitment, Concurrency and Recovery
X.700   Systems Management
X.500   The Directory
X.400   Messaging

An interesting, if not practically useful, effort is the Open Distributed Processing (ODP) project that involves activity at the ISO, at the European Computer Manufacturers Association (ECMA), and at ESPRIT (a government- and corporate-funded group of European universities). The view is that technology changes require a new set of models of computing and a new standard terminology and set of practices. Part of ODP involves rethinking computing in the face of new technology. Such an effort could be invaluable, but it is not likely the industry will modify itself to an international standards model in the heat of competition and change.

Institute of Electrical and Electronic Engineers

The IEEE is a professional organization that makes de jure standards as a surrogate for national standards organizations. It is playing a dominant role in LAN standards. A standards activity of particular interest is POSIX (Portable Operating Systems Interface for Unix). The "X" ending rightly suggests a Unix origin. However, the interface is now breaking out of the Unix niche and becoming available in a broad spectrum of operating systems, such as IBM MVS, DEC VMS, and Hewlett-Packard MPE.

Like the ISO, the IEEE has a committee structure that meets periodically to consider proposals from various vendors or consortia. Some of these proposals may be competitive and represent an attempt to promote a de facto standard to de jure status. For example, in the past, the

7.4 COMMONLY SUPPORTED ISO STANDARDS

The table below is a partial list of ISO standards supported by vendor product:

ACSE	ISO 8650
FTAM	ISO 8571
Presentation	ISO 8823/24/25
Session	ISO 8327
Transport	ISO 8073
CONS-X.25	ISO 8878
CLNS-Internet	ISO 8473
X.25	ISO 8208
Logical Link	ISO 8802-2
Token Ring LAN	ISO 8802-5
CSMA/CD LAN	ISO 8802-3
X.25 LAPB	ISO 7776
ISDN	CCITT Q.921,922,931

Pre-December 1993				
1003.0	Guide		P1003.1d	Old P1003.4b
1003.1	System Interface		P1003.1e	Old P1003.6
1003.2	Shell/Utilities		P1003.1f	Old 1003.8 Networking
1003.3	Test Methods			(File Access)
1003.4	Real Time Extensions		P1003.1g	Old 1003.12 Protocol
1003.5	Ada Bindings			Independent Interface (SNI, DNI)
1003.6	Security		P1372	Old 1003.1/LIS
1003.7	System Administration		P1003.2	Shell/Utilities (P)
1003.8	Networking (File Access)		P1003.2a	Shell Extensions (P)
1003.9	FORTRAN Bindings		P1003.2c	Old P1003.6
1003.10	Supercomputing		P2003	Test Methods (P) Old 1003.3
1003.11	Transaction Processing		P1003.5	Ada Bindings
1003.12	Protocol Independent Interface (SNI, DNI)		P1003.6	Security
1003.13	Name Space/Directory		P1387	Old 1003.7 System Administration
1003.14	Multiprocessing Application Environment Profile		P1003.9	Fortran Bindings (P)
1003.15	Batch Environment Amendments (NQS)		P1003.10	Supercomputing
1003.16	C Language Bindings		P1003.11	Transaction Processing *WITHDRAWN*
1003.17	Directory Server API (XDS)		P1003.13	Name Space/Directory
1003.18	Platform Environment Profile		P1003.14	Multiprocessing Application Environment Profile
			P1003.2d	Old P1003.15a Batch Environment: Under Revision
1993 Modifications			P1003.16	C Language Bindings *WITHDRAWN*
P1003.0	Guide		P1224.2	Old 1003.17 Directory Server API (P)
P1003.1	System Interface (P)			
P1003.1a	Systems Interface Extensions		P1003.18	Application Environment Profile
P1003.1b	Old P1003.4 Real Time Extensions (P)		P1003.19	*WITHDRAWN*
P1003.1c	Old P1003.4a		P1003.20	Old P1003.5b

OSF has presented its Motif interface standard as a candidate for an IEEE interface standard. As well, Sun Microsystems and Unix International (defunct as of 1994) proposed the OPEN LOOK interface standard.

Committees promulgate documents and hold ballots, mock (preliminary surveys) and formal, on particular documents representing standards elements.

The POSIX standard is a series of documents that describes an interface for various functional parts of an operating system (or more properly, a software complex). At any time, there is a set of documents at various levels of completion and acceptance, under negotiation or ready for promulgation. The POSIX

The 802.x series IEEE standards establish protocols for LANs. Among them are:

802.2	Media Access Control Layer (DataLink/Physical)
802.3	CSMA/CD (Ethernet)
802.4	Token Bus Media
802.5	Token Ring Media
802.6	Metropolitan Area Network Media
802.7	Broadband
802.8	Fiber
802.9	Voice/Data Integration
802.10	LAN Security

documents tend to be quite technical and specific. A commitment to the support of a POSIX standard seriously constrains the design space. Some POSIX standards affect the product, while others define methodologies for product development and test.

From time to time, cross–working group steering committees are formed to coordinate activity on a standard that straddles the current organizational structure. Such a working group, in 1993, was the Steering Committee for Windowing User Interfaces (SCWUI), which attempted to reconcile Motif, OPEN LOOK, CUA, Mac, NeXT, and Microsoft interface standards. Cross-groups try to reconcile and remove inconsistencies in various committee drafts.

The IEEE has recently (December 1993) restructured POSIX to reflect new issues and new relations between issues. This is shown in Box 7.5. The 1993 revisions reflect a reassessment of the structure of the industry.

The IEEE standards in local area networking have been enormously successful and have product support in just about everyone's LAN software.

De facto standards

The market has various mechanisms for defining a de facto standard. Mere pervasiveness establishes a technology as a de facto standard. The interfaces and behavior of a product that has 60% or 70% of a market niche unquestionably qualify it as a de facto standard.

Windows is clearly a de facto standard for desktop or laptop end user interfaces. Novell NetWare SPX/IPX local area networking protocols are clearly the de facto standard for small LANs. IBM's Customer Information Control System (CICS) is clearly a de facto standard for transaction management.

Characteristically, there are competing de facto standards. This will occur because companies share a market or because two niches have merged. An interesting example of this is the merger of the Unix and non-Unix transaction cultures. CICS and traditional Unix transaction managers (Tuxedo and Top Hat from AT&T) now directly compete with each other.

Competition affects vendor judgment about the market benefits of compatibility as opposed to value-add. Currently, competition seems to be breeding similarity and convergence rather than divergence. In order to prepare for the struggle against Windows NT and OS/2, the Unix community defined a de facto standard called Spec 1170 to provide a common look. The market will now decide whether Spec 1170 (1170 APIs) will be a dependable Unix standard, will never mature, or will go beyond Unix to become a de facto industry standard for all operating systems. Many non-Unix systems (e.g., IBM MVS) have announced their intention to comply with Spec 1170.

A de facto standard may be promulgated in a number of ways:

1 A vendor may try to publish its way into openness. The argument is that wide publication of a set of interfaces and protocols enables the development of compliant product by competitors.

2 A vendor will cross-license an interface or protocol. Secondary sources expand market coverage and position the product in niches the primary vendor could not reach. Often, the licensing is restrictive, not permitting secondary sources to add value to its version. The NFS is an example of the promulgation of a product on an aggressive, but controlled, basis (Sun Microsystems).

3 A vendor may offer a proprietary standard to a vendor alliance. The vendor alliance assures that there will be multiple sources of the technology. This is a basis of cross-vendor portability and interoperability. Organizations like the OSF exist for this purpose.

4 A vendor may promulgate a proprietary standard as a de jure standard.

Vendor alliances are the ephemera of the industry. Like shooting stars, they brighten the trade press skies and fade. But there are a few key alliances that seem stable forums of vendor technologies. These differ from joint ventures or partnerships in that no member is actually committed to any particular behavior. It is difficult to convince vendors to abandon revenue associated with proprietary products or to develop for markets that do not yet clearly exist.

Some groups, the SQL Access Group (SAG) for example, develop standards. Other groups, like X/Open, define environments (profiles) based on existing standards. The OSF provides software to vendors that is based on de facto standards. Other groups (e.g., X Consortium, IETF) try to guide de facto development. There are also organizations that test compliance and certify compliance.

The alliances and consortia allow a vendor to achieve vendor independence for a standard. By offering a technology to a consortium, a vendor demonstrates it is willing to give up control of its rate of change. What begins as a proprietary interface or protocol becomes more "open." Changes and advances to the standard are expected to come from consortium processes.

Unlike de jure standards, de facto standards tend to come from running programs. As a result, it is often possible to distribute programs. A vendor "ports" the code to its own environment from a consortium distribution in a pervasive programming language (C, for example).

The effort of porting is often underestimated. Vendors invest significant resources into adopting code for their particular environments in order to achieve acceptable performance and integration. TCP/IP in IBM MVS and in HP-UX must have the coloration of those systems regarding installation, parameterization, and administration.

Coloration is a two-edged issue. Unhappily, the "ethnic" nature of de facto standards makes them difficult to adapt and integrate into other platforms and environments. Interfaces from the Unix culture show their Unix origin and expect underlying behaviors unique to Unix. Very often the standard is "language specific," available only to programmers in C, for example.

Alliances

There is a Balkans-like history here. Alliances are bravely announced, then often fade because the problem they intend to solve is unsolvable or becomes unimportant to solve or becomes too important to solve within an alliance.

The Advanced Computing Environment (ACE), for example, could not define a useful set of standards and still satisfy the market needs of Intel, Microsoft, and DEC. Unix International, an advisory consortium to Unix Systems Laboratories, passed from the scene when Novell acquired Unix Systems Laboratories. Often, like 19th century tsars who had simultaneous defense agreements with France and Germany, companies are in alliances with conflicting goals and technologies.

The most significant relations between vendors are joint product development commitments that integrate the technology of one vendor into the technology of another. An example is the integration of Oracle7 and Sybase data bases into Novell NetWare.

X/Open

The consortium of greatest impact is X/Open, an international nonprofit organization that establishes interfaces and interface groups called "profiles."

7.7 DE FACTO CONSORTIA DIVERSE ROLES AND VIEWS
(A PARTIAL LIST)

- X/Open
- CASE Integration Services (CIS) Standards Committee
- Corporation for Open Systems (COS)
- X Consortium
- Multivendor Integration Architecture (MIA) Consortium
- Object Management Group (OMG)
- Office Document Architecture Consortium (ODAC)
- Open Software Foundation (OSF)
- Common Open Software Environment (COSE)
- SQL Access Group (SAG)
- UniForum
- Standards Promotion and Application Group (SPAG)
- IETF. The Internet: TCP/IP Users Consortia
- XAPI Mail API Consortium

The X/Open standards are de facto or de jure standards, as convenient. They are developed by identifying needed standards, selecting existing standards, and encouraging standards development as required. X/Open is the promulgator of the COSE agreements, Spec 1170. This will be used as a basis for granting a product the right to use the Unix trademark.

X/Open sponsors interfaces for software at all levels. It is owned by vendors, but a 1993 reorganization has increased user influence in order to avoid a view of X/Open as a vendor club. Members are corporations and other consortia. Key members include AT&T Global (NCR), Amdahl, DEC, Fujitsu Groupe Bull, Hewlett-Packard, Hitachi, IBM, ICL, NEC, OKI, Olivetti, OSF, Philips, Prime, Siemens/Nixdorf, Sun Microsystems, and Unisys.

X/Open selects and endorses common interfaces and coordinates the development of a Common Application Environment (CAE). It offers branding and certification of compliance. Products in the Unix culture covet X/Open branding, and as Unix/non-Unix barriers relax, products like MVS, VMS, and MPE/ix reach for X/Open compliance and certification.

X/Open structure involves requirements committees of four users, two independent software vendors, and one systems vendor. Users run all the working groups, which include efforts in transactions, security, and systems management. There is a clear desire to show user influence in the standards-endorsing process.

The prime output of X/Open, the X/Open Portability Guide, is an enormous collection consisting of 23 volumes, which total 7,500 pages, weighing around 35 pounds. There is naturally some concern that such inclusive statements tend more to be aggregations than architectures, and that inclusiveness sometimes deprives a statement of credibility. The balance between credibility and inclusiveness is hard to determine. Clearly, an organization dealing with practicality and de facto standards will tend to inclusiveness.

Open Software Foundation

Vendor alliances are often aimed at someone. They attempt to establish standards convenient to members of the alliance, and inconvenient to others. As market boundaries shift, the nature of an alliance may dramatically change.

7.8 X/OPEN PORTABILITY GUIDE/4

The X/Open Portability Guide (XPG), level 4: Interfaces (APIs) for languages, window managers, operating systems, file systems, data base managers, clients, transport layers, etc.

- ANSI C Language
- ANSI COBOL Language 85
- ANSI FORTRAN Language 77
- ISO Pascal Language
    Ada Language
- X Windows API, Display
- POSIX 1003.2 Shells and Calls
- POSIX 1003.1 Calls to Kernel
- ISAM (File Access Interface)
- SQL
- Byte File Transfer (BSFT) (FTP, rLogin)
- NFS
- NFS PC Server
- LMX Server
- X.400 Gateway
- X/Open Transport Interface Xti
- CPIC
- X.400 Message Access
- X.500 Directory

Profiles XPG+

- Base Profile
- Base Server Profile
- Workstation Profile
- Communications Gateway Profile
- Data Base Platform

The OSF was founded in 1987 to restrain the ability of AT&T Unix Systems Laboratories (USL) to unilaterally define Unix standards. IBM had (finally) decided to enter this market, and DEC saw an opportunity to substantially increase its role.

Unix had been diverging for years. The canonical Unix was controlled by USL. USL was developing System V Release 4 (SVR4), and was publishing the SVID (System V Interface Definition) API set to SV releases (not entirely POSIX).

There were a number of alternative Unix cultures—in particular, the Berkeley Software Distribution (BSD, then evolving to 4.4) and Xenix. The market and legal realities of Unix made it convenient for a vendor in the Unix market segment to use the core technology of the earlier SVR3 but provide its own extensions, ignoring SVR4. Sun Microsystems' operating system drew heavily on technology from BSD. About 80% of any Unix on the market was a combination of SVR3 and BSD technology, with about 20% of vendor flavoring. This is roughly true for IBM AIX and Hewlett-Packard HP-UX.

In 1987, IBM and DEC led the formation of the OSF. The goal of the OSF was to adopt existing standards, propose new standards, and define and publish new specifications. It would define an open process for software development, license code, provide maintenance and enhancements, and develop verification and testing specifications. A vendor

OSF TECHNOLOGY

A part of credibility in the "open" world is demonstrating a framework in which the open parts will fit, and to which product can be designed. OSF defined the structure of software as:

1 A core operating system, OSF/1, including technology for multiprocessing and internationalization, and technology for real-time and fault-tolerant mission-critical applications.

2 Distributed computing services to support distributed applications. The Distributed Computing Environment (DCE) facilitates the development of distributed applications. It consists of a client/server technology, a file system, naming services, timing services, and a process model.

3 An end user environment to define end user interfaces, graphics, text processing tools.

4 A systems managements technology to manage different vendor systems within the context of a single systems image.

OSF defined a process, RFT (Request For Technology), for the solicitation of technology. An RFT asked for member response to a particular requirement. Members could respond individually or in groups by submitting running code and documentation. A formal review would select one of the proposed technologies as a reference model for the focus area. Particular examples are Motif, submitted primarily by Hewlett-Packard and DEC for the end user interface; and DCE, submitted in various pieces by Hewlett-Packard, DEC, and Siemens. The Distributed Management Environment (DME) submitted by Tivoli, IBM, and Hewlett-Packard may be an example of a failure of the process.

would license OSF programming, contributed by OSF members, and port it to its particular product line.

The language of OSF is interesting because it is so typical of the high aims of such associations. OSF principles included:

- The development of relevant industry standards
- The open solicitation of technology
- A timely, vendor-neutral decision process
- Early and equal access to a specification
- Hardware-independent implementations
- Reasonable and stable licensing terms
- University participation to assure innovation.

Currently, the OSF result is a bit of a mixed bag. The OSF base operating system, OSF/1, has small market penetration (about 4%). Its major vendor is DEC. IBM's only attempt at an OSF/1 system was on its 390 mainframe and it was not a commercial success. On the other hand, Motif has become a dominant standard, and the Distributed Computing Environment (DCE) seems to be gaining some acceptance. The Distributed Management Environment (DME) seems ready to be abandoned. While OSF remains a distributor of code, its technology and specifications process have clearly become inoperative. There

7.10 DISTRIBUTED COMPUTING ENVIRONMENT (DCE)

1 The Global Directory Service based upon the X.500 specification with interfaces provided by Siemens Corporation. The interfaces are X/Open approved. An associated naming service (DEC Naming Service) from DEC establishes a uniform naming scheme across OSF-compliant product.

2 A network timing service (DEC Timing Services from VMS) to synchronize clocks across a network.

3 A three-party authentication system, Kerberos, primarily from M.I.T., that assures that a requester is who it claims to be and that the requested service is what it claims to be.

4 The Motif end user interface standard, a combination of technology from DEC and Hewlett-Packard.

5 POSIX-compliant threads (DEC Concert) that provides a dispatchable thread service consistent with IEEE standards.

6 Distributed File System (DFS) derived from the Andrew File System of Carnegie-Mellon, now a product of the TRANSARC Corporation.

7 The remote procedure call (RPC), based on Hewlett-Packard Apollo NCS 2.0 with extensions from DEC. Associated Interface Definition Language (IDL) from NCS 2.0. Extensions to form a TRPC (transaction remote procedure call).

seems to be a tendency for OSF to view itself as a generator of philosophical white papers, and not of operational standards.

DCE is an offering available in part on IBM MVS, VM, OS/2, and AS/400; DEC VMS/Open, Hewlett-Packard MPE/ix, Novell NetWare, and Windows NT have delivered elements. All Unix vendors are now committed, including Sun Microsystems. However, it is not clear whether all elements, particularly the file system, will be available on all committed platforms. Extensions of DCE involve enabling transaction management and supporting standards from the Object Management Group.

With the demise of the competing organizations (Unix International, the USL Advisory group), the COSE agreements, and the admittance of arch rival Sun Microsystems, the function of OSF surely will change. It is not exactly clear what its new function will be.

Object Management Group

The Object Management Group (OMG) is an attempt to establish practical standards at an early stage of object technology. Its goal is to establish standardized terminology, a common systems framework, a common reference model, and a set of common interfaces and protocols for object-oriented computing.

Its members include Apple, Borland, Canon, Deere, Fujitsu America, Hewlett-Packard, ICL, IBM, Perkin-Elmer, Sequent Computers, Software AG, Sun Microsystems, Texas Instruments, Unisys, and Wang. Its primary output is an architecture called CORBA (Common Object Request Broker Architecture), which defines interfaces and protocols for cross-language and remote object interaction.

There is considerable disagreement about whether the OMG standards have achieved cross-vendor interoperability and portability. As of this writing, a new CORBA standard (CORBA II) has been developed. There is an extended discussion of objects in Chapter 11.

Profiles

Standards are organized into sets called "profiles." A profile is a family of standards that should exist together in a particular environment. A de jure profile of some interest was an ISO profile called the Government OSI Profile (GOSIP). GOSIP is not doing well. The United States government is abandoning the profile. It is just not happening.

Putting together environments with appropriate standards is a complex undertaking. A number of efforts have been made to provide useful profiles.

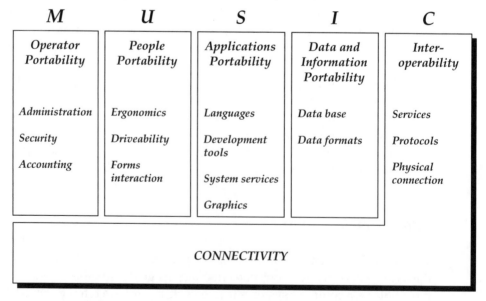

M	U	S	I	C
Operator Portability	*People Portability*	*Applications Portability*	*Data and Information Portability*	*Inter-operability*
Administration	Ergonomics	Languages	Data base	Services
Security	Driveability	Development tools	Data formats	Protocols
Accounting	Forms interaction	System services		Physical connection
		Graphics		

CONNECTIVITY

Figure 7.4   MUSIC: general structure.

Among these are the vendor profiles (e.g., SAA, NAS), X/Open XPG, GOSIP, the POSIX Open System Environment Model, and the MUSIC "megaprofile" of profiles from the British Communications Society.

Profiles are currently specific to particular functions. There is no profile for "computing," but there are profiles for application development environments, transaction-oriented production environments, etc. The profile is a systems specification with which a conformance test is associated.

Figure 7.4 shows a profile in the MUSIC structure. MUSIC partitions standards into five areas: Management, User, System, Information, and Communications. Standards associated with each area are shown in the area for each MUSIC environment. MUSIC environments are the designated profiles for various key alliances or international standards groups. By referring to the MUSIC representation, one can determine what standards are included in OSF, X/Open, OSI, and other profiles.

Higher-layer standards

The focus on "open" has shifted to layers 6 and 7 of the OSI structure. The requirements are that any application development tool be able to develop on any computing system, for any computing system; that mail and messaging programs be able to interact with any platform; that data base barriers be lowered across data models and data products; and that standard interfaces be available on any platform. Upperware is joining the game.

Application development

The requirement is a single development system on multiple platforms to develop applications for various platforms. This requirement exists across the software development life cycle. Currently, there is little ability to use specification, design, build, debug, and test tools with each other, or across environments.

There is activity toward establishing common programming environments, including tools, interfaces, and repositories for software artifacts. An example, for which many are surprised to hear there is considerable pledged vendor support, is the Programming Common Tools Environment (PCTE) of ECMA. This is a specification for a common set of interfaces that will allow program development tools to use common data formats and end user interfaces. It supports the notion of a repository of software development artifacts created at different stages of development and available throughout the life cycle.

However, the current major trend is not common programming environments. The industry is dominated by proprietary toolkits with various degrees of compliance to de facto standards. Within the proprietary environments there is the growing ability to develop across multiple platforms. For example, the Sybase toolkit allows development across multiple data base environments. There are tools vendors (for example, Smartstar and Uniface) that offer products that can develop applications to access a number of de facto data bases.

There is considerable cross licensing. Hewlett-Packard's Softbench product is available as part of IBM's AIX Case. A number of development tools from independent software vendors run on multiple platforms.

A number of software development tools are "open" in the sense that they allow access to any data base and will run on multiple systems. Tools like Borland's Delphi allow for the quick development of client/server applications across a number of client/server platforms.

Mail

Electronic mail is a key area forcing the resolution of issues in networking, multimedia, document exchange, and security. Currently, a marketplace struggle for dominance is taking place. IBM's purchase of Lotus is part of that struggle.

The intention of mail and messaging technology is to allow an end user to send documents of any kind to anyone on any platform anywhere and to allow a program developer to integrate document transfer functions into an application program running in any environment without restrictions. Cross-vendor interoperability at the top of layer 7 in the presence of new media and new information-organizing principles is involved.

The solution must involve media integration techniques allowing integrated phone and mail services with common APIs and mixed documents of video, voice, text, and graphics. It requires a reconciliation of various standards. For example, OSI X.400 for messaging has a different name/location/security structure than X.500 for directory.

There are already existing de facto standards in each of the areas to be integrated. Mail API (MAPI) and phone API (TAPI) from Microsoft are examples. There are already various consortia addressing the issue, among them APS (Asynchronous Protocol Specification) and EMA (Electronic Mail Association). There is an attempt to create a common API for mail (XAPIA).

The problems of layer 7 interoperability and portability reflect the difficulties of creating open systems at higher layers where product is most rapidly changing, most visible, and where value-add may have the most profit potential. There are a number of legacy systems and proprietary systems in the arena. Among them are IBM's Office Vision, Lotus Notes, the Unix community's SMTP, and the Microsoft products already mentioned. Some of these are network specific or operating system specific. Some are clearly fading fast.

The direction for open mail includes a "common mail call" API for send and receive on any transport, and integration of the X.500 and X.400 dictionary standards. There is a consortium for developing vendor independent interfaces (VIPs) headed by Apple, Novell, Borland, and IBM.

There are a number of interoperability products from Lotus, Novell, Wollongong, IBM, AT&T, Microsoft, and others.

Documents

Documents is another area where politics are as interesting as technology. OpenDoc (see Chapter 11) is a developing de facto standard for document exchange. It uses IBM object technology, Apple storage technology, and Novell (WordPerfect Amber) document creation technology. It provides for the exchange of complex documents across Unix, OS/2, Windows, and Mac platforms, with OpenDoc standards controlled by an OpenDoc consortium, CIL (Component Integration Lab). It will be a direct alternative to Microsoft's OLE. There will be versions for Windows 3.1 that will interoperate with OLE.

The commitment of various vendors is not clear, and the trade press reports various recantations, recriminations, and rededications in the winds of market dynamics.

Heterogeneous data base

Open systems require a technology that can not only cross multiple relational data base barriers, but extract data from a number of sources using different data models. Relational data bases and file systems must be able to act as sources of data and appear in a coherent single format to an application or end user.

Distributed data becomes more complex with different data base managers:

- different SQL dialects, perhaps at different levels of function
- different naming conventions
- different security and recovery paradigms
- different catalog organization
- different underlying communications protocols.

These differences limit the cooperation between various data base managers. Attempts to overcome limitations include communications gateways, common development languages, and "data warehouse" technology.

Various projects are trying to establish a standard set of language and capabilities for data base managers. OSI has an architecture, Relational Data Architecture (RDA), and a language project. An alliance called the SQL Access Group (SAG) has become important in establishing SQL language levels and promulgating a language standard. IBM, Borland, Novell and others are supporting a call-level SQL interface called ODAPI, and there is pervasive support for Microsoft's Open Data Base Connectivity (ODBC).

Technology is emerging in both a heterogeneous data base and a client/server form. Ingres* has had the ability to extract data from other data bases and data models (IMS and VSAM) for some time, though with some limitation on its functionality in mixed transactions. More recently, client/server technology has emerged to accomplish heterogeneous data model access and presentation.

Heterogeneous extraction has been maturing for a while. It is a technology that at its core allows an SQL query to be satisfied by data from any data base manager or file system that has a "driver" that can contribute to the answer. For example, the Information Builders, Inc. (IBI) EDA/SQL product will enable an SQL dialect to be used to form data requests regardless of the data model or data manager in which the data lies. Data will be extracted from record files, hierarchic data managers, and a set of data base managers and formed into relational tables to be shown in relational formats to an end user. Data server drivers for this technology have been delivered since late 1993.

At its limits, extraction matures into data warehouse and also involves application development and enterprise data flow analysis. An application developer must be able to determine where data is available and how data flows through an enterprise in order to effectively use a data warehouse.

chapter 8

Benchmarking migration

EXECUTIVE SUMMARY The population of computers in an enterprise should be determined by the relative costs of different populations. At times a few large systems may be more efficient, at other times a larger number of smaller ones. Rightsizing is about getting this number right and minimizing the cost of going on to a next generation.

There is a great deal of confusion about system classes, comparative hardware and software costs, and costs of migration. Apples can be compared to oranges if we can discover a common reasonable metric. The industry has tried many ways, using benchmarks of different types, to express the relative price/perform-ance efficiency of unlike systems. There are great risks in some of the comparative statements; the experimental techniques are not always what one would like to see, but we at least have some ways of comparing the performance of a single large mainframe with a set of departmental servers. It is also possible, though with somewhat less certainty, to compare software costs, software development costs, and administrative and operational costs on a reasonably normalized basis.

This chapter provides an exercise in which a mainframe workload is decom-posed across a set of candidate systems. Comparative hardware costs, software costs, and migration costs are presented to establish a base-line system cost for different populations of machines.

Investing

Investing in information technology has three fundamental dimensions: what should be acquired; when it should be acquired; and how the technology elements should be organized into a system.

Figure 8.1 shows a structure first shown in Chapter 6. Each box is a defined element of computing; each line is an interface where the network can be intro-duced to achieve distribution.

A system is a set of investment decisions across various resources. A proper investment strategy is to maximize the use of resources deemed efficient and trustworthy and to minimize resources deemed inefficient and fragile.

End user device function	End user interface standards function	Application function	Application function	Data access function	Data
(a)	(b)	(c)	(c)	(d)	(e)

n n n n n

Network

a/n/bcde	Host oriented nonprogrammable terminal
ab/n/cde	Host oriented programmable terminal
abc/n/de	Client/server (simple model)
abc/n/cde	Cooperative processing
abcd/de	Distributed database management
ab/c/c/d/de	Fully distributed

Reprinted by kind permission of MTS, Ashford, Middlesex, England.

Figure 8.1 Split points.

Figure 8.2 shows the relative efficiency of resources over time. When there is a clear constraining resource, like communications has been for many years, its use is minimized relative to other resources. Thus, in the period from 1980 to 1990, much function was moved closer to the user, at first with local mini-computers and then with desktop machines. In place of a remote interaction

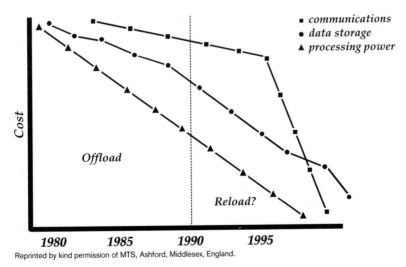

Reprinted by kind permission of MTS, Ashford, Middlesex, England.

Figure 8.2 Technology inversions.

between terminal and host every few key strokes, data could be moved over the line at the beginning or end of a transaction, or shift, or day.

After 1990, communications cost and quality improved, and constraints to dispersing resources became visible. Function began to move back from the desktop to servers. A change in the relative efficiency of communications, local storage, and local logic changed the pattern of distribution of resources.

The costing of a proposed architecture involves an assessment of the relative costs of different resources with different costs in different amounts. These cost elements are shown in Box 8.1. This chapter will present an exercise in which various system architectures were considered in developing a process by which an architecture could be evolved and economically justified.

The context

The exercise has a set of applications currently running on an older mainframe. These applications are to be either kept on the mainframe, rehosted, re-engineered, or redeveloped in accordance with a requirement to minimize cost. The cost elements considered were hardware, software, skills, and administrative. The cost of change is the cost of the new system and the cost of migration. The cost of no change is the cost of maintaining the evolution of the older system.

Communications costs for any system structure are within 15%. Communications power needed to support information processing at a certain scale across similar distances is about the same for many topologies of the system. This is true only within a particular envelope of solutions, but the network load to support the interaction between systems is surprisingly stable within the alternatives discovered by this exercise. The cost of a network is often independent of the topology of the end points.

The numbers in this chapter represent reasonable guesses as of the end of 1994. The value-add here is the framework, not the numbers in the framework. Many of the numbers used have not appeared in the literature, others have. Appearance in the literature should neither increase nor decrease confidence. The contribution of the chapter is the mental model in which the numbers are presented and the issues that are associated with them. Regardless of their specific history, all numbers should be thought of as reasonable place markers for a decision requiring some knowledge.

Hardware costs

Hardware costs is about comparing apples and oranges—something that is completely necessary to do.

No company of substantial size has a single computer. "Centralization" is a distribution model in which there is a minimum population of "data centers" with a minimum number of computers. Other distribution models involve either more data centers or more computers or both. A goal of technology assessment is to define a proper number of centers and machines. Given a need for an amount of computational power, what is the optimum way to partition computer systems to achieve the minimum hardware cost?

The hardware choices

Table 8.1 provides a hardware cost statement for various ways of achieving a given computational level. Various normalizations have been applied, as explained in Box 8.2, to achieve equivalent statements of machine power.

The table shows a small IBM air-cooled VSE/390 with a performance set at 1.0. The system has about a 9% probability of running 1.5 times as fast and an 11% probability of running 0.5 times as fast as its average performance. This is due to variations in the workload. Other systems are measured in terms of the base machine. Ratios of performance are established for a large MVS mainframe, Intel-based servers of various kinds, and various RISC-based Unix servers.

The results seem clear, but are of course hotly arguable. Argument will ensue about the equivalence of centralized and partitioned power. Partitioned

Type	Power	Peak	Prob.	Minimum	Prob.	Class
SMF	1.0	>1.5	9%	<0.5	11%	Small mainframe
BIGMF	17.3	>1.5	6%	<0.5	5%	Large mainframe
CMOSG/S 1	1.4	>1.5	11%	<0.5	14%	Small group server
CMOSG/S 2	1.7	>1.5	8%	<0.5	16%	Midsize group server
RISC D/S	3.1	>1.5	1%	<0.5	21%	Department server
RISC E/S	6.2	>1.5	8%	<0.5	14%	Enterprise server
RISC W/S	2.1	>1.5	9%	<0.5	18%	RISC workstation
PC Desk 1	1.3	>1.5	12%	<0.5	20%	Personal computer
PC Desk 2	0.4	>1.5	17%	<0.5	12%	Personal computer

Table 8.1 **Performance normalized to the small mainframe. (This is an illustrative worksheet only. The numbers are a valid statistical unitless metric derived from a performance-derivation formula involving architectural normalization and workload characterization. The methodology is proprietary to the manticore consultancy.)**

systems have a problem with peak workloads—it may be necessary to configure each machine with enough power for its peak workload. This leads to a greater total amount of power than on a centralized machine, which can trade resources between different local peaks. However, there may be business reasons why it is not necessary to guarantee peak load performance for every distributed machine. A slower transaction rate at peak times may not lose business or revenue or cause customer discontent.

There are marketplace arguments about the actual pricing of various classes of machines. As this book is written, hardware prices are becoming almost as difficult to assess as software prices or airline tickets. At the end of 1993, mainframe manufacturers were close to abandoning the idea of a list price and offering deep discounts in order to hold or attract business. However, at the end of 1994, the mainframe pricing seems to be tightening up in view of an unexpected rise in mainframe demand.

Finally, there are accounting arguments. Is the initial purchase or lease price of a computing instrument a proper standard for measuring comparable cost? What is a proper amortization period? The old practice of amortizing mainframes over periods of seven years seems to be inappropriate in a market where they lose 30% of their value every year. A related issue is what is the proper write-off period for a desktop machine as the industry doubles performance

1 Architecture: measures of path length and average cycles to perform sorting programs published in various places. Adjusted by published work on design-independent architectural power. A 32-bit architecture is assumed, with 98% cache hit ratios.

2 System Stress: workload management concerns can preoccupy a heavily shared machine. Almost 40% of the time of a mainframe can be invested in systems functions related to workload management and the presence of thousands of users. This includes resource management, list management, and recovery. All of this time is counted as nonproductive time in the normalization. Smaller systems with simpler operating systems are charged for considerably higher idle periods and low utilizations.

3 Peak to Average Load: the ratio determines the relative inefficiency of partitioning on separate machines. A shared system can trade off resources between applications as they reach peaks at different times. Distributed systems cannot do this.

4 Performance Range (Rate): the probability that the nominal MIPS rate will be exceeded or missed by a percentage at different points in the workload.

every 18 months. Accounting practices affect the perception of the relative cost of hardware. There are arguments of secondary costs involving physical maintenance, power, cooling, etc. IBM now says one can replace a bipolar mainframe with a CMOS mainframe for the cost of operating the old machine.

Given all the uncertainty and opinion, the numbers suggest that some form of "downsizing" is indeed appropriate from the view of comparative annual hardware and software costs.

The economics of distribution derive primarily from the technology change between mainframes and microprocessor-based systems. As mainframes become micro-based superservers or enterprise servers and achieve a similar cost/performance or re-establish economies of scale, an "upsizing" pattern may occur. However, the relative amount of still-unique design and manufacture in superservers may always keep them above the price/performance knee.

Table 8.2 shows the cost of systems needed to approximate the performance associated with the BIGMF system. Faster systems need more memory because they use more instructions and data more quickly.

Table 8.3 shows the net effective computing power actually provided for applications running on the system. Smaller machines tend to be underutilized and only use fractions of their power. Larger, intensively used machines invest important percentages of their power managing the workloads and sharing resources. This is discussed as System Stress in Box 8.2.

Table 8.3 shows the amount of processing power received by applications on a large mainframe to be 130 units and not 207. The Effective Price/Performance

Type	Power	Nominal Performance	Memory (MB)	Cost (dollars)
SMF	1.0	12	24	180,000
BIGMF	17.3	207	400	10,500,000
CMOSG/S 1	1.4	17	24	13,000
CMOSG/S 2	1.7	20	32	17,000
RISC D/S	3.1	37	96	42,000
RISC E/S	6.2	75	128	1,340,000
RISC W/S	2.1	25	64	8,000
PC Desk 1	1.3	16	24	3,400
PC Desk 2	0.4	5	8	1,800

Table 8.2   Cost versus performance. (The Power figures are derived from Table 8.1.)

column divides the effective performance into the given price to derive an effective price/performance number. The street price shows an adjustment applied for the small mainframe and large mainframe, but does not adjust the price/performance for other classes of machine, which are not heavily discounted.

Type	Nominal Performance	Net Performance	Effective Price/Perf. (list price)	Effective Price/Perf. (street price)
SMF	12	9	20/1	10/1
BIGMF	207	130	81/1	40/1
CMOSG/S 1	17	11	1.2/1	1.2/1
CMOSG/S 2	20	13	1.3/1	1.3/1
RISC D/S	37	23	1.8/1	1.8/1
RISC E/S	75	64	21/1	21/1
RISC W/S	25	16	1/2	1/2
PC Desk 1	16	11	1/3	1/3
PC Desk 2	5	3	3/5	3/5

Table 8.3   Net effective power. Reductions: global management 15–30%, basic management 10–15%, software complexity 5–15%, large systems effects 0–5%, and unused 10–30%.

Class	Effective Performance	Effective Price/Perf.	Number	Cost (dollars)
SMF	9	10.00	13	1,390,000
BIGMF	130	40.00	1	5,200,000
CMOSG/S 1	11	1.18	12	156,000
CMOSG/S 2	13	1.31	11	187,000
RISC D/S	23	1.83	6	252,000
RISC E/S	64	21.00	2	2,680,000
RISC W/S	16	0.50	8	512,000
PC Desk 1	11	0.32	12	41,000
PC Desk 2	3	0.60	45	81,000

Table 8.4   Composite aggregate effective: the number and cost of machines of different classes necessary to match the effective performance of BIGMF, the big mainframe.

Table 8.4 shows the number and cost of machines of different classes necessary to match the effective computing power of the mainframe. If work on the mainframe can be partitioned into 12 applications or application segments, the total hardware bill for computing power could be $41,000, the price of 12 large desktop machines. This is, of course, ridiculous for a number of reasons (e.g., storage requirements, requirements of sharing access, the number of users), but it shows the enormous discontinuity of technology pricing between old and new technologies along the dimension of processing power.

Partitioning the workload

Table 8.5 shows the structure of the workload. Each application (A, B, etc.) is shown with the number of users, data sharing, and power requirements. The column CM shows the percentage of users that are users of another application; the column Sh shows what applications share data bases; and the column D. Bases/Size shows the number of data bases and the total data base size.

Sharing users and data bases is a constraint to distribution. The strength of the constraint depends on the quality of networking that will enable remote access and on the intensity and the pattern of the sharing.

The Complexity column is a definition of the complexity of an interaction. It is given in terms of the Transaction Processing Council's standard transaction

App.	Users	CM	Sh.	D. Bases/Size	Complex.	Power	Peak	Stability
A	1,024	30%	B	5/1,000 MB	D	12	14	0.3
B	256	40%	A	3/500 MB	B	5	9	0.5
C	100	–	–	1/100 MB	A	6	7	0.8
D	340	20%	G	4/300 MB	C	21	31	0.5
E: e1	64	40%	e(n)	1/50 MB	A	3	5	0.7
E: e2	64	30%	e(n)	1/50 MB	A	4	6	0.7
E: e3	64	30%	e(n)	1/20 MB	A	6	9	0.8
E: e4	64	10%	e(n)	1/10 MB	A	4	5	0.8
F	250	–	–	4/150 MB	B	7	11	0.6
G	1,000	30%	D	3/5,000 MB	C	23	34	0.4
H: h1	54	80%	h1	1/40 MB	A	9	11	0.8
H: h2	40	40%	h2	1/30 MB	A	7	14	0.8
Totals	3,116			7,250 MB		107	156[1]	
				Composites				
AB	1,280			6/1,500 MB		17	23	0.4
DG	1,340			2/5,300 MB		44	65	0.4

[1]Peak load exceeds maximum effective capacity of mainframe–one of the reasons for this exercise.

Table 8.5   Mix partitionability: relational data base applications.

complexity levels. Very complex transactions have multiple and complex disk references that require, at the present level of communications, data to be local.

The Power column is an average requirement. The Peak column is the power needed when the application is running its peak load. The Stability column is a measure of variance (see Chapter 10) that describes the ranges of transaction complexity. The higher the number, the more processing requirements for different transactions are similar.

The Composites entries provide a profile of applications with significant common users and data sharing.

Each application is a relational data base application using a dialect of SQL. The characteristics of the applications provide the basis for mapping onto available hardware systems. Each application can run on a range of machines.

The requirements for a candidate machine:

• It can provide required storage

App.	Storage	Peak	Users	Candidates
AB	1,500 MB	23	1,280	BIGMF, RISC E/S, RISC D/S
DG	5,300 MB	65	1,340	BIGMF, RISC E/S
A	1,000 MB	14	1,024	BIGMF, RISC D/S, RISC E/S
B	500 MB	9	256	SMF, CMOSG/S 1,2 RISC D/S, RISC E/S
C	100 MB	7	100	SMF, CMOSG/S 1,2 RISC D/S, RISC E/S
D	300 MB	31	340	BIGMF, RISC D/S, RISC E/S
E: e1	50 MB	5	64	BIGMF, SMF, CMOSG/S 1,2 RISC D/S, E/S
E: e2	50 MB	6	64	BIGMF, SMF, CMOSG/S 1,2 RISC D/S, E/S
E: e3	20 MB	9	64	BIGMF, SMF, CMOSG/S 1,2 RISC D/S, E/S
E: e4	10 MB	5	64	BIGMF, SMF, CMOSG/S 1,2 RISC D/S, E/S
F	150 MB	8	250	BIGMF, SMF, RISC E/S
G	5,000 MB	34	1,000	BIGMF, RISC E/S
H: h1	50 MB	11	50	BIGMF, CMOSG/S 1,2, RISC D/S, E/S
H: h2	40 MB	14	40	BIGMF, RISC D/S, E/S

Table 8.6   Application to system class candidate matrix.

- It can provide needed computational power
- It can support the user population
- It can run appropriate software environments.

Table 8.6 is a mapping of the applications onto candidate machine classes. There will be some disagreement about whether required storage binds an application to a class of machine. There is a growing tendency for the "data farm" to be defined independently of the processing system. A storage resource can serve mainframes, LANs, and servers of various kinds. Huge, gigabyte data farms can serve any population of computers at the same per-byte cost. Data farm costs may be made topology independent.

There are no applications that require remaining on the mainframe. The exact deployment of the applications will depend on the relative resource efficiencies suggested by Figure 8.2.

Software environments

The total systems costs of a dispersion of applications will have a software environment component. In order to constrain migration costs from the existing mainframe, the exercise insists that any platform used must either run a data base or have available data base client technology allowing SQL references to a data base. This is not a severe constraint, as all classes of systems have such technology.

Other constraints:

1 All machines must be connectable by SPX/IPX and TCP/IP. Enterprise and departmental servers must have an SNA LU 6.2 option.

2 All operating systems supporting a human interface must support the Windows interface at current levels. This may be achieved by Windows, OS/2, Sun Solaris, and others in various ways.

Common systems management was not required of the aggregation of systems because it was not possible to achieve and it was not necessary across the body of the entire application set for most possible partitionings.

Software costs are much like airline prices. There is rapid change, strange deals, odd licensing terms, and very different bundlings. Baseware may be bundled with telecommunications, an end user interface, and a data base. Some software comes bundled with hardware and seems effectively free at the desktop level.

A software vendor may go after a niche by offering remarkable discounts and packages. For 100 copies of the same product, 30% discounts are sometimes available. For a commitment covering two-year needs, discounts of up to 60% can be found. A commitment to run software on all of an organization's machines can earn as much as 70%. Variations in site and user license pricing must be constantly reviewed.

There is still a tendency for Unix-world software to be more expensive that non-Unix software. What might cost $100 in the PC world could well cost $300 to $500 in the Unix world. A base Unix operating system from Novell has recently cost $500, not including communications and software development kits.

Server prices are considerably higher than desktop prices. A small server environment may cost $3,000 to $5,000. Software for an enterprise server can cost $60,000 for a complete baseware and middleware package. Servers may charge by the user. An early pricing for Novell NetWare 4.0 was: 10 users, $2,400; 100 users, $8,795; 500 users, $26,395; and 1,000 users, $47,995.

Some systems charge by processor type, by usage intensity, and by number of concurrent users. Some software is still rented on monthly charge or usage-intensity bases.

Associating a software cost with a particular system type is dangerous work indeed. At the time of this exercise, with the particular constraints imposed, Table 8.7 shows an estimate of software costs for each class of machine.

Computer	OS	DBMS	System/Mgr.	Interface	Total
BIGMF	100,000	200,000	50,000	10,000	360,000
SMF	10,000	25,000	–	2,000	37,000
CMOSG/S 1	5,000	5,000	5,000	–	15,000
CMOSG/S 2	5,000	5,000	5,000	–	15,000
RISC D/S	10,000	10,000	10,000	–	30,000
RISC E/S	20,000	50,000	20,000	–	90,000
RISC W/S	2,000	2,000	–	1,000	5,000
PC Desk 1	250	500	–	–	750
PC Desk 2	50	300	–	–	350

Table 8.7 Software costs (in dollars).

Mapping the workload onto the choices

Incrementing the current mainframe was a benchmark solution. The current hardware was running at about 85% of the processing power necessary to sustain the peak load. To bring the system up to needed resource level would cost $800,000 in memory and computer power.

Other solutions involve some further analysis of the workload. The following assumptions are made:

1 The distribution is a rehosting distribution. Subsequent restructuring within an application to form client/server configurations will occur after the primary distribution. A minimum PC desktop will provide access to the application server. Optimization of the application environment between PC and server costs will occur later in each application.

2 The distribution is constrained by the close relations of applications AB and DG. Redevelopment of these applications to achieve an integration or a new partitioning will not be considered.

3 An application will be put on the minimum machine that will handle its peak workload.

Table 8.8 shows a first step to a nominal minimum-cost dispersion of the application set. End-point costs include a basic PC and its associated software, including a Windows interface, communications, baseware, and an office

App.	Computer	HW/SW (incl. storage)	End Point	Total	Annual (over 3 yrs.)
DG	RISC E/S	1,430,000	1,608,000	3,038,000	
AB	RISC D/S	260,000	1,560,000	1,796,000	
C	CMOSG/S 2	27,000	120,000	147,000	
E: e1	CMOSG/S 1	21,000	77,000	98,000	
E: e2	CMOSG/S 1	23,000	77,000	101,000	
E: e3	CMOSG/S 1	26,000	77,000	103,000	
E: e4	CMOSG/S 1	21,000	77,000	98,000	
F	RISC D/S	60,000	360,000	360,000	
H: h1	CMOSG/S 1	30,000	60,000	90,000	
H: h2	CMOSG/S 2	35,000	48,000	91,000	
Total cost		1,933,000	4,064,000	5,922,000	1,974,000
Mainframe cost		6,480,000	934,800	7,414,000	2,471,330
Amortized cost					3,100,000

Table 8.8   First application dispersion.

package containing e-mail, spreadsheet, and word processor, but no data base manager. The software cost is about $200; the per-desktop cost is $1,200. The storage cost is $2,000 per gigabyte for all classes of system. Each system's end-point costs reflect the number of application uses.

Applications DG do not fully load the RISC enterprise server. There is opportunity for some reconsolidation. This reconsolidation is shown on Table 8.9. The application set E is moved to the big machine, and the group of group servers is eliminated. This results in software savings and some small hardware savings. Despite the fact that the enterprise server is inherently more expensive than the group server, the increments to its resources to accommodate E are less than the total costs of the E servers.

Whether other considerations will justify the reconsolidation is not clear. The savings are somewhat marginal.

Something needs to be said about the costs associated with the mainframe in Tables 8.8 and 8.9. The mainframe cost number represents a new mainframe capable of running the load at current mainframe prices. This might well be an alternative if issues of migration and cost of ownership suggest it is profitable.

App.	Computer	HW/SW (incl. storage)	End Point	Total	Annual (over 3 yrs.)
DGE	RISC E/S	1,450,000	1,916,000	3,366,000	
AB	RISC D/S	260,000	1,536,000	1,796,000	
C	CMOSG/S 2	27,000	120,000	147,000	
F	RISC D/S	60,000	300,000	360,000	
H: h1	CMOSG/S 1	30,000	60,000	90,000	
H: h2	CMOSG/S 2	35,000	48,000	83,000	
Total cost		1,862,000	3,980,000	5,842,000	1,947,333
Mainframe cost		6,480,000	934,800	7,414,000	2,471,330
Amortized cost					3,100,000

Table 8.9   Refined application dispersion.

The amortized cost line is the cost of the current mainframe, with an initial cost of $22,000,000 and three years of remaining amortization (or lease period).

It is not easy to assess what the old machine is costing. There are likely power and maintenance costs (not considered here because of the great variance in local power charges and because the point about old technology costs can be made without them) that must be included in the annual cost of the old mainframe. But what will actually be saved when the mainframe is eliminated?

We move from technology to accounting issues. A four-year-old purchased $22,000,000 mainframe might have a market price of $4,000,000. A lease turn back might be accomplished for a leased machine.

What is to be used as the "figure" to beat for the new IT technology? This will largely be determined by the enterprise culture. This book will continue with the assumption that the figure to beat is the amortized cost. Even a new mainframe will beat that. It is likely that the idea of a new mainframe and the idea of an enterprise server will have completely folded into each other by the end of the decade.

Discussion

The exercise result is interesting and equivocal. The issues that arise from it are at the core of technology investment decision-making.

How good are the numbers?

Are elements of risk, cost overrides, and changing prices factored in? Are accounting periods correct? Have calculations of the present value of money relative to interest and inflation rates been included? Is it proper to charge all systems with personal computers? Would some of these devices already exist? Are there costs of energy, platforms, and maintenance that should be added to the systems costs?

Proper accounting and reasonable alternatives

What is the accounting status of the current mainframe system? Is it paid for, on a lease, or being paid for over its depreciation period? The mainframe was depreciated over seven years at an initial purchase price of $22,000,000. It is now in its fourth year; the total cost to finish the depreciation period would be $9,100,000. The increment of $800,000 to increase its power would be depreciated over the same period at an annual rate of $266,000. The total mainframe cost would be $3,979,440. From an accounting view, extending the mainframe is not a good investment relative to downsizing. No charge is made against the mainframe for power, maintenance, and other physical costs associated with its operation. These will vary wildly from location to location but must be factored into a downsizing decision.

Benefits

It may be that the downsizing and introduction of personal productivity tools have a benefit value that increases the value of rightsizing. As we will see, increased development efficiency, professional productivity, and better decision-making may be effects of the new system.

Migration costs

There are a wide range of costs associated with the transition from the mainframe culture and technology to the rehosted technology. These include:

- Movement of data from the mainframe to the new platforms
- Movement of application function from the mainframe
- Acquisition of appropriate skills for the new platforms
- Costs of phasing-in new platforms to production.

There are many points of view about the cost of migration. In this exercise, the applications are already running on a relational data base. Data migration to other relational data bases will be facilitated by this. Tools for the migration from mainframe to server data bases already exist.

The cost of moving applications from the mainframe to the new platforms will depend on the quality of an application. If it is well documented and available in a common language like COBOL, the port can be accomplished with recompilation and some degree of tuning after it becomes operational on the target system.

Unhappily, few older programs are in good condition due to maintenance practices. The cost of migration will be seriously increased by the necessity to either redevelop or reverse-engineer the programs to determine what they do. For relational data base applications, this will be considerably easier than for applications which use other data models.

Some software economics

The costs of migration lead directly to a consideration of the economics of various software support and maintenance practices. If annual maintenance costs can be reduced by redeveloping or restructuring applications, the costs of migration might well be paid for by reduced maintenance costs.

Over 80% of mainframe applications are 5 years old or older. However, the average life of a line of code is considerably less. The half life of a line of code is six months. Large investments are made in keeping COBOL applications business relevant. In excess of 60% of the total cost of an application during its life is incurred by extension and modification after it is put into production. As much as 12% of total Information Technology budgets and 80% of total software budgets are spent on maintenance.

Table 8.10 shows estimated relative costs of development and maintenance. It shows that modifying modules in COBOL is considerably more expensive than creating new ones. Where more powerful languages are usable, the cost of redevelopment can become considerably less than the cost of modification of old programs.

The range of software maintenance costs for the current mainframe application is about $900,000 to $1,665,000.

It would be splendid if reduced software maintenance costs would pay for the migration to a new system. The smaller applications, the E and H family and C, are candidates for redevelopment using a 4GL language, which is more productive than COBOL and which could lead to lower development costs if it

Act	Develop New	Add Modules	Modify
Design and code	1.00	1.35	1.85
Test	0.40	0.80	0.80
Total	1.40	1.85	2.65
Cost/person-month	$7000	$7000	$7000
Cost/line	$4.00	$5.04	$7.40

Table 8.10 COBOL maintenance costs.

is maintained at the 4GL language level. Various programming development kits using formats closer to the problem statement and far from the computer solution statement are available.

Application program generating tools claim to be from two to five times as productive as COBOL. Table 8.11 shows a redevelopment cost for the smaller applications on small servers. Part of this redevelopment would lead to the client/server configuration, as tools are now available to achieve this.

The charge for the redevelopment includes the expenses of analysis of the current application. The actual development cost is under $3.00 per generated COBOL equivalent line, but a heavy one-time charge is made for the process of committing to the tools, understanding the application, and mastering the tool set. The initial redevelopment cost is $225,000, but the annual maintenance cost

App.	COBOL Size	Cost/Line	Total Cost	Post-Prod. Annual
C	6,000	11.00	66,000	18,000
E: e1	3,000	11.00	33,000	9,000
E: e2	2,000	11.00	22,000	6,000
E: e3	4,000	11.00	44,000	12,000
E: e4	1,500	11.00	16,500	4,500
H: h1	2,500	11.00	27,500	7,500
H: h2	3,500	11.00	38,500	10,500
Total cost	22,500		225,522	67,500

Table 8.11 Small application redevelopment.

	High	Middle	Low
Understand	588,000	280,000	2,500
Redevelop	800,000	560,000	264,000
Total	1,388,000	840,000	266,500

Table 8.12 Costs of moving the large applications.

is reduced to $67,500 for these programs. The argument is that they will be maintained at a higher level of abstraction and documentation.

Applications AB, DG, and F are larger and require COBOL redevelopment or redevelopment in some new environment involving improved CASE tools. With proper use and discipline, the CASE environments can increase productivity by around 30% and reduce later maintenance costs by more. The very large applications have around 200,000 statements.

There is a serious disadvantage to size. The cost of development and maintenance increases sharply as a function of size. There is also greater risk of erroneous cost estimating with larger programs.

A pessimistic estimate is that understanding the large programs will require an investment of about 1,500 person-days, or 7 person-years. A burdened (30%) person-year is charged at $84,000. Certain investments in re-engineering or restructuring tools and services may be required. An optimistic estimate is that some equivalent of the IBM restructuring service will make the applications suitable for migration to a new platform for about $500 per application. The range of cost estimates to prepare for the migration is an astonishing $2,500 to $588,000.

Table 8.12 summarizes large-application migration costs from various points of view. The High numbers reflect 1,500 person days to understand 200,000 lines of code and redevelopment activity at the COBOL cost of $4 per line. Middle sets understanding as the sum of understanding smaller programs with

	Mainframe Maint.	Post-Migration Maint.
Small		67,500
Large		800,000
Total	1,665,000	867,500

Table 8.13 Maintenance costs.

	First Year	Second Year	Third Year
Cumulative difference	797,000	1,594,000	2,391,000
Migration	1,065,000		
Profit	(268,000)	529,000	1,326,000

Table 8.14   Paying for the migration.

	Mainframe (based on amortization)	Best Dispersion
Hardware/software	3,100,000	1,947,133
Software maintenance	1,665,000	867,000
Total	4,765,000	2,814,133
Migration		1,065,000
Total		3,879,133

Table 8.15   Annual costs.

module sizes of around 15,000 statements. The sum of these modules is 200,000 statements, but it is considerably more efficient to understand smaller modules. Middle development reflects an increase in productivity of around 30% due to CASE tools. Low reflects the restructuring miracle and a very effective programming paradigm and tool set that achieves (as some claim objects do) a factor of 3 increased productivity.

Using the Middle numbers from Table 8.12 and the small application numbers, the total cost of software migration is $1,065,000, which is within the range of a year's maintenance of the current mainframe application ($900,000–$1,665,000).

Offsetting this cost is reduced maintenance for the smaller applications, which are now represented in more efficient notations. A reduction in cost of maintenance for the larger applications can occur as good programming practice moves the maintenance cost closer to the cost of "new" code, rather than "maintained" code. Tables 8.13 and 8.14 show the best case for the argument that reduced maintenance will pay for the migration.

Table 8.14 shows that by the end of the second year, savings in maintenance have more than payed for the migration. Table 8.15 factors in migration and maintenance costs to the change/no change choices.

chapter 9

Cost of ownership

EXECUTIVE SUMMARY   Migrating from one computer culture to another often involves a shift in the skills needed to develop applications, operate systems, and manage and administer computer resources.

Cost of ownership issues have been used by both mainframe and distributed proponents as a serious reason to stay with older systems or to move on to new ones as quickly as possible.

It is enormously difficult to assess the true cost of ownership or the true cost of moving from one platform to another. What investments in Unix skills—necessary for certain types of client/server, for example—would be necessary even if one stayed with the mainframe? To what extent are certain costs due to the changes in computing generation, and to what extent due to a shift from one style to another? Mature mainframe environments have had a long time to ride down a curve of operational costs. They were very expensive in the early days. Will client/server follow the same curve?

Investment in skills, the rate at which a company accepts new technologies, is a key indicator of aggressiveness. The cost of ownership, now more than the cost of a system, is a key gateway to different types of systems evolution.

Shifting the culture

A frequently argued issue in the cost of technology is the cost of acquiring new skills for a new technology. Skills acquisition costs are a cost of migration. Acquiring new skills is not a trivial undertaking. Moving MVS systems specialists into a Unix or Windows NT AS culture is financially and demographically difficult business.

Often one hears that moving from mainframe to client/server incurred unexpected costs because of the need for education, training, and hiring new specialists. There are some interesting underlying issues:

1 To what extent are new skills required regardless of the platform choices? Is there a shift in skills sets over time that is just an evolutionary phenomenon?

If an organization was to stay with its mainframe, would it cost less in skills development than if it downsizes, rehosts, etc.?

2 To what extent should acquiring new skills be part of an ongoing expense of IT? Shifts in culture can represent a change in the content of education but not an increase in expense. In place of going to SNA school, the staff goes to TCP/IP school, etc.

The perceived cost of acquiring skills depends on the usual education policies of the enterprise. At one time, IBM required 20 of 220 work days of education for its professional staff, approximately 9% of total salary. The cost of skills was constant regardless of the particular skills that were being taught.

When there is a culture shift, the total cost of developing new skills for the new culture (client/server or open or Unix, etc.) depends upon the levels of skill already in the enterprise. An enterprise may have:

- only proprietary/mainframe skills
- Unix skills
- LAN skills
- CASE skills
- Windows skills
- OS/2 skills
- object skills
- multimedia skills.

The perception of additional cost is defined by the degree to which good management has assured that appropriate skills, and skills awareness, is constantly being introduced into the culture. Various organizations will take different positions:

- Skills are strategic and platform independent (an investment)
- Skills are a cost of client/server (a cost)
- Skills will improve productivity
- Skills will improve my strategic position
- Skills are fundamental to business alignment.

Table 9.1 attempts to distinguish between education cost and education investment. An investment creates a skill that will be useful regardless of particular product decisions. A cost is spending on a skill that is associated only with a particular product that has no inherent strategic value. The costs are derived from a manual of courses offered by SunSoft. The dispersals attributable to current technology (the state of the art) are for skills that span platforms. The dispersals attributable to Unix client/server are specific to a technology direction

Attributable to Current Technology (the State of the Art)		
Programming in C++	2,875	5 days
Programming with Xlib	3,125	6 days
Object-oriented design	5,375	4 days
Programming OSF/Motif	2,750	6 days
TCP/IP technical	5,525	3 days
Technical introduction to LAN	3,125	2 days
Client/server DDMS	2,875	2 days
Introduction to data communications	3,375	3 days
Design enterprise networks	5,625	3 days
Totals	**34,650**	**34 days**

Attributable to Unix Client/Server		
Unix software tools	1,975	2 days
Shell command language	4,375	6 days
Novell 3.x system administration	3,825	2 days
PC-NFS 5.0	1,420	3 days
Systems administration	3,120	5 days
Totals	**14,715**	**18 days**

Costs attributable to new technology = 70%.
Costs attributable to client/server = 30%.

Table 9.1   Attribution of dispersals for education.

and are not necessarily required in any 1990s culture. Even if one disagrees with the split of Table 9.1, understanding the nature of the split is crucial.

The current technology skills are transferrable from product to product and from system to system, and represent an enterprise's participation in the technology envelope. Therefore, expenditures associated with these skills represent an unavoidable investment in keeping within current practice.

Table 9.2 shows the generality of much of the technology, and that there is a deep and broad level of current skills that cross technologies. Whether an enterprise is going to stay with MVS or move to Unix, there is a common set of knowledge that must be had in order to avoid falling out of the technology envelope.

	DCE	POSIX	X/Open	TCP	SPX	OSF	Objects
IBM MVS Open Edition	•	•	•	•	•	•	•
IBM OS/2	•	•	•	•	•	•	•
HP MPE/ix	•	•	•	•	•	•	•
DEC VMS/Open	•	•	•	•	•	•	•
AIX	•	•	•	•	•	•	•
Windows NT				•	•		•

Reprinted by kind permission of the manticore consultancy, New York.

Table 9.2   Platforms using new technologies.

Skills planning

Any technology strategy must be closely associated with skills acquisition, and this must naturally start with an assessment of the inventory and the needs. Table 9.3 is an example of a useful document providing the basis for an education plan—in this case, a three-year plan for introducing the state of the art into the culture.

Management, administration, and operations

There is considerable interest in the cost of ownership. The relative costs of various systems structures and management structures is under constant debate. Unhappily, this debate has been distilled down to mainframe vs. client/server cost per user, or cost of transaction. These simplifying measures are not really instructive, and there is considerable room for distortion in unstated assumptions, biases, etc.

Accumulated experience has informed us that there are functions that should be centralized and functions that should be dispersed. Complete decentralization either leads to chaotic increases in cost or the proliferation of mini-bureaucracies.

The need for some central control derives from enterprise needs for coherent and flexible information access and controllable costs. Other motives for centralization are a need to pool expertise and a need for a focus point from which technology can be diffused. Currently, in excess of 40% of IT activity in the U.S. is organizationally centralized in some way. About a quarter of enterprises have entirely decentralized. Others are in various states of uncertainty and flux.

	Skills Transition					
Skills	Have	Need 1 yr	Need 2 yr	Need 3 yr	Hire	Train
MF COBOL	14	10	9	3	0	0
C	3	8	8	11	0	8
C++	0	2	4	5	2	3
DB Toolkit	1	2	4	7	0	7
Server Toolkits	0	3	9	11	0	9
IPPF	10	6	2	0	0	0
X Windows/Xlib	0	2	4	7	0	7
Presentation Manager	2	3	5	6	0	3
Motif	0	2	4	6	0	6
TSO	8	5	0	0	0	0
IMS	4	3	1	0	0	0
DB2	2	3	3	3	0	3
CICS	2	4	4	5	0	5
Vendor DB	1	3	5	6	6	0
OS/2	3	5	6	6	0	3
TCP/IP	1	4	5	5	0	5
SNA LU 6.2	5	3	2	2	0	0
DCE	0	2	7	13	0	13
POSIX	1	4	7	13	0	13
Novell NetWare	0	3	4	7	7	0
Totals	57	65	71	84		

Cost of Skills Acquisition	
Study costs	$212,500
Work displacement	$100,000
Total	$312,500
Annual (over 5 years)	$62,500

Table 9.3   New technology: the shifts in skills needed to move from a proprietary environment to an open platform over a three-year period. (This is based on a particular project.)

A primary problem of centralization vs. decentralization is efficiency. Regardless of cultural viewpoints, there are issues of organizational scale that determine limits of centralization. Figure 9.1 shows a marginal utility curve,

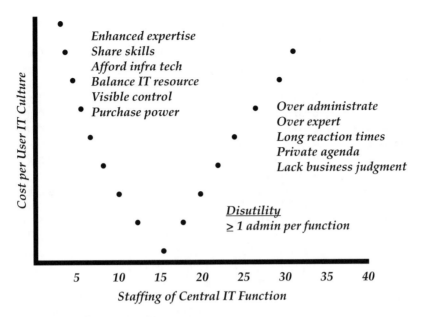

Figure 9.1   Marginal utility.

where the curve to the left of the knee represents increasing inefficiency of centralization. To the right of this knee, every increment to the centralized organization will increase the cost of systems ownership and decrease the responsiveness of the organization.

No advocate of centralized control, no matter what other arguments support the viewpoint, can defend an organization inherently inoperative. No advocate of decentralization can support an argument of increased cost without a demonstration of value added.

Systems salary and staffing

The cost of ownership is partially determined by staffing levels and salaries. Box 9.1 shows some representative U.S. salary averages drawn from Human Resources industry sources.

A cost of ownership figure may be computed for different models of computing. Different populations of skills and levels of skills will define an ongoing operational cost for various cultures and distributions. Figures 9.2 and 9.3 are two different models of computing. A third model of complete decentralization is discussed later.

Box 9.2 shows a representative staffing for a mainframe data center support-ing 3,500 users. It is very much like the data center of the downsizing exercise. The operational costs apply quite well.

Distributed, centrally managed system

Figure 9.3 shows the system described in Box 9.3, which is equal in power to that shown in Figure 9.2. The staffing for this system, shown in Box 9.4, differs from that of the mainframe system in some interesting ways:

- There is a dispersion of tasks between a centralized staff and end user depart-ments. End user departments have taken on some responsibilities and some authorities.
- There are some specialties not needed in the mainframe staffing.
- There is often a lower level of skill needed in a particular speciality.
- There is likely to be a greater reliance on consultants because of the breadth of different systems.

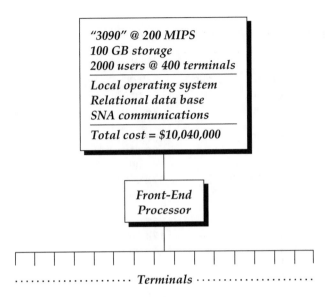

Figure 9.2   Mainframe configuration.

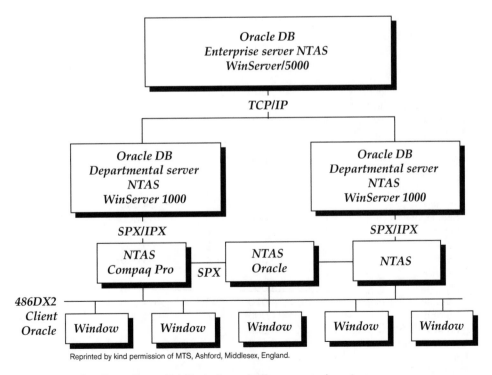

Reprinted by kind permission of MTS, Ashford, Middlesex, England.

Figure 9.3   Configuration: distributed, centrally managed system.

MAINFRAME DATA CENTER: STAFFING

	Salary	Number	Total Salary	Group Number	Group Salary
VP MIS	88,000	1	88,000		
MIS DIRECTOR	74,000	1	74,000	2	162,000
SYSTEMS AND PROGRAMMING					
Manager	58,000	1	58,000		
Project Leader	44,500	2	89,000		
Systems Analyst	42,000	2	84,000		
Programmer Analyst	34,000	4	272,000		
Programmer	28,500	5	136,000	14	639,000
APPLICATIONS PROGRAMMING					
Senior Manager	63,800	1	63,800		
Manager	58,000	3	174,000		
Senior Project Leader	55,000	2	110,000		
Software Engineer	43,500	4	174,000		
Project Leader	44,500	2	89,000		
Systems Analyst	42,000	6	252,000		
Programmer Analyst	34,000	8	272,000		
Programmer	28,500	11	313,500	37	1,448,300
TECHNICAL SERVICES					
Manager	56,000	1	56,000		
CASE Tool Specialist	48,000	2	96,000		
Help Desk	25,000	2	50,000		
Consultant	36,500	3	109,500	8	311,500
DATA BASE					
Data Base Manager	60,000	1	60,000		
Data Base Administrator	50,000	2	100,000		
Data Base Analyst	43,000	4	172,000	7	332,000
TELECOMMUNICATIONS					
Manager	57,500	1	57,500		
Telecom Specialist	44,000	4	176,000	5	233,500
OPERATIONS					
Senior Manager	49,500	1	49,500		
Manager	42,000	2	84,000		
Shift Supervisor	32,000	2	64,000		
Operator	22,000	4	88,000		
I/O Clerk	20,000	2	40,000		
Data Entry	16,500	4	66,000	5	391,500
EDUCATION					
Manager	43,000	1	43,000		
Curriculum Developer	34,000	2	64,000		
Instructor	31,000	4	124,000	7	231,000
ANNUAL HW/SW (5 years)	2,008,000				
ANNUAL DIRECT SALARY	3,748,000				
TOTAL	5,646,000				
PER-USER COSTS	2,823				

9.3   DISTRIBUTED, CENTRALLY MANAGED SYSTEM

No.	Hardware	Software Environment
2000	Personal computers	Windows, Oracle client
64	Group servers	Windows NT AS, Oracle server
4	Department servers	Windows NT AS, Oracle server
1	Enterprise server	Windows NT AS, Oracle server
		SPX/IPX LAN
		TCP/IP backbone
		SMS management system

9.4   DISTRIBUTED, CENTRALLY MANAGED SYSTEM: STAFFING

	Salary	Number	Total Salary	Group Number	Group Salary
VP MIS	100,000	1	100,000		
MIS DIRECTOR	90,000	1	90,000	2	190,000
SYSTEMS AND PROGRAMMING–CENTRAL SITE					
Manager	65,000	1	65,000		
Senior Project Leader	55,000	1	55,000		
Software Engineer	43,500	2	87,000		
Project Leader	44,500	2	89,000		
Systems Analyst	42,000	3	126,000		
Programmer	28,500	2	57,000		
PC System Developer	35,000	3	105,000	14	584,000
TECHNICAL SERVICES					
Manager	70,000	1	70,000		
Systems Programmer	42,000	2	84,000		
CASE Tool Specialist	48,000	2	96,000		
Consulting–Senior	47,000	2	94,000		
Consulting–Associate	36,500	3	109,500	10	453,500
DATA BASE					
Data Base Manager	60,000	1	60,000		
Data Base Administrator	50,000	2	100,000		
Data Base Analyst	43,000	4	172,000	7	332,000
TELECOMMUNICATIONS					
Manager	60,500	1	60,500		
Telecom Specialist	44,000	1	44,000		
LAN/WAN Specialist	41,000	3	123,000	5	227,500
OPERATIONS					
Senior Manager	49,500	1	49,500		
Manager	42,000	1	42,000		
Shift Supervisor	32,000	2	64,000		
Operator	22,000	4	88,000	8	243,500

	Salary	Number	Total Salary	Group Number	Group Salary
EDUCATION					
Manager	43,000	1	43,000		
Curriculum Developer	34,000	3	102,000		
Instructor	31,000	5	155,000	8	300,000
APPLICATIONS PROGRAMMING					
Manager	58,000	1	58,000		
Senior Project Leader	55,000	1	55,000		
Software Engineer	43,500	2	87,000		
Project Leader	44,500	2	89,000		
Systems Analyst	42,000	2	84,000		
Programmer Analyst	34,000	2	68,000		
Programmer	28,500	4	114,000	11	555,000
			CENTRAL SITE TOTAL		2,885,500
END USER DEPARTMENTS (4)					
LAN/WAN Specialist	41,000	1	41,000	4	164,000
PC System Developer	35,000	1	35,000	4	140,000
CASE Tool Specialist	48,000	1	48,000	4	192,000
Associate Consultant	36,500	1	36,500	4	146,000
			END USER DEPTS. TOTAL		642,000
			ANNUAL DIRECT SALARY		3,527,500
			ANNUAL HW/SW (5 yrs.)		1,384,000
			TOTAL		4,911,500
			PER-END USER COST		2,455

Decentralized system

Box 9.5 shows an entirely decentralized system with no IT control. IT provides only a consulting and support service. This system is based upon four departments that have defined, highly heterogeneous systems.

Box 9.6 shows a considerably reduced central staff. However, the costs incurred by each department are enormous. The duplication of effort, over-specialization of skills, and local control of enterprise-level functions have created a pathologically expensive culture. Box 9.6 also shows department staffing costs.

Table 9.4 summarizes the total costs of decentralized computing. Hardware costs approximate the total hardware costs of a mainframe, and costs of ownership are well above those of the mainframe or distributed alternative.

DECENTRALIZED SYSTEM

Department 1	No.	Hardware	Software Environment
	1000	Personal computers	OS/2, Oracle client, TCP/IP
	16	Group servers	Unix, Oracle server, TCP/IP
	1	Department server	Unix, Oracle server, TCP/IP
			SNMP management system

Department 2	No.	Hardware	Software Environment
	500	Personal computers	Windows, Oracle client, NetBIOS
	1	Department server	Windows NT AS, Oracle server, NetBIOS
			SMS management system

Department 3	No.	Hardware	Software Environment
	500	Personal computers	Windows, NetWare, SPX/IPX
	20	Group servers	NetWare 4.0
			NLMS management system

Department 4	No.	Hardware	Software Environment
	1000	Personal computers	Windows, Oracle client, SPX/IPX
	1	Department server	Unix, Oracle server, SPX/IPX
			SNMP management system

Compared costs

The staffing costs for two extreme approaches and one moderate approach to computing are shown in Table 9.5.

A column that must not be overlooked is the Profit per User column, which suggests that the horrendous costs of decentralization have been worthwhile since they generate an enormous revenue that might not be achievable in an IT bureaucratic culture. A successful enterprise must succeed in keeping this profit-per-user number central to its strategy.

Dynamics of decision making

Coherent computing requires carefully defined degrees of freedom. It is not possible to manage investment by IT fiat or high-management dictum. It can

9.6 DECENTRALIZED SYSTEM: STAFFING

	Salary	Number	Total Salary	Group Number	Group Salary
VP MIS*	88,000	1	88,000		
MIS DIRECTOR	74,000	1	74,000	2	162,000
Central Staffing					
SYSTEMS AND PROGRAMMING					
Manager	65,000	1	65,000		
Software Engineer	43,500	2	87,000		
Systems Analyst	42,500	2	85,000		
PC System Developer	35,000	2	70,000	7	307,000
TECHNICAL SERVICES					
Manager	70,000	1	70,000		
CASE Tool Specialist	48,000	2	96,000		
Senior Consultant	47,000	3	141,000		
Associate Consultant	36,500	4	146,000	10	453,000
DATA BASE					
Data Base Administrator	50,000	2	100,000	2	100,000
TELECOMMUNICATIONS					
Manager	60,500	1	60,500		
Telecom Specialist	44,000	1	44,000		
LAN/WAN Specialist	41,000	1	41,000	3	145,500
EDUCATION					
Manager	43,000	1	43,000		
Curriculum Developer	34,000	3	102,000		
Instructor	31,000	5	155,000		
			CENTRAL STAFFING TOTAL		1,467,500

only be managed by a cooperative and mutually convincing process in which the end user groups and IT define the framework for an ongoing direction.

The process is based upon an authority/function matrix, an example of which is shown in Table 9.6. The columns N, A, I, E, and Im represent levels of control for IT. For N (null), the end user function has complete authority/responsibility. For A, an end user function can consult with IT but can ignore any IT views. IT publishes "guidelines." For I, IT has escalation rights to impose its "standards." For E, IT is the final authority and enforcer of its rules. For Im, IT

Hardware/Software	$11,222,000
Annual Hardware/Software	2,244,400
Personnel	5,276,500
Total	$18,742,900
Per User	$9,371

Table 9.4　Costs of decentralized computing.

DECENTRALIZED SYSTEM: STAFFING *(continued)*

Department Staffing	Department 1	Department 2	Department 3	Department 4
SYSTEMS AND PROGRAMMING				
Manager	58,000	58,000	58,000	58,000
Senior Project Leader	55,000	–	110,000	110,000
Project Leader	89,000	89,000	–	89,000
Systems Analyst	84,000	84,000	–	84,000
Programmer Analyst	102,000	68,000	103,000	136,000
Programmer	28,500	–	–	114,000
PC System Developer	105,000	70,000	70,000	–
TECHNICAL SERVICES				
Manager	56,000	56,000	–	–
Systems Programmer	42,000	–	50,000	–
CASE Tool Specialist	48,000	96,000	96,000	–
Senior Consultant	47,000	47,000	–	94,000
Associate Consultant	146,000	36,500	73,000	–
DATA BASE				
Data Base Administration	50,000	50,000	–	–
Data Base Analyst	86,000	86,000	86,000	86,000
TELECOMMUNICATIONS				
Telecom Specialist	44,000	–	–	44,000
LAN/WAN Specialist	82,000	82,000	41,000	82,000
OPERATIONS				
Shift Supervisor	32,000	32,000	64,000	64,000
Operator	44,000	44,000	–	–
DEPARTMENT TOTALS	1,198,500	898,500	751,000	961,000
COMBINED DEPARTMENT TOTAL	3,809,000			
CENTRAL SITE TOTAL	1,467,500			
OVERALL TOTAL	5,276,500			

is the sole source of that particular function—it supplies the technology or methodology.

Various flavors of the risk/reward culture determine the matrix. Issues are:

- Where a system sits on the enterprise information flow.

	Cost per User	Revenue per User	Profit per User
Mainframe	2,823	1,947	–876
Distributed	2,455	1,400	–1,055
Decentralized	9,371	23,457	14,086

Table 9.5   Compared costs.

	N	A	I	E	Im
Recognize application	•				
Assess benefit		•			
Assess risk				•	
Establish requirements		•			
Specify application		•			
Identify system			•		
Design application (acquire)			•		
Implement application			•		
Test application				•	
Install system				•	
Migrate application			•		
Maintain application			•		
Maintain system					•
Use application	•				
Operate system				•	
End application	•				

Table 9.6   Authority/function matrix.

Reprinted by kind permission of the manticore consultancy, New York.

- The complexity of a system.
- The willingness of a department to absorb skills.

A process of regularizing decision-making starts with sessions that complete a statement of current practice. IT and end user groups agree, not at an abstract policy level, but at an actual operational level on the current split. Then reasons for the power levels of each function are presented as the basis for a reform of the matrix over time. A set of matrices for each major end user is developed to represent responsibilities as they evolve over six-month periods. As these are developed in consensus, skills acquisition and platform plans can be put into place.

IT can define its own focus functions as it forms negotiated contracts for service offerings. The role of IT is to direct the management process and assure a proper balance between cost control and entrepreneurial use. This is an attempt to discover a management architecture.

Everybody should do what they are good at: IT has no particular competence recognizing business opportunities; users have no particular competence comparing Oracle7 to Sybase or Warp to Windows 95.

chapter 10

Due diligence

EXECUTIVE SUMMARY *Rates of change in technology create a new set of conditions for investing. Associated with particular technologies and technology strategies are particular risks. More fragile vendors may not deliver usable product, industry standard products may be delayed, prices may change unexpectedly, and technology investment may become unexpectedly obsoleted.*

Current industry investment practices do not have due diligence methods for assessing the nature of technology investment risks. There is often little consideration of economic issues when choosing technologies. When costs or benefit assessments are made, the numbers are often crude and raw, reflecting crude and raw processes.

There is a collection of known statistical and mathematical techniques available to investors for assessing risk. Due diligence requires of the IT community that it use them to qualify and refine its numbers and its assessments of benefits.

Rates of change

The new information industry poses new problems: A new decision space emerges with a different set of parameters than what we have become used to. It is more challenging and more risky, and techniques for handling or assessing risk have not yet matured.

Figure 10.1 shows the percentage of total IT budget invested in "legacy" technology over time. Each enterprise should have such a chart mapping the rate of decommitment to obsolete technology. The issues associated with a rate of change are listed above the curve as systems goals, key technologies, technology links, systems environments, and skills acquisition. Solutions to these issues, and the risks associated with solutions, pace the rate of change in an enterprise. The time line below the curve shows milestones along the pathway to the new generation.

Unfortunately, there is almost no organized data on costs, benefits, and organizational efficiency. Normalized costs and a project history on software projects are rare things to find. Complete data about systems cost of ownership and the distribution of such costs is equally rare. Unfounded, inconsistent, and

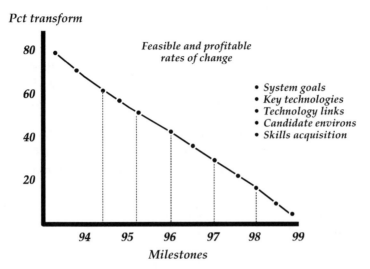

- 1994   Upper layer environment defined
- 1994   Scaffolding defined
- 1994   Education begins
- 1994   New hiring begins
- 1995   Portfolio applications identified, options analysed
- 1996   First delivery of new components, new applications in portfolio
- 1997   Second tier applications defined: ICASE Objects technology
- 1997   Global directory integrated management
- 1998   Technology evolution complete
- 1998   Desktop management in place
- 1999   Scaffolding dismantled
- 1999   Equipment replacement

Absorbing new technology

Reprinted by kind permission of MTS, Ashford, Middlesex, England.

Figure 10.1 Strategy time chart.

inaccurate statements about costs are constantly being made in unwholesome political contexts by partially informed people.

There is almost no organized technology transfer process that introduces new technology in a planned way and takes it from proof of concept to prototype to production. Money is spent on little backroom projects that are never brought to the mainstream.

Both value and cost analysis are difficult. Value analysis is frequently judgmental, qualitative, and political. Cost analysis is complicated by the fast-changing rate in technology and increasing complexity in the decision space. By and large, the tools of decision theory are not applied in mainstream information technology investment processes. Financial analysis and forecasting techniques, risk analysis, optimization theory, and queuing theory are not common practice in developing technology strategies.

Enormous sums are "invested" in information technology. Much less of this is under control than stockholders and enterprise management think.

Technology investment must have an auditable process. This process must include:

- coherent and complete strategies and architectures
- reasonable time scales
- methodically defined benefits and costs
- adequate risk-assessment refinement of costs.

Uncertainties about rates of culture change and rates of technology maturity must be factored into the decision process.

An economic framework

A business activity must have a stated economic goal, such as:

- maximize profit
- maximize revenue
- minimize cost
- bind profit goals with cost constraints.

There are admitted difficulties in quantifying benefits and measuring costs accurately. Despite these difficulties, a coherent technology investment strategy requires a statement of economic intent.

The strategy involves establishing the ratio between benefit and cost for any investment. A production function determines the output per unit of input. In macroeconomics this function describes how much oil or labor is necessary, for example, to produce a particular gross domestic product. It is a measure of the efficiency of a process.

Times of great change can involve dramatic changes in the ratio of input to output. The oil or labor needed by the U.S. to achieve a certain production

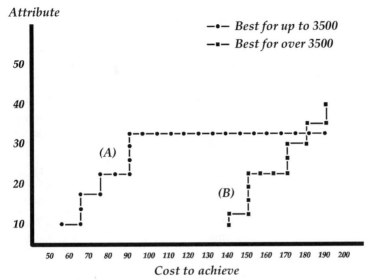

Reprinted by kind permission of MTS, Ashford, Middlesex, England.

Figure 10.2 Production functions.

level, for example, has been seriously reduced since the early 1970s. Similarly, the investment in hardware and software needed to produce a given amount of benefit has been greatly reduced since the early 1980s.

Figure 10.2 shows two production functions. The x-axis shows the investment to achieve an output (y-axis). These particular functions show the investment needed to achieve various production levels. Function A is optimal for producing up to 3,500 units. Function B is optimal for producing above 3,500 units. Function A cannot produce more than 3,500 units, but function B is inefficient for production of less than 3,500 units. To determine an appropriate investment in either the technology of Function A or B, it is necessary to know the probable level of needed production (greater or less than 3,500 units).

Figure 10.3 suggests the basis for some investment behavior. Note that the line "benefit/cost 1.7" does not intersect with a production function. This means that no investment can achieve the attribute (perhaps transactions per second, or tps) for the cost under the line. There is just no way of doing it—it is, literally, off the scale. The production function "benefit/cost .85" intersects the production function at about 175 tps. Because the benefit/cost curve intersects with the production function, there is an investment that can be made to achieve 175 tps. Unhappily, it is not a wise investment, since it only pays back $0.85 on the dollar.

It is necessary to define goals crisply. There may be a good business reason to maximize revenue even if that diminishes profit. A company in an early part of its product curve may wish to achieve market share at the cost of less total profit. When market share is achieved, the strategy may be revisited and a profit optimization goal set in place of the revenue optimization goal.

Sometimes a cost minimization goal is unavoidable, despite the possible loss of greater profits. The risk of cost minimization goals is investment at a level

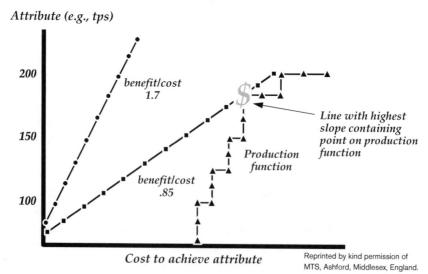

Figure 10.3   Maximize profit per unit of investment.

Reprinted by kind permission of
MTS, Ashford, Middlesex, England.

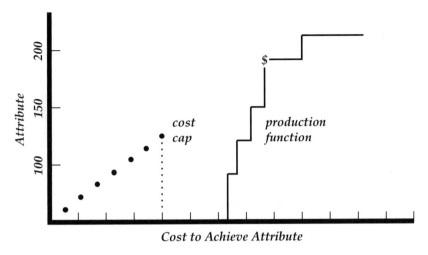

Figure 10.4 Minimizing costs and underinvestment.

that cannot achieve significant payback. That is, the funding of the production function cannot achieve a result. In this case, any money spent is pure waste.

Figure 10.4 extends the argument introduced by Figure 10.3 by showing that the maximum amount to be spent on achieving a goal does not intersect with the production function. For any benefit to be achieved, it is necessary to increase spending to the point of the dollar sign in the figure.

Figure 10.5 is another way of looking at optimum investment levels. The point at which optimum return is achieved is the point on the knee of the

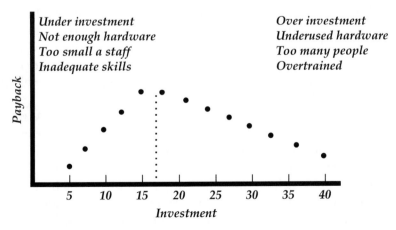

Figure 10.5 Investment level.

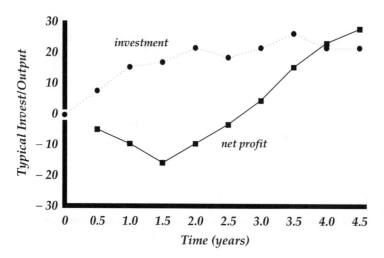

Figure 10.6   Production functions: payback of cost.

benefits/cost curve where an increase in spending generates a disproportionally large return. Beyond that point (the knee), returns are marginal; and while gross return is increased, the return on investment is decreased. Budget processes can distort an investment strategy.

On the figure (Figure 10.5), an investment at the knee generates the maximum profit that can be achieved from an investment in this technology. This maximum profit is achieved with an expenditure of around 16 investment units. Expenditure below this will produce less benefit; expenditure beyond this may increase the gross profit or revenue, but each increase will require a disproportionally large investment. A clear area of diminishing returns.

A key measurement of investment is how long it will take to recapture an investment and achieve a profit. Figure 10.6 shows a payback curve. An organization can set a limit on technology investment to technologies that will pay back within certain periods of time. If the limits are realistic and well thought out, this is not a bad policy.

The time line of Figure 10.6 shows levels of payback over time. At first, naturally, there is only expense. After 1.5 years, however, benefits begin, and the revenues become larger than the expenditures, so that they overtake in just under 4.0 years and turn the project profitable.

If the limits of payback are unrealistically short, there is a basis of serious diseconomic activity. A too-short payback period can lead to underinvestment, followed by a completely chaotic overinvestment as new technology is rushed in. There is a technology absorption rate that must be respected.

PRESENT VALUE

Information technology is an investment subject to the rules of calculating a return.

Return must be calculated with an appreciation for the current value of money over time. What is the worth of $100,000 in four years? The future worth of money is a basic calculation for economic analysis. It determines the pacing of investment, the rate of return over time in "real" dollars, and the optimum payment policy. Conversely, what is the value of $131,000 today?

$$\text{Future Worth} = \text{Value} \times (1 + i)^n$$

where Value is the current amount, i the inflation or interest rate, and n the number of years. The value of $100,000 in 4 years at 0.07 interest is $100,000 \times (1.07)^4 = $131,000.

$$\text{Present Worth} = \text{Value} \times (1 + i)^{-n}$$

Not surprisingly, at 0.07:

$$\$131,000 \times (1.07)^{-4} = \$100,000.$$

Net Present Value is a calculation using the value of money. It determines the value of revenues derived over time from investments made over time. It can be used to determine payment plans as well as investment policy—whether, for example, to pay up front or to pay over time.

Year	Revenue	Costs	Net Cash Flow	Present Value
1	1,800	1,245	555	555
2	1,800	1,245	555	516
3	1,800	1,245	555	483
Sum			1,665	1,554

Interest = 0.07
Time = 3 years
Net cash flow = $1,554
Initial cost = $1,200
Present value = $354

There may be qualitative, nonquantifiable constraints on achieving economic goals—for example, constraints in employee or customer goodwill, in the rate of availability of product, or in process life cycles. However, if maximum profit is not a goal, it is a good thing to know precisely why an enterprise is giving up maximum profit.

No accounting, statistical, or analytic technique should be inconsistent with the culture of the enterprise. Assessing paybacks, costs, and benefits is useful only if it is consistent with the "comfort" of the organization. Organizations differ widely in what makes them comfortable. An earlier chapter discussed the "aggressive," "moderate," and "conservative" enterprise. Figure 10.7 shows entirely different curves depending on whether a culture sees "lost opportunity benefits" as a risk of slow rates of change. Such an attitude marks an aggressive company. The figure shows a y-axis of costs of computing over time. One line, the upper, calculates costs, including lost opportunities due to insufficient investment; the lower line does not factor in such lost opportunity costs. An aggressive company, sensitive to the potentials of IT investment, perceives its costs as being considerably higher than a company not sensitive to unrealized benefits.

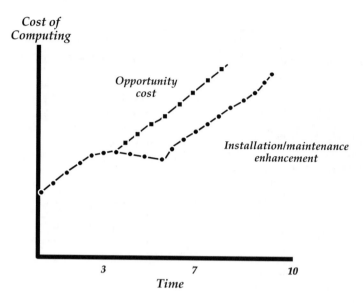

Figure 10.7   Cost of history.

Benefits

Assessing benefits is tremendously difficult. The range of ideas about what constitutes a benefit is as broad as human imagination. Some benefits that are unquantifiable at the time of an investment may turn out to be definitively important for an enterprise.

Information technology benefits may be tangible in that they show a definite accounting reduction of costs. Many benefits are intangible improvements over current practice or estimates of cost avoidance in the future. Some benefits are more abstract than others. What is the value of better decision-making or a more timely response to market need or a quicker product entry?

An issue in assessing benefit is who does it. A likely best practice is to permit the business people to determine the benefits and the IT community to determine the costs. IT has overstated its competence to be "proactive" in the business, and business units often are naive in determining costs. Everybody should do what they are good at.

Enterprise culture will determine what is perceived as a benefit. Productivity is currently a major focus, and organizations are trying to develop graphs such as Figure 10.8 for investment in information technology per employee. Productivity increases have been real and beyond expectation. Entire support

216

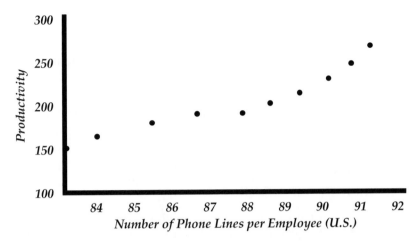

Figure 10.8 Productivity per number of phone lines/employee.

activities and specialized vendors have been eliminated, enabling principals to be able to generate their own presentations and documents. Travel budgets are reducible as workgroup computing improves its simulation of a conference.

All apparently unquantifiable areas can be "quantified" by a process of convergence called a delphi process. The best guesses of informed and responsible parties are filtered through a mechanism that achieves a consensus. With the lack of any alternative, the consensus of experts is the best one can do. Delphi processes are commonly used for disaster-avoidance consensus but may be used to quantify any area.

Cost and risk

We are more aware of the difficulty of assessing benefits than of the difficulty of assessing costs. Yet, it is more often cost overruns than benefit disappointments that dismay us.

With a fast rate of technological change and increasing systems complexity, simple assessments of cost become less and less reliable. More-sophisticated cost determination is required to support more-sophisticated decisions about technology investment. Some aspects of decision theory must necessarily be introduced to investment processes. An expanded use of financial analysis, probability and statistics, risk analysis, and optimization theory (linear programming) constituting an engineering of investment processes must support due diligence.

Nature of risk

IT seriously underestimates risk because it does not understand the degree to which it is not in control of its activities and technologies.

Risk involves uncertainty. There is "smooth uncertainty"—marginal changes in interest rates, incremental changes in product price, and slight delays in availability. But there is also singular or catastrophic uncertainty that can defeat an investment strategy—the disappearance of a vendor, equipment that is intrinsically flawed, software that is inherently nonfunctional, precipitous drops in price, or decommitment of product by a vendor.

It is necessary to factor risk into any technology investment strategy. Some assessment of future conditions and their probability of occurrence is a fundamental aspect of due diligence.

In technology, as in other investments, high risk is often a precondition for high reward. Undertakings with a high probability of success often offer only modest rewards. Degrees of risk associate with degrees of uncertainty and uncontrollability. When success depends on several uncontrollable factors whose occurrence is not known, one is at maximum risk.

10.3 RETURN ON INVESTMENT: ACCOUNTING RATE OF RETURN

Return on investment (ROI) is a widely used metric. ROI is the average present value of revenue minus the initial investment.

The table shows a present value revenue of $5,544 over five years. The average annual return was $5,544 ÷ 5 = $1,109. On an initial investment of $6,000, a return of 18% was received ($1,109 ÷ $6,000).

Year	Revenue	Present Value Revenue
1	1,000	1,000
2	1,200	1,122
3	1,300	1,135
4	1,400	1,143
5	1,500	1,144
Sum	6,400	5,544

When there is some knowledge of the probability of things going wrong, this knowledge can be used to adjust cost factors. This knowledge may be based on inferences drawn from collected data, on subjective estimates of probability, or on consensus estimates of probability.

Data and risk assessment

Data has value to the extent that it improves the quality of risk assessment. The value of data used in decision-making can be estimated. The costs of the worst possible result of the worst possible investment and the best possible result of the best possible investment can be estimated. The value of data is the difference between these possible investment decisions after data has been collected and used to refine the decision process.

It is worthwhile to collect data on the probability of negative or positive events if the cost of collecting, retaining, and processing that data is less than the difference between the worst and best seat-of-the-pants decisions.

If there is a million dollar override risk for each software project and it would cost about half a million dollars to collect and maintain software project histories in normalized form, it is clearly worthwhile to do so.

10.4 NONQUANTIFIABLE CRITERIA

Cost to quantify too high

Quantification too political

Benefit classes:

- Cost reduction or avoidance
- Error reduction
- Increased flexibility
- Increased capacity
- Improved responsiveness
- Improved management control
- Improved management planning

Risk and consensus

Without data, there can still be judgments and useful guesses. If one needs to assess the probability that a project will not be completed by a certain date, that there will be given increases in load over time, that inflation will increase or decrease, convergent expert opinion is a good guide if the consensus is achieved by a formal and controlled process.

Delphi processes are appropriate. Concerned persons and experts experience a process through which agreement is reached on the probability of an event and on the economic impact of that event, should it occur. The results can be used to derive estimates of probable costs in the face of bad surprises.

Executives, after all, get paid for judgment and leadership. Consensus estimates may be used to smooth risk somewhat.

Risk and statistics

Risk assessment, like quality control, is inextricably linked with statistics, in particular with probability. The probability theory necessary for due diligent risk assessment is less difficult to use than collecting the data used by the

PROBABILITY

INDEPENDENT EVENTS
Joint Probability of Independent Events
Prob. A × Prob. B = Joint Probability
0.10 × 0.05 = 0.0050
Probability over Populations
Probability that a unit will fail = 0.01
"Of 100,000 units, 1,000 will fail"
Not the probability of failure for one unit

NATURAL PROBABILITY (Law of Large Numbers)
Dice, pennies

ARTIFICIAL PROBABILITY
Data
Judgment

USES
Probability of not working by date
Probability of equipment cost increase over time
Probability of increase in traffic

RELATED EVENTS
C1   0.05 inflation
C2   0.12 inflation
C3   0.08 interest rate
C4   0.15 interest rate
Probability of C3 = .08, given that
C1 = .05 is "high."

probability equations. In addition to statisticians, there are uncountable computer programs able to calculate the needed elements of good risk assessment and good due diligent guessing. There is needed only the will and investment to collect the appropriate data.

10.6   SKEW AND VARIANCE

Any collection of numbers has different tendencies for numbers to group themselves. Simple measures of centralizing tendencies are average, mode, and median. Of equal interest is the tendency of numbers to diverge and vary. This can be measured by their difference from the average of the group.

The average of the numbers on the table is ≈11. AvgDif is the difference between each number and the average. Sometimes this is a positive number, sometimes a negative. The process wishes to factor out positive and negative, so it squares the numbers.

The Variance of a list is the sum of all of these squares divided by one less than the number of numbers.

$$\text{Variance} = \sum \frac{[x(i) - m]^2}{n - 1}$$

Standard Deviation = $\sqrt{\text{Variance}}$

This is a basic measure of "skew" used to estimate very key ideas about what one can expect to happen. It is also the basis of many more advanced measures of skew. Skew is a metaphor for risk.

	AvgDif	Square
10	−1	1
13	3	9
15	4	16
8	−5	25
9	−2	4
Sum 54		55

Average = 54/5 ≈ 11
Sum of squares of AvgDif = 55
Variance = 55/(5 − 1) = 13.75
Standard deviation = 3.71

Value	Probability	Adjusted Value
−10,000,000	0.10	−1,000,000
−6,000,000	0.15	−900,000
−4,000,000	0.25	−1,000,000
0	0.10	0
1,000,000	0.25	250,000
3,000,000	0.15	450,000
Expected value		2,200,000

Table 10.1   Project table of expected values.

There is a need for a few basic notions of probability, which are shown in Box 10.5. In addition, one needs some idea of the tendency of data to be different. We are familiar, from discussions in many areas, of various measures of skew and distribution (see Box 10.6).

An important idea that brings variance and probability together is the idea of an "expected value." This expected value is the probability of a series of probable outcomes times the value of each outcome. For example, consider Table 10.1. A project is to be undertaken that can work out in a variety of ways. At worst, it can cost the company $10,000,000. At best, it can make the company a $3,000,000 profit. There are intervening possibilities as well that have different economic results.

The expected value is the sum of the possible values times their probabilities of occurrence. For this to be of any use, of course, it is necessary that the possible results be correctly defined and the probability of their occurrence well understood.

The probability may be natural in that it is mathematically determined like the probability of heads or tails on a coin flip; the probability may be derived from empirical data; or it may be derived by a delphi process or from individual subjective judgment. What one does with the result depends on the culture.

Risk and strategy

A number of strategies can be used in the face of different expected values. Appropriate strategies are determined by the degree to which the organization is risk tolerant or risk adverse, that is, the degree to which it is aggressive, moderate, or conservative.

Project	Maximum Return	Minimum Return	Expected Return
System A	250,000	−110,000	70,000
System B	75,000	40,000	17,500
System C	300,000	−500,000	−100,000
System D	500,000	−60,000	40,000

Table 10.2   Potential returns for projects.

Table 10.2 shows a number of possible systems that produce potential maximum losses if they fail and maximum benefits if they work, and each has an expected return. The organization must choose.

There are various strategies that select a project. The maximize-profit strategy will select System D. The minimize-loss (cost) strategy will select System B (highest minimum return). The expected-return strategy will select System A.

The maximum, minimum, or expected return on an investment is not a direct indicator of its value to an organization. It is necessary to associate judgmental utility functions from the culture to see if the risk is worthwhile for the expected result.

People will make judgments about the utility for them: whether it is better for them, their department, or the company, in their view, to invest in A, B, or D. The utility of projects is determined by a survey of perceptions. An aggressive culture will behave differently than a conservative culture.

Whatever the economic utility, an investment must be appropriate for the culture. The culture must be up to the challenge. How an enterprise encourages appropriate risks but constrains "cowboys" is an essential problem of large corporations. Reward systems and explicit penalty systems are a great aid in this.

Risk and projection

The accounting community likes to have single cost numbers. Unhappily, true cost numbers are highly complex and represent, or should represent, curves, assessments, and probabilities. The true cost of anything is a statement such as "It will cost Y with probability A, X with probability B, and Z with probability C." Few accounting communities are up to this. What they do deserve are numbers with the risks factored in, based on wholesome risk assessment processes.

An example of a risk-modified cost assessment is Chebyshev's inequality, which is a measure of risk derived from skew. It provides an expected value for

10.7	**RISK OF PROJECT COST OVERRIDE**

Expected cost = $500,000
Standard deviation = $150,000
Number of standard deviations = k

Cost	Deviation	$1/k$	$1/k^2$	Probability
650,000	150,000	1/1	1/1	<1.00
800,000	300,000	1/2	1/4	<0.25
950,000	450,000	1/3	1/9	<0.11
1,550,000	1,050,000	1/7	1/49	<0.02

For $k = 2$, $\$150,000 \times k = \$300,000$; $1/k^2 = 1/4$
For $k = 3$, $\$150,000 \times k = \$450,000$; $1/k^2 = 1/9$

an undertaking depending on the probability of certain occurrences. It provides the probability of deviation by more than a certain amount. It is less refined, but simpler, than other techniques.

The Chebyshev inequality is a rather complex statistical concept, and only its intent need be understood. It is part of an arsenal of weapons used for statistical analysis in many disciplines and, happily, is available in various analytic and statistical software packages. Clearly, insights derived from such tools provide the definition of an envelope of risk within which decisions can be made and funding needs estimated.

For example, here is an estimate of cost for a software project. In this calculation, the expected cost is $500,000 and the calculated standard deviation is $150,000. The table in Box 10.7 shows that the probability of a cost override of $300,000 is less than 25%, and the probability of a cost override of $450,000 is less than 11%. The probability of a cost override of any magnitude is the inverse of the square of the number of standard deviations. This is in accord with Chebyshev's inequality.

One wants projects, of course, with positive net values and small deviations, which is why one wants standardized project processes and procedures, and why it is necessary to keep data on project history to compute the standard deviations.

Cost of being wrong

Technology investments involve numerous assumptions about the availability of technology components. In the current environment, for example, a project may depend upon the availability of integrated LAN management, desktop management, object design technologies, and a global directory that can be used to find all resources.

Table 10.3 shows an assessment of the probability that key technologies needed for a system will be available at certain times. On the basis of data, expert opinion, or personal judgment, the table shows that there is a certain

Technology	Probablities		
	1 Year	2 Years	3 Years
Integrated LAN management	0.4	0.3	0.2
Desktop management	0.4	0.3	0.2
I-CASE objects	0.4	0.3	0.2
Global directory	0.3	0.2	0.2

Table 10.3   Availability of key technology.

probability that each technology will be available for use in one year, two years, or three years. There is a 0.4 chance that the promised technology will be a year late, etc.

The table is an assessment of the risk of lateness of needed technologies. Table 10.4 associates values with the availability of technologies at certain times. These values may be associated with increased development costs and delays in putting a system into production, thereby shortening its life. If LAN management technology is available this year, it would be worth $1,500,000 in avoided systems cost. If it is a year late, it loses value because of incurred costs during the period of its delay.

Table 10.5 computes the expected values of these technologies, given the value at any time and the probability of their availability at any time. A cost prediction for a system based on these technologies could be done using the expected value figures for the key technologies.

Other statistics

There are various forecasting techniques for risk assessment. Simple techniques involve moving averages or weighted moving averages and exponential

Technology	Value Now	Value: 1 yr	Value: 2 yr	Value: 3 yr
Integrated LAN management	1,500,000	900,000	600,000	300,000
Desktop management	900,000	540,000	360,000	180,000
I-CASE objects	2,600,000	1,800,000	1,200,000	720,000
Global directory	2,500,000	1,400,000	1,000,000	720,000

Table 10.4   Time value of pacing technologies.

Technology	Now			1 Year			2 Years			3 Years		
	Value ($million)	Probability	Expected Value ($million)	Value ($million)	Probability	Expected Value ($million)	Value ($million)	Probability	Expected Value ($million)	Value ($million)	Probability	Expected Value ($million)
LAN management	1.5	0.1	.15	.9	0.6	.54	.6	0.7	.42	.36	0.8	.04
Desktop management	.9	0.1	.09	.54	0.6	.32	.36	0.7	.26	.18	0.8	.02
I-CASE objects	2.6	0.1	.26	1.8	0.6	1.4	1.2	0.7	.84	.72	0.8	.57
Global directory	2.5	0.2	.50	1.4	0.7	1.0	1.0	0.7	.80	.72	0.8	.57

Table 10.5   Expected value of key technologies over time.

smoothing (adjusting a forecast with a percentage of a previous period's deviation from actual). More-sophisticated techniques involve correlation, regression, and general linear programming models.

It is not necessary, or advisable, to do everything by the numbers, and often formal techniques have not been useful because their use depends on a simplification of reality that often renders them naive. However, technology investment is about value and cost, profit and loss, and risk and reward; and it is impossible to avoid the use of some level of economic statistical techniques if we are to determine strategies with confidence.

There's no safety in numbers (or in anything else)

All difficult choices involve danger. For an aggressive company, there is the danger that new technologies may not be at industrial strength; they may lack tools and services; they may introduce new forms of complexity; and they may prove more difficult to establish than expected. For a conservative company, there are the dangers of falling out of the competitive envelope because of bad technology. Applications will continue to be late with maximum maintenance costs; and there will be productivity lags, missed strategic opportunities, and an unwholesome reliance on vendor strategies.

Decisions must be made. How much can or should be invested in qualifying each number remains unclear. The value of information is what it earns us. We must know what is necessary to know.

Should systems be built to peak performance or average performance? Is it worthwhile spending the money to determine if a delay at the peak will cost business, customers, and revenue? How much should be spent to determine if it is useful to break up linked applications, or to redevelop applications completely? How much should be spent on technology tracking, modeling, risk assessment, prototyping, etc.?

Each enterprise must answer these issues in its own value system. What must be true, however, is that the process of technology investment be in some sense controlled and that it reflect the orderly procedures of sensible people practicing due diligence.

chapter 11

Software development
and objects

227

EXECUTIVE SUMMARY   There seems always to have been a software crisis and a set of promises about how to resolve it. Clearly, there has been progress in programming methodology, quality, technology, and management since 1955, when the first programming started. High-level languages like COBOL and PL/I have permitted large populations of people to become "programmers." However, there is a feeling that the state of the art has been pretty much unmoved for some time. There is a great sense of disappointment with two decades of promises about new techniques to improve the productivity of programming or the quality of code. There is some feeling that the best thing one can say about programming is that now one can do less of it; that is, solutions can come from buying packages, or from extensions to the data base technology, that eliminate a good deal of traditional programming. Much information can be accessed through nonprogrammer queries to data bases that once would have required program development projects.

In general, it may well be true that a problem of delayed access to information, delayed projects, etc. may be best solved without placing hope in software development methodologies. This observation, however, comes at a time when we have a new set of dramatic promises about software development breakthroughs. "Objects," we are told, will finally bring it all together and provide the technology we have been looking for. This chapter explores that claim and concludes it is probably not so. Objects leave unsolved many of the underlying problems with the software development process.

Another software promise, Rapid Development, enables quick "slicing and dicing" of data from many systems. It is closely associated with data warehousing techniques, as it has the ability to draw from multiple data bases.

What is most maddening about this area is that there is so little solid and usable data, and there have been so few intelligent experiments conducted over the vast experience we have had with programming. We roam in a wilderness of wild claims and counterclaims and no useful data at all.

CHAPTER 11:   SOFTWARE DEVELOPMENT AND OBJECTS

Software development

This topic deserves, and has received, volumes of its own. The true cost of software development has so many aspects that it is difficult to even find agreement on proper metrics. Many have despaired of any finer measure than whether or not the programs were delivered on time. There is almost no carefully kept normalized corporate data on development experience, and a very small body of serious experiment. Comparative numbers for different techniques usually involved comparisons of projects with absolutely no control at all over other variables, population characteristics, project complexity, etc.

In general, software development cost involves an appreciation of:

1 *Productivity issues:* What makes people productive when they conceive, create, test, and support software? In addition to the processes, methodologies, and technologies of software development, there are myriad sociological, demographic, and psychological concerns.

2 *Complexity issues:* What makes a program complicated? Why are some programs inherently more expensive to create than others? Is the complexity of the problem the root of complexity, or is there something about the nature of programming that adds complexity to the solution of even simple problems?

3 *Organizational issues:* How should the activity be organized and managed? Should program developers work for professional IT management or for the business management that has the problems?

These issues must be addressed in a time of rapid technological change. Data bases have simplified programs by removing the necessity of navigating through unneeded data. There are constant changes (and promises) in the area of software development tools and technology. Each decade has its own miracle cure that seems eventually to fade into history, leaving COBOL programming practices unchanged. There seems to be no program development methodology so bad that it is not more efficient in its last use than its "improvement" is in its first.

There is no software crisis in that software problems are chronic and continuing. However, there are some helpful principles:

1 There are known curves, such as the Rayleigh curve (an empirically derived equation for the behavior of software projects), that help achieve estimates of cost and models of resource allocation. They are rarely used. There are also known curves for mapping development costs over various times for

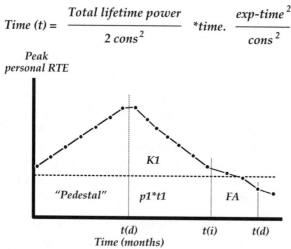

$$\text{Time } (t) = \frac{\textit{Total lifetime power}}{2\ cons^2} *time. \frac{exp\text{-}time^2}{cons^2}$$

Begin at non-0
Total Development $=k=k1+P1*ti+Ka+FA$
Constant$=$ artificial to force peak at $T(d)$
  39% effort done at this point
Peak $= K/t(d)^e$

Figure 11.1 A proper allocation of resources to a software project at different stages. The total development investment is a function of people, time, and productivity. This figure is not intended for use in calculation but to illustrate the existence of well-known resource use patterns.

projects of various sizes. The equations are based on large amounts of empirical data, they are counterintuitive, and they are much better than the simple and inadequate cost techniques most commonly used. Figure 11.1 shows a Rayleigh curve. Maintaining normalized data of project history (a rare practice) would improve costing enormously. But repositories of normalized project data usable to estimate new projects are rare in America.

2 Technology for software development is a great element in the array of factors affecting cost. But programmer quality, experience, and use of good programming practices can have an equal or greater effect. Introducing a powerful new methodology into an environment where good software practices are not used will not improve software development.

3 The most effective way to maximize cost and minimize quality is to schedule a project with a too-short duration and try to solve the problem by increasing staff size. Figures 11.2 shows that as the due date of a project is compressed the maximum number of people needed to achieve it becomes dramatically

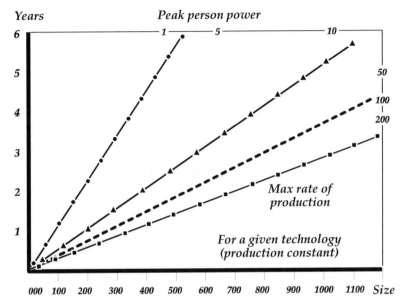

Years   *Peak person power*

Flow rate: max size/time
As time increases, power peak decreases
Gradient establishes minimum time: effort/duration sq =14.7

Figure 11.2 **The relationship of time, peak person power, and maximum project size. (The right vertical axis is an extension of the upper horizontal axis.)**

larger. For a project of 400 modules ("Size" on the horizontal axis) to be completed in 6 years, a peak staffing of 2 people is required. For the same project to be completed in 1 year, 200 people are required. Figure 11.3 shows how additional staffing actually delays projects and increases costs.

4 The metrics are not reliable and often do not reflect what true cost or scale is. Never trust KLOCS (thousands of lines of code) or Function Points, as they do not state true complexity or productivity, are biased toward batch-oriented concepts of complexity, and are usually reduced to numbers of statements in known programming languages anyway.

5 Software development cost must be minimized by tools in the earliest stages of an application. Good design technology minimizes maintenance costs and maximizes quality.

6 The payback period for significant improvements in methodology and technology is too long for most organizations to wait. Figure 11.4 shows this.

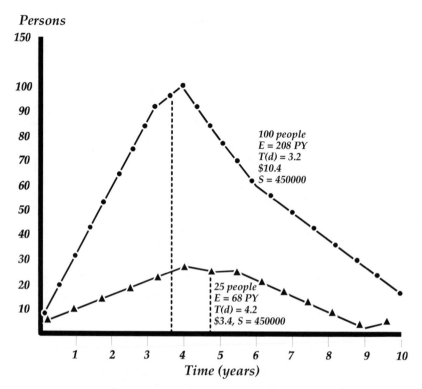

Figure 11.3 A comparison between two similar projects, one staffed with 100 people and one staffed with 25. The larger project took longer and cost over twice as much.

7 Most attractive tools do not scale. The organization has the choice, as it has always had, to abandon tools for projects that are too large, or to limit projects to those that the tools can handle. A larger number of companies "do not do large apps."

8 Buy when you can. Or look to data base technologies to address issues of sudden needs for new slices of data.

The software development cycle

There are various articulations of the sequences of events that occur from the idea of a computer application to operational, business-relevant code. In a general way, people agree that there should be the following:

232

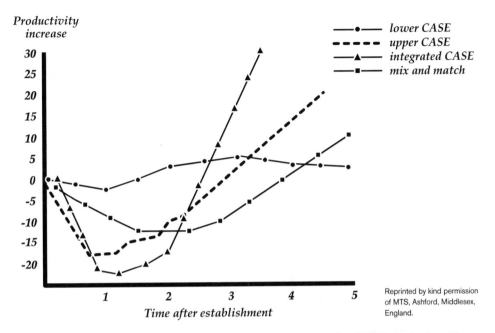

Productivity
increase

Legend:
——•—— lower CASE
— — — upper CASE
——▲—— integrated CASE
——■—— mix and match

Time after establishment

Reprinted by kind permission of MTS, Ashford, Middlesex, England.

Figure 11.4 Costs and technologies across the life cycle: the CASE strategies. There are increases and decreases in software development productivity for different development technologies over time. The greater the potential impact of the technology, the later a benefit occurs.

- statement of requirements—what is needed
- specification—what requirements will be met
- design—a description of how specifications will be achieved
- build—how programs will be developed to honor the design
- test—how the programs will be shown to fulfill the specification
- maintenance—how programs will be kept business relevant.

But despite general agreement on these abstractions, there is little consensus on exactly what is done in each phase of development, what the relative cost is of each phase, how productivity is measured across phases, where errors are introduced, and how the long-term cycle, the efforts after first production, should be managed. Figure 11.5 shows some ideas of the "life cycle."

The classical cascade cycle involved a complete artifact at every level. A statement of requirements was produced that supposedly constrained the specification. The specification, in turn, supposedly constrained the design. The design constrained the development, etc. For many years this was considered the proper, and only, way to develop software. It had some serious drawbacks.

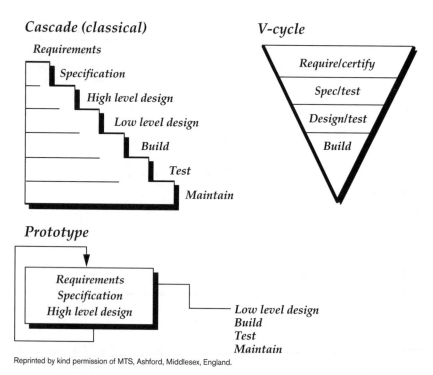

Cascade (classical)

Requirements
Specification
High level design
Low level design
Build
Test
Maintain

V-cycle

Require/certify
Spec/test
Design/test
Build

Prototype

Requirements
Specification
High level design

Low level design
Build
Test
Maintain

Reprinted by kind permission of MTS, Ashford, Middlesex, England.

Figure 11.5   Life cycle: cycle concepts.

The artifacts at different phases were generally narrative documents. There was no way to assure that they were complete, consistent, and correct. There was also no way to assure that they truly constrained the work of the effort that came after them. How does one assure that programming respects design intent if the statement of design intent is informal and fuzzy? Another negative of the cascade cycle is that many of the best design ideas occur late in the development cycle, when more is understood about an application.

The notion of rapid prototyping develops as techniques for approximate descriptions of intent mature. The process involves a series of iterations on the requirement or specifications until there is agreement that the software functions as desired. Then a production process is entered to create a robust version of the software whose function is understood. It is a technique profitably practiced across the application interface elements of a program.

The V-cycle of the figure addresses a notion that the life cycle should be symmetric, and the processes of building software factored into the processes of designing. In the classic cascade, testing and later-stage activities were not

Analysis	12%
Specification and early design	18%
Detailed design	15%
Code and debug	20%
Testing	35%
All preproduction costs	34%
All postproduction costs	66%

Table 11.1 Distribution of costs.

addressed until late in the cycle. In the V-cycle, these activities are integrated with design so that the underlying structure of the software can facilitate testing.

There is little uniform opinion on the distribution of costs across all of the phases. The author has found the numbers in Table 11.1 to be useful and to stand up to tests of experience.

The astonishing fact that two-thirds of total programming costs occur in the "maintenance phase" should focus attention on how that phase is being managed. Many feel the concept should be defined out of existence—that maintenance, since most of it is program revision, is best understood as iteration over the development cycle, by the same quality of team that originally developed the application.

The numbers should also focus attention on how little payback there is in improving development programming as opposed to improving specifications and design. This is the basis for interest in the "upper CASE" tools that address activities in the early phases.

CASE

CASE (Computer Aided Software Engineering) is a catchall phrase for tools that improve software development processes. CASE tools span a wide variety of type and function. Upper CASE tools are those that provide support for specification and high-level design activities. Lower CASE tools provide support for activities closer to programming. Integrated CASE tools attempt to span the entire life cycle.

CASE tools (see Box 11.1) come from different communities with different viewpoints. Some are very attached to a programming language. COBOL editors, for example, come with particular COBOL compilers. Some are associated with a method such as Composite Design or Structured Analysis. They are language independent and often require the hand development of code based upon their output. Others provide a methodology, such as matrix manipulation or finite-state machine definition, by which a problem solution can be stated in a quite formal manner. The tool generates code from the formal description of the problem and its solution.

11.1 SOFTWARE DEVELOPMENT ENVIRONMENTS–DIFFERENT SOURCES

Language-Centered
- Built around one language
- Interactive through life cycle

Structure-Oriented
- Language independent
- Manipulate program structures
- Application generators
- Matrix/state diagram

Toolkit Environments
- Collection of tools
- Configuration management
- Version control
- Language independent

Method-Based
- Particular specification and design methods
- Project management
- Structured design and analysis

11.2 CASE TOOL CHARACTERIZATION: "PERSONAL TOOL"

- Use PC as development platform
- Single-platform development
- Single user, small group
- Premium ease of use for casual users
- Quick learning curve
- Effectively generate GUI
- Coding in Basic for non-GUI
- SQL not in environment
- Quick prototype, rapid development
- Little emphasis on Information Engineering
- Run on "client side" only
- Cost $100–10,000
- Visual Basic
- ObjectVision
- Powersoft PowerBuilder
- Easel Workbench
- SQLWindows

Some tools come from the data base community and are specifically associated with particular data bases or data models. They are often associated with the SQL data access language and represent an attempt to reduce the programming problem to a data query and data access description problem.

In the current environment, with vast numbers of personal computers on laptops and desktops, a set of programming development tools has emerged for the single user of a single computer. They are characterized by easy usability, by appropriateness for small applications, and by the assumption that the PC is a closed and complete environment. The characteristics of these tools are given in Box 11.2.

There is an increasing number of client/server development tools aimed at applications requiring a service from a networked server. They are characterized in Box 11.3.

The taxonomy of tools is truly more complex than the scale or life cycle positioning of a tool. Various tools are aimed at professionals in various subject areas—at data base professionals, at end users, at "paraprogrammers," etc.

Many tools have significant penetration in particular envi-

11.3 CASE TOOL CHARACTERIZATION: "CLIENT/SERVER TOOL"

- Run in multiple environments (Unix, VMS, OS/2, Windows)
- Multiple team developers/workgroups/large projects
- Function for development organizations
- Extensive learning curves for professional user
- Desktop clients sections (multiple)
- Server sections (multiple)
- Oracle, Sybase, Ingres, Rdb, etc.
- Reliance on Information Engineering
- SQL inherent
- Provide heterogeneous DB access
- Integrates 3GL or 4GL with SQL
- Cost $2,000–200,000
- Uniface
- Smartstar
- ASK Ingres
- Windows 4GL
- Sybase
- Oracle

11.4 OBSTACLES

Tools do not scale

Cultural resistance
- Existing practice
- Existing tools

No hard proof of payback

Long-term cost insensitivity

Acquiring skills

Confusion of alternatives
- Differing technologies
- Differing methodologies

Organization
- User/developer relations
- Up-front cost
- Pilot requirements

ronments. Tool investment is a disputable thing in many companies. Some companies feel that tools should be standardized as an enterprise investment. Others feel that particular projects should pick (and pay for) their own tool sets. It is no easy thing to measure the economic impact of a particular tool investment. Calculating return requires an understanding of the true initial outlay, the ongoing costs, the costs of training, and the curve of achieving competence. One must have a carefully defined life cycle, a set of formalized methodologies, and a careful way of determining the impact of a tool.

A tool may increase productivity for only a given percentage of projects. For example, a particular tool may reduce effort by 0.30 in a phase that has 0.30 of costs, but be usable in only about 40% of the projects. Such a tool's payback is about 0.036 $(0.30 \times 0.30 \times 0.40)$ across the entire software development community across the life cycle. If the cost of programming without the tool is $1,000,000 across applicable projects, the savings with the tool will be $36,000, reducing the cost to $964,000. The savings per programmer-year must be more than the costs of purchase, training, etc. In general, tools become profitable rather late, and the more they address real issues the later they pay off.

Box 11.4 shows why so many IT people have become so difficult to convince about new software revolutions. Box 11.5 suggests why so many believe the process is not manageable.

Applications strategies

There must necessarily be a strategy relative to the development and management of an application portfolio. This strategy must address various dimensions:

1 Managing the portfolio.

2 Defining development activities.

3 Defining development architectures.

Each of these dimensions is an area of intense disputation and astonishing counterexample. Some companies are exploring the application portfolios to see what can be retired, what can be left alone, and what must be replaced, regardless of what implications this has for the hardware base. Other companies are assuming that whatever is now running must always be running. Some companies are continuing with decade-old COBOL-based methodologies on mainframes, while many are moving away from the mainframe as a development platform and even as a development target. Box 11.6 summarizes some issues in application architecture.

It is clearly necessary to determine what corporate standards are necessary to achieve the degrees of application migratability, portability, and interoperability deemed necessary over the next technology era. An architecture must specify the protocols and interfaces to be used in application development, and what protocols and interfaces to use in the run-time environment. In this way, a direction to open can be defined and sustained.

Box 11.7 characterizes application development activities by firms that may be considered aggressive, mainstream, or conservative.

APPLICATION STRATEGIES

Aggressive
- No more large applications
- Workstation/client/server development
- Old application redevelopment in CASE
- Abandon old applications
- Portability required (XPG/4)
- Client/server or distributed data base
- Production in objects with OOA
- Object data base pilots
- No new applications on mainframe

Mainstream
- Identifying client/server applications

- COBOL development mainstream
- Object pilots in C++
- Lower CASE tools
- Relational mainstream
- Increasing workstation use
- Increasing package acquisition

Conservative
- Primary COBOL project
- Mainframe used as development system
- Not yet big relational commitment
- Little off-load

Commitment to tools, movement from the mainframe, and interest in objects seem to be the defining criteria.

In all companies, the intrusion of data base–oriented tools is impressive. More than 50% of the new applications of some companies are derived from data base tools; and in about 25% of major companies, more than 75% of new applications come from data base tools.

There are also instances of re-engineering and reuse of old code, a subject to be taken up with objects.

Objects

The idea of an object is variously represented, from formal definitions to vague notions of a synonym for "thing." Different groups have different ideas about what an object is and what object-oriented is.

Objects have been the subject of some recent hype. Once again we have a miracle drug in software development, end user interfaces, and distributed computing. Objects are to give us revolutionary increases in productivity, usability, and interoperability. They can, according to *Business Week* cover, enable a diapered child to create programs.

The core idea of an object is that data is encapsulated by the actions that can be taken upon it. In Figure 11.6, the actions surrounding the data are programs (methods). All references and changes made to the data must be made by these programs. No other program can get to the data except by requesting an action

Create instance		Delete instance	
Calculate taxes	Employee name Employee salary Employee location Employee dependence		Modify salary
Modify dependents		Modify location	

Figure 11.6   Object.

from the surrounding methods. The data is encapsulated in the sense that it lives in a cocoon defined by the programs that can refer to it.

The idea of encapsulation and data hiding is quite old and has been a principle of software engineering for about twenty years. A newer idea of objects is that an object is a template, a model, from which instances can be generated. The name and address of the object "employee" provides a model for instances of "employees," as shown in Figure 11.7. Each time a new employee is created, the instance is created on the template of the object. The template represents data of a certain class or type.

A third idea of objects is strong typing. Each data element must have a type associated with it, and there are rules for the actions that can be taken on a type. This is a feature of 1970s academic programming languages. By typing, one means the essential nature of the object and the behavior one expects from it. At a very primitive level, a decimal number is a type of number whose behavior differs from a floating point number.

Create instance		Delete instance	
Calculate taxes	Brown, John $50,000 New York, N.Y. Spouse, 3		Modify salary
Modify dependents		Modify location	

Figure 11.7   Instance.

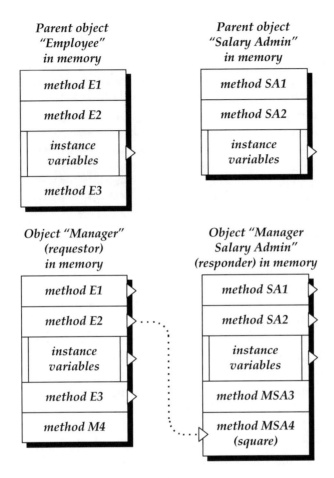

Parent object
"Employee"
in memory

| method E1 |
| method E2 |
| instance variables |
| method E3 |

Parent object
"Salary Admin"
in memory

| method SA1 |
| method SA2 |
| instance variables |

Object "Manager"
(requestor)
in memory

| method E1 |
| method E2 |
| instance variables |
| method E3 |
| method M4 |

Object "Manager
Salary Admin"
(responder) in memory

| method SA1 |
| method SA2 |
| instance variables |
| method MSA3 |
| method MSA4 (square) |

MESSAGE: "Manager" to "Manager Salary Admin": square of 9
MESSAGE: "Manager Salary Admin" to "Manager": 81

Figure 11.8 Objects in memory. Objects send messages to each other to invoke behaviors and request the results of those behaviors.

Objects may also use each other. An object wishing to invoke the behavior of another sends it a message, as in Figure 11.8.

Figure 11.8 is a representation of objects in memory. Object Employee is the parent object of object Manager. Object Salary Admin is the parent object of object Manager Salary Admin. The methods E1, E2, and E3 of object Employee are inherited by object Manager. Any activity of Manager involving the functions of E1, E2, and E3 will use the programming of object Employee. This is the true sense of inheritance. A derived object uses the same programming for its functions. Method M4 is the specialization of Manager that makes it a perfect subtype of Employee. Employee and Manager follow the strict rules of inheritance in that wherever Employee may be used in a system, Manager may be substituted for it. A similar relation is seen between Salary Admin and

Manager Salary Admin. Manager Salary Admin inherits two methods and is extended by its own methods MSA3 and MSA4.

None of the structures in Figure 11.8 have real data in them. Real data is represented in instances of these objects. The objects must point to their instances or exemplars for real operations. Exemplars of Employee, Manager, Salary Admin, and Manager Salary Admin are the true employees and managers of the enterprise.

While Manager is running, it requires the squaring of a data value in the instance for John Jones. The value for Jones is 9. It sends a message to Manager Salary Admin asking for the square of this value. Manager Salary Admin responds. The message contains the name of the object to do the activity, the activity that is to be done, and the value it is to be done on.

Encapsulation, template, and type are fundamental to object-based systems. Object-based systems have been in existence for some time, both commercially and in advanced technology. The IBM AS/400 and its predecessor, the S/38, are object based, meaning the system is organized into encapsulated structures with very particular characteristics.

Object-oriented

Object-based systems become object-oriented when objects have defined relations. Well-defined relationships are key to object-oriented simulation, analysis, design, or programming.

Objects also have relations. For an end user, a relationship involves ideas of containment, embedding, and co-occurrence. An object can be embedded in

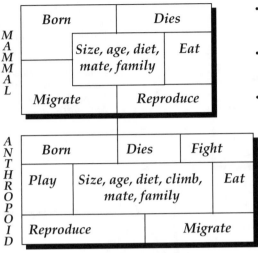

- *Anthropoid inherits born, dies, eat, migrate behavior from mammal*
- *It has fight, play, climb behaviors unique to itself and not common to all mammals.*
- *Some of the inherited behaviors may be more complex with anthropoids than with the generic mammal in some systems.*

Figure 11.9 Inheritance: mammal/anthropoid.

another object to form a complex document. Objects can be linked to form a group that always occurs together on a screen. Microsoft OLE (Object Linking and Embedding) is a popular example of this capability.

Objects can be thought of as a subset of the entity–relation model. There is a core relation between objects called "inheritance." An object passes its data model and its methods to a "child." The child, sometimes called a "subclass," inherits from its parent.

Figure 11.9 shows an inheritance relation between an object "mammal" and an object "anthropoid." An anthropoid is a more specific creature than a mammal. However, it inherits some of the properties of its parent in that it breathes, feeds its young, and dies. However, an anthropoid has some data and some behaviors that are unique to itself—climbing trees and good stuff like that. The child achieves some of its behaviors by using the methods of its parent. Inheritance is the basis of reuse and programmer productivity.

The application of inheritance is shown in Figure 11.10. An additional child object, "humanoid," is derived from the anthropoid object. It has some of its behavior through inheritance and other through unique methods. The creation of the new object was facilitated by the mammal and anthropoid behaviors and inheritance between the three generations. Box 11.9 shows the dispute between different schools about the liberality of inheritance. This is the basis for some IBM/Microsoft market disputes.

The degree to which behaviors in generations (nature vs. nurture) can diverge is disputed. Those one might call classicists insist that every child is

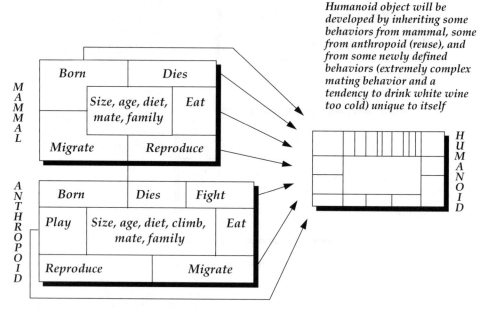

Humanoid object will be developed by inheriting some behaviors from mammal, some from anthropoid (reuse), and from some newly defined behaviors (extremely complex mating behavior and a tendency to drink white wine too cold) unique to itself

Figure 11.10   Creating humanoids.

11.9   DIFFERING SCHOOLS OF INHERITANCE

1   The Classicists (OMG): An inherited method must be identical in the child and the parent. Only new methods can be put in the child. The child must be substitutable for the parent in all cases, so only new methods are added.

2   The Revisionists: Inherited methods may be redefined but must have the same name and give the same result. A particular method with a particular interface can be implemented different ways.

3   The Radicals: Methods can be redefined as necessary. They may give different results and can have differing names.

4   Impact: The ease with which children can be derived and, as a consequence, the degree of re-usability.

identical to its parent except that it may have additional behaviors. More radical theorists remove almost all constraints.

Getting the issue of liberality in generation relations right is key to the success of objects. A rigorous methodology embedded in a crisp technology will solve some problems quite well. However, some things will be awkward and difficult to do. In order to facilitate certain solutions and enable others, one relaxes the discipline, softens the constraints, and makes the methodology more flexible. As a consequence, the methodology loses its rigor and merges into other (already failed) methodologies.

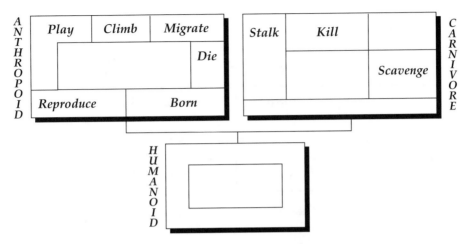

Figure 11.11   Multiple-inheritance anthropoid carnivore.

There is concern about the degree to which a child object is insensitive to changes in its parent. Ideally, because of information hiding, the behavior of a parent should be changeable without affecting a child who inherits. However, there are possible dangers and some known exposures for a child object if its parent changes. As a result, some object designers prefer a methodology that Microsoft calls "aggregation." With aggregation, a relation between a parent and a child must be explicitly stated by a programmer.

Some object languages allow the concept of "multiple inheritance," as in Figure 11.11. The object humanoid here inherits characteristics not only from the object anthropoid, but from the object carnivore also, since a humanoid is a deviant of an anthropoid, the only carnivore of the family. To derive a humanoid, it is useful to inherit from both objects. The need for multiple inheritance is related to the liberality of the derivation laws and to the way that methods are defined. Surely, EATMEAT might be an augmented method of a humanoid, as would STALK, KILL, etc., and still respect classical rules of substitution. However, specific behaviors for humanoids would minimize reuse.

The hierarchic inheritance relation provides a structure from which new objects can be made and instances generated. There are different organizing principles for the hierarchy. The hierarchy structure discussed so far is an "is a" structure, indicating that a human "is a (kind of) anthropoid." There is an alternate structure called a "has a" structure, which is a map of componentry.

Figure 11.12 shows "has a." A humanoid is depicted as having a head, a torso, and appendages; and in turn, the head is depicted as having eyes, a nose, a mouth, and a brain.

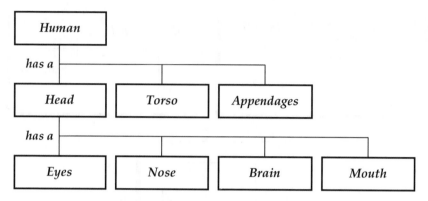

Figure 11.12 "Has a" heirarchy.

"Is a" and "has a" structures are two significant relations. There are others that can be defined. Objects can be cast into the entity–relation model, where an object is an entity and inheritance is one of the relations.

At this point, the crispness of objects begins to fade and seems to merge into a class of methods based upon smart network data semantics. The inheritance relation in various forms is one of many relations that objects can have with each other. This will be discussed again in Chapter 12.

When running, objects have a relation like that of programs that do not share memory spaces. An object invokes the behavior of another object by "sending it a message" that activates it, causing it to run and return a value to the invoker.

Basic object technologies

The programming model suggested by Microsoft OLE is enormously appealing. Clicking on an envelope to put a mail function into an application, clicking on a lightening bolt to put a communications function, etc. are natural end points of re-use. In effect, the management and development of a document and of an application merge with each other. Creating an application is creating a document with active elements.

We are far from this in the bigger arena. As is true of many technologies, attributes of the concept are confused with attributes of products that represent versions of the technology. Objects are associated with a number of notational systems with particular sets of characteristics and problems.

The most disciplined notation is a language developed in the early 1980s called Smalltalk. Objects in their aspects of inheritance are most formally represented

ABSTRACT AND CONCRETE

A concrete object has usable computer programming that can be delivered into a software structure. In the classicist's model of inheritance, an object at any point in the inheritance tree can be concrete. Coding for the methods of a parent and child are identical.

Some believe it is useful that only the "leaf" nodes, those at the bottom of the inheritance tree, are concrete, deliverable objects, which may have actual instance. Other objects are "abstract" objects, which serve as sources of methods but represent abstractions too indefi-

nite to operate upon. The abstract object "account" would have data instance data and methods usable for checking or savings accounts, but there could not be an instance of an account. Only a checking account or a savings account object can have instances.

Increased liberality and polymorphism is a feature of trees of abstract objects. Leaf objects contain specializations of framework methods of the abstract parent, sometimes breaking the rule that a method with the same name is identical in all generations.

---

in Smalltalk notation. It is pure in the sense that it is impossible to create programs without staying within the paradigm. It imposes the discipline.

Perhaps the most extensively used representation of objects is a language called C++, which is an extension of the C language that permits the declaration of inheritance relations. There are object extensions to other languages, for example, COBOL and Ada. In these languages, the paradigm shift is not enforced. It is relaxed to the point that it is possible to create C++ programs with effectively no objects.

Characteristics of C++, Smalltalk, and other notations are often taken as characteristics of objects. For example, in C++, the addition of a new object requires the complete recompilation of a program. In C++, objects are not persistent; they do not exist independently of running applications. They have "process duration." Often the peculiarities of the programming language or environment are held to be inherent peculiarities of objects

11.11 SEEKING THE PARADIGM SHIFT

Object buffs speak of a "paradigm shift," a fundamentally different way of thinking about programming. There is some truth, and much hype, to this. The author endured a number of C++ and Smalltalk courses that did not reveal it. It is difficult to see in microcosmic views of programming. Good procedural programs provide encapsulation, reuse, data hiding, etc. They can have well-defined specific functions. They can manipulate highly typed data.

However, when one looks at the actions and data of a problem at large, objects create a profoundly different population of modules and mappings. If one thinks of data types as rows in a matrix, and of action as columns, procedure-oriented programming will tend to map a function across multiple data types, while object-oriented programming will tend to map multiple activities across a single data type.

This leads to quite a different set of modules (objects) within a program structure. In effect, the paradigm shift is a rotation of the matrix.

11.12   OBJECT METHODOLOGY

A number of books discuss methodologies appropriate for object analysis and design. Some are fairly useless reriggings of old data-driven or structural analysis techniques that have little to do with objects as such. The following works are considered seminal by some:

Booch, Grady. *Object-Oriented Design with Applications*. Benjamin/Cummings, 1990.

Jacobsen, Ivar. *Object-Oriented Software Engineering*. Addison-Wesley, 1992.

Meyer, Bertrand. *Object-Oriented Software Construction*. Prentice-Hall, 1988.

Rumbaugh, James, et al. *Object-Oriented Modeling and Design*. Prentice-Hall, 1991.

Taylor, David. *Object-Oriented Technology, A Manager's Guide*. Addison-Wesley, 1991.

There are now many trade publications and a vast literature of seminars, proceedings, etc.

and are treated as a barrier to going on to the new technology. Many of the C++ problems are unique to C++.

A generation of visual object tools is developing on the desktop. Data base vendors such as Oracle and Sybase have extended their data models to take on an object flavoring and have provided appropriate development tools for the extensions.

Visual C++, PowerBuilder, and Delphi are among a set of tools that provide a visual paradigm for creating programs. This visual paradigm involves browsing over a defined structure, selecting elements, and including elements into a complex object.

What is not clear is the extent to which the object programming languages constitute design languages. Some very ambitious projects have been undertaken to model vast enterprises with Smalltalk. But a programming language remains a programming language, unsuitable for design.

All of the major vendors have an object visual technology of some kind on the desktop and in the systems structure. IBM, Sun, Hewlett-Packard, DEC, Novell, and NeXTstep have application development toolkits closely associated with visual user interfaces. Reconciling these various products and concepts has become an industry problem.

There are some differences of opinion about how mature the object technology kit already is. Box 11.13 describes a mature environment in which objects and upper CASE tools technologies have entirely fused.

Clearly, the payoff in objects will be based on the same dynamics as the payoff with any other software development methodology. The payoff must come late in the life cycle, but it must be set up by good design, good practices, and good documentation. Objects will be mature when there are true object-oriented analysis and design tools. C++, COBOL++, and other programming languages will surely not provide the level of productivity improvements that are being talked about.

A MATURE OBJECT DEVELOPMENT ENVIRONMENT

This box describes a set of object concepts derived from a project at a major vendor that undertook to discover how software might be and how it might be created at the beginning of the 21st century.

Stable Structures with Multiple Interfaces and Protocols. The inheritance tree consists of abstractions of increasing particularity as one descends the tree. For example, in the figure the root object is "system," then "communications system," "connection-based transport," "TCP," and finally Version "A" TCP. A complete subtree of connection-based transports contains all known transports. Each has declared public interfaces corresponding to available APIs.

Advanced Browsing Capability. It must be possible to efficiently browse object libraries for necessary attributes and relations. Browsing must be done at high levels of abstraction with pictorial navigation through various representations. The browser should be able to follow "has a," "is a," and other relations in arbitrary patterns. Sustaining a high "find" ratio is critical. Discouraged browsers will not achieve reuse. New objects will ruin the integrity of the structure and the coherence of the library. Found usable objects should be "clicked" into an emerging structure.

Knowledge-Based Technology. This is fundamental to objects. Knowledge can be expressed in a set of rules representing a "browsing apprentice." The browsing apprentice can help novice browsers achieve high hit ratios and systems integrity. As a system matures, sophistication and knowledge about it grow, and

efficiency of recapture can be maintained by representing this knowledge.

Software Configuration Management. The system browses and assembles appropriate libraries. The creation of a system is a rules-driven CONSTRUCTION from class libraries. Protocol and interface rules select which protocol and API elements will be used. Distribu-

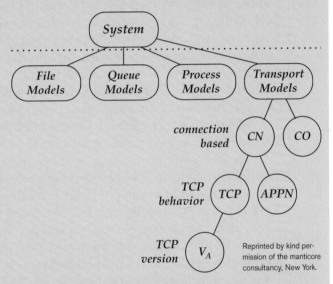

Reprinted by kind permission of the manticore consultancy, New York.

tion rules describe the population of objects around the network or cluster.

Multidirectional Design. There must be some use of "bottom-up" design, where abstract objects are "extruded" from sets of similar base objects. Software development is always done at different levels of abstraction simultaneously over the life cycle.

Live Objects in Context. The developer must be able to watch families of objects operate together. A workbench must support early simulation of the behavior of the design. A designer must be able to see object behavior at chosen levels of abstraction.

Underlying economics of objects

Particular difficulties of software are:

- it is labor intensive
- it is not manageable
- it is never finished.

Imposing a "standard parts" architectural metaphor on programming misses the point that over its life an application is modified in a manner comparable to evolving a garage into the Empire State Building. This constant modification is the root of the unwholesome economics of software. Methodologies must address the key issue of constant change.

The payback of objects is reuse, not productivity gained in initial program development. Over 60% of total software cost is experienced in modification and enhancement after the first version. For objects to be the promised breakthrough, they must provide a software process achieving reuse, re-engineering, and configuration management. Objects must provide an enduring and understandable structure on which to perform modifications.

Since objects are primarily a re-use technology, payback comes late in the introduction cycle, following the unhappy curve of Figure 11.4 (on page 233). Patience is required to achieve benefits for deep changes in software development technology. Objects must be introduced elegantly to avoid disappointments. One cannot buy Turbo C++ and go. The proper selection of the right projects, of appropriate size and careful definition, is key. A careful training process is necessary, and a premature commitment to production code is fatal. There is a slow learning curve here, and patience is required.

The great coup of reuse is design reuse. But to have reuse one must have understandability and easy ways to browse through a structure to find usable elements. Unhappily, C++ is not readable, and one can expect relatively little reuse with raw C++. COBOL++ might be better, since COBOL is fundamentally more understandable than C.

There are different views about the basic premises of objects. Some think the neat top-down flow of objects is unworkable, and that if it was workable, programming problems would have been solved years ago without objects. Some think the top-down bias is not realistic, since many good design ideas occur late in the cycle where accumulated knowledge leads to better insights.

There is currently no reliable metric for measuring the efficiency of objects: rate of code production is counterproductive, since new code production is not what one is out to achieve. Some emerging measures of object efficiency only

11.14 SOM/DSOM

IBM has developed the System Object Model (SOM) and Distributed System Object Model (DSOM) to be available for various object-oriented languages and on all IBM platforms.

SOM provides language-neutral support of object hierarchies and inheritance. It is a system for defining hierarchies and invoking methods. At run time, SOM run-time components intermediate between object calls, locating objects and passing parameters. SOM addresses a problem of cross-language and cross-compiler inheritance and invocation by providing mediation at run time.

SOM eliminates the necessity for recompiling entire hierarchies because of changes to parent objects. It allows new methods to be added without recompilation of children. An extension, DSOM, runs on various communications protocols to provide cross-network object linkage. SOM is CORBA compliant and will interact with HP, DEC, and Sun objects if those objects are developed to understand messages that are passed. The SOM aim is to link objects anywhere to objects anywhere else across language and compiler boundaries.

A visual browser for SOM is forthcoming. In addition to SOM, IBM has pledged support for OpenDoc. This is primarily an Apple object technology that uses SOM as its object framework.

measure object technologies against each other. Function points do not become more convincing in the presence of objects.

Slowly, over the decade, objects in some form are likely to have an impact on programming practice. While only about 2% of the programming budgets of large companies are invested in objects in 1994, there is a projection that by 1999 well over 75% of the total programming budget will be invested in objects. It is not clear that those answering these questions have a clear idea of exactly what objects are or what they are going to do about them.

Objects and open distributed computing

Objects affect the culture of open distributed computing in a number of ways:

1 There are distributed versions of Smalltalk that enable a Smalltalk class library to be dispersed across a network.

2 There is a de facto standard, CORBA (Common Object Request Broker Architecture), that establishes a technology for objects to communicate across a network, and even across various language and environment boundaries. This standard was in its second version as of the end of 1994. Unhappily, it has not provided interoperable objects between object compilers and libraries, but CORBA II promises some improvement.

3 There is emerging manufacturer technology, some within the CORBA culture, that provides for cross-environment and cross-network object interaction. Among these are IBM's SOM (Systems Object Model) and Hewlett-Packard's DOMF (Distributed Object Management Facility) and, under agreement, objects from Sun, DEC, Novell (Hyperdesk), and other participants in the COSE agreements. OMG has approved a set of standards for cross-vendor interaction called COSS (Common Object Services Specification), primarily from Sun Solaris.

4 The use of the object model as a vehicle for various functions of distributed computing is expanding. The narrative for the OSI/CMIP systems management standard is cased largely in object terminology, and some systems management product is moving toward CORBA architecture. IBM Karat and Sun Encompass are object-oriented revisions of systems management technology. There are object aspects to the directory technology in that browsing for attributes is organized on an object basis.

5 Objects as an interface paradigm is rapidly emerging as mainstream, especially driven by the needs of compound documents and multimedia messaging. Object-like technologies are emerging as part of client/server application development tools.

Netting it out

Objects is an organizing principle for software elements that has its major payback in achieving reuse. There is in fact a shift in programming style, but that shift should not make much difference in the productivity of a programmer already using good programming practices in traditional programming. In fact, without the institution of good programming practices as a precondition to using objects, there is not likely to be any improvement in productivity across the life cycle at all.

The methodology of objects focuses on classification and cognitive processes that are difficult for many people to do. Bad objects are as bad as anything. There are likely to be more C++ programs in the world than well-defined object hierarchies.

There is a strong sense of déjà vu about some aspects of objects. Smalltalk, after all, is fifteen years old, and the simulation environments that some object theorists talk about stem from SIMULA in the late 1960s. Some literature uses terminology and concepts that are direct borrowings from works on operating systems in the 1970s.

The single new idea, perhaps, is controlled derivation in a well-structured library. But some mighty big promises are being made for this notion whose effectiveness is not yet well understood.

Rapid application development

There have long been tools for "rapid prototyping" of smaller applications. These tools come from both the tool industry and the data base industry. For small applications ("one shots") or as a way of evolving the behavior of an application, these rapid prototyping tools have been useful.

The problems have been that the tools are largely interpretive, do not scale, and only rarely are capable of operating in client/server environments. Recently, there has been some advance in the technology, leading to a set of rapid application development tools that seem to scale and have good performance and are usable in a client/server environment. These tools can extract data from a multiplicity of data bases, work with object-oriented technologies and interfaces, and run in standard end user environments.

The apparent star of this set, and an excellent example of the technology, is a product called Delphi introduced by Borland.

It is an amalgam of a number of techniques, including visual programming, objects and object browsing, and SQL local and remote data base access. It can use Oracle, Sybase, SQL Server, Informix, and Borland Interbase data management systems. It permits simultaneous viewing of visual and text representations of programs, and uses a technique once called "incremental compilation" to generate high-quality code as elements are defined or included in an application. Data bases can be moved without changes to programs. The tool seems to scale and has many of the features of Box 11.13. It can interoperate with other tools, and higher-level interfaces are used for program modification and extension.

Such technology moves us from rapid prototyping to rapid development, integrates object technology with CASE, provides what is needed for reuse of objects, integrates data warehousing features with rapid development, and seems to suggest, finally, the realization of technology long suggested and long promised.

chapter 12

Accessing resources

EXECUTIVE SUMMARY The trail from sign-on to data access involves a number of technologies. The personality of a system is defined by its end user interfaces and the technologies used to interact with humans. After accessing a system, a user or program surrogate must locate resources on the network with some kind of directory function. The user then encounters data in various forms and encodings.

Various standards, practices, and states of the art obtain in each of the areas of access, directory, and data models. The usability of a system defines its inherent attractiveness as a problem-solving tool. Various vendors and alliances have defined interfaces, which are roughly similar, based upon a common paradigm of windows in which text and graphics may appear and which may tile or overlap each other. These windows, when not in the direct attention of the user, may be represented by icons that suggest their function.

Traditionally, every data management system has had its own directory service. This leads to separate naming conventions and formats that make it difficult to access data in different systems across the network. An emerging standard from the OSI, X.500, provides a common naming convention and notation for all resources in a system. Slow to start, vendors are now beginning to pay some attention to it.

The modeling of data has provided various concepts. Standard practice is now the relational data model, where data is presented as two-dimensional tables. The limitations of this model—its inability to represent images, for example—has led to the development of object-oriented data bases. An interesting and closely related data model is the entity–relation, which many believe to be the underlying proper model for objects.

Data warehousing and on-line analysis are closely related ideas for accessing data orthogonally to its underlying organization. New "slices and dices" of data in different formats from different data systems in different models can be brought together to support new views of the business.

CHAPTER 12: ACCESSING RESOURCES

Transaction management concerns rigidly controlled access to data of different types in a synchronized manner so that a particular computer event leaves all data it modifies across files in time-stamp synchronization.

Overview

The technologies of this chapter define the path from accessing a computer to accessing its data.

End user interfaces determine the productivity, quality of work, morale, and health of workers who use computers. Learnability, rememberability, attractiveness, and forgivingness are aspects of systems that connect people and electronics.

Directory is a technology for locating resources in a network. Until now, data products, communication products, and many applications have had private directories for indicating the location of the resources within their domain. This has made it difficult, even on a single machine, to find out what the system has. Finding resources available in a network is key for distributed open systems.

Data representation has always been key in computing, more so than ever because of the current focus on dynamic reconfiguration of data, the integration of new forms, and the creation of compound documents.

"Objects" is a technology that has had everything promised for it. In this chapter, it is an enterprise modeling technique. Entity–relation data base is a form of smart semantic network data base from which some believe the object model should derive. Data warehousing is the attempt to unify data of different types and models behind a uniform interface so that new views can be taken.

User interfaces (the end user interface model)

This technology defines the look and feel of a computer to a user. The metaphors of usage are overlapped multiple windows, menus, icons, and focus windows. The technology enabling this are all-points–addressable screens of high resolution, large memories enabling image representation where as many as 24 bits can represent a single point on a screen, and light pens and other graphics drawing devices. Voice, video, and three-dimensional graphics are quickly entering the domain of the interface.

12.1 USABILITY ARCHITECTURE

- Semantics–the behavior of the interface. Semantics defines the functions provided, how the functions are organized, and the model of elements and actions.

- Syntax–the notation of the interface. Syntax defines panel design, menu tree definitions, and interface style. It defines the spatial and graphic attributes of the interface. It determines the balance between menu and command, voice, and touch.

- Physical–defines the function key mappings, color highlighting, and the placement of objects on a screen. It maps the ideas of usability on the physical characteristics of devices.

End user models are commonly used to create the usual business artifacts (pie charts, histograms, etc.) or to enable visualizations of scientific data in ways that suggest new relations. The importance of visualization is brought home by chaos theory. The irregular, but enticingly near-cyclic, patterns of the butterfly and other representations of chaos theory were first represented by a computer plotter. Raw numbers could never have shown the underlying patterns, which suggests that small events and round-off error variations can destabilize large systems.

The end user model is defined by standards that define how a window will look, the quality of fonts and colors, the icons, the messages, etc. The underlying model comes from early work in Xerox Park and is thought by many to be best represented by the Macintosh, although the elegance of the Apple interface is now being approached by others.

Elements of usability

The elements of usability are what the user perceives, what the user can do, what the user must know, and what the user must do. For a general purpose interface, these elements must be defined for a variety of populations and tasks.

There is far to go. There is constant complaint about computer behavior—odd and unexpected character traits that show through the formal interfaces. It is not clear whether programmers developing interfaces understand what psychologists are telling them. It is not clear what is an acceptable level of complexity and skill, and whether it remains the same across generations. It is not clear if mental models are stable over time, if an electronic interface should try to masquerade as the electromechanical instrument it is replacing or go on to new behaviors.

Usability is an iceberg. What is above the surface accounts for about 30% of the full range of its issues. It is a compound discipline, involving elements of human factors, ergonomics, cognitive engineering, psychology, anthropometry,

12.2   EXAMPLE STANDARDS

CGI	ANSI X3.161
	ISO 9636
CGM	ANSI X3.122-1986
	FIPS PUB 128
GKS	ANSI X3.124-1985
	FIPS PUB 120
	ISO 8805-1988
GKS FORTRAN Binding	ANSI X3.122.1
	ISO 8651-1
GKS Ada Binding	ANSI X3.122.3
	ISO 8651-3
GKS Pascal Binding	ANSI X3.122.2
	ISO 8561-2
GKS C Binding	ANSI X3.122.4
	ISO 8561-4

pyscholinguistics, the sociology of small groups, usability engineering, and technology for display, storage, and the network.

An interface must be built around the human and the task that the human is to perform. A "knowledge worker," involved in creative or research tasks, must deal with complex representations and multimedia documents. The environment needs flexibility, an easy transition from context to context. On the other hand, the "production worker" requires an interface that enforces structure focused on a specific task.

In group work, the group must interact naturally, share documents of diverse complexity, modify documents as a group, and comment on each other's work. The interfaces must simulate meetings and conferences. This requires a deep understanding of how people interact and considerable bandwidth on the network.

Current technology might be characterized as "at the looking glass." The keyboard, mouse, stylus, joystick, voice recognition, natural speech, and interactions are all derived from some model of human interaction with another device.

Principles of usability

There are some principles understood to be key at an interface. The system must maintain a consistent personality from task to task and from application to application. A consistent systems persona was not a part of the interfaces of early personal computers. Baseware allowed upperware to develop its own personalities. A user of multiple applications faced deep shifts of style between a data base manager, a word processor, a spreadsheet, and other applications.

A reason for the success of the Macintosh is the consistent personality within which its applications perform. The IBM/Microsoft world was very late in recognizing the need for this. A common persona did not emerge from IBM or Microsoft until the very late 1980s.

A system must limit the number of its "states." The variety of conditions a user may face, and what can be done about it, must be constrained to a memorable set. Constraining the number of states minimizes the conceptual load on a user. The actions required to use the system must be perceived as "natural" or "intuitive."

The end user must be interrupted with care and flow of thought not disturbed. The personality of the system is minimally intrusive. A period waiting for a cursor or an arrow to move is one in which the worker is diverted from the task. Unpredictable response times, or inappropriately long response times, also break flow and have a serious negative effect on knowledge worker productivity.

Specialized use of punctuation is disturbing. That symbols % and $ have special systems meanings—a favorite device of the 1970s—violates a rule of neutral punctuation, in which all symbols naturally in the repertory of the user have only the meanings they have in natural language.

The actions to be taken must simulate some "intuitive" or well-known mental model. A checkbook balancing program may be built around the image of a check. Throwing out documents might simulate the act of carrying them to the basket.

Above all, the system should be predictable in success and failure. No surprises are allowed.

A necessary pattern of early user focus, early and continuous user testing, and iterative design is not part of the classic program development style. The programming community is insufficiently sensitized to the process of creating good interfaces.

No strategic application headed for the desktop or laptop of a client can have an interface roughly guessed at by systems programmers whose major qualification is knowledge of C or C++.

The failure of early operating systems to provide adequate personas has forced various products to develop with quite different looks and feels. As a result, spreadsheets, word processors, and document managers have diverged. Now the key upperware vendors are offering integrated "office suites" of e-mail, word processor, spreadsheet, and/or data base with an increasingly consistent look and feel. Lotus, Microsoft, and others have made an investment in similar personalities across the major applications.

Usability software

"Interface managers," or "user servers," are a fundamental part of a platform. There are a number of major standards, styles, and products associated with providing end user interfaces (EUIs) and graphical user interfaces (GUIs).

IBM CUA (Workplace Shell) is an evolving standard associated with the IBM Presentation Manager on OS/2. Other interfaces include those of the Apple Macintosh, Windows 95, Sun OPEN LOOK, NeXT, Hewlett-Packard VUE, and Motif, which is associated with almost all Unix products. The Common Open Software Environment (COSE) has defined a Common Desktop Environment (CDE). Taligent waits in the wings.

Usability software has different relations with the underlying operating system. The OS/2 Presentation Manager was designed to be unique to OS/2, and is deeply integrated into its structure. At the other extreme, X Windows is a presentation manager that will run on many operating systems, including OS/2, Windows, Windows NT, MVS, VM, and all of the major Unix systems.

End user software provides, in addition to an end user touch and feel, an API used to create the EUI. This API provides functions that define graphics, colors, fonts, etc. There are kits of tools used to create graphics, define window and screen composition, integrate multimedia elements, etc. There are de facto standards emerging in this area, particularly the API for X Windows (endorsed as an X/Open standard) and the Microsoft XAPI.

There are a number of industry standards, de jure and de facto, affecting end user interfaces. The de facto standards are constrained by de jure graphics and end user standards from a number of international bodies. Among these are standards for graphics libraries, language bindings, etc. (see Box 12.3).

Multimedia

The introduction of audio (music, voice, sounds) and visual (image, graphics, animation, motion video) reopens issues of what interface methodologies are appropriate for what tasks. Computing, interactive television, and games become intertwined at this point. Developing industry relations reflect this.

The applications now beginning to emerge for education, simulation, direct sales, and information dissemination seem unlimited. Yet somehow, perhaps because of all of the options, and perhaps because of the intercrossing of communications technologies—television, telephone, computer, and the entertainment industries—periods of apparent intense progress intertwine with periods when all of the promises seem remote indeed.

The core computer industry seems to be the fastest moving segment. With the integration of the telephone and the television set, as well as the fax machine, CD-ROM stereo is a clearly progressing development, as is the connection of the computer to cable television lines as well as to telephones. Large flat screens and "information walls" are becoming available in specialized environments.

12.3 X WINDOWS

X Windows is a set of interfaces, protocols, and libraries for multiple operating systems. It can support multiple EUIs. X Windows allows a context for looking at local or remote applications. It is able to reconfigure so that it can be run on a single workstation, on a system where the application is across the wire, or on a system (X terminal) where only the basic services are local and all other elements are across the wire.

X Windows has a "server" side, which is on the desktop or laptop, and a client side on a system running an application. It has a set of protocols for interaction with the client and server; a library of widgets, basic graphics building blocks; a library for higher-level interface abstractions, for example, those of Motif; and a

set of functions that drive an end user device. The figure shows an X Windows structure. This structure can be configured to run on a single workstation, to run with the application remote from the toolkit and X server, or to run with the application and toolkit remote from the X server.

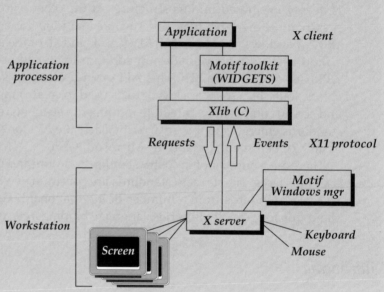

The displays are achieving greater and greater resolution and size. (There are 2K × 2K monitors available. The VGA standard is 640 × 480 pixels, Super VGA is 800 × 600, XGA (Extended VGA) is 1024 × 768.) Displays and the compression/enhancement technology behind them permit animation that may soon be indistinguishable from image. CD-ROM expects an order of magnitude increase in capacity in 1995 and is being joined by video disk and other optical storage as a visual media.

All this technology requires a software response providing authoring languages as well as usage conventions for the multidimensional environments that will be developing within this decade. All major operating systems, including Macintosh, OS/2, and Windows now have multimedia extensions. IBM is delivering multimedia PM/2 and Microsoft is delivering Microsoft Multimedia Windows (MME). The IBM/Apple venture, Kaleida, is developing multimedia programming capabilities.

A great danger to IT is misjudging the rate of intrusion of multimedia. "Soft" multimedia magazines suggest what can be done with the media combinations. Games are a leading test ground of multimedia applications as well. Delivery of CD-ROM–based information services, games, and encyclopedias has begun to be mainstream, and publishing applications with multimedia capability are now available.

Coming technology

One might think of the future stages of human/machine interaction as "through the looking glass." The images of the computer and the perception of three-dimensional real space begin to fuse. The industry hopes for total sensory involvement based upon the availability of speeds and storages orders of magnitude beyond present capability.

Three-dimensional immersion in images indistinguishable from true solids will surround us. Our perception of them will be adjusted by the sensing of our body positions. We will affect the objects by gesture and will feel tactile and kinesthetic responses from the objects and ourselves. We will be wearing our computers and everything will be wired; fiber optics will course through our clothes.

The technologies for much of this are already in place in experimental laboratories. Wired gloves and clothes, head-mounted displays, force balls, 3-D sound boards, ultrasonic, inertial, and optical sensors afford (for example) NASA advanced space behavior simulation.

Economics of usability

Productivity metrics are not good. We know how to measure keystrokes per minute, but not how to measure the number of design errors per computer response delay and the reduction in product profit resulting from these.

As computer interfaces become increasingly associated with consumer electronics, expectations will be brought to the office from the home. An enterprise will find it expensive and disruptive not to install the interfaces that are commonly expected by its employees. To be using back-level interfaces would be as odd as providing company cars with levers rather than a steering wheel for determining direction.

The economic advantages for the knowledge worker are improved quality and creative productivity. How this is measured is part of corporate culture, but it often must be measured not as an attribute of the work of the employee but as an attribute of product profitability. A late product with defects will earn less in the market than an on-time product without defects. If elegant knowledge worker interfaces lead to better product, they have quite high value.

The value of usability is an aspect of the mainframe vs. client/server struggle. The underlying question is when do good interfaces produce revenues. If low-paid employees are going to do transaction entry, there may be no argument for investing in high-quality interfaces. If customers are to do the transaction entry, attractive interfaces may be a key business requirement.

An issue for vendors is the emergence of "non-defect-related problems." These are product barriers created by a user dislike of certain features. Users commonly do not report discontent, they discontinue use of the product. Determining what feature negatives are constraining sales is quite expensive. Even without this problem, support costs for products in the field are enormous. Toll-free numbers, help lines, etc. and all the paraphernalia of a highly competitive consumer industry with low profit margins now appear.

Directory

A user or an application program must locate documents, files, data bases, and other resources on the network. This is done through a directory function, which provides location information through "white pages" and "yellow pages" functions.

Directory functions have traditionally been part of file or data base systems or of network systems representing resources through the network. Each system has had private naming conventions, and made private decisions about what information it would maintain. Typically, a system knows where a file is, who "owns" the file, when the file was last used, when it was last modified, its size, etc.

A de facto directory product for the Unix culture is the NIS (Network Information Services) of the Open Network Computing architecture. It is pervasive across Unix platforms. Outside of Unix, there has been recent intense activity in the directory area. Novell NetWare 4.x has considerably expanded its scale and capability in the directory area. Microsoft is developing enhanced directory services for Windows NT. StreetTalk, from Banyan VINES, has long been a scalable network directory service.

In distributed open computing, the lack of a common directory service is a serious constraint. One effort to establish network-wide common directory

12.4 DIRECTORY

"A service providing access by name or attribute to resources throughout the network. Defines a consistent, human intelligible, location independent naming scheme, a Universal Naming Convention (UNC). Associates with an Information Model that describes relations between Directory and resources. Involved in Application Management, Security, and Logon Services. Provides the basis for Resource Registry, Lookup Services, Yellow Pages, and White Pages."– *International Standards Organization (ISO).*

services is the ISO X.500, which establishes standards for naming and organizing network-wide directory systems. The intent is to enable users to find all resources in the network from a consistent directory service.

Directory plays a role in determining who is an "enterprise" vendor and who is a "niche" vendor. In the "New Age," a way for companies to grow beyond their niche is to offer credible renderings of a directory consistent with the concepts of X.500. Novell, Sun Microsystems, and Microsoft are using global, scalable, network directory capability as part of their strategy to play a more central role in IT culture.

The underlying concepts of directory:

- Everything has a name.
- There is a global name convention for everything.
- This convention can coexist with existing conventions.
- The directory service is integratable in systems structures.

The topology of the directory is built around the notion of a cell. A cell is an administrative domain defined by a management culture. Figure 12.1 shows a cell. A local directory provides local naming services for a cell. A Global Directory Service links cells into an apparently seamless structure.

Figure 12.2 shows a directory. The directory provides the name of a resource, the location of the resource manager, and the location of the resource. It can be used for lookup in the style of a white pages telephone directory, or for attribute browsing in the style of a yellow pages. Physically, the directory is distributed into subtrees across the network, although it provides an image of a single unified directory. Each node has partial knowledge of the network resources and pointers to other nodes.

Naming and information

Figure 12.2 shows the hierarchic naming convention. The root nodes of an organization must be registered with an international authority. The layers of the hierarchy are root, organization, and domain. The root level contains country,

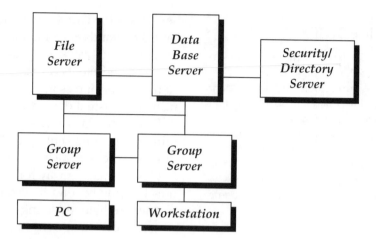

Figure 12.1   Cell.

locality, and/or organization. The organization level contains organizational schema and partitions to administrative domains. The domain level contains domains, directories within domains, actual resources, and a domain schema. The schema contains the definitions of resources, their attributes, and definitions of their attributes. Actual data base managers and file systems are "mounted" to the domain level.

To accommodate local naming conventions, the naming scheme permits local names to be used within a domain. Thus, CO=USA, ORG=Manticore, LOC= NYC, Organization Unit (OU)=PUBLISH, USER=LORIN/pub/IT/chap12 would be the full name of the file representing this chapter on the system.

There are two types of information: information about the structure of the directory system and about objects in the directory. Each entry has information about its attributes, the nature of its attributes, and permissible values for the attributes. Entries are organized in a highly typed way, with rules for attribute definitions. There are resource and service classes and an inheritance structure.

Directory interfaces

A Directory Services Interface from Siemens has been taken up by X/Open. This interface defines directory functions for data access, update, and control. Attributes can be browsed and compared to criteria; data can be added (a new object instance), removed, and read; schema can be modified and extended.

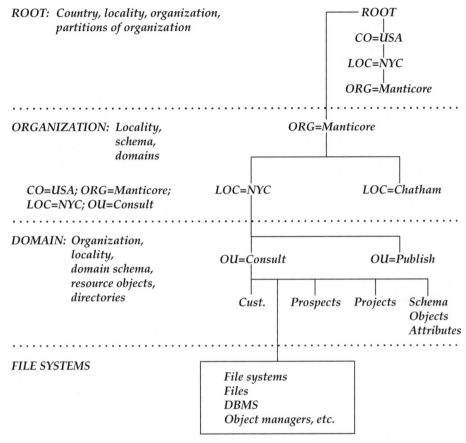

ROOT: *Country, locality, organization,*
partitions of organization

ROOT
|
CO=USA
|
LOC=NYC
|
ORG=Manticore

ORGANIZATION: *Locality,*
schema,
domains

ORG=Manticore

CO=USA; ORG=Manticore;
LOC=NYC; OU=Consult

LOC=NYC   LOC=Chatham

DOMAIN: *Organization,*
locality,
domain schema,
resource objects,
directories

OU=Consult   OU=Publish

Cust.   Prospects   Projects   Schema
                                  Objects
                                  Attributes

FILE SYSTEMS

File systems
Files
DBMS
Object managers, etc.

CO=USA; ORG=Manticore; LOC=NYC; OU=Consult/lorin/demeter/objects

Figure 12.2   Directory.

Directory and open distributed systems

A barrier to enterprise networking has been the lack of a common directory to identify resources across the network. Some systems require a user to sign on to various systems and conduct a "manual" search by browsing local system or file directories. Some systems assume small sets of resources and nodes and represent all resources on all systems. Early IBM CICS applications represented all "home" and "away" files at each system. Clearly such approaches are not appropriate for networks of serious size. While methods like Unix remote

SEARCHING THE DIRECTORY

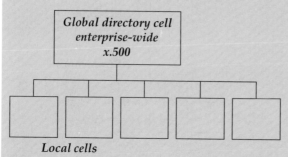

*Global directory cell
enterprise-wide
x.500*

Local cells

The upper figure shows a global directory service and cells.

The directory may be searched by multicast, leaf following, or neighbor request.

In a multicast search, a node requests of all, or a defined subset of other nodes, whether they have the element. The node that has the element responds; other nodes either send negative messages or do not respond. If no response is received within a set time, the search may be tried again.

Leaf following is a technique of "mounting" local entries to each other's subtrees. The lower figure shows the "mounting" of a subtree on node A from node B. The full name of entries at node B is the name of the tree at A and the names on the tree at B. When an element is searched for and not found at a local node, the search continues across the network to the remotely mounted tree at node B. If it is not at node B, a return is made to the requesting node. Some systems do not permit B to continue a search to C, but will have B pass up the link to C to A to continue the search. Mounting searches are common in the Unix environment.

Neighbor request is an ordered search where each node is considered to have a defined set of "neighbors." In a four-neighbor sys-

tem, A's neighbors are B, C, D, and E. When A starts a search, it asks all for an element. If B does not have it, it asks its neighbors, A, F, G, and H. As the search widens, some nodes will be asked twice for the same element. On second request, they delete the request. In this way, requests are killed off as the search widens until a success occurs.

Searching conventions and naming conventions are related. In some distributed data bases, the system-wide name in the data base directory is used as part of the search strategy. For example, in IBM mainframe DB2, the system-wide name contains the name of the user who created the data base and the node on which it was created. The name of the node is called the "birthnode." When data bases are searched for, the search strategy is to ask the birthnode, identified by the birthnode name in the system-wide name, first. If the data base is not there, the birthnode will know where the data has migrated. Such name-based methodologies are a reason for leaf node escape.

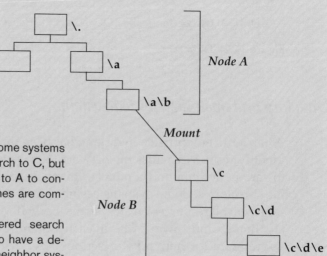

mounting might scale a bit better, the technology does not permit heterogeneous connection.

To be effective, the directory must be used. This requires organizational activity of considerable magnitude. Smaller organizations do not have the habit of defining enterprise-wide naming schemes and schema. Larger organizations have considerable inertial resistance. Applications must be disciplined to use the technology. Since the availability of the directory is environment dependent, it is difficult to know exactly when the disciplines should be put in place.

It is an enormously difficult undertaking to organize an enterprise-wide directory. The effort has started slowly, but there is now enough perceived need and vendor interest to lend some credibility to the X.500 image as a link between administrative domains.

Novell is offering a NetWare Directory System intended to serve as an enterprise directory, as is Banyan's StreetTalk. These are not directly interoperable with X.500 but require a gateway. The OSF/DCE-oriented vendors (Hewlett-Packard, DEC, IBM, et al.) are offering product based on the DCE directory standards, including a Universal Naming Convention interoperable with X.500. Sun has considerably enhanced its directory services in ONC+.

Data

The history of data modeling involves a number of various levels of abstraction and conceptualization. The base abstraction of data is the Unix sequential flow of bytes where information is laid out linearly from byte 0 to byte n, and is accessed by pointing to a byte position.

Record-oriented file systems define the idea of a record. A record is a well-defined element of a file containing a key (used to locate it) and a set of data items. A file consists of a group of records, usually ordered in some way.

A good percentage of the data in the world is still in byte-oriented or record-oriented file systems. Chapter 6 discussed some file systems used in distributed computing to gain remote access.

Organizations of data more easily manipulatable than file data have been with us for many years. Among these are the hierarchic data base managers, which represent data elements as occurring in well-structured trees ("employee is a descendent of department"); the smart network semantic data bases, which represent data in terms of complex relations between elements; and the relational data model, which represents data as two-dimensional tables.

The current state of the art is the relational model. Its great advantage is that it eliminates the need for programs to "navigate." However, the recent interest in graphic and image data, and a sense that 80% of the data yet to be made electronic will be unstructured image data, raises questions about the completeness of the relational model. The data access language SQL is seen to be easily usable across other data models, and extensible for other data classes. There is growing interest in the use of SQL for more inclusive data models. Among these are object-oriented data bases.

Entity–relation data model

This is a well-known data model in the set of semantic net data models. There has been a good deal of advanced technology and some product. There is more significant use of the model as a design and modeling tool than as a production data base. However, any model that can be defined by entity–relation can be transformed by some balance of application code and data base logic into relational, object, or even flat file.

The model derives from the notion of an entity and a relation. An entity is a unit of being having a name and attributes. It is a template for the creation of "instances" of the entity. It has relations of various types with other entities. These relations may be used to show process flow, structural status, events that begin behaviors, etc. Figure 12.3 shows two entities with a relation.

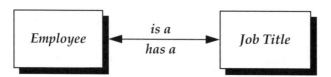

Figure 12.3   Two entities and their relations.

In the figure, an Employee has an "is a" relation with a Job Title. Conversely, a "has a" relation may exist between the Job Title and an Employee.

Different implementations and publications about the model differ in many details. In the most general concept, entities and relations have attributes. In effect, the picture might be more properly drawn as Figure 12.4. This more properly represents the notion that the relation is a kind of filter between the entity Employee and the entity Job Title.

Different kinds of attributes can be defined for entities and for relations. Some natural attributes for an Employee are: Name, Sex, Age, Address, Date of Employment, Last Raise, and Time in Grade. Some natural attributes for a Job

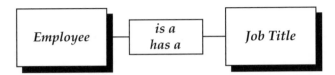

Figure 12.4 Relations have attributes.

Title are: Name, Grade, Salary Range, Reporting Structure, Organizations Where Found, What Data to Access, and How. A natural attribute for a relation is whether it is one to one, one to many, many to one, or many to many. In the most flexible systems, the attributes and relations can be dynamically defined as part of the design tool.

A complex data structure is formed by defining the relations between different kinds of entities. A design tension exists regarding what is an attribute and what is a relation. For example, the organization in which a job title exists may be an attribute of the Job Title entity. This could be true if there were no other interest in the organizational structure of the enterprise. However, if organizations have information for a data base, then there would be organizational entities. The department in which a job code appeared would be indicated in an "exists in" relation. This is shown in Figure 12.5.

The above describes the association of employees with job titles and the association of job titles with organizations. Whether a unique "exists in" relation need be defined or whether the semantics of "has a" can be used in both places depends upon the details of the relations.

An employee may have a relation with an organization independent of job title. For example, organizations have "head counts" to which employees are assigned, tables of organization, and manning in which an employee participates. A person may have skills uniquely required by the organization.

Clearly, the simple chart in Figure 12.6 is subject to countless variations in attribute and relation. The entity–relation model in and of itself does not provide guidelines for the identification of entities, the definition of attributes, and

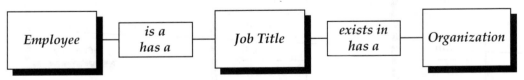

Figure 12.5 Job Titles exist in Organizations. The Job Titles of the enterprise are dispersed among Organizations. This is expressed by the "exists in" relation. Conversely, Organizations have Job Titles. This is expressed by the "has a" relation. There is as yet no relation between Employee and Organization.

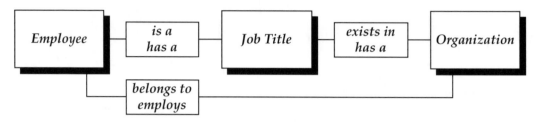

Figure 12.6 Employees (with Job Titles) work for Organizations.

the identification of relations. For this, some topic area guide is needed. For an asset management data base, sources like the SNMP MIB (Management Information Base), the OSI MIT (Management Information Tree), and the OSI GDMO can be useful (see Chapter 13).

Naturally, each of the entities, Employee, Job Title, and Organization, must have instances or exemplars that follow the model (Figure 12.7). A design tension is the degree of generalization associated with the template entities, that is, how much variation in characteristic is an exemplar allowed to still be an instance of "employee."

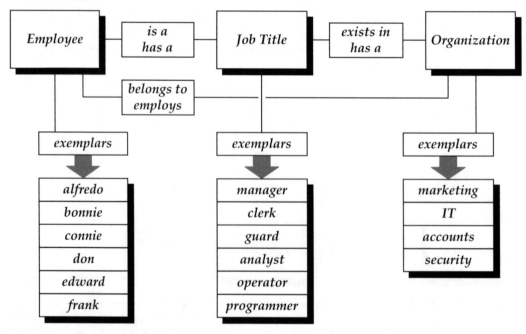

Figure 12.7 Real Employees.

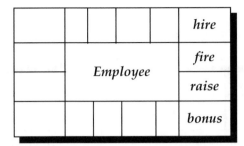

Figure 12.8   Entity Employee as an object.

Entity–relation and objects

Object concepts are natural to entity–relation:

1 An entity can be organized as an object.

2 The derivation (inheritance or aggregation) relation is possible in the entity–relation model.

This discussion will continue without distinguishing between Microsoft aggregation and OMG inheritance.

Consider the actions that can be taken upon an employee. He or she can be hired, fired, transferred, promoted, demoted, experience a change in job title, etc. If these actions are thought of as encapsulating the entity, then the entity has behavior as well as attributes and is consequently an object.

Figure 12.8 shows the entity Employee as an object. In such a context, the attributes of relations would contain a statement of which actions on the object Employee a related object can take.

Object derivation can be represented by an inheritance relation that indicates what data variables and what behaviors a subtype can inherit. There are differences of opinion in this area about degrees of freedom between subtypes and parents. This discussion will follow the OMG standard that a subtype must always be substitutable for its parent, and that it is always a perfect superset of its parent as regards behavior and data. There are many systems that allow more liberality in the "allomorphism" of subtypes.

Consider the desire to define different types of employee. All employees have some things in common. They are all hired, belong to departments, receive salaries, etc. However, managers may have some attributes and relations that nonmanagers do not have, and executives some attributes and relations

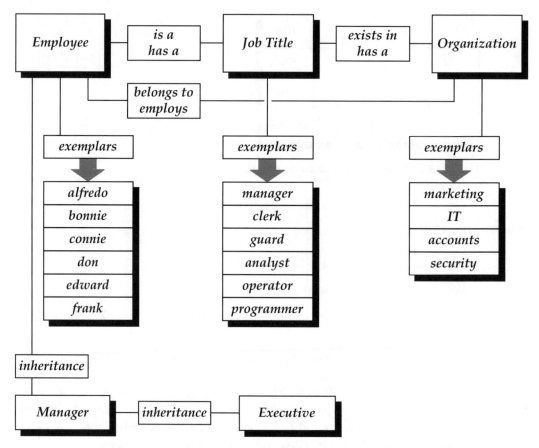

Figure 12.9 Managers are derived from Employees. Manager inherits behavior from Employee but adds some specialized behaviors. Executive inherits behavior from Employee and Manager but adds some specialized behaviors.

that managers do not have. Object people say that managers are derived from employees and executives are derived from managers (Figure 12.9).

Naturally, the subtypes defined by the inheritance relation can participate in a full range of other relations. That is, they can have "is a," "has a," and "uses a" relations as needed.

Object-oriented data bases

Entity–relation models form the underpinning for object data bases. These are coming into interest because the relational data base is limited as to what data

12.6 OMG DATA BASE STANDARD

The OMG initiated an Object Database Management Group to develop a standard for object data base systems. The developed standard, ODMG-93 1.0, currently has no de jure status and is independent of efforts at the American National Standards Institute to develop standards of object information systems. However, ODMG does provide some insight into the developing nature of this technology.

It addresses the need for an object data model, definition language, and manipulation language. It provides for bindings of these languages to Smalltalk and C++ so that statements of the languages can be embedded in these programs in much the same way SQL statements can be embedded in programming languages.

Key to the construction of an object data base is the definition of a schema. Objects must be defined and their interfaces created. In addition, methods must be developed for inclusion in the libraries used to generate Smalltalk and C++ code. Data query is handled by an SQL-like language that performs operations on the attributes of objects much like the operations of relational data bases.

types it can handle. There is interest in including various types of image and voice data into systems that can manage all information types behind a uniform data model. Extensions to SQL that would enable it to manipulate types like "picture" are receiving attention.

An additional motive for a new data technology is the need to solve problems of persistence in C++, where an object does not have a lifetime beyond an executing program that brings it into being. There is a need for a permanent repository of objects that have data base duration and whose attributes are stable and known.

Object-oriented data base management systems (OODMS) intend to provide appropriate representations for the object model and integration between the relational data base and objects. The OODMS stores object attributes and persistent representations of data. The lifetime of an object is "coterminus with the data base" and not the procedure or process running against it.

The fundamental principles of object data bases are

1 Objects can be "complex," formed from heterogeneous elements like text, pictures, etc.

2 Objects are always referenced by an object identifier (OID) assigned by the system. This identifier exists for an object's lifetime in the data base.

A number of object-oriented data base products have come to market. Some are "vertical" in the sense that they are specialized for a particular industry; others are intended as cross-industry servers. Among them are UniSQL, Gemstone, ObjectStore, Versant, and OpenODB. There are rather few of these in use in mission-critical applications.

Some of the relational data base managers (Ingres, Sybase) are being extended to support object-oriented concepts. UniSQL undertakes to unify relational and object-oriented concepts. OpenODB is an extension to relational data bases from Hewlett-Packard and Informix.

Some believe OODMS are not truly "objects" in that the methods associated with behavior are external to the object data base and must be linked to them when an application is to be run. This link may be done across a network in a client/server fashion, or on a local system. Despite some objections, this does provide an ability to map different object attributes and actions on data that can participate in more than one object.

Data warehousing

Data warehousing is a complex concept involving some ideas about the application life cycle and some ideas about the integration of data resident in diverse data base managers and file systems. In the idealized versions of data warehousing, the business enterprise analysis functions of the front of the life cycle are supposed instances of various types of information around the functions of the enterprise. The instances are supposedly captured in such a way as to build a usable and browsable directory of related and integrated data elements. These data elements can then be combined in the warehouse regardless of the system environment in which they exist. The combination allows new views and new dimensions, leading to decision insight.

The data warehouse is viewed as a permanent structure, a sort of "enterprise information factory," consisting of storage, data base, and management decision support technology sitting just below decision support applications, as shown in Figure 12.10.

The data warehouse provides accessibility to diverse collections of data through the use of a common API based on SQL. An application running on Windows, Unix, or OS/2 can access data residing in various servers across various communications protocols. Such a capability is provided by Information Builders' EDA/SQL (Enterprise Data Access/SQL). The ability of an application to access diverse data collections through SQL is considered by some to be the basis of data warehouse.

The extraction of data must be associated with an integration function that resolves conflicts in names, representations, etc. The data warehouse consists of snapshots and replications ("slices and dices") of data extracted from production data bases and used for decision support. The set of notions and technologies associated with extracting data for decision-support processing is now sometimes referred to as OLAP (On-Line Analytical Processing), where

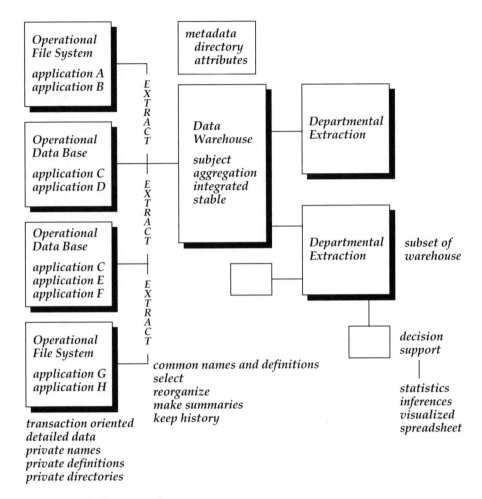

Figure 12.10 Data warehouse.

long and complex queries slice, dice, summarize, and aggregate (like super spreadsheets) elements extracted into the data warehouse.

The Hewlett-Packard Intelligent Warehouse is an example of the edge of the art in data warehousing. It takes an open data base call and analyzes the request to provide:

- Row-level security.
- Summarizations, averages, and other functions.
- Browsing of summaries and end tables.
- Interface with Excel, Access, Powersoft, and Visual Basic.

This is a tool closely related to rapid development tools.

Transaction processing

A group called the Transaction Processing Council (TPC) has undertaken, primarily for benchmarking, to define transaction complexity. They have defined, or are in the process of defining, four transaction types: A, B, C, and D.

These are important because the industry now uses transactions per second and cost per transaction as competitive numbers. Related to issues of comparative speed and cost are issues of industrial strength and scale. Legacy vendors are anxious to carve out a niche in transactions as the only reliable industrial-strength vendors. IBM VSE, for example, is positioning to maintain market share with versions of CICS running on VSE with the benefits of unattended operation. On-line transaction processing is the last fortress of proprietary, mainframe, text-oriented systems. The weapons are metrics like cost of migration, cost per transaction, and cost per user. Unhappily, the metric is never profit per transaction or profit per user, and that is why we are sometimes misled.

The technology

Interactive applications have an ongoing set of interactions driven by the user. Actions are completed, aborted, or terminated when the user decides. Examples are editing a document, creating a graphic, and writing a program.

Transaction applications have interactions structured into definite events called "transactions." A transaction is complete when the activities associated with it have been successfully performed. The computer system transaction manager guarantees "all or nothing" completion. If any activity cannot be completed, the transaction is aborted and all previous activities are "undone." A transaction is atomic in the sense that it is indivisible. During a transaction, no program or user may refer to affected data until the transaction is completed or aborted.

Transaction management may be provided by a file system or a data base manager. Alternatively, transaction capability may be provided by a transaction manager. A transaction manager is a manager of managers. It calls upon various resource managers, such as file systems, data base managers, recovery managers, etc., for transaction services. In this way, complex transactions that straddle data bases and environments can be supported by the transaction manager.

There are many products that fit into one of the above models, or somewhere between them. IBM's CICS (Customer Information Control System) offers an

TRANSACTION MODEL

The figure is a model for transaction processing. It includes a file system, data base manager, and recovery server. A transaction manager is a co-ordinator of servers. The transaction manager has the following functions:

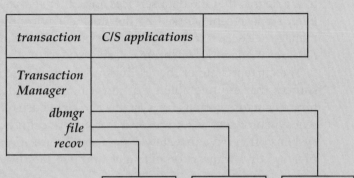

1 An application may have different transaction types with different processing needs. The transaction manager recognizes a transaction type.

2 It decomposes the transaction into services required from each server and passes service requests. It may do the service request serially or concurrently, depending on its own abilities to assure synchronization and integrity.

3 Successor transactions are precluded from seeing data to be changed by a current transaction until it is complete. Some "locking" relationship must exist between the transaction manager and the servers.

4 The transaction manager receives completion notices from the servers as they finish and (perhaps) return results.

5 When all servers have completed, the transaction manager "confirms" the transaction.

Commitment is a confirmation of any changes made during transaction processing. A common protocol is "two-phase" commit. In a two-phase commit, the transaction manager issues directives to servers after it has received confirmation of correct completion. Until then, the servers are prepared to abort the transaction. The commitment is firm; even if the server goes down as it accepts a commit, it will finalize data changes as part of its recovery process.

6 If any server reports trouble, all changes must be abandoned, and any changes in the permanent system must be reversed. This assurance of integrity, and all or nothing, is a primary role of the transaction manager.

API for transaction management and a set of local and distributed transaction services. It is now moving from its 390-only environment into OS/2, AIX, and HP MPE/ix. Other transaction capabilities include Tuxedo, a Unix de facto standard, and Top End. Example applications are all point-of-sale, inquiry, or on-line service applications.

The elements of a transaction processing environment include an API for data access (and an associated file or data base system) and APIs for synchronization, recovery, and security. Other APIs may be used by the application to gain the operating system services it requires. Current environments differ as to the degree that the data services and other services are linked to each other. Even some recent work, like the Encina environment, links the transaction manager closely to a particular file system. The transaction manager calls on resource managers, synchronizes, and recovers.

The current state of the art does not permit much diversity in the data resources that are referable by a transaction. Obstacles are differences in functionality across various file systems and data base managers, lack of cross-system synchronization and recovery protocols, different data formats, etc. These systems often have private views of synchronization and recovery difficult to preempt by a transaction manager, and overlapping any process built into recovery servers.

File systems are isolated entities, and traditionally, transaction managers have been built around their own file systems. This remains true, for example, in the latest transaction technologies from OSF and from Microsoft. The OSF transaction monitor, Encina, uses a record-oriented file system that differs from the distributed file system of OSF DCE. Transaction processing must use the transaction processing shared file system, a specialized RPC (the transaction RPC), in order to work with the Encina executive and monitor technology.

Distributed transaction management introduces the notion that a server or servers may be accessed across the network. The required synchronization and integrity guarantees of the transaction manager are not relaxed. It must still be true that no data can be seen by another transaction until a current transaction has gone to "commit," and that all actions, or none of the actions, of the transaction are completed. However, a whole new class of failure—network failures—are introduced.

There is a complex set of options for distributed transactions depending on the nature of the server(s) to be involved. Pure SQL relational data base transactions may rely on the relationships of homogeneous relational data bases doing distributed units of work and using private commit and recovery protocols as a group. Heterogeneous data bases do not currently do a two-phase commit together, and a transaction manager must accomplish the synchronization and recovery. Some of the transaction manager functions may be required of clients attempting to access data from more than one data base.

chapter 13

Systems management

EXECUTIVE SUMMARY   Systems management is a highly sensitive and political area. Often, deep issues of who is responsible for IT and the split of work between IT and users are argued out in the context of systems management.

Systems management is also an area where vendors compete for an "enterprise-level role." A vendor can be assured a central role by being a source of systems management technology. The competition for such a role is intense. Three major players are IBM, Hewlett-Packard, and Sun Microsystems, with Novell and Microsoft making serious advances. Also, countless companies provide systems management "applications" in the areas of storage management, recovery, archiving, and security, which run stand-alone or in systems management frameworks.

There are various aspects of management: the resources to be managed, the managing components, the distribution of management, management in heterogeneous systems, and standards to be used to do the management. Historically, systems management has been fragmented across diverse elements of software. Operating systems, library systems, mainframe administration systems, and network management systems have all undertaken to manage resources on a single machine or across the network.

There has been a division between "node" and "network," reflecting the division between operating systems and communications systems. The personality of an MVS mainframe is clear when node functions of data, work load management, and local security are undertaken. A different systems personality is seen with Netview managing traffic, recovery, and systems resources on the network. The integration of systems management across resources is far from being achieved.

Systems management

One can take a large view of systems management, in which case it becomes synonymous with asset management, or a small view, in which its only functions are network, fault, and performance management. Figure 13.1 shows some elements in a system requiring management.

Many systems and software vendors offer systems management frameworks or tools. A framework is an environment in which various management tools run together. The framework offers a set of protocols and interfaces for the use of the tools. Examples are IBM SystemView, Hewlett-Packard Open-View, Novell NetWare, DEC Polycenter, and Microsoft SMS. These products differ in what platforms they run on, the degree to which they may be centralized or distributed, and what resources they manage.

There has been a some activity directed at developing standards that would allow greater heterogeneous systems management and greater accord in the definitions of the resources and functions of management. Various products reflect many of these standards.

The seamy boundary between network and systems management is associated with something of a fuzziness about the issues that are naturally part of systems management. Current technology involves concepts like "backup management," "application management," "data management," and "storage management," as well as "systems management" and "network management." It is not clear precisely how various aspects of management relate to each other.

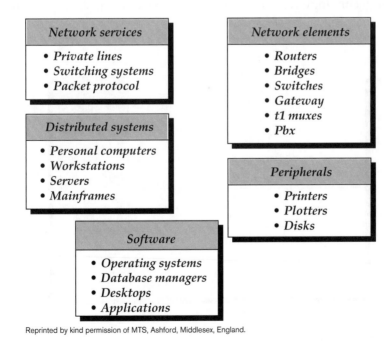

Reprinted by kind permission of MTS, Ashford, Middlesex, England.

Figure 13.1   What is to be managed.

A comprehensive and understandable image of the full range of systems management issues comes from the conceptual material of visions like IBM's SystemView. Despite the difficulties SystemView has had as a product set, it presents an elegant image of the grounds.

Figure 13.2 shows the SystemView dimensions: end user, application, and data. A systems management framework must define how it will appear to an end user, what data is to be collected and how it is to be organized, and what system management operations are to be mapped upon the data.

The dimensions are mapped across disciplines. The disciplines are: business, change, configuration, operations, performance, and problem. Each of the disciplines has a set of defined management tasks and corresponding functions.

Business management includes inventory management for the control of information technology resources, end user services control, accounting, and security.

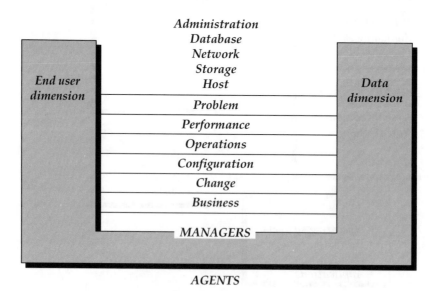

Figure 13.2   IBM SystemView picture.

SYSTEMS MANAGEMENT

There are a number of definitions of systems management function. They differ in how they group particular activities. Here is an alternative grouping:

Planning
- Linking technology and business strategies
- Developing systems architectures and structures
- Integrating systems components
- Defining systems management functions and objectives
- Budgeting and systems acquisition

Administration
- Control user services, accounting, and registration

- Configure hardware and software to support services
- Configure network to support services
- Monitor performance to assure user satisfaction
- Monitor security
- Control software use, including licensing and distribution
- Install and test systems
- Charge systems for computer and network use

Operations
- Fault and status monitoring
- Security monitoring
- Failure recovery
- Systems and network reconfiguration

Change management includes the delivery of resources (programs and files) from host processors (servers) to clients. It provides license management, copy management, and delivery tracking.

Configuration management is at the core of an integrated statement of systems and network management. It includes network configuration and particular machine configuration functions.

Operations management provides system and network work load control, operator automation, and fail-soft work load transfer. It positions the "host" or "server" as a backup and archiving server for workstations. Performance provides systems-centered utilization and service monitoring.

Problem management provides failure analysis for the network and machine-specific systems.

OSI and ISMA views of systems management

OSI has published the X.700 standards. These define dimensions and behaviors for a management framework. The OSI model has a number of functional areas. The following table shows how they correspond to SystemView disciplines:

OSI	SystemView
Accounting management Security management	Change management
Configuration management	Change management Configuration management Operations management
Performance management	Performance management
Fault management	Problem management

OSI has defined a management information base, Management Information Tree (MIT); protocols for relations between managing and managed systems, Common Management Information Protocol (CMIP); and a schema for the development of information bases, Guide Development Management Objects (GDMO).

There are a number of other standards efforts in the systems management area and a number of standards organizations working on aspects of systems management. These include the OSF Distributed Management Environment (DME), the Network Management Forum OMNIPoint, and X/Open. The X/Open systems management API, XMN, has been promised as an interface by a number of frameworks and products.

Perhaps the most comprehensive statement of systems management activity comes from the Information Systems Management Association (ISMA). ISMA states specific "processes" that can be organized into the larger "disciplines" of OSI and SystemView. This list is given in Box 13.3.

Basic technologies and protocols

There are three fundamental elements of systems management:

1 A management information base (MIB) with an attendant set of rules that define the meaning and representation of information in the data base. The structure of the data base follows a set of rules, SMI (Structure of Management Information), to define how managed elements are represented.

2 Managing and managed systems. A managing system runs management functions that collect information and issue directives to managed systems. An agent of the managing system is resident in the managed system. This agent has the capability to respond to requests for data and to perform directed actions.

3 Protocols defining the actions and responses of managing and managed systems. Two important sets of protocols are SNMP (Simple Network Management Protocol), now pervasive across systems management products, and CMIP from OSI, whose future is less certain.

As of the end of 1994, SNMP protocols are heavily dominant in available product, with almost trivial intrusion of CMIP. SNMP comes from the Unix community. SNMP data representation uses an international notational standard called Abstract Syntax Notation (ASN.1) to describe managed elements. SNMP also defines behaviors and operations between managed and managing systems. These include directives to obtain information about particular resources, to change the values associated with the status of particular resources, to respond to directives by reporting compliance, and to report unsolicited information to a managing system for defined critical events.

SNMP is pervasive in Unix, but it is also the basis for many non-Unix systems management products. It has just been extended (SNMP 2) to increase the degree of its object orientation, to extend its functionality, and to enable it to be present on more platforms. It is the current core technology of IBM NetView products as well as those of Hewlett-Packard, Sun, DEC, and other major tool vendors.

The core of the OSI technology is generically called CMIP. It is a considerable extension of SNMP, both in its object orientation and in its functionality. Managers and agents (system management application entities) run at layer 7 (application) in the OSI structure using protocols of the CMISE (Common Management Information Services Element) and the ROSE (Remote Operations Service

---

13.3   ISMA

- Application procurement and upgrading
- Architecture definition
- Audit planning
- Budget planning
- Business strategic planning
- Capacity planning
- Change control
- Customer services
- Data planning
- Distribution
- Education/training
- Financial administration
- Hardware/facility installation and upgrading
- I/S strategic planning and control
- Management systems monitoring
- Management systems planning
- Problem control
- Production
- Production and distribution scheduling
- Recovery planning
- Resource and data inventory control
- Resource and data performance control
- Security planning
- Security evaluating
- Service level planning
- Service marketing
- Skills planning
- Staff performance
- Systems planning
- Tactical plan management
- Tuning and systems balancing

Entity), and the usual connection/session services of ACSE (Association Control Service Entity), which supports "dialogues"—the OSI equivalent of conversations.

The data base supporting CMIP is organized into object classes representing significant extensions of SNMP object types. Each object has a set of operations that can be performed that enable requests for information, setting information, and general object management and definition functions. Inheritance rules apply over the body of the CMIP MIT.

Issues of systems management

Systems management now looms as a major element of cost of ownership for client/server systems as it did for mainframe systems years ago. Hidden costs of client/server are characteristically costs associated with inadequate systems management in first generation client/server systems. Lack of interoperability and uniformity of product is a primary constraint for the further evolution of distributed systems. In various trade surveys, nearly 40% of companies undertaking client/server and interoperable networks cite network management as a primary problem.

Network management is labor intensive, with in excess of 30% of many network budgets devoted to personnel and with uncountable expenses in client and decentralized environments not properly supported.

There are diverse views of who should run the network. Industry surveys suggest that about half of networked companies use IT to administer networks, and about 30% have some separate "networking" function. About as many permit the using departments to run networks as do not know who is running the network.

In the background is the issue of what constitutes industrial strength. Products developing for mainframe platforms extend older systems like MVS with backup and archiving capabilities for clients, providing industrial strength to the network. However, companies such as OpenVision, Epoch, and Legato, as well as IBM, have products that enable smaller servers to provide the same industrial strength backup and recovery as older mainframes.

The development of distributed heterogeneous systems gives rise to the need for management systems to cross a number of difficult boundaries. Traditionally, particular management protocols have been associated with particular communications stacks (SNMP with TCP, CMIP with OSI), and particular products have been associated with particular operating systems and architectures. Each management product family has privately organized MIBs and APIs. It is

	OpenView	AIXnet V6000	NWMS	SunNet Mgr.
Platform				
AIX	Y	Y	N	N
DOS/Windows	Y	N	Y	N
HP-UX	Y	N	Y	N
SunOS	Y	N	N	Y
ULTRIX	N	N	N	N
Windows NT	N	N	Y	N
Interface				
Motif	Y	Y	N	N
OPEN LOOK	N	N	N	Y
OS/2 PM	N	N	N	N
Windows	N	N	N	N
Communication				
DECnet	Y	N	Y	Y
SPX/IPX	Y	Y	N	N
OSI	Y	N	N	Y
TCP	Y	Y	Y	Y
SNA	Y	N	N	Y
Management				
CMIP	Y	Y	N	Y
RMON MIB	Y	Y	Y	Y
SNMP 1	Y	Y	Y	Y
SNMP 2	N	N	N	N
X.700	N	N	N	N
License				
By user group	Y	Y	Y	N
Per site	N	N	Y	N
Per user	Y	N	Y	Y

Table 13.1   Management platforms.

characteristically necessary to have multiple management systems and to have separate LAN and WAN management systems.

There is now a need for interoperability so that heterogeneous systems can be managed as a coherent entity. A requirement for mature systems management is:

- All dimensions and disciplines are organized into a coherent framework with common interfaces, data representation, and protocols.
- The system runs on a multiplicity of managing system platforms, including diverse communications protocols, operating systems, and architectures.

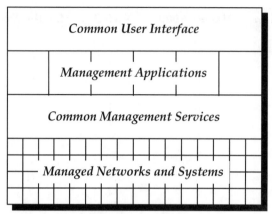

Reprinted by kind permission of MTS, Ashford, Middlesex, England.

Figure 13.3 OpenView structure.

- The system manages a multiplicity of platforms across all aspects.

The diverse history of systems management product makes systems management coherence sometimes seem an unachievable goal.

Table 13.1 shows some current systems and attributes of platforms. It is taken from the trade press in 1994. It is very likely obsolete by publication, but it provides a useful framework for understanding interoperability.

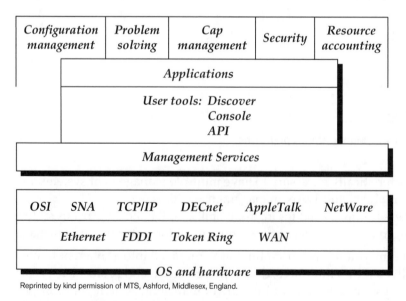

Reprinted by kind permission of MTS, Ashford, Middlesex, England.

Figure 13.4 SunNet Manager structure.

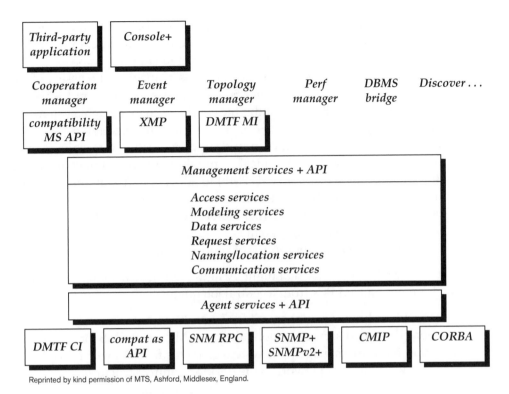

Reprinted by kind permission of MTS, Ashford, Middlesex, England.

Figure 13.5 Emerging architecture.

A management platform, although not using a particular operating system as a host, can manage a number of different operating systems by placing agents in their context.

Unhappily, this high-level summary does not suggest the true complexity of this area. Framework providers (Tivoli, IBM, Hewlett-Packard) intersect and cross license each other, whereas tool providers in various disciplines do not work within frameworks or on particular platforms.

Each of the major vendors is pursuing an apparent strategy of interoperability with major competitors. Yet each has its own MIB structure and set of constraints and limitations. Despite the excellent foil sets, coherent cross-system systems management remains a major constraint to integrated scalable systems.

Figures 13.3 and 13.4 show high-level frameworks for HP OpenView and SunNet Manager. Figure 13.5 is a conceptualization of a standards-driven, fully interoperable systems management architecture.

As a result of product immaturity, many customers must rely on minimum technology or use multiple management systems. Companies using three, four, or even five different management systems are not rare. Companies using different backup tools, for example, for different systems is common. The use of different systems for LAN and WAN management is common.

A key aspect of systems management is managing the assets of personal computers. There are now about 50 million PCs installed on LANs, of which only around 3.5 million are under the control of management systems. Costs of badly managed desktops in terms of end user time, excessive software licensing, remote software installation, and support functions are claimed by some to make client/server uneconomical. A number of vendors have formed a Desk Top Management Task Force (DTMF) to address issues on the desktop. These include IBM, Intel, Microsoft, and Novell among some 300 others. The attempt is to define a desktop management interface for PCs that allows a PC to behave as an agent in a managed system.

Currently, there is a potpourri of product that:

1 Allows PCs to be used at night by network schedulers that distribute work among unused PCs from a central job queue.

2 Provides license management for LANs by monitoring the use of software on clients and servers. Among these are Microsoft SMS for Windows NT and NetWare management system elements from Novell. Novell and Intel are working on a network-wide desktop control structure.

3 Provide fault-tolerant configuration and backup/archiving for a designated server. Among them are Epoch, Legato, OpenVision, and IBM Distributed Storage Manager.

Progress in interoperability, desktop management, and integration is a key gating function of computing evolution and a key competitive piece of the action.

Applications

The framework vendors are joined by a large population of application vendors who develop applications aimed at various aspects of systems management. There are vendors who have developed product in security, storage management, recovery, archiving, etc.

These applications often lack the integration that would be desirable in a coherent management set, but they do provide adequate tools for viewing the network, synchronizing and scheduling backup and recovery, and monitoring security. Other applications provide software licensing and distribution management.

Directions

New versions of systems management capability are coming to the market. These have features that considerably extend their use of object-oriented technology and use of OSI standards. IBM Karat provides a common interface and information structure across a subset of SystemView products and will run on a number of non-IBM platforms. Sun Encompass is a considerable extension of the SunNet Manager.

Increased integration of applications, wider interoperability, and more common application look and feel are visible parts of the direction.

There is also a tendency for "agents" to become more intelligent and to disperse some management functions toward the managed systems. Some hierarchic notions of multitier management are beginning to mature, with zones and domains of control more flexibly defined to support distributed systems management.

In the winter of 1994, Compaq announced that each personal computer would come bundled with software based on the DMI interface (from Intel and Novell) that would permit all of its PCs to be queried from a central site that could determine their hardware configuration.

chapter 14

Some systems players

EXECUTIVE SUMMARY There are countless vendors in the niches, naves, and apses of the computer business. Many are niche vendors, resellers of others' technologies, or service companies. Many are dominant within their niche. For example, very strong data base companies like Sybase, Oracle, Informix, and Gupta are coequal players with companies that span more niches. Communications companies like Wellfleet, Cisco, and 3Com are also significant technology pacesetters and trendsetters.

Despite this, the dramatic events and changes of the last decade seem to spotlight a handful of companies whose fortunes (rising and falling and rising again) seem to be metaphors for the industry. Some are companies that have come from nowhere to dominate a part of the business; others are traditional multisegment leaders; while still others are inventors of their own niches.

The nine companies discussed in this section were chosen by the author from a grouping of around 20 that he tracks for seminars and clients with the intent of giving a snapshot of the industry.

Apple

Major challenges:

- Increase penetration into the corporate mainstream
- Provide increased perception of "open"-ability, interoperability, and portability
- Increase server ability
- Maintain and/or increase usability advantage
- Separate hardware and software revenue flow
- Re-establish superiority as a graphics and publishing vehicle.

Apple holds a dominant position in the consumer segment of the market. However, the total product shipped is small compared to the total of all Intel-based systems and Windows systems running on Intel. The position of Apple in the PC market is not entirely unlike that of the AS/400 in the midrange market—a system much admired, but with problems related to current trends.

Surely the most dramatic recent event for Apple has been its commitment to the PowerPC chip and its agreement on a set of standards that will make Apple and IBM PowerPC personal computers compatible. During 1994 and 1995, Apple introduced systems that could take on Intel-based capability and run Windows software on a coprocessor basis seamlessly with Macintosh software.

Over the last few years, Apple has moved to reposition itself as a more open vendor. It now provides a Unix offering, A/UX, and it is beginning to attract greater ISV attention. In general, there is a rich set of the "usual" applications for Macintosh, many of which come from Microsoft. There have been some nasty interchanges between the two companies. The latest versions of Microsoft Word run quite poorly on the Macintosh. Apple accuses Microsoft of threatening to withhold application software if Apple aggressively pursues the OpenDoc alternative to OLE.

Apple seems interested in a broader range of systems and in leading in new interface hand-held systems. In this arena, products like Newton find competition from consumer electronics companies (Sharp) and some concern about what the devices are best at doing. The introduction of Newton met with some disappointment. It seemed to have a handwriting recognition learning curve for which the market was not adequately prepared, and its limited communication abilities restricted a number of natural uses.

Apple has for some time moved from its single-system personal user stance with a set of communications protocols (AppleWorks), and is attracting increasing support from servers supporting AppleWorks. It is also now possible to connect Apples with other than AppleWorks protocols. Apple has achieved connectivity to many major servers and larger systems including DEC, IBM, and Hewlett-Packard. Apple protocols are part of TCP/IP and NetWare.

There is a focus on 3-D graphics and multimedia and conferencing, with an attempt to establish Quickdraw and QuickTime as early integrated environments.

AT&T Global (NCR)

Major challenges:

- Extend enterprise penetration at the server level
- Gain acceptance of 3600-level architectures with integration of data base engines
- Establish serious Windows NT role
- Gain wider reputation as a leader in objects.

This section will discuss that part of AT&T Global that was National Cash Register (NCR). NCR was an enterprise player before IBM, and still has a major presence in banking and financial industries, where it was never entirely dislodged in the period of wild IBM growth. It is a respected technology leader, credited by some for making Unix accepted in the business marketplace.

NCR hardware is Intel architecture based. It is possibly the only major provider of enterprise-level servers that uses an industry standard bus architecture. It offers a wide range of product from desktop to enterprise server and some interesting systems architectures that integrate NCR servers, the specialized Teradata Data Engine with disk array and mainframe interconnection. Wherever advanced technology groups are interested in exploring alternatives and new models of computing, there is a frequent NCR presence.

The product line scales from Model 3200 desktops through 3300 workstations, 3400 SMP servers, 3500 enterprise servers, and the loosely coupled, clustered 3600s that can form the basis for distributed transactions and enterprise level client/server.

NCR is a major SVR*n* provider and an important instrument for introducing Unix into business environments. Its Top Hat transaction manager is a de facto standard for Unix-based transactions. Despite its Unix presence, NCR is also positioning itself as a major Windows NT player. This gives the company a Windows NT or Unix solution for scalable Intel-based software. It is offering migration services to Windows NT in cooperation with Microsoft. NCR is a major service company.

NCR systems interoperate with IBM using CPI-C interfaces over LU 6.2 and other LUs. There is support for IBM SQL dialects, token ring, and OSF DCE. NCR interoperates with Novell clients and provides a shared server where Unix OCCA elements and NetWare server elements coexist. Interoperation is supported over TCP/IP and SPX/IPX protocols with mappable APIs. OCCA provides Apple protocols up to the file level.

This is a serious player, and more so now with AT&T's resources and communications technology merged with it. It can run a significant part of a business as a primary strategy vendor.

DEC

Major challenges:

- Achieve introduction of the Alpha product line across a range of prices with minimum loss of VAX and DECstation revenues

- Establish role as group and enterprise server source
- Build software revenue flow for other platforms.

There was a time when IBM marketeers looked with awe on VAX/VMS, DECnet, the relational data base managers, the development tools, VAXclusters, and IBM marketeers trembled at "NAS" (Network Application Support), "DEC has it now," and the "Open Advantage." In the early days of IBM angst, DEC seemed still to be flying high.

Now, after some disappointing relapses, and after apparent turnarounds, deep questions remain. Profitability seems elusive despite the unquestioned quality of their products, their leadership in key areas, and their generally good relations with their clients.

DEC has the world's fastest chip, a 1.2 billion instructions per second instrument. They seem finally to be marketing DEC Intel-based PCs with some success, but the market penetration is small. There are Alpha-based PCs that might give DEC a more aggressive desktop posture, but these have not been getting the general attention of PowerPC-based desktop machines from Apple, Motorola, and IBM.

The main action at DEC is bringing in the Alpha-based product line. It must hold the VAX base as Alpha systems become mainstream. DEC must show that migration to Alpha, Alpha Unix or Windows NT Advanced Server, is a good strategy for VAX/VMS. It has recently seriously restated and reduced its commitment to VMS/Open on Alpha.

All of this includes a large effort to port middleware and baseware into a multioperating system strategy. The preoccupation with the VAX-to-Alpha transition has ironically left DEC unable to attack IBM legacy mainframes.

VMS/Open seems committed to a rich range of POSIX support, including drafts at the 1003.4 level. It has announced XPG4 support and is a major source of DCE elements (parts of the RPC, naming services, thread services, timing services, and elements of Motif). DEC claims that aspects of the Alpha architecture were designed to optimize VMS performance.

But as of the summer of 1995, DEC seems especially interested in showing its Windows NT posture and assuring its market of timely ports of key DEC software to Windows NT on Alpha enterprise and departmental servers. This includes Rdb, the DEC data base manager, DEC LAN Manager, DECmessage, C++, DECmail, and other formerly VMS-particular or ULTRIX middle- and upperware.

DEC, possibly because of its very close relations with Microsoft, was late and seemed a bit tentative in joining the COSE process. Often DEC takes a bridging and mediating position between the Microsoft and non-Microsoft worlds. It offers, for example, to build bridges between Microsoft COM and CORBA-compliant systems. DEC has had some particular uncertainties about its Unix strategy. ULTRIX has been "stabilized," and attention has shifted to the OSF/1 Mach-based microkernel system. It now seems committed to bringing OSF/1 to Alpha. Despite DEC's early positioning with RISC-based worksta-tions, it did not hold leadership against Hewlett-Packard and IBM, and has slipped from being second to Sun.

One aspect of DEC that remains unchanged is the excellence of its network offerings. Pathworks offers multiprotocol support on a number of platforms, a shared file system (Pathworks DOS File System), and integrated systems man-agement of LAN Manager and NetWare servers from a PC. FrameWorks pro-vides consistent network images and terminologies.

The proud and aggressive history of this company, its unusually large set of firsts, and its tradition of industry leadership encourage one to expect a revival. But until the Alpha gains deeper penetration and some successes are scored with the servers, there seem to be shadows here. By and large, downsizing sto-ries and rightsizing tales do not seem to involve the Alpha. Much depends on the success of the Alpha port and on some wins with Windows NT at the top of the line.

DEC remains a full source strategic company capable of supplying and inte-grating product at enterprise architectural levels. It is going through agonizing restructuring events in its attempt to find the "new DEC," and one can only wish it well.

Hewlett-Packard

Major challenges:

- Establish itself as an enterprise player
- Increase market share at minimum cost in the departmental and small enter-prise server area
- Maintain a role as leader in LAN management, objects, and graphics software
- Increase its role as a personal computer vendor
- Increase the integration of product offerings.

There do not appear to be too many problems here. Hewlett-Packard, aside from its printer business, is a major systems player in an aggressive posture, gaining great results from attacks on vulnerable IBM midsize older 390s. There does seem to be a return to the "core business" attitude settling in at the end of

1994. There also seems to be a turning away from notions of "desktop" Unix as Hewlett-Packard PC sales begin to surge and it begins to achieve a nontrivial part of the Intel/Windows market.

Hewlett-Packard is two companies at the systems level. One company, the marketer of the HP 3000 line with the MPE/ix product line, has product positioning problems not unlike IBM and DEC. MPE/ix supports XPG/4 and the usual DCE/POSIX/Unix paraphernalia (except that, as of the end of 1994, it lacks a Spec 1170 announcement). The perhaps more-dramatic part of the company comes from the Apollo Computing Company—an early innovator in objects, distributed computing, and open systems. The Network Computing System (NCS) of Apollo provided the base technology for the OSF DCE and RPC and its associated IDL (Interface Definition Language), now a mainstream standard. The operating system platform is HP-UX, a proprietized Unix based on elements of SVR3, BSD, OSF, and Hewlett-Packard technology. It runs with X11R5, supports Sun ONC+, and NetWare client and server. It is respected as a high-quality Unix, capable of OLTP, and support of very large SMP enterprise servers.

Hewlett-Packard is a major software development, graphics, and end user source. Softbench is a major industry CASE framework, licensed to IBM and others. It is a major leader in objects with the DOMF (Distributed Object Management Facility) and support for CORBA standards. It is delivering second-generation CORBA software (Hewlett-Packard ORB+) to provide C++ language bindings to DOMF. It is shipping versions of Distributed Smalltalk. It is using object technology to provide data warehouse functions behind Open-Object Data Base. Hewlett-Packard claims this product can integrate all data regardless of format, complexity, or location. It will work with IBI EDA/SQL tools that provide access to 50 data bases or file systems, including IMS and DB2. Hewlett-Packard's aggressiveness in graphics and multimedia matches its aggressiveness in objects.

A major area of strength for Hewlett-Packard in positioning itself as an enterprise player is the network management technology OpenView. It is a serious competitor to IBM NetView (in fact has been licensed by IBM) and SunNet Manager, with a somewhat richer coverage of systems managed and wider range of platforms (see chapter 13). Hewlett-Packard is expected to move to an object-based version of OpenView. It has announced a relational data base repository using Oracle7 that will permit the distribution of management data and common management of data bases.

Hewlett-Packard was a leader in the organization of COSE, and claims to have the nearest-to-compliant Unix product. Its interface, Hewlett-Packard VUE, is part of the common desktop environment. It was a co-definer (with DEC) of Motif.

This is a robust, growing, aggressive enterprise player, encouraging down-sizing to its enterprise-level servers, leading with object, graphics, and development technology. It has the respect of its growing customer base and, from time to time, the admiration of Wall Street. It has a full-range product line, from laptop to enterprise server, and some credible plans to help people get off older mainframes.

Of course, there are always downsides. There is some concern about the PA-RISC chip which, like Alpha, has small penetration outside its creator and is not keeping up with Alpha or other chips in performance. Hewlett-Packard is working with Intel on a "post-RISC" wide-word machine. This might create some migration problems for PA-RISC–based software. The delay of new generation systems management technology in early 1995 was taken badly by many loyalists who feel that Hewlett-Packard is now seen as slipping behind IBM and Sun. Still, the Asset Management Offering, in which Hewlett-Packard offers to take on systems management from its own center, is an innovative notion.

Hewlett-Packard is becoming a leader in intelligent data warehousing. It supplies a graphical browsing tool that supports up to 2,000 users across a number of data base elements, including Oracle, Sybase, CA-Ingres, Informix, and Red Brick on HP-UX.

There is a sense that Hewlett-Packard feels that it has gotten the low-hanging IBM fruit. It has been spectacularly successful edging out older midsize IBM mainframes. It may be turning its attention to some low-hanging Sun Microsystems fruit, represented by older Unix workstations.

IBM

Major challenges:

- Integrate product offerings
- Overcome lag in key technologies
- Phase out old-technology 390s and base culture on new technology with minimum revenue loss
- Find new revenues in consumer and entertainment markets
- Achieve credibility as an "open" vendor.

IBM remains a dominant player. It offers product in more segments of the industry than any other vendor, and for many companies is by far the primary vendor. While no longer the vertically integrated standards maker that defined the industry, it has recoiled from the (bad) notion of breaking itself into niche companies.

The reports of the death of IBM have been greatly exaggerated. Although the 1994 mainframe revenues are about half of the 1990 revenues ($5 billion vs. $11 billion), the company is maintaining revenue in a time of transition. It is building a good services business. IBM is clearly a company in transition. There are still signs of confusion and being out of step between product lines.

A number of people hold titles with the word "strategy" in various offices in Somers, Atlanta, Tarrytown, and in Europe. Naturally, there is some diverse opinion in this group and quite a range of pessimism and optimism. An IBM strategy must address the question of what business IBM is in. It is among the companies searching for a core business.

The major strategic investments in the opening years of the 1990s have been to position product in an "open" market. APIs and protocols from outside of IBM have been added to every major platform (MVS, VM, OS/2, AS/400, AIX), and alliances have been formed, joined, and abandoned. IBM has intensively participated and undertaken the leadership of both de jure and de facto standards groups. It is a member of OMG, a founder of OSF, and a leader in forming COSE. It claims to have 1,300 employees on 1,200 committees of ANSI, AWOS, CCITT, COS, ESPRIT, EWOS, IEEE, ISO, NIST, OSF, X/Open, and OMG. It has positioned new proprietary technologies, for example, CPI-C and MQI, as candidates for de jure or de facto protocols. It has included standards from OSI, OSF, and IEEE in all of its major baseware and, where appropriate, middleware.

IBM has been extraordinarily successful at choosing a competitive technology to license, filling its product line with that technology, and then, in a development window this strategy creates, coming forth with its own state-of-the-art technology. It has done this with Mail, first riding on Lotus Notes and then moving away from it, only to return.[†] It has done this with systems management, first licensing Hewlett-Packard OpenView and then coming forth with its own Karat.

At its best, IBM tries to present the image of a company providing whatever solutions are appropriate to a customer. It claims to be a supplier of a broad range of its own and industry technology. It still must make some major investment decisions. It must understand more fully what is an appropriate time to

---

[†] IBM's acquisition of Lotus, viewed as a good thing by Wall Street, may not look so good if Lotus software gives way to Microsoft, CompuServe, etc. as a primary mail system. If IBM manages Lotus the way it did Rolm, there will be disaster.

wait for profits and what are the balances of profit vs. market share in various marketing cycles.

An underlying question for IT here is whether, and for how long, IBM will underwrite technology for the 390 proprietary-software culture that IT can afford. At stake are decisions about if, and how quickly, there must be planning to migrate or redevelop applications or acquire skills to move onto an alternative PowerPC-based superserver.

The strategy seems to be to position the 390 culture as a credible option with a future. Still, AIX products are presented as "downloading" alternatives more frequently than in the past, and there is strong client/server marketing activity. However, the notion that a mainframe may be replaced at some time by very large AIX PowerPC servers is not mainstream at this time.

The message is that an evolutionary shift to microchip-based 390s and RAID technology will bring the mainframe customer into the hardware mainstream, and that the evolution of MVS, VM, CICS, and the Network Blueprint will bring the customer into the software mainstream. It is a credible story, but like all stories it has some gaps and some glosses.

There are persistent IBM issues. The high percentage of IBM revenue from mainframes remains a key concern. The AS/400's transition to an "open enough" system seems to have been well managed. In the minds of many, the AS/400 has a "niche" problem and did not seem to be as "modern" as Unix, Windows NT, and other players. IBM seems to have succeeded in protecting its base and growing it slightly by committing AS/400 to Spec 1170 APIs and opening the communications. The underlying hardware of the AS/400 will be the PowerPC, providing a common machine base for it and AIX systems.

IBM OS/2 seems one of the Cinderella stories of the industry, and must be counted a great triumph for IBM. OS/2 "Warp" version 3.1 has impressed the industry at a time when there is growing concern abut the availability of Windows 95. Even at the OS/2 2.1 predecessor level, OS/2 had become a serious desktop and small server competitor, with an important intrusion into key industries like banking.

While OS/2 in all markets (consumer and corporate) seriously lags Windows, it is a formidable corporate contender, with a developing reputation for robustness and (surprisingly) performance compared to Microsoft Windows NT for common applications software.

OS/2 is nearing 8 million copies. It is a true 32-bit operating system that runs on the hardware of over 60 vendors, including the IBM Micro Channel, PCI, and EISA buses. It supports PCMCIA. It is coming to the PowerPC. It provides concurrent support of DOS, Windows, and OS/2 applications, permitting data exchange and sharing between them. It has integrated telephony, CD-ROM, audio, and video windows. It is pledged to support the IBM Network Blueprint. It has a fast file system, transaction processing with CICS, a family of data base managers, support for DCE (except the file system), reasonable support from independent software vendors, and both client and server versions. A basic OS/2 system will run with 4 MB of memory and needs 30 MB of disk space and a 386 microprocessor.

In 1994, IBM had yet another reorganization. This one returned the company to a previous incarnation based on a vertical industry orientation. There is likely no permutation or combination of its various operational units that IBM has not yet tried. They never seem to get it quite right. There are always seams that are visible and annoying to customers.

Yet the current top man is clearly uncountable levels above the management that presided over the demise. Some key bad guys have left (and, not surprisingly, some good ones), and the move from the mausoleum in Armonk may do something more to make this bank look like a technology company. Still, the word from inside is that it is not clear what has changed. A recent client of mine said of IBM that "they just seem tired."

Microsoft

Major challenges:
- Achieve role as an enterprise player
- Increase penetration at server and mission-critical levels
- Maintain operating system dominance in the face of increasing competition to itself and to Intel-based platforms
- Sustain application market position and the ability to set de facto standards
- Resist public policy efforts to constrain relations between applications and operating systems
- Successfully penetrate the home market with networking and television-related services.

Microsoft is the dominant multitiered software company of the 1980s. It is a major player at baseware, middleware, and upperware levels. At the upperware layer, it offers spreadsheets, e-mail, word processors, CD-ROM–based encyclopedias, dictionaries, games, and publishing packages for Windows/MS-DOS baseware, Mactintosh, and OS/2. As of end of 1994, it was shipping 2 million MS-DOS/Windows–based systems per month, and 80% of the Intel-based personal computers are running MS-DOS. There are in excess of 40 million Windows users.

Microsoft's major platform product is the Windows family. It is commonly packaged with hardware offerings by hardware vendors who also include upperware. In July 1994, Microsoft agreed with the Justice Department to modify certain licensing practices with PC vendors. The agreement leaves Microsoft intact as a platform and applications supplier. When it is not packaged, Windows can be purchased for $99. It is likely that most readers of this book have and use a copy of Windows 3.1 on MS-DOS in their homes.

Windows has resisted the increasingly "Unixy" flavoring added to other systems. It has made no commitment to support Spec 1170. Windows does provide much of what is needed for interoperability (TCP/IP, SPX/IPX, NetBIOS) and some APIs, from POSIX and DCE. For the most part Microsoft generates proprietary de facto standards by virtue of their pervasiveness in the marketplace. Microsoft APIs for data base call (ODBC), telephone, mail, etc. are effective de facto standards, and other software and systems vendors must confront them. Some of them are supported and others are emulated; yet others cause the formation of alliances to offer an alternative that is certified by some vendor neutral organization.

The beginning of 1995 has seen a review of an agreement that resolved the threat of "breaking up" Microsoft into applications and platform companies. By agreeing to cease some licensing practices, Microsoft has maintained its single identity. It is clearly interested in revenue from non-Windows platforms, is a dominant vendor of Macintosh software, and is rarely accused of manipulating the application strategy to impact the platform strategy, although such an issue has been raised by Macintosh users with regards to version 6 of Word.

Microsoft has shown its ability to visualize new opportunities and to move into them aggressively. It is now working with systems companies like Hewlett-Packard to establish itself as a major software vendor for their desktop TV technology. It has declared an interest in providing on-line services to compete with Prodigy, CompuServe, and America Online, and in actually building a private network to do this, deciding to confront the government after backing down on the acquisition of Intuit.

On the downside, the company has stumbled at times on delivering high-quality versions of new systems on time. Windows NT had a rough introduction, and Windows 95 has been the subject of a number of disappointments and delays.

It is not clear how large this company can grow. So far it has made every bet right. It is positioned for content-oriented software as well as application- and systems-oriented software and seems, regardless of how the Justice Department issue goes, to be able to anticipate everything and make the plays.

Novell

Major challenges:

- Move profitably out of its traditional niche and establish itself as an enterprise player
- Prevent being blindsided by upperware offerings from other vendors and squeezed out as the first-generation small client/server systems begin to evolve to larger systems
- Position itself as a multisegment vendor operating at multiple levels.

This is a company trying to redefine its role in the industry. It seems to have a clear vision of the risks involved in its present niche and of the steps necessary to redefine its business. It pursued the position of an "all-niche" vendor aggressively until the arrival of its new CEO, Robert Frankenthal, from Hewlett-Packard. He has brought something of a "core-business" strategy and a lowering of the confrontational stance relative to Microsoft.

Novell is the dominant player in the niche of LAN-based small client/server systems. Its major competition in this niche is IBM and Microsoft LAN Manager and LAN Server products. It also has competition for larger networks from Banyan (and others) and from small Unix servers.

Novell has made some dramatic moves within the past few years. It has acquired Unix Systems Laboratories and is now the owner of SVR5, although it has given up trademark control to X/Open. It has participated in the COSE agreements. Novell has the intention that all Unix will have NetWare protocols, all NetWare will have Unix protocols, and there will be free intermixture of clients and servers with minimum ISV effort. Novell hopes to achieve a single code stream. A scalable undertaking in this direction is UnixWare, which aims at the complete integration of NetWare and Unix at all system levels.

The company has entered cooperative projects to extend its LAN protocols to WANs through agreements with AT&T and with router vendor Wellfleet. AT&T will take Novell LANs out to the telephone system through its PBXs, and Wellfleet will provide WAN routing technology that could lay the basis for an SPX/IPX Internet. Novell has begun to acquire and make alliances to give itself a greater visibility to the client.

Novell has made a determined move to upperware visibility with the announcement of Novell AppWare. AppWare is a challenge to Microsoft WOSA. It provides visually based cross-platform tools, code builders, CORBA compliance, and Hyperdesk objects. There was an early commitment to AppWare, which through UCS (Universal Component System) will develop client applications that run on "anything," including major versions of Unix, Mac, Windows, and OS/2, as well as serve as NetWare Loadable Modules (NetWare server applications). This commitment has since been softened. The acquisition of WordPerfect is part of Novell's upperware strategy.

Novell may not really have managed the introduction of its level 4.0 product as well as one might hope. It is not clear whether Novell understands how to play enterprise. Also, its delivery of a scalable server operating system is well behind the industry.

Sequent Computing

Major challenges:

- Establish itself as a true enterprise player
- Match the software richness of direct competitors like HP and IBM
- Form and maintain a proper set of alliances for emerging functions
- Define value-add for its packaged system
- Balance Unix and Windows NT Advanced Server opportunities.

Sequent is yet another company "redefining" itself and attempting to "play" enterprise. It has experienced a number of transformations and counter-transformations in the past three years in attempting to position itself as a company capable of working at strategic IT levels with large companies. It has had some recent successes, and it is found as a secondary vendor in a broad range of financial, technical, and manufacturing companies. Lately, it has been able to engage some potential clients in enterprise-level architecture projects.

Traditionally, the heart of the Sequent product line is a set of Unix-based systems—the Symmetry series, Symmetry 2000 and Symmetry 5000—spanning desktop to enterprise server. These systems are based on Intel processors and are configurable in large multiprocessor populations. A top-of-the-line server can serve 3,000 on-line users. Costs are in the $3 million range for a server of this class when fully configured, which is directly competitive with top-of-the-line Hewlett-Packard enterprise servers.

Sequent's strong suits are symmetric multiprocessing and clustering. Sequent has been an unquestioned leader in high levels of multiprocessing with their proprietized version of Unix, Dynix/ptx. Their ptx/Clusters allows close associated and fast memory-to-memory transfer (SDI) between elements of a cluster. This extremely useful configuration for data base management is aimed at attracting the support of Oracle Parallel Server. Versions of the clustering technology can be made high availability with the use of ptx/EFS (Enhanced File System), which provides highly efficient recovery.

Sequent positions itself as an "open" vendor, and it is open in multiple senses. The Dynix/ptx system is an aggressive Unix product, highly respected by Novell Unix Systems Laboratories and OSF. The multiprocessor features of Dynix will influence both System V multiprocessing and new versions of OSF/1.

The company is now also offering WinServer, a software platform based on Windows NT. This positioning will allow it to see how the wind blows as regards the intrusion of NT at server levels. The NT line does not scale as high as the Symmetry line.

Historically, Sequent has had an On-Line Transaction Processing (OLTP) orientation. Recently, however, it has shown keen interest in a position in data warehousing and new-generation decision support systems, On-Line Analytical Processing (OLAP). It has announced various OLAP products in subject areas such as financial data (DecisionPoint for Financials).

Sequent is participating vigorously in the alliance and consortium field. In the past, it was both a Unix International and an OSF member, and has consistently achieved X/Open branding for its Dynix product.

It has a relation with just about every producer of major elements of the software environment. It seems to work most closely with Oracle, but there are Informix, ASK Ingres, and Sybase versions for Sequent product. There is an implementation of the Network File System. IBI EDA/SQL Access will run with Dynix.

Sequent is a serious player facing very difficult competition from the megaplayers (HP, IBM, DEC) and oncoming competition from Sun. As a primarily Unix vendor, it clearly has a strategy problem about how much to invest in supporting Window NT Advanced Server, and whether to ensure that all the facilities of Dynix/ptx are available with NT. Industry commentators often talk about the quality of Sequent's relation with its "partners."

While the product line is clearly broadening—OLTP and OLAP, Unix and Windows NT—an equally important aspect of the strategy is the positioning as an enterprise player. The Innovative Business Institute provides executive-level seminars on the alignment of the technology and business. Sequent's consulting service business is develping rapidly, and it is experiencing success as a strategic vendor. But this is also a highly competitive business populated by megaplayers. The struggle to expand beyond the "platform" level may be difficult.

No member of the Unix culture with a data warehousing or transaction interest of significant scale would not want Sequent to be on the list of vendors receiving a request for proposal.

Sun Microsystems

Major challenges:

- Maintain workstation business while building server and Intel desktop revenue
- Remove concern about SPARC's future
- Establish Solaris as a major Unix desktop product
- Maintain dominance in systems management
- Manage entry to commercial accounts.

Sun Microsystems and major divisions like SunSoft and SunConnect are the leading Unix-environment workstation vendors. Sun's enterprise presence permits it to dominate certain aspects of a business, especially those that are computationally intense. The technology has grown from an engineering and design culture to financial institutions, brokerage houses, and other businesses where mainstream tactics and strategies involve sophisticated computation. It is an enterprise player by its existence as the primary technology in many aspects of a business. It rolls back mainframes in key areas.

Sun is the source of ONC (Open Network Computing), the industry-pervasive de facto standard for client/server, file-oriented computing. ONC+ consists of the NFS (Network File System) and an enterprise-level directory.

Sun has been successful in building a community of SPARC packagers and in promoting SPARC as a platform. SPARC seems to be the architecture of choice for Japanese mainframe companies looking for alternatives to 390-based systems. There are a number of other workstation packagers and a large set of semiconductor companies competing for fast versions of SPARC (among them Texas Instruments and Cypress). Sun has been very successful in attracting independent software vendors to the SPARC culture, and there is a full range of desktop applications.

In the past few years, however, there has been some concern about Sun. There has been a slight dip in workstation market share in the face of intense competition. There has been some concern about the SPARC architecture's ability to grow to 64 bits, and to compete on benchmark bases with Hewlett-Packard, Alpha, and PowerRISC chips. Sun is now trying to increase its presence in the server market and to establish a presence in the PC market to augment its workstation position.

There have been a number of server announcements and considerable interest in reassuring the market about SPARC performance. It is not clear how Sun will succeed in the server market as a follower of IBM and Hewlett-Packard.

However, its customers are devoted. Many have made deep psychological commitments to Sun as part of their struggle to refresh the legacy, and the introduction of servers into their workstation environments should not be impossibly difficult. The success of Solaris in Intel markets is less sure. However, Wabi, the Windows emulator, is now becoming a de facto emulation standard, and will be found in other Unix environments.

Sun Solaris is a packaging of SunOS, communications, and OPEN LOOK. At the version 2 level, its underlying operating system is SunOS 5.x, the first SVR4-based SunSoft Unix. It is available in desktop, group server, and enterprise server versions. Solaris 2 is not backward compatible with Solaris 1, which was a BSD-based system. Sun is trying to position itself as a PC player as well as a server player, and Intel-based packaging of Solaris is a key strategy. A Solaris will also be available for PowerPC architecture, and there are PC emulation licenses out to SCO, Hewlett-Packard, and USL. It is a participant in the COSE agreements. It is associated with efforts to converge object technologies with IBM, Apple, Hewlett-Packard, and DEC. SunOS groupware is called ShowME (Shared Interactive Environment). It provides for wide-area group separation within an OpenWindows framework.

Sun is a leader in network management tools with SunNet Manager. It is deeply respected for its functionality, and is clearly the dominant system in terms of worldwide installed base. The recent announcement of Solstice removes any concern that Sun was slipping behind IBM and Hewlett-Packard in this area.

the basics book: chapter 1

The queen in the hive

EXECUTIVE SUMMARY IT cares about basic component hardware because issues of performance, compatibility, and support of software impact the budget significantly. One goes from one computer generation to another with expectations of improvement. There is real danger that improvement will not be achieved unless care is taken to understand the conditions under which existing software will actually run faster and new software will be enabled. There is equal danger of underestimating the extent to which there is danger in moving from one hardware culture to another.

In a world as perfect as vendor statements of direction imply, hardware is hidden by layers of software, and the properties of hardware are irrelevant, except for measurements of how fast certain software elements run on different machines. But the "devil in the detail" here is that there are potential versioning, licensing, availability, and pricing issues that tie very directly to hardware properties.

There are a number of pervasive industry hardware cultures that offer the basis for populations of packaged computers. Computers differ from each other in their fundamental set of operations (architecture), their design (layout of architecture on technology), and in the technology used to construct them. Various computers with the same architecture, design, and technology may be packaged with different features and with different levels of proprietarization that make them preferable to others in certain circumstances.

Architecture, design, and technology

All of the elements of a computer—processors, memory, storage, interfacing devices, printers, etc.—have aspects of architecture, design, and technology.

Architecture is what hardware looks like to software: the rules that a program must obey to perform on a machine, for example, how big a number can be added to another, how elements in memory are addressed, and the particular operations that can be performed. The portability of a program from one

THE BASICS BOOK: 1. THE QUEEN IN THE HIVE

machine to another is determined largely by the architecture, which makes two machines look similar or dissimilar to a program.

Design is how circuits are used to map the operations of the architecture onto technology. The number of circuits determines whether the machine will be cheap, fast, or somewhere in the middle. Design determines what can be done in parallel—whether some complex operations can be disproportionately fast for special applications. Design will influence technology, since newer technologies usually cannot support the densities (circuits per micron) of older technologies. There is often a trade-off between less-sophisticated design on faster technology and more-sophisticated design on slower technology.

Technology determines how the design is implemented in the physics and chemistry of semiconductor substances. This determines the manufacturing cost of the machine, its basic speeds, the cost of elements like power, cooling, water, air or exotic gas encapsulation, etc. Technology has the least direct impact on software, but it does affect software performance, how much effort must be put into programming to recover from failures, and in a general way, what new software ideas can be introduced in a generation of computers.

Architecture

Architecture defines how a machine looks to a program. Table B1.1 shows some industry-pervasive architectures and the computer systems in which they are available. One can see a reasonable range of "scalability" for various architectures. The Intel Pentium, for example, is available in laptop computers and is also used in higher-performance enterprise servers where 16, 32, 64, or more are combined to produce a more expensive and more capable system.

RISC architectures achieve speed with very fast, simple instructions cleverly sequenced by a compiler. CISC architectures achieve speed by very powerful instructions that reduce the number of instructions that must be performed.

The "personal computer" is dominated by Intel CISC x86 architecture. There are over 700 packagers of the Intel architecture, including IBM, Compaq, Dell, ASR, NEC, and Toshiba. "Intel Inside" is a clear industry standard. Users of the Intel architecture may acquire the chips from Intel licensees or may manufacture them themselves under license. Often, leading vendors will attempt to add unique value by using specialized elements and packaging that provide superior capability or price effectiveness.

As of this writing, a challenge to Intel dominance is being made by the IBM, Apple, Motorola Somerset Consortium, which has developed a RISC chip called "PowerPC." Apple is already marketing desktop systems using a version of

Architecture		Packaging Range ($)	Characterization
IBM "S/390"	CISC	75,000–6,000,000	midsize to mainframe
IBM AS/400	CISC	10,000–1,000,000	small to midsize
IBM PowerPC	RISC	5,000–3,000,000	laptop to superserver
DEC VAX	CISC	3,000–4,000,000	desktop to midsize
DEC Alpha	RISC	4,000–1,000,000	workstation to enterprise server
Intel 386	CISC	800–2,000,000	laptop to parallel
Intel 486	CISC	1,500–2,000,000	laptop to parallel
Intel Pentium	RISC/CISC	2,500–2,000,000	laptop to enterprise server
SPARC	RISC	4,000–1,000,000	workstation to enterprise server
HP PA-8000	RISC	3,000–1,000,000	workstation to enterprise server
MIPS RS4200	RISC	5,000–750,000	workstation to enterprise server

Table B1.1 Architectural examples. A CISC architecture has many powerful instructions that attempt to do things with the fewest instructions. A RISC architecture has very simple instructions and achieves speed by doing many of them in parallel.

this architecture. IBM intends to do so in 1995. Late 1994 agreements between the Somerset members will lead to the marketing of effectively identical machines under the IBM and Apple names.

On the other hand, the workstation industry is dominated by RISC architectures. RISC processors are vendor specific, available from a single vendor or from a smaller community of vendors under license. Hewlett-Packard PA-8000–based systems are available only from Hewlett-Packard, and Alpha-based systems are available only from DEC. PowerPC-based systems will be available from more sources. SPARC is generally more available—in systems from Sun, Amdahl, Solbourne, and others—because of a Sun desire to make SPARC an industry standard.

Larger machines—servers of various sizes—may be Intel architecture or RISC based. There has been a strong tendency for servers running versions of Unix to be RISC based and servers running OS/2, Novell NetWare, or MS-DOS to be Intel based. There are important exceptions.

The end of the RISC–CISC dichotomy seems at hand. The successor to the Pentium, the P6, is essentially a RISC machine that executes the CISC instructions as a series of RISC instructions in a RISC manner.

A similar technique of "emulation" with lower-level RISC-like instructions can be used to intermix programs written for different architectures on the same "chip."

Design

Design is the mapping of the architecture on the technology of the system. In any particular technology period, within a range of architectures there is an economy-of-scale curve. A smaller version of an architecture is cheaper but disproportionately slower than a larger version, which itself is slower but more price effective than a still larger version. The constancy of this economy of scale, despite the apparent inversions of recent years, is surprising.

In CISC machines, much of the circuitry is dedicated to enabling the operations of the architecture. In RISC machines, a higher percentage is dedicated to improving the speed at which the more-simple operation set can perform.

The goals of contemporary design are:

1 Minimize time by doing as much as possible in parallel.

2 Minimize time needed to get a value from memory to the processor.

The two major design elements that achieve these goals are "pipelines" and "caches." A pipeline divides an instruction into simple stages so that there can be an overlap between successive instructions. That is, instruction 1 can be performing while data is gathered for instruction 2 and while instruction 3 is analyzed (see Box B1.1). A cache provides a smallish but very fast storage area for instructions next to be executed (or data recently used) so that a processor can introduce an instruction into the pipeline in one cycle, keeping "air out of the pipe," an empty stage without an instruction to process. Air in the pipe reduces the rate at which instructions are completed.

Computers are not built on a single chip. They are built from a chip family that includes memory chips, processor chips, and various specialized chips that provide particular capabilities. Among the specialized chips are mathematics coprocessors that provide a "floating-point" capability; there are also chip sets to interface with keyboards, printers, and disk drives and other to provide video, stereo, voice, etc. capability. Computer manufacturers have packaging choices about which of the specialized chips to use in their product and how to integrate various capabilities. Various packages may or may not include integrated video, imaging, CD-ROM, fax modems, answering machines, etc.

PIPELINES

The figure shows a simple pipeline. Such a modest pipeline will approach one operation per cycle. More aggressive pipeline designs will do 4 operations per cycle, and top-of-the-line pipes approach 10 operations per cycle. More aggressive designs involve duplicate pipelines (Intel Pentium) or special-purpose pipelines (DEC Alpha). The key is avoiding intervals in which a stage of the pipe is empty. This makes it necessary to optimize programs to conform to the structure of the pipeline.

A key issue is how to handle conditional branches. Some kind of prediction must be made about the branch to avoid "stalling." This is done with a more or less sophisticated algorithm, which in its most complex form remembers the history of the last 512 branch instructions and predicts based on recent behavior.

Cache Memory

| operation 9 |
| operation 8 |
| operation 7 |
| operation 6 |
| operation 5 |

operation 4

decode | *operation 3*

develop data address | *operation 2*

access data | *operation 1*

execute

Operation	Cycles
Decode (determine what is to be done)	1
Develop data address (find out where data is in memory)	1
Access data (get data from memory)	1
Execute (do the operation to the data)	1
Complete 1	4
Complete 2	5
Complete 100	103

Cycles per operation = 1.03

Key to pipeline success is the cache, which holds the next instruction to be performed so it can be transferred into the pipeline in 1 cycle.

Technology

Much of the change in the industry structure is due to a technology shift that has allowed the digitalization of many devices at low cost. Digital telecommunications, digital television, digital cameras, and digital radio join the digital computer as users of digital semiconductor technology.

Earlier computers, especially those intended for high performance, were based on technologies appropriate for small markets. Each computer generation involved a unique design on a uniquely chosen technology. The goal was a technology/design that would lead to the fastest high-performance machines. The microchip, on the other hand, provides a basis for an industry with

THE MPC601

Memory
- 4 GB logical space
- invisible 256 MB segments
- block of 128 KB to 8 MB
- page of 4 KB

Memory Master (MMU)
- 256-entry 2-way SA TLB (page load/store)
- 4-entry BLTB, ITLB (block, instruction)
  - read queue (2); write queue (3)

Cache
- 32 KB unified cache
- 8-way set associative
- 64 byte line
- 2 eight-word sectors
- physical address search
- store-in (specified write-through)
- cache coherence protocol

Instruction Unit
- 8-instruction queue
- up to 8 per reference
- issues to FPU, BPU, IU bottom half
- chaotic execution: FPU, BPU, IU
- Q0 decode stage

BPU	FU	IU
Branch folding	IEEE 754	Integer, bit, L/S
Unconditionals	5 stage	3–4 stage pipe
Conditionals	• buffer	• Q0
Branch predict	• decode	• > buffer
Static loop	• execute 1	• > execute
	• execute 2	writeback
		32-register GPR
		block bypass
		L address calc
		Dual write

a huge marketplace and consumer electronics dynamics. In computer design, performance is achieved by uniquely combining populations of essentially identical units.

The existence of the microchip and its first use in smaller computers introduces a discontinuity in pricing between classical mainframes, built on older technology, and newer systems built with microchip technology. Many of our arguments about the "death" of various classes or sizes of machine derive from whether we see this discontinuity as temporary or permanent.

The fundamental characteristics of a technology are its cost, its switching speeds, and the density of circuitry that can be placed on it. Secondary characteristics that affect the efficiency of digital devices are how hot the technology runs, what it costs to cool it, what it costs to package it, to modify it, etc.

The speed of a technology is now commonly expressed as how fast it can be "clocked." The clocking speed defines the time of a basic cycle. Personal computers are clocked in a range from 25 MHz to 150 MHz. Machines informally called workstations may be clocked to 400 MHz. A clocking of 100 MHz means that a technology can switch 100 million signals per second.

There are basic choices in semiconductor technologies. Gallium arsenide (GaAS) is the fastest but most expensive, and there have been some disappointments getting it to general manufacture. Bipolar is the technology for traditional mainframe computers, and is the preferred technology for computers that are to have limited populations, can tolerate high power needs, and can afford exotic packaging.

CMOS is the technology of the microprocessor. It has low power needs, can be manufactured in large numbers on an attractive learning curve, and seems the ideal technology for a mass market. "Experts" guess that a CMOS computer can deliver one-half to one-third the performance of a bipolar mainframe, but at one-third to one-tenth the cost. It is largely the disproportionate efficiency of CMOS microprocessor technology that has so unsettled the industry.

There is always fascination with the future. Table B1.2 shows a projection of the number of transistors per microprocessor available with Intel technology and design. It explains what has happened and suggests what is yet to come.

Bill Joy, chief architect at Sun Microsystems has projected that the growth in the number of MIPS (millions of instructions per second) will follow the curve $2^{(Year-1984)}$. Therefore, in the year 1994 there should be 2^{10} MIPS on our desks. The industry is about an order of magnitude off this mark, but the rate of change is increasing: new speeds are announced in less than 15 months, down from 18 months, and there may well be a doubling every year in the near future.

Table B1.3 is an Intel statement, using an Intel benchmark, of the power relation of various Intel processors. The Intel benchmark is a combination of a number of industry benchmarks.

Year	Type	Transistors
1970	4004	1,000
1975	8080	10,000
1978	8086	100,000
1983	80286	200,000
1985	80386	800,000
1988	80486	1,000,000
1993	P5 (Pentium)	3,000,000
1995	P6	10,000,000
2000	P7	100,000,000

Table B1.2 Intel packaging densities—historical and projected.

Processor	Rating
Pentium 100	815
Pentium 90	735
Pentium 66	550
Pentium 60	510
486 DX2 66	280
486 DX 50	250
486 DX 33	170
486 SX 25	100
386 DX 25	50

Table B1.3 Intel iCOMP rating based on Spec92, ZD Bench, and Power Meter.

THE WIDE-WORD MACHINE

In 1994, Hewlett-Packard and Intel announced a joint effort to build a "post-RISC" machine that would be more efficient than RISC. The class of machine they are to develop is commonly called a "wide-word machine," also sometimes referred to as a "programmable-logic machine." Such machines have been hiding in the literature since the 1960s.

The principle involves a very long word in which basic logic functions are embedded. "Long" is a relative term. In 1970, a long word would have been 128 bits. In 1994, a long word might be 128 *bytes*.

Embedded in the long word are basic logic functions that together define an operation that can be done in parallel. In effect, the machine dynamically defines its own set of operations with long words that combine logic functions into united directives. Horizontal microcode and program logic arrays are similar concepts.

The speed of such a machine lies in the higher parallelism than is possible with a RISC machine. Also, the mechanisms for achieving parallelism can be less complex and expensive. The job of a compiler is to infer proper logic building blocks from high-level programs. An inefficiency of such an architecture is the incomplete long words with which sufficient parallelism could not be defined.

In the late winter of 1994, Intel is giving an early view of the P6, which is the successor to the Pentium. This technology will nominally run more than double the speed of the current chip with memory and bus to around 300 MIPS.

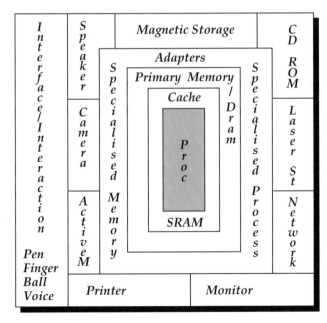

Figure B1.1 The queen in the hive.

HARDWARE AND SOFTWARE

Traditionally, software was developed and optimized for particular hardware. Sometimes it was written in a programming language developed for a particular architecture or machine family. In the new industry, there is more software developed to run across different packaging of the same architecture, and even across different architectures.

The portability and general availability of software and software development tools are key interests. However, there are limits to the notion that everything runs on everything. For independent software vendors like Lotus or Borland or Sybase, the cost to port a program across architectures is greater than the cost of versioning for different Intel-based architectures. Software vendors must be convinced of the marketplace opportunity of non-Intel architectures to invest in versions for the PowerPC or other RISCs.

This is true not only for application programs but for operating systems. Microsoft estimates that to move the Windows NT operating system from a packaging of Intel architecture to another architecture should involve about a 1% change in the program, but to move from an Intel-based machine to a non-Intel–based machine would require about a 10% change in the programming for Windows NT.

Within an architecture family, some generational changes are critical. A key architectural aspect is the size of the architectural unit. The industry is completing a movement from 16 to 32 bits, with 64 bits well upon us. The impact on software organization is huge. It takes some time for software to use the capabilities of an increased word size and addressing range.

Pipeline and cache have a direct effect on program performance and, consequently, on program portability. Programs will not perform as hoped unless they are recompiled to take advantage of new-generation pipeline and cache characteristics. Portability is a design as well as an architectural concern. Scaling programs up from laptops to servers in different designs of an architecture encounters the same issue of limits on improved performance.

One hears the question "Is it time for a Pentium-based processor?" If the Pentium is intended only to improve program performance there may be disappointments. Programs not recompiled for the Pentium pipeline will not achieve Pentium performance. Pentium chips not using fast pathways to and from memories will not get data and instructions fast enough to keep them busy.

The technology will provide two levels of caching, a 128-bit bus, and RISC-like emulation for the complex instructions of the previous processors.

System components

Full computers consist of memories, buses, and storage units, as well as processors. Each of these has architecture, design, and technology attributes that affect the price and performance of a computer.

A useful way of thinking about machines is shown in Figure B1.1. The processor is at the heart of components that become progressively slower as one

PERFORMANCE OF A PROCESSOR

The calculation of the speed of a processor within a computer is marvelously simple:

$$P = F \times C \times T$$

where P is performance, F is the number of operations required to perform a function, C is the number of cycles for each operation, and T is the time for each cycle.

CISC (complex instruction set computer) architectures attempt to optimize P by minimizing F. Many powerful instructions make programs small (important when memory is limited and expensive) and minimize the number of instructions that must be taken from memory. Since memory is slower than processors, taking instructions from memory delays the processor.

A problem with CISC is that compilers that translated from languages like COBOL and FORTRAN to machine architecture did not use most of the powerful instructions. Perhaps 6% of the possible instructions were generated 95% of the time. Therefore, the rich, powerful instructions of CISC were rarely used. Architectures like the DEC VAX, IBM 390, and Intel x86 were never used to their full ability.

As memory became larger, the need for small programs became less critical. Also, a technology called "cache" provided a small fast memory where instructions could be accessed quickly. This reduced the need to minimize the instructions that were needed. Microchip technology matured and fast clocking rates could be achieved, minimizing T.

These factors led to the idea that minimizing C was more important than minimizing F. A program made up of many very simple instructions could be made to run faster with fewer circuits. Invest money, the RISC (reduced instruction set computer) pioneers said, in design not in architecture. Clever design could execute the simple instructions at very high rates and require less circuitry than trying to perform complicated instructions at high speeds.

moves from the center to the edge. An SRAM (static random access memory) provides a cache just about as fast as the processor in which recently used data and upcoming instructions are held. The size of this cache can run from about 4 to 512 KB (in 1994).

The primary memory, DRAM (dynamic random access memory), is considerably slower than the processor and SRAM. This is why SRAM is needed as a staging area for DRAM. For a DRAM memory to respond to a processor data request may take as many as 8 processor cycles. SRAM may be thought of as a buffer for DRAM. DRAM, despite its slow speed, however, can be huge. Even the smallest off-the-shelf personal computer now will have 4 MB, and larger personal machines can scale to 64 MB. Larger servers may be configured with DRAM memories in the area of 1,000 MB.

As SRAM is a buffer for DRAM, DRAM is a buffer for the storage and other devices built in or attached to the system. Referring to a disk unit can take milliseconds and slow the processing units to a crawl. Larger DRAM allows larger amounts of data and instructions to be held in RAM, reducing the frequency with which the processor must refer to the disk storage unit. Access to

BUSES

The basic characteristics of a bus are its data transfer rate, width (number of bits moved across it in parallel), how it "arbitrates" (grants use to competing requests from processor, disk controller, etc.), and how it "packetizes" bytes between the elements it is connecting (whether it sends 8, 16, 32).

Bus characteristics are a key marketplace issue. Most of the scientific and engineering workstations (range of about $5,000 to $15,000) use RISC processors. Various RISC architectures (SPARC, Alpha, PowerPC, PA-RISC) have specialized high-performance buses associated with them—the S-Bus, the Alphabus, the IBM Micro Channel, etc. These buses are generally high-performance buses with wide data paths and high clocking rates, allowing up to 256 MB per second. Portability of hardware and software between these systems must overcome a bus barrier.

On the other hand, there are industry standard buses, ISA and EISA (Extended Industry Standard Architecture) which are 16- and 32-bit buses, respectively, with lower performance levels at low clocking rates. These are common in Intel environments, sometimes in surprisingly large systems in the marketplace midrange. The advantage to an industry standard bus is that it improves binary portability. Some programs may have dependencies on bus characteristics and cannot be ported across buses. A key difference between a clone and a compatible (which does not guarantee all programs will port at the binary level) is often found in the characteristics of the bus.

Intel has a new bus technology, PCI bus, that considerably speeds pathways in Intel architectures. PCI bus is clocked at 33 MHz. With a transfer width of 32 bits, PCI can transfer 132 MB per second. This will enable considerably expanded imaging and multimedia capability in PCs. Such bus speeds make the Pentium chip a potential competitor for applications previously only possible on a workstation.

An important new bus technology is associated with a standard called "PCMCIA." This allows devices like additional memory, storage, or whatever one can think of to be placed on cards looking much like credit cards and plugged into the system.

CD-ROMs, optical storage units, and the devices at the human interface is even slower than magnetic disks.

The ring containing specialized adapters, processors, and memories is interesting in that it represents components that interact directly with cameras, speakers, and communications lines. Sometimes these components are more powerful computers than the central processor. An imaging processor, for example, may be considerably more powerful and require a larger and faster memory to manage images than that available on the central processor.

Buses

The bus is the pathway that connects the processor(s), memories, specialized video, and other elements to each other. These pathways are the backbone of a

MEMORY

The faster a processor, the more memory it needs, as it requires more data and fresh instructions at a faster rate. The software environment also influences memory requirements. As operating systems and other software grow functionally richer, they require more memory.

In late 1994, small and medium machine memory costs were about $50 per megabyte. The amount of real memory on a machine is determined by the capacity of memory chips and by how many chips can be plugged into the system. In the Pentium processor, up to 4 GB can be directly addressed in the architecture; however, physical memory on desktop or laptop computers ranges from 4 to 64 MB.

A key force in the electronics industry is the fall in price and expansion in size of RAM. Box B1.8 is a projection of the increase in DRAM capability over time. The memory chip density doubles about every three years.

system. Figure B1.2 shows some bus structures. The various bus structures determine the nature of data flow; degree of overlapped operations between disks, processors, memories, video chips, etc.; and the number of different functions that can be configured into a system.

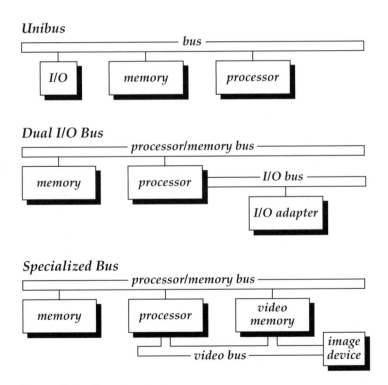

Figure B1.2 Bus structures.

Combined estimates–bits per chip:

1970	2^{12}	(4K)
1975	2^{13}	(8K)
1980	2^{16}	(64K)
1982	2^{18}	(264K)
1985	2^{20}	(1M)
1988	2^{22}	(4M)
1991	2^{24}	(16M)
1994	2^{26}	(64M)
1997	2^{28}	(256M)
2000	2^{30}	(1G)

In a unibus design, all information from or to a processor flows on the same bus pathway, regardless of whether it is going to memory or to an I/O (input/output) adapter. In a multibus design, there is a different bus flow between the processor and memories and between the processor and I/O adapters. In elaborated multibus systems, like that shown in the final drawing of Figure B1.2, there are specialized buses between specialized imaging processors, their private memories, and the rest of the system.

The market politics of buses are awesome. A reason for the IBM/Microsoft tension was the desire of Microsoft to run DOS on all Intel-based computers. IBM wanted an operating system

B1.9   CACHE

In order to balance the speed disparity between primary (DRAM) memories and the processor, a smaller high-speed memory is used. It is called "cache" because it is essentially hidden from a program. Its contents are managed by hardware that tries to assure that the cache holds the instructions and data the processor is most likely to want in the immediate future. Hardware algorithms that manage the contents of the cache come from a family called "least recently used" or "least frequently used." They attempt to order units of the contents of cache by last usage. The prediction is that the data most recently used will be most immediately needed in the future. When space is needed for new data, the oldest changed data is written back out to memory.

Caches differ in a number of ways. They may be on the processor chip (level 1 cache) or on the memory (level 2 cache) or both. They will have different units of transfer from the memory and will have different rules about where a memory address may go in the cache. A fully associative cache will permit any memory location to go anywhere in the cache. This is very efficient, but requires many circuits for large caches. Some caches have n-way "set associativity"; that is, a particular zone of memory addresses may go to n different places in the cache, but not anywhere.

Caches differ as to when changes in the cache are reflected in the memory. Some caches are "write-through" and store the data in the corresponding memory location as soon as a change is made. Other caches are "write-in" and hold the data in the cache until the least recently used algorithm selects the cache location for writing back into memory to make room for more recent data.

Some caches hold both data and instructions. Other caches are specialized for data and instructions. The problem in mixing data and instructions is that processor references for data will encounter and delay processor references for instructions. Machines like the PowerPC 601 that mix instructions and data may have an additional buffer area for instructions in order to minimize conflict.

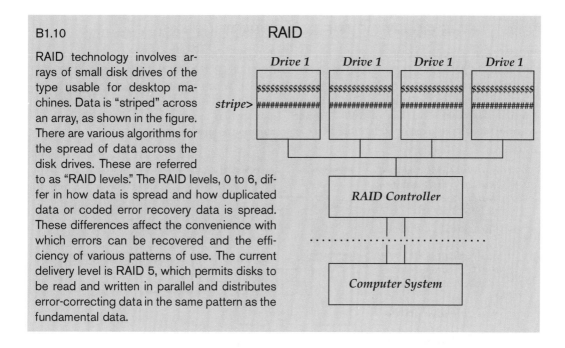

B1.10

RAID technology involves arrays of small disk drives of the type usable for desktop machines. Data is "striped" across an array, as shown in the figure. There are various algorithms for the spread of data across the disk drives. These are referred to as "RAID levels." The RAID levels, 0 to 6, differ in how data is spread and how duplicated data or coded error recovery data is spread. These differences affect the convenience with which errors can be recovered and the efficiency of various patterns of use. The current delivery level is RAID 5, which permits disks to be read and written in parallel and distributes error-correcting data in the same pattern as the fundamental data.

special to its own versions. At the heart of the issue was the IBM Micro Channel bus and the Intel industry standard bus.

Bus issues are at the center of compatibility and performance concerns and may affect software availability for particular computers in all market segments.

Storage

The magnetic disk is the primary storage technology for computing systems of all classes. Small machines have single internal hard drives of 80 to 400 MB (representing about 12,000 to 72,000 8.5" × 11" pages of 3,600 characters per page). Large machines have "disk farms" of uncountable trillions of bytes allocated across different drives clustered behind various control units and pathways.

There are significant differences between disks. The internal hard disks of desk and laptop systems are similar to the common diskette. The performance of 3.5" drives is around 11 to 13 milliseconds average access time (the time it requires a read head to move across the surface of the disk) and 5 to 8 milliseconds latency (the time it requires for the desired data on the rotating disk surface to move under the waiting read head). Data is transferred at millions of bits per second, ranging from 10 to 30 Mb per second.

THE GLORY OF THEIR TIME, PART II (SEE BOX 3.3, page 61)

The figure is a schematic of a large mainframe–oriented "data farm." These data farms are enormous on mainframes, running into terabyte (millions of megabytes) ranges. Over 15% of mainframes have in excess of 500 GB, and over 40% have in excess of 100 GB. The in-put/output processor(s) of the mainframe connect to channels, which in turn connect to controllers, which in turn connect to disk drives. Each disk drive has many platters. There is a megabyte of memory in the controllers and perhaps in the disk drive.

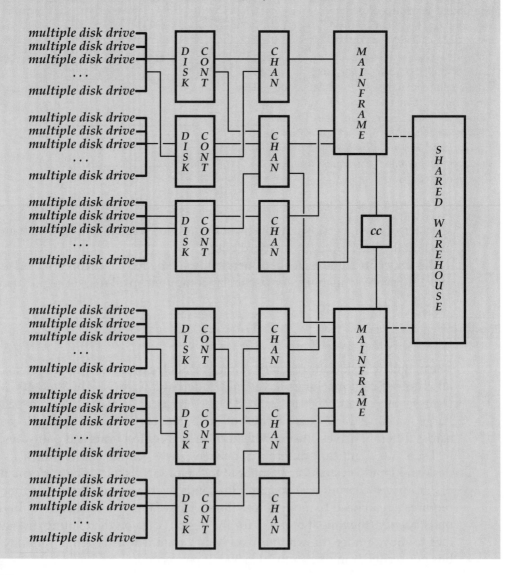

B1.12 STORAGE

Storage information from various industry surveys:

Magnetic Storage
- One-year product cycles
- 50% annual capacity increase
- 10% quarterly price decrease
- 1995 capacities:
  - 5.25" 1500 MB
  - 3.5"   1000 MB
  - 2.5"   500 MB
  - 1.8"   400 MB
  - 1.3"   100 MB

Magnetic-Optical
- Capacities:
  - 1990 650 MB
  - 1993 1.4 GB
  - 1995 2.5 GB
  - 1996 5.1 GB

There is a tremendous performance discontinuity between disks and RAM memories. The industry has been seeking to fill this gap for over two decades. Many technologies have come and gone. The latest is a memory device called "flash memory" that provides very large, inexpensive storage at nanosecond speeds and can be put on a PCMCIA card.

The great endurance of the magnetic storage disk drive is due to the rate at which its capacity has increased over time. There is almost an annual doubling of density, and smaller and smaller units can hold greater amounts of data at very low per-megabyte costs.

Storage has had a role in the economy of scale wars. In the late 1970s, when the efficiencies of minicomputers relative to mainframes were first noticed, it was thought that the efficiencies of large-scale on-line storage were so great that mainframe systems could never be seriously challenged from a total cost viewpoint. The cost per byte of storage on a mainframe disk unit was about an order of magnitude less than the cost per byte on a smaller disk.

In 1994, the estimated cost for a megabyte of storage on mainframe technology is $4 per megabyte, for small system storage $2 per megabyte. Large and intermediate system technologies are beginning to merge on a model that is borrowed from small systems, RAID (Redundant Arrays of Inexpensive Disks), a new model for magnetic disk technology.

CD-ROM technology is similar to disk technology, except that the surface is organized as a continuing spiral. The great advantage of CD-ROM is its enormous capacity for digitized information. The great disadvantages are extremely low speeds (slower than disk access times) and the difficulty of re-recording. This is a WORM (write once/read many) device.

CD-ROM is clearly becoming important in the computer industry as a distribution technology for information, games, and software. CD-ROM technology is usable in a private CD-ROM world. Phillips and other manufacturers create total CD-ROM systems. However, personal computers are now more and more frequently equipped with a CD-ROM capability as part of their basic packaging. Apple has an integrated CD-ROM unit, and IBM is now distributing versions of its software on CD-ROM.

Optical technology may come in either WORM or rewritable forms. It is commonly offered as a package of 1 to 64 disk surfaces providing from 650 MB to 40 GB of storage for prices in the $10,000 to $20,000 range. It is extremely slow. Drives with multiple disk sets require multiple seconds to position a disk under a reader and have a 35 millisecond access time thereafter. However, the technology is believed to have enormous potential.

the basics book, chapter 2

Communications review

EXECUTIVE SUMMARY *Interconnecting computers is a precondition for interoperability and resource sharing. Much of the behavior that dominates networking comes from software written to support de facto or de jure industry protocols and interfaces.*

The fundamental idea of a protocol is that of an agreement between end points and intermediaries who wish to communicate. This agreement defines the language to be used, the style of presentation, the rules of good behavior, etc.

In the communications community, a set of protocols from the International Standards Organization (ISO) provides a canonical model for communications. The protocol comes in seven layers, each layer responsible for a particular set of behaviors having to do with the physical hardware, the nature of a message, the topology of the network, and the rules for presenting data to applications.

Communications

Computer networks using underlying analog telephone technology developed as an element of computing in the late 1960s and had reached some maturity by the mid 1970s. Also, there has long been computer use of radio transmission at assigned frequencies under public policy control.

There is a wide range of transmission media. Technologies include cable, wireless, radio spectrum broadcast, and satellite broadcast. Society has traditionally had institutional, regulatory, and investment boundaries between the radio model and the telephone model of communications. These barriers are now decomposing. Governments struggle to define appropriate policies as local telephone companies, long distance telephone companies, cable companies, entertainment companies, computer companies, retail video chains, graphics technology companies, and software companies dance around each other in a great mazurka in search of possible profits, which sometimes seem far off indeed.

In the current era of network-oriented computing, the boundaries between computer and network have blurred. A network is largely a collection of software functions dispersed among computers. IT computer and networking decisions are inseparably intertwined as the definition of a system involves trade-offs and balances between investment in computer power and investment in network power.

Above the physical media of communications, in the layers between the wire and an application program, software-defined networks acquire attributes from protocols (behaviors) built into programming. These protocols originate in major systems vendors like IBM or DEC, or in international organizations like the ISO or IEEE. Machines wishing to communicate over a network use software on the sending and receiving sides that understands a common set of protocols.

Communications protocols and interfaces

Most communications behavior is software defined. Software protocols define what can be sent (voice, text, graphics, image), how a receiver recognizes what is sent, how it is sent (formats for data and control information), how receivers are addressed, how data transmission is synchronized, how receipt is acknowledged, etc. There are two aspects to software communications systems: protocols and interfaces.

Protocols

Software must define or respond to:

1 Physical media attributes. Various physical media have various speeds, reliabilities, convenient distances, and costs. Software must be able to manage the hardware characteristics of the media.

2 "Topology"—the shape of the network, its patterns of interconnections, what can talk directly to what, and what must talk through an intermediary node. Software takes responsibility for routing messages through the network.

3 "Addressing conventions"—the rules by which names of units on the network are formed. Networks have differing conventions for naming systems and forming an address.

4 "Control protocols" that define sequences of interaction, acknowledgment, and response to various events. Software defines the "handshaking" rules by which sender and receiver confirm that proper information has been transferred.

Send a message	Application content	Receive a message
Put message in proper format. Indicate start/end	Agree on negotiation, start/end signals, etc.	Present message
Parcel message into packets	Agree on how many per message	Collect packets into message
Send a packet	Agree on packet size	Receive a packet

Figure B2.1   Protocol viewpoint.

5 "Message formats," which define the structure of a message. Messages contain "headers" in addition to their data. These headers define the start of the transmission, the beginning and end of the pieces (packets) into which messages are broken up for transmission, etc. Software on both sides must understand the conventions and encoding of the messages.

Protocols are behaviors that must occur—the semantics of communication. They represent permissible patterns of interaction and transitions between communicating end points. Compliance with protocols enables systems to communicate, even if many aspects of their environment are quite different. The protocol viewpoint is represented in Figure B2.1. It is shown as a correspondence between layers at different ends of the wire. The receiving transport layer must be able to recognize, decode, and process data and control signals developed for it by the sending transport layer, etc.

Interfaces

Another aspect of communications is the programming interface used to activate communication software. Programs that communicate over common protocols may use quite different interfaces to these protocols in their own software complex. Just as a telephone system interface (dials, buttons) is distinct from the behavior of the network, a software communications interface is distinct from the protocols beneath it. The interface is the syntax of communication.

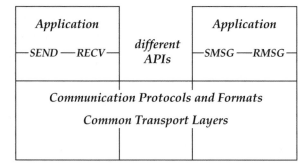

Figure B2.2 Different interfaces.

The relations between syntax and semantics in communication are subtle, as they are in the study of language and sociology.

Figure B2.2 shows an application in system 1 and an application in system 2 interacting with each other over a common protocol, but with different views of how to start or respond to a communication sequence.

As a protocol determines communicability, an interface determines portability, the ability of a program to move from one system to another and sometimes from one protocol to another.

The communications community has largely focused on behaviors and ignored programming interfaces. Portability is not a communications issue. The systems programming community has now come forward with interface standards that allow software to port from one protocol environment to another.

Protocol families

Protocols have been developing since the early 1970s. In 1974, IBM announced its Systems Network Architecture (SNA), and at about the same time the ISO promulgated the Open System Interconnection (OSI) protocols, and DEC developed Digital Network Architecture (DNA, or DECnet).

These early protocols were built on an assumption of quite slow and relatively unreliable communications media. They made "pessimistic" assumptions and developed elaborate schemes for recovery and error control. The software that embodied these protocols was developed by a programming community not yet integrated into the operating systems world. As a result, many of the functions of operating systems are duplicated, often in clumsy ways, in early communications software.

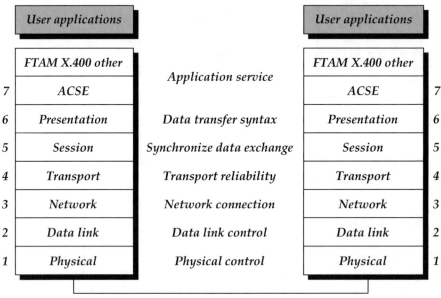

	User applications		**User applications**

	FTAM X.400 other		FTAM X.400 other	
		Application service		
7	*ACSE*		*ACSE*	7
6	*Presentation*	*Data transfer syntax*	*Presentation*	6
5	*Session*	*Synchronize data exchange*	*Session*	5
4	*Transport*	*Transport reliability*	*Transport*	4
3	*Network*	*Network connection*	*Network*	3
2	*Data link*	*Data link control*	*Data link*	2
1	*Physical*	*Physical control*	*Physical*	1

Figure B2.3   The OSI model is a standard for interconnecting computers of different manufacturers that provides a structured architecture defining formats and protocols.

In the early days, major vendors invested more effort in their own proprietary protocols (SNA, DNA, etc.) to enable their own hardware to communicate rather than in OSI protocols that enable communications across vendors. Of course, this was more true of IBM, which dominated the market, than of other vendors who had to coexist with IBM.

Local area networks (LANs) and their software developed late in a different product set based on different standards (IEEE) than software for wide area networks (WANs). A boundary between LANs and WANs consequently developed. This boundary is just now fading.

Bottom layers

The ISO OSI model provides a definition of layers in which certain behaviors occur. Despite redefinitions due to new hardware technologies and new interoperability concepts, the OSI model remains the model against which other models are mapped and compared.

The OSI layer framework is shown in Figure B2.3. A way of thinking about the relations between layers is that on the way down, on the sending side, each layer adds some information or processing necessary to commit data to the network. On the way up, on the receiving side, each layer determines that all is well and strips off the control information until the message arrives, pristine, at the ultimate receiver.

Layer 1: Physical

The physical layer provides access to the connection media. This may be cabling, fiber optic technologies, radio transmissions, or microwave transmissions. The protocols include various standards for interacting with media of various kinds and speeds. They can provide for fax, for the integration of data and voice, and for LANs.

Layer 2: Data link

Data link layer conventions determine how systems start and stop transmitting, whether they can transmit asynchronously, and how data is "framed" with headers and broken up into "packets." A number of de jure and de facto conventions apply, including start/stop, BiSynchronous, OSI HDLC, and IBM SDLC.

Layer 3: Network

The network layer provides addressing conventions and routing functions. To send a message from a starting point to an ending point, it is necessary to know (or to know someone who knows) the network address of the ending point and the path that must be taken from sender to receiver if they are not adjacent to each other. A message moves from a node to an adjacent node along a path to the receiver. This path is defined by the routing algorithm of the network layer. The cleverness with which the routing function is performed is a competitive issue for various communications architectures. The goal is to find the best pathway that has the fewest number of stops and the least utilization.

Upper layers

The lower three layers provide pretty much all that is needed to move a message from one computer to another. Communications above these provide increased guarantees of correct transmission (transport), more complex relations

ROUTING AND PACING

There are a number of aspects to routing. Routing may be static or dynamic. In static routing, a fixed route is determined, and all information flowing between sender and receiver must follow that fixed route. Dynamic routing allows a "best available" route to be determined at various stages in the transmission. Each message, or each part of a message, may move from the initial to the end point by a different routing. There are various algorithms for determining the "best available" route. Open Shortest Path First attempts to identify the shortest route with the lowest load between two nodes. A problem with allowing different routing is that a message or group of messages may arrive out of order, or that elements may be lost without the knowledge of the sender or receiver.

The network layer also controls the "pacing" of message elements to assure transmission does not override available memory space at the receiver, and that no data is lost because message elements overlay each other in memory. Network layers differ in whether they reorder packets. For example, IP, widely used in Unix environments, does not order packets. X.25 does order packets—at the network layer.

between groups of senders and receivers (session), some data access conventions (presentation), and some particular communications applications (application), such as network management.

Layer 4: Transport

Relations between senders and receivers are established by the transport layer. It provides end-to-end control, packet and message reordering, and some address conversion. In some protocol families, this layer is directly used by an application program.

An important aspect of a transport layer is whether it is "connection" based or "connectionless." A connectionless transport is an extended message handler offering a service called "datagram." A message is sent, much like a letter. There is no additional message implied, nor is there the expectation of an answer. The delivery of the message may be guaranteed, but there is no concept of a continuing relation between sender and receiver.

A connection-based transport establishes a relation much like a telephone call. This connection has attributes of charge, recovery, continuity, and coherence, beyond the contents of the messages that are flowing.

Layer 5: Session

A session is built upon connections. It provides for complex relations between senders and receivers and groups of senders and receivers. Equivalents of conference calls, group calls, and other "fancy" variations are defined by the session layer.

EVOLUTION OF LOWER LAYERS

X.25 is an early standard for packet switched networks. Packetizing is a basic notion of transmission that enables a message to be broken into logical units (e.g., 128 bytes) for transmission. In X.25, the packets are dynamically routed, and standards exist for retransmission, flow control, and error detection based on behaviors in layers 1, 2, and 3. X.25 permits variable-length packets and assures proper sequencing.

Frame relay and cell relay, new lower-layer concepts, are much "lighter" than X.25. They do not neatly map onto the traditional OSI layer structure. Because of the speed and reliability of the new technologies, some older ideas have been abandoned in the new protocols. In particular, cell relay uses small, fixed-size packets (no longer necessary to optimize overhead) and the same routing (no time to reroute), and does not retransmit if a small packet is lost from time to time. Such a convention is appropriate for video transmission or image transmission at a very high speed, where the information in a particular packet is a quite small percentage of the total information of the message.

Frame relay does assure that frames will arrive in order. Because of the speeds required, flexible alternate routing is often not needed and permanent fixed routes are used. This avoids the overhead of dynamic routing for very small, very many units of transmission.

Frame relay is a considerable simplification and speeding of X.25. Cell relay goes a considerable step beyond. A cell is a 53-byte structure that contains 48 data bytes and 5 header bytes for circuit and path identifiers. Every unit of information (voice, image, etc.) is split into fixed-size cells. Fixed-size cells are sent on a fixed route and in a fixed order. If a cell is lost, it is not retransmitted because it represents a trivial amount of lost image information.

This layer has ideas of "dialogues" and "conversations." These are continuing identified relations between end points. Synchronous or asynchronous transmission is possible within conventions for determining who sends and who listens at any time.

Layer 6: Presentation

This layer is visible to application programs. It presents data to programs so that they do not need to know whether the data was local or remote. This involves data translation or common data formats when data is moving from quite different environments. This layer is used by application programs that are part of the communications culture or by applications that require industrial-strength communication.

Layer 7: Application

This layer is occupied by programs outside of the communications culture or by extensions to it. There are various "applications" that are inherently network oriented. Among these are file transfer services, mail services, telephone services, and systems management functions. All protocol families have products that operate at this layer as part of their culture. Some of these are discussed as part of systems management.

Local area networks

Local area networks (LANs) are physically based on cable, fiber optic, or wireless transmission and are primarily based on a model of networking provided by Ethernet or token ring. The protocol standards for LANs come primarily from the IEEE and are mapped onto the OSI model with some effort. Figure B2.4 shows the LAN protocol structure. The physical is divided into two layers, the top layer providing a physical interface to the media. The data link layer is similarly divided. The logical link layer provides a "lighter" version of the services offered in OSI layers.

LANs come in various topologies and technologies. The fundamental styles are token ring and Ethernet. These are generic names for LANs having properties more or less in conformance with IEEE standards.

Token ring defines a network as an apparent circle. On the circle at any time is a "token" that moves in an orderly fashion around the ring. A computer may transmit information on the ring when it has the token. But it cannot keep the token indefinitely, and must pass it on to a successor. The token moves around the ring, giving each station a chance to transmit. As data moves around the ring, stations listen for messages addressed to themselves. Physically, underneath the abstraction, the network is implemented as a "star," with point-to-point connection through a central station. Current token ring speeds are 4 and 16 Mb per second.

Ethernet is a bus that uses an algorithm called CSMA/CD (Carrier Sense Multiple Access/Collision Detection). All computers wishing to send messages may do so, but they must listen for a "collision." If they hear a collision, they must wait a bit and try again. The odds are they won't wait the same time exactly and they won't collide again. Current Ethernet nominal speeds are 10 Mb per second, but a standard for 100 Mb per second is already in place.

Boundary crossing

The boundaries of essentially similar networks may be at the media layers or at the addressing layer. Bridges and routers perform an adequate network integration function. Higher-level boundaries, allowing interaction between systems that have layer 4, 5, or 6 divergences, must be done by gateways.

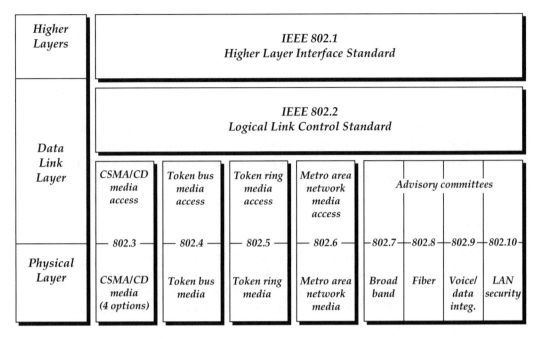

Figure B2.4 LAN standards.

With the fragmentation of the industry and the ability to put microchips into functionally specialized packages, the role of communications-oriented companies has considerably increased. New network systems offerings have emerged to help offload functions from applications machines, and to help integration across various network protocols. Companies unknown in the first form of the industry—3Com, Cisco, Asante, Wellfleet, SynOptics, Tivoli, Net-Labs, and ODS Infinity (to name a few, almost randomly chosen from a large set)—have joined IBM, DEC, Hewlett-Packard, and AT&T, in the business of forming networks. The routers, bridges, and gateways come largely from the group of industry specialists. Many vendors have offerings that support, or extend product that comes from, the major systems vendors.

Bridges

A bridge is a layer 1 and 2 (Media Access layers) function that enables two LANs to appear as one. It is possible to bridge across geographic distances, but in general, bridging is a local function. In a bridged network, the addresses of each station are expanded to include a network identifier. The bridge transfers frames across the networks. A station on a token ring must know the end point address across the bridge. On an Ethernet bridge, the bridging function will provide the address.

Routers

Routers operate at layer 3 and are used to move messages across networks divided by addressing schemes. Multiprotocol routers will support the routing functions of various protocol stacks, but will not move messages (perform a gateway function) across protocol stacks.

Gateways

These instruments perform conversions at transport, session, and presentation levels. They commonly contain protocol stacks for a source and a target (bidirectional) stream (e.g., LU 6.2 to TCP/IP) and a conversion program that converts an incoming stream using one set of protocols into an outgoing stream using another.

Other network instruments

A physical network consists of a variety of devices, seemingly always changing as the nature of the networking problem changes. Concentrators take a set of many low-capacity lines and combine them into traffic on a single high-speed line. Deconcentrators, of course, do the opposite. Multiplexers and demultiplexers decompose or integrate signals in time. Modems translate analog to digital signals (and vice versa) when analog networks are being used.

There are hubs and switches that control the pacing, addressing, and segment sections of messages.

The population of intelligent, programmed devices on the network is often hidden by our focus on the end points, the clients, or the servers. There is a complex web of intervening technology capable of failure and requiring management.

Metropolitan area networks

Filling the gap between WANs and LANs is a technology called MAN, metropolitan area network. In MAN technology, a user interfaces to the network over a subscriber interface (SNI). Behind the interface is a metropolitan switching system using protocols associated with SMDS (Switched Multimegabit Data Services). SMDS provides source and destination address services and multicast, and various access paths to equipment on customer premises.

The MAN extends the range of a LAN across a city. It interconnects various LANs across media and protocols, and defines a new geographical distance between the LAN and WAN of up to about 35 miles (50 kilometers).

Operating systems basic functions

*E*XECUTIVE SUMMARY *An operating system in its aspect of baseware performs a number of underlying functions to coordinate hardware use, protect data from careless destruction, synchronize I/O, manage memory, provide communications, and provide security. These functions are reviewed in this chapter.*

The structure and function of selected operating systems is discussed. The systems selected are Unix, Windows NT, and, as an example of a mainframe system emerging from the previous generation, IBM MVS for the IBM 390.

Process and program management

The "process model" defines the abstraction, process, whose characteristics define how programs will run on the computer, how they will share resources, and how they will protect themselves against each other.

A domain is a collection of resources, and a process represents the domain that a set of programs can access. A process is a steward of resources that "threads" (the active agents representing running programs) can use. This terminology is from the academic and standards community. Unhappily, not all systems use this terminology. In some systems, "processes" are both stewards and active agents; in others, words like "task" are used with meanings somewhere between process and thread.

At the heart of an operating system is a list of processes and threads that define the workload to be managed. An operating system divides the hardware resources of the system between the processes, which divide the times to use the resources between the threads.

In a single-user system, the operating system multiplexes between the printer, keyboard, and disk unit, and between applications running in various windows, balancing the use of systems resources between tasks in a way most convenient for the user.

In a multi-user system, the operating system must sequence between sharing users so that it provides satisfactory response times to each while using the resources of the system in accordance with priorities. The operating system must share resources "safely" so that users cannot contaminate each other's domains.

An aspect of the process model is the relationship between processes. Processes must be able to send each other messages when they do not share memory. Part of the definition of a process model is the way processes can communicate on the same computer or across a network. The flexibility of interprocess communication is a key technology issue for complex systems in environments where diverse applications may wish to share data.

In its aspect of defining relations between processes, the process model is readily extensible to the network. Interprocess message-passing activities that are built around queue management between shared process queues, such as Unix pipes, are now coming onto the network so that remote processes can interact as if they were local.

The memory and storage model

The storage model determines how data is allocated to devices. Memory management defines the relation between "disk"-like devices and the primary random access memory (RAM) used by a running program. The memory model defines how RAM "looks" to a program.

Systems software has three fundamental responsibilities in defining the memory model:

1 It must support the concepts of the hardware.

2 It must manage what is in RAM.

3 It must enforce protection within and across address spaces.

The support of hardware concepts involves the management of an artifice called a virtual memory. The virtual memory is an image of RAM laid out on disk. In any particular computer, the size of the RAM may be smaller (or larger) than the virtual memory. A machine with an address space of 4 GB may have only 4 MB of actual RAM. The operating system must determine what parts of the virtual memory (or virtual memories) are actually in RAM at any time. It is responsible for strategies that assure a working set (most needed data and instructions) is in RAM to minimize delays in transferring images of the virtual memory from disk as they are needed.

There are various models of virtual memory. A single virtual memory in a single space enlarges the apparent addressing of the system. All programs and data are mapped into this single apparent address space, which is as large as the physical addressing of the hardware.

A multiple virtual memory provides particular users and their environments with unique virtual memories. A group of program-development users might share an address space, while a group of data entry persons would share another address space. Further division may be made so that each user has an address space, and access to other address spaces is made through interaddress space mechanisms that permit a user to access multiple address spaces.

Software is responsible for assuring that programs do not make unauthorized references to the memory space of other programs. Here there must also be appropriate hardware that sets boundaries whose attempted violation can be observed by the operating system.

The workload management model

The workload management model schedules work across shared resources. A system has a number of workload management models. Work must be distributed across a network as well as managed on a single system. A macro model plans the management of a workload for days or shifts. Particular operating systems have long-term schedulers that plan workloads for upcoming minutes or seconds, intermediate schedulers that plan for milliseconds, and short-term schedulers that worry only about the immediate future and decide which thread is next to run.

Long-term schedulers create lists of work from a pool of possible work to be done in the system. On the basis of resource requirements and scheduling constraints, they form a population to which the system will grant resources over the next few seconds or minutes. Only those dispatchable units on the "IN" lists will receive attention over that time. At the end of the time, the workload is analyzed again and a new IN list is created. The work on the IN list is kept in memory during the working period to the extent allowed by system resources.

An intermediate scheduler will select from a set of candidates for work on the basis of their recent history, their demonstrated pattern of use of input/output devices, and their general effect on the immediate load on the system.

A short-term scheduler will select from candidates chosen by the intermediate scheduler on the basis of which candidate is ready to run, which is waiting for some event, etc.

The recovery model

This is the capability of a system to recognize errors and to restore resources after an error has occurred. It is a key element of the idea of "industrial strength" and, consequently, of the politics of information technology.

Mainframe defenders argue that only the older technologies have proven to be industrial strength and can guarantee recovery in complex workloads for different conditions of failure. Client/server or distributed computing protagonists argue that the old mainframe software contributes nothing to network recovery and that products like NetWare are much more robust on the network than products like MVS, which performs little archiving, backup, etc. on a network basis.

The basic technology of recovery is to recognize that an error has occurred and then to fix the error. The nature of the error determines the extent of the recovery process. The basic paradigm is that the system takes checkpoints from time to time or records events in a log so that there is a known point of integrity to which the system can be restored. When an error is recognized, the recovery technology backs out of everything that has happened since the known checkpoint.

Traditionally, major middleware components have their own recovery capability. This is particularly true of data base managers and file systems. Base operating systems, however, also take on a good deal of recovery responsibility. The boundaries between middleware and baseware recovery have never been well defined. The amount of special knowledge a data base manager must have to recover failed data base operations, for example, and whether the base operating system could undertake such a recovery, is a matter of design dispute.

Recovery across the network is difficult technology, especially if there is heterogeneity in the elements that must be commonly recovered. If a failed program has modified data at machine A and a cooperating program has modified data at machine B, the data at A and B must be restored. If the environment of A and B have different ideas of checkpoints and logging, coordinated recovery will be impossible to achieve.

The authorization and security model

Authorization is the procedure involved in registering an end user or organization of users with the system and enabling them to access particular resources in a particular session. The intent of the model is to constrain system access to legitimate users, and, after access, to identify the particular resources to which a user or set of users has rights. Some system structures treat security as an aspect of the systems management model.

An end user commonly must provide a password to gain access to the system. Certain systems require two identifiers, one the name by which the system and all others know the user, and the other a private personal identifier that convinces the system that the person is legitimate.

The authorization model determines what "logging-on" achieves. Many environments include programs requiring specific authorization beyond access to the system. Each element of a software complex may have its own authorization function. The current technology direction is to provide common authorization services across software elements—single system log-on; but this direction is not yet fully mature. In environments where a user may need resources from a network of computers, it is sometimes necessary for the user to "log-on" to each system server or even individual services within a server.

Some environments, for example, IBM MVS, have independent products such as RACF (Resource Access Control Facility) that provide for authorization controls. In other environments, authorization is a secondary function of a central directory system.

The authorization mechanism provides a mapping of users and resources. This mapping may be "subject to object" or "object to subject." The subject-to-object mapping provides a list of authorized users, the resources each can use, and how it can use them. An example is the IBM AS/400 User Profile. The object-to-subject mapping provides a list of resources, and states what users or using organizations can do to each resource. Object-to-subject mapping is a de facto industry practice common to RACF, Unix Access Lists, and other products. It is part of the emerging de jure operating system standard coming from the IEEE.

Security has three aspects: authentication, authorization, and encryption. Systems differ as to whether there is a single security service or whether diverse elements have private security models—each file system, each data base manager, each networking manager, etc.

Once a user is identified, authorization determines what rights the user has in the system. Authentication is about assuring the true identity for both subject and object. There is an emerging de facto standard for authentication called Kerberos (from the Massachusetts Institute of Technology). Kerberos provides a three-party authentication system in which there is a trusted authenticator who must be convinced the subject and the object are what they claim to be.

Encryption is the transformation of information so that it can be retranslated into intelligible form only if the "key" of the encryption is known. There are various standards for encryption.

The various governments of the world have devised classifications for security levels and procedures for certifying how secure a system is. In the United States, the ranking system goes from D (no knowledge exists about how easy it is to penetrate this system) to A (this system is provably secure, provably correct, and follows the formalisms of a provably secure system). Most commercial systems are at the C1 or C2 level, which is called "discretionary security." This is achieved with reasonable functionality such as passwords, access lists, etc. B1 requires only that security classifications be shown on every image or document. Beyond B1, there are structural and software engineering requirements to achieve mandatory security levels B2, B3, A1, etc. There is some uncertainty about whether the highest levels could ever be achieved in general purpose systems giving satisfactory performance.

The data model

A system must provide access to data. Data is organized into a number of mental models, which determines how it will look to end users or programs. A basic notion is a file. A file is a named entity representing bytes mapped onto a device (tape, magnetic disk, optical disk). It has attributes of format, length, ordering, and internal structure. There are two fundamental kinds of file systems, byte stream and record oriented. A byte stream file, common to the Unix community, is one in which the bytes of the file are viewed as a continuous stream—byte 0, byte 1, byte 2, etc.—and operations on the file are done in terms of movement within the stream.

In a record-oriented file, there are elements called "records." Records have keys by which they are identified, and they have size and orderings of fields. A file may be ordered with regards to alphanumeric values of the keys of the records. An example is a record of information about an employee in an employee data file. There are different access methods available for retrieving records from a file; these may be simple, such as "GET" the next record, or quite complex, such as "GET all the records that have keys within a range."

Data bases represent models of data of a number of basic types: hierarchical, network, relational, and object oriented. In the industry, Microsoft, IBM, DEC, and some others are both operating system and data base vendors. For the most part, however, the data base vendors are separate from the operating systems group.

In a relational data base, data is presented as a two-dimensional table, with rows and columns containing data that accord with a set of data selection rules. The presentation is essentially in the form of a table of values. SQL (Structured Query Language) is the de facto data access and definition language for relational data bases.

Data base managers are primarily provided by companies specializing in that layer. As a result, they tend to run on multiple platforms and within multiple contexts. Oracle, Sybase, Informix, Ingres, and others are widely available for different machines of different scale with different operating systems.

Unix as a model

"Unix" is used with various meanings. Some intend to refer to a quite specific system that supports de facto standards developed by the Unix Systems Laboratory (now a part of Novell). These standards define a version of Unix called System V Release 5 (SVR5), the canonical Unix from which so many depart. A number of systems are Unix in the sense that they share with Unix a fundamental view of life—a style, many functions, and programs—but they diverge in details that are either helpful or annoying, depending on one's viewpoint. Among these systems are Hewlett-Packard's HP-UX, IBM's AIX, OSF/1 from DEC, and (naturally) many others. There are also more and more systems that "look" like Unix in that they provide Unix APIs and utilities, but are not Unix in their very souls. They have other programming styles in their deep places. Among these are Hewlett-Packard's MPE/ix, DEC's VMS/Open, and IBM's MVS Open Edition. This leads us to the question, "What makes Unix Unix?" There are a number of concepts associated with the word.

1 The Unix kernel: the base system within the base system. The kernel provides the file system, security, communications, process management, and device management. The kernel state is basic to Unix operation.

2 Unix directory: a particular directory with particular names. Naming is according to /root/dir1/dir2/dir3/file, where root is a pointer to a directory that has a pointer to another directory or to a file.

3 Unix networking focuses on TCP/IP and UDP/IP.

4 Systems calls: APIs that provide an interface to the kernel, which are defined by SVID (System V Interface Definition) for SVR5 systems.

5 Unix shells: the Unix on-line command language used by a user to interact with the system. It has three basic forms: the C-shell, the Bourne shell, and the Korn shell.

6 Unix utilities: While specific utilities vary with different versions, there is a core set that is so much a part of the culture it is thought of as part of the base system. These include various editors, mail programs, and file transfer routines.

7 Unix programmer support: Some program development toolkits also seem basic to the Unix community and inseparable from the base system. This includes the SSCS (System Software Control System) and other utilities to manage and link programs together.

8 The C language: This is a C culture, and C programming mentality is pervasive. The source language is C, the programming toolkits largely generate or assume C, the libraries are in C, etc.

9 X Windows: A late comer, X Windows is a central part of the Unix culture, an assumption of a Unix environment.

10 SNMP (Simple Network Management Protocol): An industry de facto protocol for systems management. See Chapter 13.

Unix commands (shells)

The shells are the underlying interface to Unix and its utilities. They are both a command language and a programming language, with features generally found only in programming languages (e.g., if, do while, case). Each verb of the language is a command that is run as an independent dispatchable unit. The notation of commands and the syntactic inconsistencies between commands have caused general dismay in nonorthodox circles for some time. The commands are cryptic and often comic. They have complex lists of associated options and arguments.

There are over 200 commands, providing access to utilities as well as to Unix services. The programming languages are accessed through commands, as are the basic line and screen editors, and the software development tools.

The basic concepts of the shell are I/O redirection (naming files as substitutes for standard-in and standard-out files), pipes, filters, shell procedures, shell variables, and command substitutions. Together they provide an enormously flexible environment that can be made enormously elegant by a clever professional user. The notion of using a command language as a programming language, integrating many runtime APIs and storing executable command lists with dynamically provided variables, was quite something in 1974.

An essential concept of the shell is the pipe. The shell permits the output of one program to be directed to another. In this way, chains of programs can be built in the shell, each piping its output to a successor. Utilities to convert data formats or otherwise modify output to be input can be interspersed in the pipe as filters. The intent of this feature was to be able to build complex applications

System Call Interface	
Kernel level	

File system
   Directory
 	
  File
  I-nodes
  Access lists
  Open, Close,
  Read, Write
  Chmod, Chown
  Buffering
	Process system
	   Fork
	   Exec
	   Join
	   Wait
	   Signal
	
	   CPU scheduling
	   Demand paging
	   Virtual memory

'Raw I/O' (character devices)	
Terminals Device controllers Real memory	
Kernel interface to hardware	

Figure B3.1 The kernel.

at the shell level by stringing together families of simple programs in a pipe. It supports a programming philosophy of application construction now with us again as objects.

The kernel

The primeval Unix kernel was constructed with C and assembler, grew to around 300,000 statements, and was used by members of the Unix community as a storage area for just about anything. The kernel provided the semantics of the file system, the communications system, the I/O system, the security system, the processes, memory management, and anything else anyone wished. It is entered with a system call API, which was expanded by a compiler to map it to needed primitive operations. Figure B3.1 shows the kernel and its functions.

As Unix evolved toward a significant market role, concern developed about the traditional Unix kernel. A number of new Unix kernels, among them the SVR4 kernel, were developed in the late 1980s. Major vendors developed new kernels (e.g., IBM for the RS/6000 AIX) to add features and restructure functions for efficiency and installability. The OSF/1 kernel and the Chorus (Chorus International) kernel were "microkernels" whose intent was to provide a basis for greater flexibility, scalability, and security in Unix environments.

Unix file system

The file system is "byte oriented." It has no concept of records or of record access methods. Unix file systems have a pointer that points to a byte that is the current position in the file. References to the file are derived from the pointer.

Everything is a file. The network and I/O devices are special files. Directories to the file system are just specially used files. All programs exist in files. Files have path names whose sizes differ in various versions. Files are parceled over disk space in fixed-size slices, and parts are located by a particular search scheme.

Access control and security are built into the file system. Each file has a definition for its owner, for the workgroup of its owner, and for other persons. The owner of a file may make it available to members of the workgroup and others on a read-only, read/write, and/or execute basis. There is widespread violation of access rules, as there are well-known ways to bypass protection constraints to gain access. Various versions of Unix have tried different ways to plug known and well-documented security holes.

Unix processes

The classic Unix process is "an image in execution." A process is encapsulated in an address space holding program text, data segments, and a run-time stack used to pass parameters between programs. There is a one-to-one relation between the dispatchable unit and the memory image.

A process is created by a "fork." The fork creates an identical image (child) of its creator (parent). All resources associated with the parent are associated with a child. The "fork" command is almost universally followed by an "Exec" command, which differentiates the parent and child and can cause a new child image to be brought into memory. A "spawn" creates a dispatchable unit (thread) within a domain.

Process management is a key technology for larger servers. The canonical model for server process management is called N-Level Feedback Cyclic Queuing. It is typical of 1970's time-sharing systems. It is developed to distinguish between short, medium, and long jobs and to provide a shortest-job-first bias.

A dispatchable unit may be in a number of states. In the Unix SVR4 model, each process is either executing in user mode or kernel mode. It is ready to run, sleeping (waiting on an event but blocked until the event occurs), ready but needs swapping, or waiting and swapped in. It may also be in start state, in transition, not ready to be run. A final state is the "zombie" state, in which it

CHORUS

The microkernel associated with Unix SVR4 is Chorus, a product of Chorus International, headquartered in Paris. It runs on Intel and PowerPC, and Motorola is announcing the availability of Chorus on a chip.

Chorus consists of a small (around 50 KB) nucleus with the usual microprocessor functions: task switching (with a good deal of scheduling), memory management, event response, processor communications, and basic communications. It consists of two layers, supervisor and executive/manager. The supervisor is machine dependent, but the managers above it (IPC, memory, etc.) are portable.

On top of the nucleus are families of "servers"–file managers, Streams and Sockets API servers, and even device drivers. Groups of servers are subsystems representing the full capability of a particular operating system, such as SVR4.

Chorus has some features aimed particularly at distributed computing. It has a notion of segment-oriented memory in which the segments may be dispersed across the network but still be shared by actors (the Chorus equivalent of a process). Systems functions can be split across populations of machines, with logically conjoined users and system spaces.

Unix Systems Laboratories is among a large group of software vendors interested in Chorus. Others include Unisys, Tandem, SCO, and Cray Research.

still exists but will not again be dispatched and is waiting for systems data collection.

The kernel state in Unix has a special meaning, one that has been a problem for Unix in transaction processing and in real time. Functions like process creation, scheduling, communications, and file reference are done in the kernel state. A process wishing these functions runs them on its own dispatch list in kernel state, which is not preemptable. The kernel state is not terminated until the kernel functions release the system. This has meant that it was impossible, in Unix, to respond to an external event while a process was in the kernel state.

Unix memory management

Memory management is very much influenced by hardware characteristics. Therefore, its details are likely to diverge more than other functions of an operating system. There are, however, a number of higher-level abstractions common to all systems, and to all Unix systems in particular.

In Unix System V, the kernel is always in memory. An executing process is partially in memory, subject to swapping and demand paging. Space is organized into two major areas: the kernel space, which is nonswappable and nonpageable, and user space, which is both swappable and pageable. Programs in the kernel space see a combined-process address space of user and kernel portions as if it were a single space. Each user program is in a virtual memory of its own. There are sharable regions in SVR4. Each memory is organized into three regions: a sharable text region for programs, a sharable data region, and a stack region for parameters and systems control. SVR4 is primarily a swapping system that does paging, whereas BSD is primarily a paging system that does swapping.

Unix communications

The fundamental communications technology of Unix is TCP/IP, including IP and a family of physical and link layer protocols, and UDP and TCP as transport layers. Novell SPX/IPX local area protocols are now available with some versions of Unix, as are LU 6.2 (for IBM versions) and other vendor-specific protocols.

Unix provides a number of interfaces to its transport layers. Streams is a higher-level interface popular within the SVR4 community. Sockets is a lower-level (more technical looking) interface dominant in BSD-influenced systems.

Unix development

A large family of CASE and object tools are now available for Unix, in particular, or for Unix and other operating systems. In reality, a tool market has developed that is operating system independent, so the idea of Unix-specific development tools is not as key as it was some years ago.

However, there are some Unix development fundamentals that are traditionally a part of the Unix culture. Part of the development environment are directory-oriented commands that list directory contents, move files, remove files, or copy files. These are used in connection with library functions associated with software development. There are also some classic file processing functions such as "grep," a pattern search function, and "vi," the visual editor.

Programming languages associated with Unix include assemblers for various architectures, the C programming language, a pattern-matching report generator, and an early compiler compiler called "YACC" (Yet Another Compiler Compiler). Unix manipulates program and system building with "make," which constructs a program file from elements, and the Source Code Control System.

Unix and open

For many years Unix and "open" were almost synonymous terms. As open became a mainstream market issue in the late 1980s, Unix took on importance, as it is open in a variety of ways:

1 It is portable across scale and architecture.

2 It is available from many suppliers for various architectures.

3 It is interoperable through TCP/IP.

4 There is an API standard, SVID.

5 There is a large number of common de facto protocols across versions.

6 There is a large number of international de jure standards supported by all versions.

7 There are de jure and de facto standards groups working with assumptions of the Unix culture; among these are IEEE, X/Open, and OSF.

Structure of Windows NT

Figure B3.2 shows the structure of Windows NT. It contains a Hardware Abstraction Layer (HAL), which creates a common machine abstraction for machine-independent layers. Microsoft claims that it is possible to port from any version of Intel architecture to any other version with a 1% hit on coding, almost all of which is confined to the HAL. Above the HAL, is the NT kernel, with basic functions of thread scheduling, interrupt exception dispatching, and multiprocessor synchronization. The NT kernel contains some primitives that higher layers use to implement higher-level objects.

Resting directly on the HAL are a set of basic operating systems services—file systems, cache drivers, device drivers, and network drivers. Each of these presents an abstraction to higher-level elements relative to local or remote input and output. The file system accepts file-level requests (Get, Put, Read, Write) and prepares them to be submitted to a device. The cache manager stores recently read I/O in memory. Device drivers directly drive specific I/O devices, and the I/O manager projects a device-independent model for basic I/O functions. Network drivers transmit I/O requests to the network. A function called a network redirector provides translations to various network protocols for interoperability.

Windows NT can handle multiple file systems. Its primary system is NTFS (New Technology File System), but it provides support for the OS/2 High Performance File System and the File Allocation Table. NTFS has transaction logging for recovery, and can be used as a transaction file system. It provides long names and enormous file sizes (up to 17 billion gigabytes).

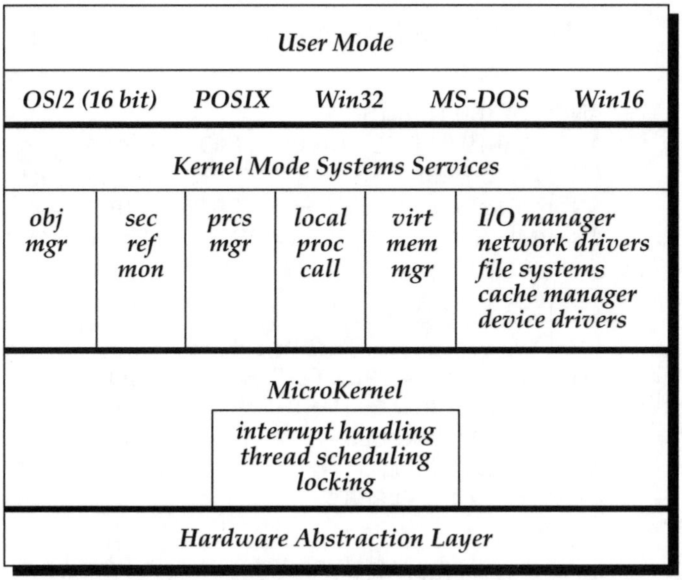
User Mode
OS/2 (16 bit)
POSIX
Win32
MS-DOS
Win16
Kernel Mode Systems Services
obj mgr
sec ref mon
prcs mgr
local proc call
virt mem mgr
I/O manager
network drivers
file systems
cache manager
device drivers
MicroKernel
interrupt handling
thread scheduling
locking
Hardware Abstraction Layer

Reprinted by kind permission of the manticore consultancy, New York.

Figure B3.2 Windows NT architecture.

Supported by the kernel, with no access to HAL, is the highest layer of the NT executive (that part of NT that runs in kernel mode). This layer consists of elements that are structured by a vertical, rather than a horizontal, paradigm. These elements might be called "servers." Like Unix, kernel-mode elements do not run in their own processes, but as functions running in a thread as a result of a request or an event. Sometimes referred to as native services, these "server" elements consist of:

- Virtual memory (VM) manager: This element creates a virtual address space for each process and provides protection from address space to address space. It is supported by a paging mechanism running least-recently-used algorithms.
- Process manager: creates and deletes processes and threads, and suspends and resumes threads, using the facilities of the kernel. NT provides preemptive multitasking (except for 16-bit Windows applications) permitting concurrent operation of many threads, asynchronous I/O, etc.
- Local procedure call (LPC) facility: This service passes messages between processes on the same machine; it is the core interprocess mechanism, a local version of an RPC.
- Security reference monitor: provides common security services for local resources. Each object in the NT executive has an access control list checked

B3.2   UNIX AND STANDARDS

Language standards

C-Draft	ANSI C #X3j11/88-159
FORTRAN	ANSI x3.9-1978, FIPS PUB 69-1, ISO 1539-1980E
COBOL	ANSI x3.23-1985, FIPS PUB 21-2, ISO 1989-1985 (High Level)
Pascal	ANSI770x3.97-1983, FIPS PUB 109, ISO 7185-1983
Ada	ANSI/MIL STD 1815 A-1983 FIPS PUB 119, ISO 8652

Graphics standards

CGI	ANSI x3.161, ISO 9636
CGM	ANSI X3.122-1986, FIPS PUB 128
GKS	ANSI ANSI X3.124-1985, FIPS PUB 120, ISO
GKS FORTRAN Binding	ANSI x3.122.1, ISO 8651-1
GKS Ada Binding	ANSI x3.122.3, ISO 8651-3
GKS Pascal Binding	ANSI x3.122.2, ISO 8561-2
GKS C Binding	ANSI x3.122.4, ISO 8561-4

Data access standards

SQL	ANSI X3.135-1986, FIPS PUB 127

Communications standards

TCP	RFC 793
IP	RFC 791
SNMP	RFC 1065, RFC 1066, RFC 1098
SMTP	RFC 821, RFC 822
Telnet	RFC 854, RFC 855, RFC 856
FTP	RFC 959
IEEE 802.3	
IEEE 802.5	
X.25	FIPS PUB 100

by the security monitor to determine if a running process has the right to use or modify the object. NT meets government C2 requirements.

- Object manager: creates, manages, and deletes objects running in the NT executive. It is a highly typed generator of executive abstractions with models of "process," "access token," etc. from which it provides instances. Sharable resources in the NT executive are objects. When an application starts within a subsystem (see the paragraphs directly below), it calls the process manager to create a process in which the application will run. The process manager, in turn, calls the object manager to create a named instance of a process.

Each of these servers is designed to have maximum independence from other elements at this level. Microsoft claims that interfaces are carefully controlled, and it would be possible to replace any of these servers. A design principle clearly has been maximum encapsulation and information hiding.

Above the systems servers are the user-mode environment subsystems that present an operating system to an end user. These are:

- Win32 (the primary personality)
- MS-DOS
- OS/2 16-bit
- Win16
- POSIX.

The emulation environments (DOS, Win16, OS/2) provide virtual machines in which these emulated systems can perform.

The Win32 environment, which looks like Windows 3.1, provides the user interface and is an environment for 32-bit applications developed for Win32. When Win32 recognizes an alien application, it calls the appropriate subsystem to run it in a virtual machine (VDM) so as to emulate an MS-DOS, Win16, or other environment. All subsystems must communicate through Win32, which controls the display. NT can run a theoretically limitless number of fully pageable MS-DOS applications providing full screen display or windows with copy and paste. Sixteen-bit Windows applications run in Win16 (Windows on Windows, or WOW). WOW is a multithreaded virtual DOS machine where each application runs as a thread. The single virtual machine emulates the Windows 16-bit environment. Windows 16-bit and 32-bit (Win32) applications can share data with no visible difference to a user.

Each of the subsystems creates an image of memory that its applications expect, and each abstraction is supported by the NT executive. Each executive address space is 4 GB, divided into 2 GB for the system and 2 GB for applications.

Some features are particular to NT Advanced Server. These include support for file replication, which will automatically replicate files and directories on other servers when specified, and disk mirroring, which writes two copies of a file on disks on the same disk controller, or disk duplexing, which mirrors files across controllers. NT Advanced Server also supports RAID 5 protocols.

Windows NT networking

Windows provides integrated multiprotocol networking with some additional options. TCP/IP and NetBEUI is built in, as is a superset of the Windows for Workgroup services, including file transfer, e-mail, and printer sharing. Microsoft Mail is built into NT. (Although NT Advanced Server is the scalable SMP server system, any NT station can perform as a group server.) Access to DOS and OS/2 systems is achievable through computability with LAN Manager and support of NetBIOS and NetBEUI technologies.

Microsoft permits stack crossover. Presentation layer interfaces can use various transport protocols behind the transport driver interface (TDI) layer. Session and transport layers share the media access layers.

Windows NT offers optional connectivity to SNA, DECnet, NetWare, and Banyan clients. SNA support includes LU 6.2 and other LU support, NetView services, and a variety of (not all) options at various protocol layers. DEC is porting DECnet to Windows 3.1, and Novell and Banyan have (Microsoft claims) committed to appropriate support product. At the interface level, NT offers a DCE-compatible RPC and a version of Sockets (WinSockets), as well as Streams over TCP/IP and SPX/IPX. It does not support the ONC RPC.

Windows NT can act as a client to NetWare servers using an NT element called the NetWare Workstation Compatible Server (NWCS), which allows an NT client to access data and printers on NetWare networks from all platforms (Intel, Alpha, etc). Applications make requests through Win32 APIs, which are redirected (NWCS is a network redirector) to NetWare networks.

Windows NT Advanced Server can communicate with NetWare clients without disturbing client environments. NetWare functions (NetWare Loadable Modules) can be ported to NT. NetWare Mechanisms run on Windows NT Advanced Server NWLink, an SPX/IPX–compatible protocol stack.

Microsoft provides interconnection with Macintosh clients by direct connection with AppleTalk networks, emulating the behavior of an AppleTalk network. Windows NT services for the Macintosh allow PCs and Macintoshes to share files and printers.

IBM MVS: Multiple Virtual Storage

MVS was for years the IBM flagship system, one of the SAA systems and the software technology focus of IBM. It is a complex, robust, sophisticated platform that runs, in various versions, on systems costing from about $250,000 to about $20,000,000. As the growth of desktop machines has enabled Unix on the PC desktop, the growth of smaller 390 machines has enabled MVS on the mid-size air-cooled machine. It is likely that an "entry version" MVS will someday run on all models of the 390.

The system has gone through many changes, many in response to changing machine architecture, some in response to changing patterns of use. The line of machines that has evolved from the 360 over the past 30 years has had both design and architectural changes. MVS has had to react to these changes. MVS also has responded over time to changes from batch to interactive- or transaction-oriented users, connected from remote locations.

One of the great complexities of MVS evolution has been the necessity to remain backward compatible with programs running on earlier versions. This has led to a matrix of "modes" and to the retention of many mechanisms that are clearly obsolete.

Various parts of the MVS culture are developed around the world. Putting together a coherent software system within this geography is likely to be beyond the ability of humankind in this stage of evolution. The relations between DB2, VTAM/NCP (communications), CICS, and baseware parts of the MVS culture are discouragingly ragged.

The end user model

The MVS end user model is visible from a 3270-type terminal or when a personal computer is emulating a 3270-type terminal. By the nature of the terminal, all screens are textual; but there is color, and some interfaces have been brought into conformance with a low-level text form of CUA.

To a large degree, each subsystem defines its own interface style for end users and for the systems/administrative community. Large mainframe systems of this type assume a staff of specialists and operators, and offer a wide range of installation and tuning parameters. The major baseware subsystems are:

- JES (Job Entry Subsystem), for submitting and controlling batch jobs
- TSO (Time Sharing Option), for interactive professional activity
- RMF (Resource Manager Facility), which collects performance data to support tuning and capacity management
- HSM (Hierarchical Storage Manager), which provides backup, archiving, and "percolate and trickle"
- RACF (Resource Access Control Facility), which provides an object-to-subject access control mapping.

Each of these has a more or less private language, more or less similar in form to the command language of MVS, JCL (Job Control Language). There are some ease-of-use utilities that permit easier creation of terminal screens and easier to use interfaces. Among these are ISPF and IPPF, screen dialogue generators for text interaction. But even the usability tools assume a high degree of professional training. In general, tools for this kind of system aim at increasing the productivity of the professional, not at empowering the amateur.

Naturally, there is an increasing relation between MVS and desktop users with DOS, Windows, and OS/2. There are a number of tools that permit the transfer of files between MVS and a desktop operating system, and even the extraction of data from MVS files into local data bases. Local operating systems also show MVS windows on their screens. Some transparency and access is achieved through data base software and through client/server software from major data base vendors and file systems. MVS can act as an NSF (but not a full ONC) server. There is a version of X Windows that will run with MVS.

The IBM strategy at this time seems to be to withdraw the visibility of MVS behind developing client interfaces as part of its enterprise server positioning of the product.

Authorization and security

Authorization is somewhat dispersed in MVS. Each subsystem has its own access control function somewhat independent of the basic file access control mechanisms in the baseware. CICS (Customer Information Control System), IMS (Information Management System), TSO, and DB2 maintain partially separate security mechanisms, although the RACF function can be used to support TSO.

MVS as a base system has sufficient security to be certified B1, the highest of classifications that does not require demonstrations of structural properties. It has sufficient journaling and logging to trace security violations, and it has excellent encryption capability. IBM is an industry leader in encryption.

IBM has committed MVS to the support of Kerberos authentication as part of the DCE model of distributed services.

Data

The MVS data model is a complex record-oriented file model that permits access to records by position, by key, and by some attribute definition. The access facility is provided by access methods generated into programs, the most sophisticated of which is VSAM (Virtual Storage Access Method). This is inverted file indexing software that enables a number of pathways to records. It still requires a program to "navigate" through data. MVS also provides NFS server function. Data base capability is provided by DB2 and by major data base vendors such as Ingres and Sybase. There are versions of CODASYL (network) data bases (ADABAS) and hierarchic data managers (IMS) available.

IMS is a transaction manager and hierarchic data manager. In a hierarchic data manager, data is organized with parents and children in an object data base–like way. It is still a key product in the mainframe community, although it was never an SAA system. It is one of the products supported by data warehouse and EDA/SQL. It is possible to acquire an SQL shell to run as an IMS API.

CICS is surely the most successful of the middleware products. It has broken its link to 390 and is available on a number of IBM platforms (AIX, OS/2) and from other vendors. It is a reasonably respectable candidate in the open transaction manager sweepstakes. In non-MVS environments, however, there are such differences in systems attributes under the CICS APIs that it is difficult to judge how portable, or migratory, CICS applications will be.

The communications model

The primary communications capability of MVS has been SNA 6.2 supported by VTAM and NCP. MVS capability has grown as SNA has grown to support ISO protocol stacks, TCP/IP, and LAN technology. MVS is committed to full support of the IBM Network Blueprint, which provides multiprotocol support.

The program and process model

The MVS process model is rich and complex, with complex relations between domains, virtual memories, and dispatchable units. The basic model is this: a virtual memory can contain a number of dispatchable units. The tasks are not truly POSIX threads because they can define a subdomain of resources within a virtual memory. A virtual memory is a domain of resources, like a POSIX process. Within a virtual memory, different tasks can carve out different resource domains.

The latest memory model, ESA (Enterprise Systems Architecture), adds some complexities. The potential addressable space for a running application actually consists of a large number of 2 GB addressable units initially called virtual memories. Up to 32 GB are simultaneously addressable theoretically, but the full address space is essentially limitless (4K by 2 GB, theoretically.).

A task lives in a home virtual memory and has the usual subdomain of resources. However, a task can roam around virtual memories in the address space, and as it does, its domain shifts depending on the virtual memory within which it is executing.

The scheduling model can be construed as a very sophisticated rendering of cycle feedback. It exists on two distinct levels: an intermediate scheduling level called the APG (Automatic Priority Grouping), which balances I/O utilization, political priority, and the work group to manage a set of "active" tasks, and a long-term scheduler called the SRM (Systems Resource Manager), which plans intermediate work groups and moves tasks on and off active lists. The SRM is the highpoint of mainframe systems workload management.

The memory model

MVS is a demand paging and swap system with three levels of abstraction. An address space is a collection of virtual memories defined in the processor and in tables in memory. A virtual memory is a defined addressable unit with a name of 32 bits and an offset of 31 bits. A segment is a defined unit of a virtual memory, and a page is a defined unit of a segment. MVS assures a working set size for a program to be dispatched and endeavors to keep the pages of active programs in memory. It frees memory for active programs by "swapping out" the memory spaces of nonactive programs, or by "page stealing" from other active programs when necessary.

The workload management model

In addition to the SRM, RMF, and JES, there are a large number of workload management tools offered by IBM and other vendors. These include automated operations, performance monitoring, and administrative interfaces.

The recovery model

MVS is an industrial-strength system with a number of fail-soft and recovery mechanisms. It has full journaling and logging, and various states of partial and complete recovery and reinitialization. It has backup and archiving technology for supported nonprogrammable terminals. The Data Storage Division of IBM has developed a backup capability for desktop systems called DFMS (Distributed File Management System).

The systems management model

Taking this to mean network management, IBM NetView is the prime network manager for MVS. See Chapter 13.

The application model

There are software development activities ongoing on MVS. AD/Cycle posited a large set of tools and data collections that would be mainframe resident across the life cycle. Outside of the AD/Cycle context is a large number of programming language environments, lower CASE tools, and upper CASE tools that matured in the early to mid 1980s. Major interactive development is done through TSO.

The object model

IBM has announced (in June 1994) its intention to fully support objects in an MVS context. That involves C++, COBOL++, and other object-oriented compilers, as well as MVS support for OMG standards and the IBM Systems Management Model, which provides language-to-language object relations across a network.

The future

IBM is undertaking to position MVS as an open server—MVS Open Edition. This strategy has a number of components:

1 Announcement of intention to support Spec 1170. This is a big commitment for an older system.

2 Support of POSIX 1003.1, 1003.2, and 1003.4, which pretty much matches what anyone else is doing.

3 Support for DCE, including RPC, directory, and file systems. The MVS version of DCE/DFS is IFS developed with Michigan University. Early development workshops and seminars are underway.

4 Participation in the IBM Network Blueprint, including TCP/IP, SPX/IPX, NetBIOS, and OSI protocols, with protocol adaptation and the ability to use various layer 3 and 4 facilities with various layer 5 and 6 facilities.

5 Support for SunOS, ULTRIX, A/UX, Macintosh, and other workstation and PC clients.

IT acronyms

ACE	Advanced Computing Environment
ACF	Advanced Communications Function
ACSE	Association Control Service Entity
AD/Cycle	Application Development/Cycle
APG	Automatic Priority Grouping
API	Application Program Interface
APPC	Advanced Program-to-Program Communication
APPN	Advanced Peer-to-Peer Networking
APS	Asynchronous Protocol Specification
ASN	Abstract Syntax Notation
ATM	Asynchronous Transfer Mode
B-ISDN	Broadband Integrated Services Digital Network
BSD	Berkeley Software Distribution
CAE	Common Application Environment
CASE	Computer Aided Software Engineering
CCITT	Consultative Committee for International Telephony and Telegraphy
CDE	Common Desktop Environment
CICS	Customer Information Control System
CIL	Component Integration Lab
CISC	Complex Instruction Set Computer
CMIP	Common Management Information Protocol
CMISE	Common Management Information Services Element
COM	Component Object Model
CORBA	Common Object Request Broker Architecture

COSE	Common Open Software Environment
COSS	Common Object Services Specification
CPI	Common Programming Interface
CPI-C	Common Programming Interface for Communications
CSMA/CD	Carrier Sense Multiple Access/Collision Detection
CUA	Common User Access
DCE	Distributed Computing Environment
DFMS	Distributed File Management System
DFS	Distributed File System
DIA	Document Interchange Architecture
DME	Distributed Management Environment
DMI	Desktop Management Interface
DMTF	Desktop Management Task Force
DNA	Digital Network Architecture
DOMF	Distributed Object Management Facility
DS1	Digital Signal 1
DSOM	Distributed System Object Model
ECMA	European Computer Manufacturers Association
EDA	Enterprise Data Access
EISA	Extended Industry Standard Architecture
EMA	Electronic Mail Association
ESA	Enterprise System Architecture
EUI	End User Interface
FTP	File Transfer Protocol
GaAs	Gallium Arsenide
GDMO	Guide Development Management Objects
GOSIP	Government OSI Profile
GUI	Graphical User Interface
HAL	Hardware Abstraction Layer
HDLC	High-level Data Link Control
HSM	Hierarchical Storage Manager
I-CASE	Integrated CASE
IBI	Information Builders, Inc.
iCOMP	Intel COmparative Microprocessor Performance
IDL	Interface Definition Language
IETF	Internet Engineering Task Force
IMS	Information Management System
IP	Internet Protocol
ISMA	Information Systems Management Association
ISO	International Standards Organization

ISPF	Interactive System Productivity Facility
ISV	Independent Software Vendor
ITU	International Telecommunications Union
JCL	Job Control Language
JES	Job Entry Subsystem
LEN	Low Entry Networking
LPC	Local Procedure Call
LU 6.2	Logical Unit 6.2
MAPI	Mail Application Program Interface
MHS	Message Handling Services
MIB	Management Information Base
MIMD	Multiple-Instruction Multiple-Data
MIT	Management Information Tree
MME	Microsoft Multimedia Windows
MPE	MultiProgramming Executive
MQI	Message Queuing Interface
MVS	Multiple Virtual Storage
NAS	Network Application Support
NCP	Network Control Program
NCR	National Cash Register
NCS	Network Computing System
NetBEUI	NetBIOS Extended User Interface
NetBIOS	Network Basic Input/Output System
NFS	Network File System
NIS	Network Information Services
NIST	National Institute of Standards & Technology
NTFS	New Technology File System
NWCS	NetWare Workstation Compatible Server
ODAPI	Open Data Application Program Interface
ODBC	Open Data Base Connectivity
ODMG	Object Database Management Group
ODP	Open Distributed Processing
OID	Object IDentifier
OLAP	On-Line Analytical Processing
OLTP	On-Line Transaction Processing
OMG	Object Management Group
ONC	Open Network Computing
OOA	Object-Oriented Analysis
OODMS	Object-Oriented Database Management System
ORB	Object Request Broker

OSF	Open Software Foundation
OSI	Open System Interconnection
PBX	Private Branch Exchange
PCI	Peripheral Component Interconnect
PCMCIA	Personal Computer Memory Card International Association
PCTE	Programming Common Tools Environment
POSIX	Portable Operating System Interface for Unix
PU	Physical Unit
RACF	Resource Access Control Facility
RAID	Redundant Arrays of Inexpensive Disks
RDA	Relational Data Architecture
RFT	Request For Technology
RISC	Reduced Instruction Set Computer
RMF	Resource Management Facility
RMON	Remote Monitoring MIB
ROSE	Remote Operations Service Entity
RPC	Remote Procedure Call
RTP	Routing Update Protocol
SAA	System Application Architecture
SAG	SQL Access Group
SCO	Santa Cruz Operation
SCWUI	Steering Committee for Windowing User Interfaces
SDLC	Synchronous Data Link Control
SIMD	Single-Instruction Multiple-Data
SMB	Server Message Block
SMDS	Switched Multimegabit Data Services
SMI	Structure of Management Information
SMP	Symmetric Multiprocessing
SMTP	Simple Mail Transfer Protocol
SNA	Systems Network Architecture
SNADS	SNA Distribution Services
SNA/MS	SNA Management Services
SNMP	Simple Network Management Protocol
SOM	System Object Model
SONET	Synchronous Optical Network
SPP	Sequenced Packet Protocol
SPX/IPX	Sequenced Packet Exchange/Internet Packet Exchange
SQL	Structured Query Language
SRM	Systems Resource Manager
SSCP	System Services Control Point

SSCS	System Software Control System
SVID	System V Interface Definition
SVRx	System V Release x
TAPI	Telephony Application Program Interface
TCP/IP	Transmission Control Protocol/Internet Protocol
TDI	Transport Driver Interface
TPC	Transaction Processing Council
TPS	Transactions Per Second
TRPC	Transaction RPC
TSO	Time Sharing Option
U-CASE	Upper CASE
UCS	Universal Component System
UDP	User Datagram Protocol
USL	Unix System Laboratories
VDM	Virtual DOS Machine
VINES	VIrtual NEtworking System
VIP	VINES Internet Protocol
VM	Virtual Memory
VMS	Virtual Memory System
VSAM	Virtual Storage Access Method
VTAM	Virtual Telecommunications Access Method
Wabi	Windows Application Binary Interface
WfWG	Windows For WorkGroups
WORM	Write Once/Read Many
WOSA	Windows Open System Architecture
WOW	Windows On Windows
XAPIA	X.400 API Association
XPG	X/Open Portability Guide
YACC	Yet Another Compiler Compiler
4GL	Fourth-Generation Language

guide to publications

Over many years, at uncountable meetings, seminars, consulting sessions, presentations, etc., I have formed a vision of the industry. This book represents that image.

The book has been influenced by other books, trade and academic journal articles, and much other published material. It has also been flavored by verbal and situational interaction with diverse people in the industry, including business executives, strategists, architects, planners, designers, programmers, and (even) end-users in using and producing companies. Often, it is truly impossible to trace a particular view or fact to a particular document or person.

This appendix undertakes to indicate some of the books and articles that have influenced the text. They are sources of viewpoints, facts, assessments, guesses, and good explanations. The author recommends them to the reader seeking to form an independent vision of the industry, or to understand from what I have built mine. Caution: some of the articles from the trade press have no particular merit or insight. They are listed merely as examples of the issues and trends being discussed.

One of the great issues of computing, reflected in its chaotic industry and systems structure, is a proper topology of knowledge. The organization of knowledge is knowledge, and many problems result from bad intellectual maps. Unfortunately, a good topology of knowledge is beyond us, or at least beyond me. I do not like most other peoples' topologies, and therefore, I propose some simple classifications that seem to make sense:

- Data technology and methodology
- Communications technology and methodology
- Interface and usability

- Application development technology and methodology
- Systems architecture technology and methodology
- Management and investment issues and methodology
- Industry dynamics.

Below is a list of publications grouped according to these subjects.

Data technology and methodology

ACM Computing Surveys, special issue on Heterogeneous Databases. **22** (3), 1990.

Anderson, D. P., Y. Osawa, and R. Govindan. "A File System for Continuous Media," *ACM Transactions on Computer Systems*. **10** (4), 311, 1992.

Butterworth, P., A. Otis, and J. Stein. "The Gemstone Object Database Management System," *CACM*. **34** (10), 64, 1991.

Chorafas, D. N. Intelligent Multimedia Databases. Prentice-Hall, Englewood Cliffs, NJ, 1994.

Deinhart, K. "SAA Distributed File Access to the CICS Environment," *IBM Systems Journal*. **31** (3), 516, 1992.

Demers, R. A., J. D. Fisher, S. S. Gaitonde, and R. R. Sanders. "Inside IBM's Distributed Data Management Archtecture," *IBM Systems Journal*. **31** (3), 459, 1992.

Demers, R. A. and K. Yamaguchi. "Data Description and Conversion Architecture," *IBM Systems Journal*. **31** (3), 488, 1992.

"Directory Service for a Distributed Computing Environment," White Paper. Open Software Foundation, Cambridge, MA, Apr. 1991.

"Distributed Remote Data Architecture," SC26-4651. IBM Distributed Data Library, 1990.

Inmon, W. H. *Building the Data Warehouse*. Wiley, New York, 1992.

Inmon, W. H. and R. D. Hackathorn. *Using the Data Warehouse*. Wiley, New York, 1994.

Levy, E. and A. Silberschatz. "Distributed File Systems: Concepts and Examples," *ACM Computer Survey*. **22** (4), 321, 1990.

Mohan, C., Pirahesh, W. G. Tang, and Y. Wang. "Parallelism in Relational Data Base Management Systems," *IBM Systems Journal*. **29** (2), 349, 1994.

"NFS: Network File System Protocol Specification," RFC 1094. Sun Microsystems, San Francisco, 1989.

O'Connell, B. "Mandating the Multiplatform Database," *DEC Professional*. **12** (4), 22, 1993.

Qadir, I. "Distributed File Systems," Course project in Advanced Operating Systems Design, Hofstra University, Spring 1992.

Rangan, P. V. and H. M. Vin. "Designing File Systems for Digital Video and Audio," *ACM Operating Systems Review*. **25** (2), 81, 1991.

Riley, M. F., J. J. Feenan, J. J. Janosik, Jr., and T. K. Rengarajan. "Design of Multimedia Object Support in DEC Rdb." *DEC Technical Journal*. **5** (2), 50, 1993.

Satyanarayanan, M. "Scalable, Secure, and Highly Available Distributed File Access," *Computer*. **23** (5), 1990.

Satyanarayanan, M., J. H. Howard, D. A. Nichols, R. N. Sidebotham, A. Z. Spector, and M. J. West. "The ITC Distributed File System: Principles and Design," *Proceedings*. 10th Symp. on Operating System Principles, ACM, Dec. 1985.

Silberschatz, A., M. Stonebreaker, and J. Ullman, Eds. "Database Systems: Achievements and Opportunities." *CACM*. **34** (3), 110, 1991.

Singleton, J. P. and M. M. Schwartz. "Data Access within the Information Warehouse Framework," *IBM Systems Journal*. **33** (2), 300, 1994.

Stein, R. M. "Object Databases," *BYTE*. **19** (4), 74, 1994.

Zachman, J. A. "Business Systems Planning and Business Information Control Study," *IBM Systems Journal*. **21** (1), 31, 1982.

Communications technology and methodology

Awuah, P. "Overview of Remote Access Services for Windows NT Advanced Server," Document NT103, *Microsoft Tech Ed '94*, Microsoft Corp., Redstone, WA.

Black, A. P., E. D. Lazswoska, H. M. Levy, D. Notkin, J. Sanislo, and J. Zahorjan. "Interconnecting Heterogeneous Computer Systems," *CACM*. **31** (3), 258, 1988.

Comer, D. *Internetworking with TCP/IP*. Prentice-Hall, Englewood Cliffs, NJ, 1988.

Cort, R. "Advanced Networking within Windows NT," Document No. NT301, *Microsoft Tech Ed '94*, Microsoft Corp., Redstone, WA.

Cypser, R. J. "Evolution of an Open Communications Architecture," *IBM Systems Journal*. **31** (2), 161, 1992.

"DECnet/OSI Transition Planning for Open Networking." Digital Equipment Corporation, Maynard, MA, 1991.

"Directory Service for a Distributed Computing Environment," White Paper. Open Software Foundation, Cambridge, MA, Apr. 1991.

Harrison, B. T. "Multiprotocol Highways," *DEC Professional*. **10** (13), 38, 1991.

Harrison, B. T. "Using DCE," *DEC Professional*. **11** (1), 44, 1992.

Hedrick, C. L. *Introduction to the Internet Protocols*. Rutgers University, New Brunswick, NJ, 1988.

"High Speed Networking Technology," GG24-3816. International Technical Support Centers, IBM Corp., Research Triangle Park, NC, Mar. 1992.

"Information Processing Systems—Open Systems Interconnection—File Transfer, Access and Management," ISO 8672. International Standards Organization, Oct. 1988.

IPX Router Specification, Part No. 107-000029-001. Novell Corp., Provo, UT, Sept. 1992.

Janson, P., R. Molva, and S. Zatti. "Architectural Directions for Opening IBM Networks: The Case of OSI," *IBM Systems Journal*. **31** (2), 313, 1992.

Lorin, H. "Personal Computers and Communications," *IEEE JSAC on Communications for Personal Computers*. **7** (2), 1989.

"Midyear Update—Cost-to-Use Midrange and PC LAN Systems in the Network Enterprise." International Data Corporation (IDG), Framingham, MA, 1992.

"Multiprotocol Transport Networking (MPTN) Architecture," Technical Overview GC31 7073. IBM Corp., Research Triangle Park, NC, 1993.

Nance, B. "OS/2 and Windows Networks," *BYTE*. **18** (12), 117, 1993.

"Networking," *Proceedings*. 1991 European Conference, Paris, Cap Gemini Institute, Nov. 1991.

Nicolaou, C. "An Architecture for Real-Time Multimedia Communications System," *IEEE Journal Selected Areas of Communication*. **8** (3), 413, 1990.

"Open Systems Interconnection Application Layer Tutorial," ZZ81-0194-00. International Technical Support Centers, IBM Corp., Research Triangle Park, NC, 1987.

Ramos, E. and A. Schroeder. *Contemporary Data Communications, a Practical Approach*. Macmillan, New York, 1994.

Schwarz, M. *Telemmunications Networks, Protocols, Modeling, and Analysis*. Addison-Wesley, Reading, MA, 1987.

Stallings, W. *Local and Metropolitan Area Networks*, 4th ed. Macmillan, New York, 1993.

Stallings, W. *Local Area Network Standards*, 2nd ed., Vol. 2 of *Handbook of Computer Communications*. Macmillan, New York, 1990.

Stallings, W. *The OSI Model and OSI Related Standards*, 2nd ed., Vol. 1 of *Handbook of Computer Communications*. Macmillan, New York, 1990.

Voss, F. W. "APPC/MVS Distributed Application Support," *IBM Systems Journal*. **31** (2), 381, 1992.

Interface and usability

Adam, J. A. "Virtual Reality Is for Real," *IEEE Spectrum*. **30** (10), 22, 1993.

Berry, R. E. "The Designers Model of the CUA Workplace," *IBM Systems Journal*. **31** (3), 429, 1992.

Berry, R. E. and C. V. Reeves. "The Evolution of the Common User Access Workplace Model," *IBM Systems Journal*. **31** (3), 414, 1992.

Bourne, P. E. "Visualization: From Promise to Progress," *DEC Professional*. **11** (7), 46, 1992.

DeFanti, T. A., D. J. Sandin, and C. Cruz-Neira. "A 'Room' with a 'View.' " *IEEE Spectrum*. **30** (10), 30, 1993.

Mandelkern, D. "GUIs: The Next Generation," *CACM*. **36** (4), Apr. 1993.

Marchs, A. "Human Communications Issues in Advanced UIs," *CACM*. **36** (4), 100, Apr. 1993.

Nielsen, J. "Noncommand User Interfaces," *CACM*. **36** (4), 82, Apr. 1993.

Ramanathan, S. and V. Rangan. "Integrating Virtual Reality, Teleconferencing, and Entertainment into Mulimedia Home Computers," *IEEE Transactions of Consumer Electronics*. **38** (2), 1992.

Rangan, P. V. "Software Implementation of VCRs on Personal Computing Systems," *IEEE Transactions of Consumer Electronics*. **38** (3), 1992.

Reisman, S. and W. A. Carr. "Perspectives on Multimedia Systems in Education," *IBM Systems Journal*. **30** (5), 280, 1991.

Udell, J. "Computer Telephony," *BYTE*. **19** (7), 80, 1994.

Application development technology and methodology

Biggerstaff, T. J. and A. Perlis. *Software Reusability*, Vols. 1 and 2. Addison-Wesley, 1989.

Binstock, A. and D. Burnette. "Porting at the Binary Level," *Unix Review*. **10** (6), 25, 1992.

Birrell, A. D. and B. J. Nelson. "Implementing Remote Procedure Calls," *ACM Transactions on Computer Systems*. **2** (1), 39, 1984.

Boehm, B. *Software Engineering Economics*. Prentice-Hall, Englewood Cliffs, NJ, 1981.

Davis, A. M. "Impacts of Life Cycle Models on Software Configuration Management," *CACM*. **34** (8), 104, 1991.

Freeman, P. A. and M. C. Gaudel. "Building a Foundation for the Future of Software Engineering," *CACM*. **34** (5), 30, 1991.

Gellock, S. "Developing Distributed Applications with Windows NT," Document NT303, *Microsoft Tech Ed '94*, Microsoft Corp., Redstone, WA.

Gould, J. D., S. J. Boies, and C. Lewis. "Making Usable, Useful, Productivity Enhancing Computer Applications," *CACM*. **34** (1), 74, 1991.

Jacobson, I., M. Christerson, P. Jonsson, and G. Overgaard. *Object Oriented Software Engineering*. Addison-Wesley, Reading, MA, 1992.

Knox, S. "Modeling the Cost of Software Quality," *Digital Technical Journal*. **5** (4), 9, 1993.

Lorin, H. "Application Development, Software Engineering and Distributed Processing." *Computer Communications*. Jan. 1990.

Lorin, H. "Dangers in Unsophisticated Use of Objects," *OMG First Class*. Nov. 1992.

Lorin, H. "An Extended Approach to Objects," *ACM Operating Systems Review*. **20** (1), 6–11, 1986.

Lorin, H. "Some Issues in Software Management," *Proceedings*. Computer Measurement Group Conference (CMG XIV), Dec. 1984.

Lorin, H. "Toward Distributed Applications," *Proceedings*. SHARE 71, Vol. 1, Aug. 1988.

Lorin, H. "Toward Usable Objects," *OMG First Class*. May 1993.

Marzullo, K., R. Cooper, M. D. Wood, and K. P. Birman. "Tools for Distributed Application Management," *IEEE Computer Journal*. **10** (8), 42, 1991.

Meyer, B. *Object-Oriented Software Construction*. Prentice-Hall, New York, 1988.

Mills, H. D. *Software Productivity*. Little Brown, Boston, 1983.

Mooney, J. D. "Strategies for Supporting Application Portability," *Computer*. **23** (11), 59, 1990.

"NAS Handbook: Developing Applications in a Multivendor Environment." Digital Equipment Corporation, Bedford, MA, 1990.

"NCR, Your Scalable Solutions Partner." Presented at Microsoft NT Symposium, New York, 1992.

"Novell AppWare," white paper. Novell Corp., Provo, UT, 1993.

"Open Systems Interconnection Application Layer Tutorial," ZZ81-0194-00. International Technical Support Centers, IBM Corp., Research Triangle Park, NC, 1987.

"Remote Procedure Call: Technology, Standardization and OSF's Distributed Computing Environment," Technical Paper. Open Software Foundation, Cambridge, MA, Jan. 1992.

"Remote Procedure Call Using OSI," Final draft, 2nd ed., ECMA-127. ECMA, Jan. 1990.

Richardson, J. "Escape from POSIX," *Windows/DOS Developer's Journal*. **4** (4), 20, 1993.

Riley, M. F., J. J. Feenan, J. J. Janosik, Jr., and T. K. Rengarajan. "Design of Multimedia Object Support in DEC Rdb." *DEC Technical Journal*. **5** (2), 50, 1993.

Rofrano, Jr., J. J. "Design Considerations for Distributed Applications," *IBM Systems Journal*. **31** (3), 564, 1992.

"RPC: Remote Procedure Call Specification," RFC 1050. Sun Microsystems, San Francisco, 1988.

Rumbaugh, J., M. Blaha, W. Premerlani, F. Eddy, and W. Lorensen. *Object-Oriented Modeling and Design*. Prentice-Hall, Englewood Cliffs, NJ, 1991.

Soukup, J. *Taming C++*. Addison-Wesley, Reading, MA, 1994.

Udell, J. "IBM's Assault on Distributed Objects," *BYTE*. **18** (12), 125, 1993.

Voss, F. W. "APPC/MVS Distributed Application Support," *IBM Systems Journal*. **31** (2), 381, 1992.

Wayner, P. "Objects on the March," *BYTE*. **19** (1), 139, 1994.

Systems architecture technology and methodology

"AIX Distributed Environments," IBM GG 24-3489. International Technical Support Centers, IBM Corp., Research Triangle Park, NC, 1990.

Aken, B. "MVS Futures." Presented at the Operating System Symposium, IBM Systems Research Institute, 1987.

"Alpha AXP Architecture and Systems," *Digital Technical Journal*. **4** (4), 1992.

Arfman, J. M. and P. Roden. "Project Athena: Supporting Distributed Computing at M.I.T.," *IBM Systems Journal*. **31** (3), 550, 1992.

"A Technical Overview of Microsoft Windows NT 3.1," White paper at the Business Solutions Conference and Expo, New York, 1993. Available from Microsoft Corp., Redstone, WA.

Awuah, P. "Overview of Remote Access Services for Windows NT Advanced Server," Document NT103, *Microsoft Tech Ed '94*, Microsoft Corp., Redstone, WA.

Bourne, P. E. "Bridging the VMS–Unix Gap," *DEC Professional*. **10** (13), 62, 1991.

Brady, K. "SVR4.1ES: Making Unix Airtight," *Unix Review*. **11** (4), 31, 1993.

Cappel, M., C. Higgins, and C. Whitmer. "SPARCserver 1000 Aims to Divide and Conquer," *SunWorld*. **6** (11), 61, 1993.

Cerutti, D. and D. Pierson. *Distributed Computing Environments*, McGraw-Hill, New York, 1993.

Chang, H. "MACH: Distributed and Multiprocessor Operating System," IBM Operating System Symposium, Thornwood, NY, Feb. 22, 1991.

Cole, T. "Porting Large Scale Applications to Alpha," *DEC Professional*. **11** (9), 44, 1992.

Custer, H. *Inside Windows NT*. Microsoft Press, Redstone, WA, 1993.

Dichter, C. "Moving C from DOS to Unix," *Unix Review*. **10** (6), 29, 1992.

"Directory Service for a Distributed Computing Environment," White Paper. Open Software Foundation, Cambridge, MA, Apr. 1991.

Donovan, J. "Operating Systems Trends," *BYTE*. **17**, 159, Oct. 1992.

Febvre, J. "Single Server Systems: Overview." OSF Design Review Workshop, Cambridge, MA, Feb. 1991.

Fountain, D. "The Chorus Microkernel," *BYTE*. **19** (1), 131, 1994.

Gehringer, E. F., D. P. Wiewiorek, and Z. Segall. *Parallel Processing, the Cm* Experience*. Digital Press, Maynard, MA, 1987.

Geihs, K. "The Road to Open Distributed Processing (ODP)," European Networking Center Technical Report 43.9002. IBM Corp., Zurich, 1989.

Goscinski, A. *Distributed Operating Systems: The Logical Design*. Addison-Wesley, New York, 1991.

Grubb, L. "Chorus," Presentation at IBM Operating System Symposium, Thornwood, NY, Feb. 1991.

Hampel, T. L. and A. K. Weldon. "Can Windows NT Coexist with Unix?" *Unix Review*. **11** (11), 43, 1993.

Harrison, B. T. "Multiprotocol Highways," *DEC Professional*. **10** (13), 38, 1991.

Harrison, B. T. "Using DCE," *DEC Professional*. **11** (1), 44, 1992.

Hayes, F. "Personality Plus: Multiple Operating System Personalities Are Here to Stay," *BYTE*. **19** (1), 155, 1994.

"IBM 9076 Scalable POWERparallel 1," GH26-7219. IBM Corp., Kingston, NY, Feb. 1993.

"IBM Scalable POWERparallel Systems Reference Guide," G325-0648. IBM Corp., Kingston, NY, Feb. 1993.

Kennedy, R. C. "Windows NT," *Unix Review*. **12** (4), 63, 1994.

Lent, A. "Guide to Top Software for Windows and OS/2," *BYTE*. **18** (12), 151, 1993.

Leslie, I. M. "Pegasus—Operating System Support for Distributed Multimedia Systems," *ACM Operating Systems Review*. **27** (1), 6, 1993.

Lorin, H. "Application Development, Software Engineering and Distributed Processing." *Computer Communications*. Jan. 1990.

Lorin, H. *Aspects of Distributed Computing Systems*, 2nd ed. Wiley, New York, 1988.

Lorin, H. "Distributed Computing," in *Models of Distributed Computing*. (D. Cerutti and D. Pierson, Eds.) McGraw-Hill/Manning Publications, New York, 1993.

Lorin, H. "Distributed Processing: An Assessment," *IBM Systems Journal*. **18** (4), 382, 1979.

Lorin, H. "Emerging Security Requirements," *Computer Communications*. **8** (6), 1985.

Lorin, H. "Impact of Technology on User Issues," *Proceedings*. European Systems Research Institute Seminar, July 1986.

Lorin, H. "The Limits of Distributed Computing," *Computerworld*. **25** (45), Oct. 19, 1991.

Lorin, H. "A Model for the Recentralization of Computing." *Computer Architecture News*. **18** (1), 81–98, 1990.

Lorin, H. "Systems Architecture in Transition," *IBM Systems Journal*. Jan. 1987.

Lubart, B. "AIX/ESA Foundations for 2000," Private presentation at IBM Corp., Kingston, NY, 1989.

Martin, B. E., C. H. Pederson, and J. Bedford-Roberts. "An Object Based Taxonomy for Distributed Computing Systems," *IEEE Computer Journal*. **10** (8), 17, 1991.

"Midyear Update—Cost-to-Use Midrange and PC LAN Systems in the Network Enterprise." International Data Corporation (IDG), Framingham, MA, 1992.

Moran, B. "A Technical Review of the Architecture of Windows NT," Document NT101, *Microsoft Tech Ed '94*, Microsoft Corp., Redstone, WA.

Moran, B. "Windows NT for the UNIX at Heart," Document NT206, *Microsoft Tech Ed '94*, Microsoft Corp., Redstone, WA.

Morrison, D. "With Middleware, Maybe You Can Get There from Here," *Beyond Computing*. **3** (3), 18, 1994.

Morse, K. D. and P. A. Naecker. "Preparing for Migration to Alpha VMS, Part I," *DEC Professional*. **11** (7), 54, 1992.

Morse, K. D. and P. A. Naecker. "Preparing for Migration to Alpha VMS, Part II," *DEC Professional*. **11** (8), 54, 1992.

Nance, B. "OS/2 and Windows Networks," *BYTE*. **18** (12), 117, 1993.

"NCR, Your Scalable Solutions Partner." Presented at Microsoft NT Symposium, New York, 1992.

"Network Computing System Reference." Apollo Computer, Inc., 1987.

Nicolaou, C. "An Architecture for Real-Time Multimedia Communications System," *IEEE Journal Selected Areas of Communication*. **8** (3), 413, 1990.

Nussbaum, D. and A. Agarwal. "Scalability of Parallel Machines," *CACM*. **34** (3), 56, 1991.

Nutt, G. J. *Centralized and Distributed Operating Systems*. Prentice-Hall, Englewood Cliffs, NJ, 1992.

O'Connell, B. "Alpha: RISC to the Rescue," *DEC Professional*. **11** (1), 64, 1992.

O'Connell, B. "Simplify, Simplify, Simplify," *DEC Professional*. **11** (10), 34, 1992.

"Open Cooperative Computing Architecture (OCCA)," OCCA Specification ST-2116-75. NCR, Dayton, OH, 1991.

"POSIX: Portable Operating System Interface for Computer Environments," Federal Information Processing Standards Pub. FIPS PUB 151. Dept. of Commerce/NIST, U.S. Government Printing Office, Washington D.C., Sept. 1988.

Pountain, D. "A Different Kind of RISC," *BYTE*. **19** (8), 185, 1994.

Rannenberg, W. and J. Bettels. "The X/Open Internationalization Model," *DEC Technical Journal*. **5** (3), 32, 1993.

"RISC System/6000 Technology," SA23-2619. IBM Corp., Austin, TX, 1990.

Scherr, A. L. "SAA Distributed Processing," *IBM Systems Journal*. **27** (3), 1988.

"Security in a Distributed Computing Environment," White Paper. Open Software Foundation, Cambridge, MA, Apr. 1991.

Sherman, S. "The New Computer Revolution," *Fortune*. **129** (6), 56, June 14, 1993.

Stefanou, L. P. "Survey of Windows NT," Thesis for Advanced Operating System Course, Hofstra University, Spring 1994.

"Support Environment for Open Distributed Processing" (SE-ODP), ECMA TR/49. ECMA, Jan. 1990.

Swanson, M.D. and C. P. Vignola. "MVS/ESA Coupled Systems Considerations," *IBM Journal of Research and Development*. **36** (4), 667, 1992.

Tanenbaum, A. S. and R. van Renesse. "Distributed Operating Systems," *ACM Computing Surveys*. **17** (4), 379, 1985.

Thelen, R. "The PowerMac's Run-Time Architecture," *BYTE*. **19** (4), 131, 1994.

"The SAA and Open Software Spectrum," Special Edition, *Spectrum Reports*. Vol. 5, Rpt. 5, 1992.

Thorson, J. "Win32 Memory Management," Document No. NT306, *Microsoft Tech Ed '94*, Microsoft Corp., Redstone, WA.

Tomlinson, P. "Windows NT Virual Device Drivers for Hardware Dependent 16 Bit Applications," *Windows/DOS Developer's Journal*. **4** (5), 6, 1993.

"Towards a Worldwide Distributed Computing Enviroment," White paper. Open Software Foundation, Cambridge, MA, Jan. 1992.

Ubios, J. "The Big Pipe," *SunWorld*. **6** (11), 86, 1993.

Udell, J. "Is There a Better Windows 3.1 Than Windows 3.1?" *BYTE*. **18** (12), 85, 1993.

Udell, J. "Windows for Workgroups 3.11," *BYTE*. **19** (2), 180, 1994.

Umjar, A. *Distributed Computing, a Practical Synthesis*. Prentice-Hall, New York, 1993.

"Unix and Open Systems," *Proceedings*. 1992 European Conference, Paris, Cap Gemini Institute, June 1992.

UnixWare Product Announcement: Pricing and Availability, Document 2015. Novell Corp., Provo, UT, Oct. 1992.

UnixWare Product Information: Company and Product Overview, Document 2010, Novell Corp., Provo, UT, Sept. 1992.

UnixWare Product Information: UnixWare Application Server, Document 2030, Novell Corp., Provo, UT, 1992.

UnixWare Product Information: UnixWare Compatibility Handbook, Document 2035. Novell Corp., Provo, UT, 1992.

Van Dam, T. "Windows NT in a NetWare Environment," Document No. NT102, *Microsoft Tech Ed '94*, Microsoft Corp., Redstone, WA.

Van Renesse, R. "Amoeba System," Presentation at IBM Operating Symposium, Thornwood, NY, Feb. 21, 1991.

Varhol, P. D. "Small Kernels Hit It Big," *BYTE*. **19** (1), 119, 1994.

Walker, M. "VM Technologies and Strategy." Private presentation at IBM, Endicott, New York, 1990.

Wheeler, E. F. and A. G. Ganek. "Introduction to Systems Application Architecture," *IBM Systems Journal*. **27** (3), 1988.

Wilkes, M. V. "The Long Term Future of Operating Systems," *CACM*. **33** (4), 23–25, Apr. 1993.

Winters, G. B. "International Distributed Systems—Architectural and Practical Issues," *DEC Technical Journal*. **5** (3), 53, 1993.

"XDR: External Data Representation Standard," RFC1014. Sun Microsystems, San Francisco, 1987.

Zachman, J. A. "Business Systems Planning and Business Information Control Study," *IBM Systems Journal*. **21** (1), 31, 1982.

Zahorjan, J. and A. Karshmer. *Lecture Notes in Computer Science—Operating Systems of the '90s and Beyond*. Springer-Verlag, Berlin, 1991.

Management and investment issues and methodology

"A Framework for Success." Digital Equipment Corporation, Bedford, MA, 1990.

"A Guide to Building Open Systems," Digital Equipment Corporation, Bedford, MA, 1991.

"Characteristics of Leading-Edge Users," Diebold Research Programs Management Implications Series 239M. Diebold Group, New York, 1986.

Cini, A. "How to Be a Systems Integrator," *DEC Professional*. **11** (1), 38, 1992.

Cole, T. "Porting Large Scale Applications to Alpha," *DEC Professional*. **11** (9), 44, 1992.

Conner, W. D. "The Right Way to Rightsize," *Unix Review*. **11**, 50, May 1993.

"DECnet/OSI Transition Planning for Open Networking." Digital Equipment Corporation, Maynard, MA, 1991.

Fogarty, K. "Taking Stock, Users Get a Sobering Look at I.T.'s Future," *Network World*. **11** (25), 1994.

Geihs, K. "The Road to Open Distributed Processing (ODP)," European Networking Center Technical Report 43.9002. IBM Corp., Zurich, 1989.

George, J. F. and J. L. King. "Examining the Computing and Centralization Debate," *CACM*. **34** (7), 62, 1991.

Hoffman, T. "Getting There from Here," *Computer World Client/Server Journal*. **1**, 20, May 1994.

Lent, A. "Guide to Top Software for Windows and OS/2," *BYTE*. **18** (12), 151, 1993.

Lorin, H. *The Economics of Information Processing*. Vols. 1 and 2. (H. Lorin and R. Goldberg, Eds.), Wiley, 1982.

Lorin, H. "Impact of Technology on User Issues," *Proceedings*. European Systems Research Institute Seminar, July 1986.

Lorin, H. "Leading Edge Organizations," *Proceedings*. SEAS, Autumn 1986.

Lorin, H. "The Limits of Distributed Computing," *Computerworld*. **25** (45), Oct. 19, 1991.

Lorin, H. "Management Approaches to New Information Environments," *Data Processing* (Butterworth Scientific Journal). **25** (4), 1983.

Lorin, H. "A Model for the Recentralization of Computing." *Computer Architecture News*. **18** (1), 81–98, 1990.

Lorin, H. "Some Issues in Software Management," *Proceedings*. Computer Measurement Group Conference (CMG XIV), Dec. 1984.

Lorin, H. "What Cost DDP?" *Computerworld* (In Depth). Oct. 12, 1981.

Lorin, H. "Why Distributed Processing Fails," *Datamation*. Feb. 1981.

Marion, L. "Keeping Your Balance: Managing a Multivendor Client/Server Shop," *Beyond Computing*. **3** (2), 18, 1994.

"Midyear Update—Cost-to-Use Midrange and PC LAN Systems in the Network Enterprise." International Data Corporation (IDG), Framingham, MA, 1992.

Morrison, D. "CEOs & PCs: Do They Compute?" *Beyond Computing*. **3** (1), 30, 1994.

Morrison, D. "With Middleware, Maybe You Can Get There from Here," *Beyond Computing*. **3** (3), 18, 1994.

Mullins, C. S. "The Great Debate," *BYTE*. **19** (4), 85, 1994.

Taylor, D. A. *Object Oriented Technology, A Manager's Guide*. Addison-Wesley, Reading, MA, 1990.

"The Premier 100: The Most Effective Users of Information Systems," *Computerworld* (Special Section). Sept. 14, 1992.

"The Premier 100: How the Best are Playing the New Business Game," *Computerworld* (Special Section). Sept. 13, 1993.

Tulk, J. "Making the Switch to a Success," *Open Systems Today*. July 6, 1992.

Ubios, J. "The Big Pipe," *SunWorld*. **6** (11), 86, 1993.

Wreden, N. "Re-engineering: The Ultimate Test of Skill," *Beyond Computing*. **3** (3), 30, 1994.

Ziegler, K. *Distributed Computing and the Mainframe: Leveraging Your Investments*. Wiley, New York, 1991.

Industry dynamics

Bebar, J. A. "DEC Strategy and Product Overview," Presentation at IBM Technical Education Center, Thornwood, NY, Sept. 1992.

Broadbent, C. and H. Jesperson. "Emerging Standards," *Unix Review*. **10** (3), 31, Mar. 1993.

Coffee, P. "Unix Quiet Success Leads to Gains for Open Solutions," *PC Week* Special Report, Dec. 21, 1992, p. S30.

"DEC Software Strategy," Interview with David L. Stone, *DEC Professional*. **11** (10), 48, 1992.

"IBM's Shake-Up," *The Economist*. **321** (7735), 19, 1992.

"IBM Transformation," Presentation to customers, IBM International Executive Briefing Center, IBM Corp., White Plains, NY, 1993.

"Information Technology," *Fortune*, Special Report. July 11, 1994.

King, P. "Sun's Secret Weapon," *SunWorld*. **6** (11), 54, 1993.

Linderholm, Owen, and Reinhardt. "Novell Gets Serious About Unix," *BYTE*. **17**, 23, Mar. 1992.

Loomis, C. J. "IBM—The Real Story," *Fortune*. **127**, 41, July 15, 1991.

McCarthy, M. "The Unix Crossroad," *Advanced Systems*. **7**, 10, 1994.

Morse, A. and G. Reynolds. "Overcoming Current Growth Limits on UI Development," *CACM*. **36** (4), 72, Apr. 1993.

"Multimedia Distributed Computing," G229-7340. IBM Corp., Research Triangle Park, NC, Nov. 1992.

Musciano, C. "Getting COSE," *SunWorld*. **6** (12), 92, 1993.

"New Day At Digital," Interview with Robert B. Palmer, *DEC Professional*. **12** (4), 1993.

Pollack, A. "Japanese Computer Giants See the Danger of Following IBM," *New York Times*. Sec. 3, p. 8, Feb. 21, 1993.

Reinhardt, A. "Pentium Changes the PC," *BYTE*. **18** (7), 80, 1993.

Romeo, M. "UnixWare Enters the Desktop Wars," Term paper CSC 256. Hofstra University, Spring 1993.

Schubert, K. "Operating System Competitiveness for the 1990s," IBM Operating System Symposium, Thornwood, NY, Feb. 1991.

Segervall, L. C. "Can Sun Microsystems Recover?" *Advanced Systems*. **7** (6), 152, 1994.

Smith, B. and T. Yager. "Is Unix Dead," *BYTE*. **17** (9), 1992.

Snell, N. "The New MVS: Tuned to Serve?" *Datamation*. **76**, July 15, 1992.

Thompson, T. "New Mac Blazes Technology Trails," *BYTE*. **19** (7), 197, 1994.

Udell, J. "Justifying NT," *BYTE*. **19** (4), 149, 1994.

Vaskevitch, D. *Client/Server Strategies*. IDG Books, San Mateo, CA, 1995.

"Within The Whirlwind—A Survey of the Computer Industry," *The Economist*. **326** (7800), insert after p. 58, 1993.

Woods, A. "The Making of a Dynasty," *Infomart Magazine*. 17, 1st Quarter, 1994.

index